PROTEST

PROTEST

Studies of Collective Behavior and Social Movements

JOHN LOFLAND

Transaction Books
New Brunswick (U.S.A.) and Oxford (U.K.)

Library of Congress Catalog Number: 84-23941
ISBN: 0-88738-031-X (cloth)
Printed in the United States of America

Library of Congress Cataloging in Publication Data

Lofland, John.
  Protest: studies of collective behavior and social
movements.

  Bibliography: p.
  Includes indexes.
  1. Collective behavior—Addresses, essays, lectures.
2. Social movements—Addresses, essays, lectures.
3. Opposition (Social sciences)—Addresses, essays,
lectures. I. Title.
HM281.L66   1985   303.4'84   84-23941
ISBN 0-88738-031-X

Contents

List of Figures

Preface and Acknowledgments

This volume collects fifteen of my previously published studies addressed to aspects of social protest, crowd or collective behavior, and social movements. Even though the studies are diversely cast, they exhibit preoccupation with a single and overarching question: When and how do people object collectively in some fashion to conditions prevailing in their society? Although stated as a single question, this is actually many questions, both on the surface and in the successive layers of complexity that emerge in pursuing analysis.

Four specifications of this overarching question have been of special concern to me, and they are the four around which the fifteen studies in this volume are organized. Forming its four parts, these questions are:

1. What are larger contexts and immediate circumstances in which people define collectively a need for concerted action of an oppositional character?
2. In such collective behavior contexts, what are the social processes through which people undergo the sharply discontinuous changes in social and personal identity we call "conversion"?
3. When people form themselves into social movement organizations, what is the range of structural forms for doing this?
4. Considered systematically, what are the organized actions movements undertake in pursuit of oppositional change?

Detailed analysis of these four questions can become quite specialized and technical. Perspective can thus be "lost," as it is conventionally put. In an effort to counterbalance and mitigate this unavoidable tendency, I have prepared introductory materials that strive to situate the studies in relevant, broader contexts. In addition to the connections drawn in the brief introductions to each of the four parts, in the general introduction I undertake (1) to bring the literature on the concept of protest to a new level of clarity and (2) to align my more microstructural work and orientation with more macrostructural approaches.

Advisory reviewers of this volume in manuscript have suggested that the single concept of protest does not clearly capture the range of issues that the fifteen studies address or provide an integrating framework that is sufficiently detailed and broad. They have warned me that readers will criticize the title and framework as providing a "coupling" that is too "loose."

I must agree that the concept of protest does not provide an entirely satisfactory mode of integration *if* one demands an especially stringent or "tight coupling" of the materials. My affection for protest as the overarching theme is nonetheless undiminished. Despite numerous indirections and even misdirections, the phenomenon of human objection by means of collective escape or attack—exit or voice—has provided for me the social-psychological agenda underlying all the works in this volume. It is the abiding preoccupation that is perhaps beneath the surface in some places, but which is there nevertheless. Thought of in the classic terms provided by Herbert Blumer, the concept of protest as used in this volume is thus more sensitizing than definitive, more a suggestive and flexible orientation to the subject matter than a rigid and detailed depiction.

I hope these inquiries prove of interest to several distinct yet related audiences, audiences I believe to possess significant common concerns although they are frequently not aware of that fact. Indeed, a central aim of this work is to foster a "consciousness of kind" among kindred inquirers not now very aware of their kinship. First and most obvious, there are students of crowd or collective behavior and social movements per se. Second, the interests of such scholars overlap and crosscut importantly with those of social scientists of religious movements and gatherings. Third, flanking but separate and approaching form yet another direction there are political scientists and political sociologists who focus on interest groups, interest group politics, and protest. Fourth, more philosophically attuned and action-oriented, there is the tradition of scholarship addressing nonviolent, direct action both as a way of life and as a central mode of seeking fundamental social change.

A key argument of this volume is that, despite the diverse interests and the separation of these four audiences, the objects of their analyses form a single, fruitful domain of inquiry. The new juxtapositions achieved in constituting them in a single realm will stimulate new insights into the dynamics of all the interests and topics I have just mentioned.

In addition to these more scholarly-analytic audiences, I would also like this volume to be useful to activists—to people who are making practical decisions about organizing and acting to achieve progressive social change. I subscribe to the old adage that "there is nothing more practical than a good theory," and I am hopeful that the studies presented here can provide a variety of clarifications of options-for-acting in diverse nuts-and-bolts situations.

Fifteen scholarly undertakings cannot but generate an enormous range of debts to people who have allowed themselves to be studied and to colleagues in scholarship. In continuing recognition of my thanks to them, the acknowledgments originally appearing with each publication have been retained.

Five of the fifteen chapters have junior authors. I am grateful to each of them for permission to reprint their contributions: Michael Fink, Michael Jamison, James Richardson, Norman Skonovd, and Rodney Stark.

Lyn H. Lofland read the entire manuscript and made a large number of cogent substantive and editorial suggestions that I have adopted. As in many other projects, her love, optimism, and insight have sustained me in the process of drawing this work together.

Irving Louis Horowitz's enthusiastic faith in this venture, despite our differences of opinion on some matters, has been a continuing joy to me. I am profoundly grateful to him for his genial encouragement and sagacious advice.

Bill Brigham, Lyn Lofland, Gary Marx, John McCarthy, Clark McPhail, and David Snow did me the enormous favor of critiquing the new, introductory material—critiques that led to significant changes and rescued me from many faux pas. It is accurate rather than merely perfunctory and obligatory to report, moreover, that I have not accepted significant portions of their suggestions and that they are therefore not responsible for faults that remain.

Wava Haggard typed and retyped the manuscript with unwavering good humor, superhuman accuracy, and astonishing capacity to correct the most atrocious misspellings rendered in my bad typing and barely legible handwriting.

The original publishers of the materials have generously given gratis permission to reprint articles and chapters on which they hold copyrights. All are credited below:

Chapter 1, "Collective Behavior," in M. Rosenberg and R. Turner (eds.), *Social Psychology,* Basic Books, 1981, pp. 411-446; and Chapter 4, "Becoming a World-Saver," *American Sociological Review* 30 (December 1965):862-875, are reprinted by permission of the American Sociological Association.

Chapter 2, "Crowd Joys," *Urban Life* 10 (January 1982):355-381; Chapter 5, "Becoming a World-Saver Revisited," *American Behavioral Scientist* 20 (July/August 1977):805-818; and Chapter 13, "Sociol-

INTRODUCTION: PROTEST AND THE PUBLIC ARENA

The studies collected in this volume address diverse aspects of, first, social protest—of collective and unorthodox dissent—and second, collective behavior and social movement phenomena variously related to protest. In this general introduction I want to provide an orientation to protest and to the larger range of social movement matters that are treated. I do this in two sections.

In the first section, I strive to clarify the concept of protest itself. Several traditions of study have evolved in relative isolation of one another. The upshot is an array of conflicting conceptions that need to be collated and clarified. In addition, the treatments I offer in subsequent chapters grapple selectively with the gamut of problems posed in the study of protest, and I therefore need to specify how my efforts are specialized.

In the second section, protest is conceived as but one significant variation on (or dimension of) the major elements making up the public arena of societies: human gatherings, citizen organizations, the macro-structure, central institutions, and mass opinion. The analyses presented in this book deal in a focused fashion with each of these elements. I therefore need to explain how this is so and I also want to call attention to additional and recent works that are germane.

CONCEPTIONS OF PROTEST

Like other ideas treated social-scientifically, scholars employ the term *protest* in diverse ways. Fortunately, elucidation of this diversity can itself serve to advance our understanding of protest. We are wise to begin by recalling what the "folk" had in mind before the likes of we social analysts got hold of some of their better words and turned them into labyrinthine "concepts." Several dictionaries provide these themes of meaning, first as a noun, then as a verb: a solemn declaration of opinion and usually of dissent; a complaint, objection, or display of unwillingness usually to an idea or course of action; a gesture of extreme disapproval; declaration by a party especially before or while

1

paying a tax or duty or performing an act demanded of him which he deems illegal, denying the justice of the demand and asserting his right and claim to show that his action is not voluntary; to declare formally in public; to make a formal written declaration of nonacceptance or nonpayment; to vow; to promise to undertake solemnly; to demand as a right.

Several dimensions are evident in these dictionary depictions of protest: (1) dissent or objection; (2) that is relatively extreme in the context; (3) strongly felt; (4) directed to some person or institution with power over one; (5) in a solemn and formal fashion; (6) that is done publicly; (7) and is based on a sense of injustice. With this anchoring in conventional usage, let us examine how social-scientific investigators have complicated the concept in striving to cope with snarled social realities.

SUBJECTIVE LABEL VERSUS OBJECTIVE PHENOMENON

Arising from labeling theory studies of deviance in sociology, a distinction is sometimes drawn between protest as (1) an "objective phenomenon" and as (2) a label imputed to the action of others (Turner 1969:817). As an imputed definition of action, the notion of protest competes with such alternative labels as "crime" and "riot" as a way to define and explain certain collective acts, namely mass violence, looting, and disruption. The empirical referents of protest are, in this conception, whatever people popularly say they are.

More specifically, to impute one or another of these labels is to impute *causes* or *intentions* of such problematic collective action. Thus, in titling his book *Violence as Protest,* Fogelson (1971) was asserting that Black ghetto riots of the sixties were "far from being meaningless outbursts by black riffraff, [instead they] were articulate protests by ordinary blacks" (Fogelson 1971:xii). The subjectivist approach to Fogelson's assertion treats it as *data,* as a type of response to events in the world, and then goes on to inquire into who will use this or some other definition under what circumstances. As Turner (1969:817) observes, analysis of protest as public and subjective definition "contrasts—but is not incompatible—with studies in which protest is defined and explained as an objective phenomenon."

UNITS OF REFERENCE

Confining our attention to protest as an objective phenomenon, we find the concept used to refer to quite different *units of social organization* and that such "units of reference" often shift within and between analysts without their being aware of this.

1. Most microstructurally (and following directly from the dictionary conceptions just quoted) is focus on specific, circumscribed *acts* of individuals of the sort inscribed in the Western tradition by Henry David Thoreau and exemplified forcefully in more recent times by Rosa Parks on a Montgomery, Alabama bus in 1955.
2. More commonly, human *gatherings* (a large number of people in the same place at the same time) are the referent, as in marches, rallies, pickets, sit-ins, riots, stormings, and so forth (e.g. McPhail and Wohlstein 1983; Tilly 1981; pts. 1, 4, this volume).
3. Such gatherings combined with organized action carried out over weeks, months, or slightly longer, make up protest *events,* as in a boycott, strike, or vigil (as described, for example, in ch. 12 below).
4. An interrelated series of such protest events taking place over some months provides a *campaign,* as in the one guided by Martin Luther King and centered on Selma, Alabama, in the spring of 1965 (Garrow 1978).
5. A series of campaigns focused on a common objective and taking place over many months in diverse locales, reaches the level of a protest *wave,* as in the sit-down strike wave of industrial workers in 1936-37 and the sit-ins of civil rights activists of 1960-61 (these and other examples are described in ch. 12 below).
6. Following the analysis of Tarrow (1983a:10-11, to whose clarity I am more generally indebted), some few waves combine with other waves in periods of a "general heightening of social conflict" and the invention of "new weapons . . . of protest" that diffuse through several sectors of the public arena. Tarrow (1983a) calls these "cycles" of protest and has analyzed Italy between 1966 and 1975 in such cycle terms (terms pioneered by Tilly and Tilly 1981; Tilly 1978).

   The six units just listed make up a distinctive class that consists of progressively more complex, populated, and temporally prolonged series of actions. We may refer to the six of them taken as a class as *protest action.*
7. Shifting the unit of reference significantly, one encounters the concept of the protest *organization,* as in, for example, Useem's (1973:18-28) study of a draft resistance organization and Schwartz's (1976) analysis of The Southern Farmers' Alliance. More commonly in recent times, protest organizations have been called "social movement organizations" and jargonized as either "SMOs" or "MOs" (a practice I follow in this volume).
8. Least encountered and most ambiguous is the idea of the protest *movement,* a usage sometimes meaning a protest organization, but sometimes also intending something broader, as in Herbele's (1968:439) characterization: "Protest movements . . . are, as a

rule, limited in spatial expansion, being mostly of local, regional, or national character, for example, many " 'radical' farmers and peasants' movements." Boulding (1969:viii) uses the term distinguishing "between protest movements and educational movements, the one designed to crystallize a change for which a society is ready, the other to push the society toward a change for which it is not yet ready. The techiques of these two movements may be very different. A protest movement needs to be shrill, obstreperous, undignified, and careless of the pattern of existing legitimacy which it is seeking to destroy in the interest of a new pattern which is waiting to emerge. Educational movements have to be low-keyed, respectful of existing legitimacies—tying into them wherever possible, and chary of arousing counter-protest."

SCOPE OF REFERENCE

Crosscutting units of reference are variations in the scope or range of *substantive* acts, gatherings, events, etc. the analyst is prepared to group under the label.

Singularly narrow is Lipsky's (1968:1145-46) well-known formulation of protest as political action (a) "characterized by showmanship or display of an unusual nature" that is (b) undertaken by "relatively powerless groups." Operationally, in this use protest refers mostly to histrionic press conferences, hearing room posturings, and abrasive press releases in the mode documented so well by Brill (1971) and Wolfe (1971). Such activities as boycotts and strikes are specifically excluded since they are by definition actions of relatively more powerful groups (Lipsky 1968: 1146).

At the opposite extreme, protest is a catch-all for the gamut of violent and nonviolent modes of objection. Most sweepingly, Piven and Cloward (1977:23-24) include "strikes and riots" alike in their treatment of protest as "mass defiance" that provokes "serious institutional disruption."

Despite the fact that both of the above usages are treated quite seriously by scholars of protest, both are statistically rare in actual employment, even idiosyncratic. Much more common and mainstream are attempts to set protest apart from violence on the one hand and some formulation of ordinary politics on the other. In his classic essay, James Q. Wilson (1973:282), for example, thus juxtaposes "bargaining, protest and violence," defining protest as "a process whereby one party seeks by public display or disruptive acts to raise the cost to another party of continuing a given course of action." (This revises his formulation in "The Strategy of Protest," 1961:293, which included violence as a form of protest.)

In another classic, Peter Eisinger's (1973:13) effort to use the term "technically to refer to a conceptually distinctive set of behaviors" counsels that the "basic dynamics" of protest and violence are so different that they must be considered separately.

PLANNED, ARTICULATE, AND SUSTAINED, VERSES UNPLANNED, INARTICULATE, AND EPISODIC

Using the idea of the "movement" as the unit of reference, protest movements have been contrasted with those of withdrawal, reform, and revolution (Gusfield 1970:85-89). Protest movements are set off from others by virtue of being "less permanent forms of collective action" and being "spontaneous, unplanned, and episodic" (Gusfield 1970:86). In addition, protests such as "riots, insurrections, spontaneous demonstrations, and strikes often seem unrelated to programs or goals" (Gusfield 1970:86). This use compounds the three dimensions of planning, persistence, and degree of goal orientation, adding in violence to boot. In addition to excluding violence, contrasting usages tend to *allow for* protest that is unplanned and episodic but also to include protest actions that are planned. Moreover, contrasting treatments tend also to insist that even unplanned protest actions are goal-directed and articulate. (Although they use the term *rebellion* rather than *protest,* Gamsom, Fireman, and Rytina [1982] lay out clearly this contrasting complex of features.)

OTHER TRADITIONS

Further to complicate the world, there are many studies of protest and entire traditions of protest studies that do not travel under that rubric. Despite the fact that the authors of these works are talking about virtually identical empirical materials, they ignore one another— at least in print. Two such roses by other names are particularly conspicuous.

Nonviolent Action. The first tradition uses central terms such as "nonviolent action" and "direct action" instead of protest. Its intellectual forebearers are religious and humanistic social activism rather than mainstream political science and sociology. Its central text is Gene Sharp's *The Politics of Nonviolent Action* (published in 1973—an apparently vintage year since two political science classics also appeared then). Like James Q. Wilson (1973) but apparently independently of him, Sharp (1973:66-67) sets nonviolent action apart from "conciliation and appeals" and negotiations on the one side and violence on the other. Positively, nonviolent action consists of symbolic protest (e.g. processions, assemblies, pickets), social, economic, and political noncooperation (e.g. strikes, boycotts), interventions (e.g. blockades, occupations), and alternative institutions (e.g. of transportation and economic systems). (For elaboration, see ch. 12 below, and Sharp [1973].) Further, nonviolent action is "usually extra-constitutional; that is to say, it does not rely upon established institutional procedures of the State" (Sharp 1973:67). (Other contributions to this tradition include Carter [1973], Lakey [1973], Gregg [1959], and numerous "how to" manuals, e.g. Hedeman [1981].)

Collective Action/Contentious Gatherings. A second conspicuous (and celebrated) name for our rose is "collective action," the central term of Charles Tilly (1981:17) et al., a concept defined as "all occasions on which sets of people commit pooled resources, including their own efforts, to common ends." In many of the Tilly (1981:39, 49) empirical inquiries, the notion of collective action is pared down to the idea of "contentious gatherings" which are "occasions on which people assembled . . . and made visible claims on other people via declarations, attacks, petitions, symbolic displays, or other means" or "an occasion on which a number of people gather in a publicly accessible place and visibly make claims which would, if realized, bear on the interests of some other person(s)." For purposes of making the massive codings of long historical periods for which this genre is noted, contentious gatherings are identified by a "series of concrete rules" that "capture just about every event a historian or contemporary observer would call a 'riot,' a 'disorder,' a 'disturbance,' a 'protest,' or something of the sort. However, they also bring in a number of parades, processions, ceremonies, festivals, rallies, organized meetings, and other gatherings in the course of which people make claims" (Tilly 1981:49).

Tilly (1981:17) recognizes the similarity of the concepts of collective action (contentious gatherings) and protest, but rejects the use of the latter for two reasons:

> First, the conventional vocabulary—not only "protest" and "rebellion" but also "disorder," "disturbance," and similar terms—prejudges the intentions and political position of the actors, usually from the perspective of authorities. The idea of collective action applies more or less equally to actors who are determined to tear down the system and those who seek minor reforms, to the outcast and the privileged, to the successful and the ineffectual. Second, collective action covers a wide range of behavior whose connections and common properties deserve attention: not only almost all behavior which authorities call "protest," "rebellion," or one of the other disparaging epithets, but also petition-

ing, parading, bloc voting, and any number of other ways of acting together which authorities tolerate or even encourage. In the history we are examining, a number of forms of action have crossed the line between illegal and acceptable behavior; witness the legalization of the strike in country after country. Why let the boundary of our subject matter depend on the attitude of the authorities?

Leaving aside the "disparaging epithet" charge (which is something lodged in the eye of the beholder), the boundaries of the two concepts do in fact appear to be somewhat different even if they are close. Tilly is correct in saying protest refers to some but not all "political positions" in most usages—the positions of those opposing people in authority. He elects to be more inclusive. His second reason incorporates violence under the "collective action"—which is fine—but he then goes on in the passage just quoted erroneously to assert that legal forms of opposition are excluded from study under a protest conception.

These two independent roses by other names converge, overlap with—and diverge from—the more mainstream notion of protest in some important ways. First, nonviolent action analysts agree with protest analysts in isolating three main classes of action which are, roughly, ordinary politics, protest, and violence. Second, both these traditions are mainly concerned with protest as action rather than as organizations or movements. In particular, both tend to focus on *gatherings* and *events*. However, unlike the nonviolent action tradition, the collective actionists strive to integrate their quantified compilations of gatherings into larger-scale actions, particularly entire *cycles* of protest. Finally, collective actionists have a much broader scope of reference for their central concept, one that includes the actions of all parties in the political arena (not just the "challengers," as in the protest practice) and violence.

Other Terms and Practices. There are several other terms for the domain before us that vary as to focus and the degree to which the usage seems to have been studied.

In the tradition of political psychology we find, as reviewed by Alan Marsh (1977:39ff), such studied labels as "unorthodox political behavior," "unconventional political behavior," "disorderly politics," "political disobedience," and "civil disobedience."

Encompassing a variety of perspectives, we find many words and their usages that do not seem to have been especially thought through, studied, or reflected on. On the one hand, we encounter the term *protest* employed in relatively unspecific and omnibus ways. For example, William Gamson's *The Strategy of Social Protest* (1975) does not define the term or supply extended discussion of empirical referents. Violence, however, does seem to be a form of protest (Gamson 1975, ch. 6 and pp. 181-82, the code for "Col. 58: Means of Influence"). On the other hand, there is an assortment of terms in the literature that seem roughly to refer to one or another unit of reference or scope of protest, but it is often difficult to determine what exactly these might be, as in "insurgency" (e.g. Jenkins and Perrow 1977), "mobilization" (e.g. Oberschall 1973), "rebellion" (e.g. Gamson, Fireman, and Rytina 1982), and global references to "strategy" and "tactics." (Even the late and great guru of protest practice—Saul Alinsky [1969, 1972]—was an intuitive genius about the social psychology of protest, but lacked an articulate, written conception of the object to which he devoted his life.)

HIERARCHY OF SERIOUSNESS

Irrespective of the particular label, most treatments of the empirical materials at issue give relatively little attention to questions of order among the items studied. Can and should the constituents of the category "protest" (or whatever label you like) be meaningfully arrayed along some at least ordinal continuum or should they be treated as infinitely interchangeable?

Despite neglect, two investigators have searched for order and deserve our attention. The first is Gene Sharp (1973), who arranges protest into (what I construe as) four ascending classes of seriousness and degree of organization: symbolic protest, noncooperation, intervention, and alternative institutions. This ordering attempt is elaborated in his *magnum opus* (and summarized in ch. 12 below). Suffice it here to say that his scheme remains a major point of departure and I employ it in part 4 below.

The second effort, by social psychologist Alan Marsh, consists of extensive survey research in which people have been asked such questions as: "Think about protest. Generally speaking, how far are you prepared to go?" Respondents are asked this question after being given a set of ten cards, each containing an act of protest. They arrange the ten in terms of "how far (they are) prepared to go" (Marsh 1977:48). Using this and other devices, respondents are found to have definite conceptions of the relative seriousness of the ten acts and to exhibit "a dimension of unorthodoxy passing through a series of thresholds away from conventional politics toward violence" (Marsh 1977:45). The five "threshold acts" in order of increasing, perceived seriousness (and declining proportion of endorsement among the British adults surveyed) were: signing petitions, lawful demonstrations, boycotts, rent strikes and unofficial strikes, and occupying buildings and blocking traffic (Marsh 1977:50).

These two efforts are theoretical (Sharp) and social psychological (Marsh). A next step is the employment of such conceptions of hierarchy in the study of actual protest acts, gatherings, events, organizations, and the like. Some work in this direction at the level of organizations is set forth in part 3 below, on differing levels of "corporateness," and therefore seriousness, exhibited by movement (protest) organizations.

POLITE, PROTEST, AND VIOLENT STRUGGLE AS DRAMATURGY

As my remarks thus far convey (and I elaborate in part 4), I accept a tripartite conception that in some fashion sets off violence and ordinary politics from protest. The phrase "in some fashion" is key, for I am uncomfortable with the exact schemes of distinction set forth by James Q. Wilson (1973), Ralph Turner (1970), and others. As these and other people propose the tripartition, I fear they conflate aspects of *organizations* and their resources with aspects of forms of *action*. We need to distinguish among organizations *and* actions in terms of their bargaining persuasion/polite features versus their protest or violent features. In so doing, we can perceive, as Tarrow (1983) has observed, that otherwise conventional organizations may employ protest actions; otherwise protest-oriented organizations may use violence, and so forth through many complicated "loose couplings" of organizational orientation and action.

Uncoupling organizations and actions helps us to focus more sharply on actions and then to appreciate that our tripartition is not only substantive (the degree of having the resources to bargain and the like) but *dramaturgic*—forms of presenting a case, modes of displaying one's preferences and desires. Substantive factors obviously structure or conduce choice of actions, but these are nonetheless separate matters. As Erving Goffman and others have taught us so well, action is form and style as well as substance, even though there are substantive causes and consequences of form and style (cf. Snow, Zurcher, and Peters, 1981).

There is a second sense in which the tripartition is dramaturgic and not simply substantive. As we move across the three classes of actions (and perhaps also of organizations) matters become more *dramatic,* as in Eisinger's (1973:28) reference to "the drama of protest." Risks escalate and the immediate fatefulness of the consequences of action increase. Such escalation has a substantive meaning, obviously, but it can precipitate qualitatively different definitions of the situation, definitions we refer to generically as "collective behavior situations" (and which are defined and discussed in chs. 1, 2, 15).

In chapter 14, I explore an instance of this dual uncoupling (the separation of organization and action and substance and dramaturgy). What is there termed "crowd lobbying" is engaged in by: (1) polite interest groups with (2) more than sufficient resources to bargain or whatever (the substantive aspect), but who nonetheless (3) stage gatherings and events that have protest qualities (the dramaturgic aspect).

I hope that these dramaturgic amendments make the substantive tripartitions offered by others more accurate by locating their lacunae and suggesting some of the other matters that need to be addressed.

The variations in unit and scope of reference, degree of planning and goal orientation, terminology, hierarchy of seriousness, and substance I have just reviewed are of enormously more than scholastic or historical interest. They reveal a thicket of confusions that retard communication both among people interested in the same topic but who may not realize it and among people who do address one another but who, unknowingly, are not talking about exactly the same thing.

Having propounded, then, that protest is a throny patch of bramble in which we must make our way slowly and with ever-alert caution, let us take another step.

THE PUBLIC ARENA

Protest is but one aspect of some of the major elements making up the public arena of a modern society. Put differently, in order best to understand protest, we must place it in the several kinds of contexts provided by the public arena.

By the term *public arena* I call attention to the five major components of the public realm that scholars conventionally identify when studying protest, collective behavior, and social movements. These are: (1) human gatherings—occasions of humans assembling face-to-face in relatively large numbers; (2) citizen organizations—enduring citizen associations that are relatively independent of controlling, central institutions; (3) the macrostructure—the economic, demographic, political, geophysical, and other large-scale arrangements that structure possibilities for and limitations on human organization and action; (4) central institutions—the organizations that control public order, most saliently, the government, the military, and the police; (5)

mass opinion—the sentiments (as best they can be known) of the public at large.

These five components make up a complex, interactive system of reverberating connections. Tracing specific forms of these connections constitutes an analytic agenda that encompasses significant portions of several social science disciplines. Explication of all such connections is a huge task vastly beyond the purpose and scale of this introduction. My aims here are necessarily the more modest ones of suggesting how the studies contained in this volume relate to the components of the public arena and hence to the larger and multidisciplinary project of describing and explaining the nature, causes, and consequences of protest and associated phenomena in modern societies.

HUMAN GATHERINGS

In the beginning is the human gathering, the occasion of people assembled in face-to-face proximity for whatever purpose. This is "collected" rather than "collective" behavior in its most fundamental sense. When such copresences are of substantial size, humans commonly speak of them as audiences, crowds, or even throngs. Leaving aside the social-psychological meanings of large numbers of people in copresence (discussed in ch. 14), I here only observe that humans themselves identify collecting together as happenings important enough to notice, comment on, regulate, actively stage, and often, prohibit.

Structures. Human gatherings conceived in this specialized way—as collected behavior—themselves display numerous important variations only two of which are at the moment pertinent.

The first is the degree of preplanning. The most obvious and commonplace is the ordinary social occasion, be it a work site, a play, a classroom meeting, a rally. Following Goffman's (1953) seminal discussion of gatherings, there are regulations about who can participate, a preknown beginning and end, a contour of involvement, and assignment of responsibility for starting, guiding, and terminating. In sharp contrast are emergent occasions or "episodes" that have few of the features of planned occasions. Instead, out of unfocused copresence (and perhaps media instructions), an "episode" takes shape. It is these episodes that scholars commonly identify as collective behavior. Many forms of it occupy a large part of the "crowd" sections of chapter 1 below, including such classic episode-gatherings as crowd panics, lynchings, ghetto riots, and ecstatic upheavals.

Second, Crosscutting the degree of planning is the motif—the substance, emotional tenor (or perhaps) the purpose of the gathering. There are five as yet crudely identified but nonetheless central forms of this. Amalgamating the distinctions between fear, hostility, and joy explained in chapter 1 with the tripartition of diplomatic, protest, and violent action previously discussed (and making other adjustments), we have the following.

1. *Workaday* or task gatherings are the ordinary congregations of everyday work that occur ubiquitously in such places as plants, office complexes, and stores.
2. *Celebrations* "honor . . . some jointly appreciated circumstances" (Goffman 1983:7). A dozen forms of these are described in detail in chapter 2 below, including revivalist and reverent "crowds."

   Workaday gatherings and celebrations are marked off from items 3-5 just below, by the relative degree to which they do not direct demands for change toward agents of central institutions. Instead, participants in celebrations, in particular, target their own or supernatural resources and satisfaction more than mass opinion or agents of central institutions. The three below do target the latter and are, in the nice term used by Tilly (1981), "contentious."
3. Focusing the tripartition of action made above, the mildest of contentious gatherings is diplomatic, staid, and *polite,* as in ordinary meetings of legislative bodies.
4. Radically in contrast, are the many forms of *violent* gatherings depicted in chapter 1 below, occasions where the motif consists of hostile emotion and the breaking of physical objects and human bodies.
5. As important as these four other forms of gathering are, it is the fifth, the *protest* gathering, that is of special interest in this volume and which figures centrally in part 4 both as a general class of gathering (ch. 12) and as an object of detailed case analysis (ch. 14 on crowd lobbying and ch. 15 on symbolic sit-ins).

Dynamics and Issues. The conjunction of the two dimensions of planned versus unplanned and motif or purpose identifies ten major forms of human gatherings among which there are many dynamic relations, as well as complex relations with other forces of the public arena.

Strain at the Margin. There is a strain at the margin between protest and diplomatic gatherings in that forms of protest gatherings tend to evolve features of diplomatic gatherings and vice versa. This is the thrust of the notions of crowd lobbying set out in chapter 14 below, and symbolic sit-ins depicted in chapter 15. In the former, diplomatic gatherings subtly became protests in character and in the latter, protest is tamed into more diplomatic guise. Both these forms of struggle "strain at the margin," even though both approach the margin between the two classes of action from different directions.

Repertoires of Collective Action. Societies vary markedly in the frequency, forms, and dynamics of the gatherings that their populations form. At one theoretical if not empirical extreme, gatherings in a society may be infrequent, confined to a limited range of possible purposes, and be very constrained in emotional and behavioral expression. At the opposite extreme, the population of a society may generate gatherings almost constantly, for a wide variety of purposes, and display a vast gamut of emotional arousals and collective acts. All societies fall between these poles, but vary strikingly along such dimensions as frequency, purposes, emotional content, and levels of affective arousal.

A first key task in the understanding of gatherings in cross-national perspective is the construction of a rich yet precise inventory of the range of possible gatherings. The schemes so far proposed, including those set forth in chapters 1 and 2 below, are highly provisional and incomplete, as are attempts in the cross-national politics tradition (e.g., Gurr and Ruttenberg 1969; Taylor and Hudson 1972).

A second key task is the development of a language that facilitates meaningful compositing of the gathering profiles of societies. For this, one of the most helpful conceptions at hand is Charles Tilly's (1978, 1979, 1981) notion of "repertoires of collective action." It serves elegantly to suggest a learned range of ways of acting collectively that is but a limited array when viewed against the panoply of theoretically possible actions. Tilly provides us an especially strong sense of this by comparing how forms of protest gatherings change in the same society over time. Consider for example these generalizations for Western Europe based on the massive and tedious codings of public records that Tilly (1981:19-20) and his associates have performed on eighteenth- and nineteenth-century materials:

> In western Europe, the prevailing eighteenth-century repertoire differed significantly from the modes of collective action Europeans employ today. Its most dramatic recurrent forms were the food riot, concerted resistance to conscription, organized invasions of fields and forests, and rebellion against tax-collectors. Less visible, but in some ways more influential, were established public festivals and rituals during which ordinary people voiced demands or complaints.

The repertoire which came to dominate nineteenth-century collective action looked quite different. Its most visible recurrent forms were the demonstration, the protest meeting, the strike, the electoral rally—essentially the means by which aggrieved Europeans today air their grievances collectively.

The waxing and waning of numerous other forms of gatherings reviewed in chapters 1, 2, 12, and 15 below, provide many other puzzles to ponder. For example, why the virtual disappearance of lynchings (chapter 1) and the true old-time revival meeting (chapter 2)? There is a generic question of why and how all such shifts occur. The most general answer ordinarily involves an important change in the macrostructure of the public arena and the behavior of central institutions. Tilly's (1981:47) account of the shift he describes just above exhibits the essential form:

> The character of collective action in the eighteenth-century western city reflected the character of the city itself: The city was segregated into small subcommunities, organized politically as an interlocking set of corporate interests and patron-client networks, accustomed to doing much of its business (and pleasure) in the street, and peopled largely by poor, illiterate workers. Such a city produced a web of collective action which capitalized on authorized public gatherings such as markets, hangings, and ceremonies; which used street theater, ritualized mockery, and garish symbolism generously; and which frequently consisted of a crowd undertaking actions which, in the view of ordinary people, the authorities themselves should have performed. The borrowing of authoritative forms of action frequently extended to the ritual details: burning in effigy, displaying the head of an executed traitor, posting of decrees, and so on. With the growth of the nineteenth-century industrial city and the concomitant reorganization of urban politics, these distinctive features of eighteenth-century popular collective action faded away.

Chapter 3, on the youth ghetto, provides a more specialized account of changes in an arena's macrostructure creating "ghettoization" as a generic circumstance productive of several forms of, especially, planned and unplanned celebrations and protests, as well as violence.

CITIZEN ORGANIZATIONS

Citizen organizations are any reasonably enduring human associations that possess a significant measure of independence from the central institutions of society.

Structures. For current purposes we need to distinguish five main forms of citizen organizations, which parallel somewhat the forms of gatherings. First and most common are *workaday* organizations, the conventional, noncontentious associations in which most citizens spend their ordinary days: plants, businesses, warehouses, stores, schools, military bases, etc. The second type (and the mildest form of contentious organization) is the (organized) *interest group,* lobby, or pressure group. These are often the creatures of workaday organizations, but organizationally distinct from them and staffed by their own specialized personnel. Characteristic features of this pattern are spelled out in chapter 13 below. Third, and the center-stage object of the eight chapters making up parts 2 and 3, is the *social movement organization* (termed "SMO" or "MO" in contemporary social science jargon). It might more accurately be called "protest organization," for I want to distinguish this ordinary modern MO from a fourth type, the contentious organization employing *violence* as the central element of its strategy. Instances of this type are also termed terrorist bands, guerrilla armies, undergrounds, or liberation movements, depending on one's political point of view. Fifth and last, one important sort of citizen organization is barely organization at all and sloppily but unavoidably crosscuts the polite-protest-violence tripartition. Especially in circumstances of unplanned human gatherings, emergent, ad hoc, and sometimes short-lived circles of cooperators both stimulate and to a degree guide emergent protest and violent gatherings especially (Tarrow 1983b:4, Gamson, Fireman, and Rytina 1982). Ill-understood, such ad hoc groups are nonetheless a key form of citizen organization.

A second kind of variation also requires attention. As elaborated in chapters 7 and 8, citizen organizations vary in the degree of the intensity of commitment and involvement they extract from most of their members, ranging from asking and getting a few hours a week or month up to taking "the whole of their lives," to use the phrase of Lenin made famous by Benjamin Gitlow (1965). The significance of this variation will become clear momentarily.

Dynamics and Issues. The following are among salient dynamics and issues.

MO Instability and Change. The central and classic generalization about MOs asserts their tendency to become either interest groups or workaday organizations. In chapter 7, James Richardson and I try to make this highly abstract generalization more precise for the case of the religious movement organization (RMO), where it has historically been formulated as the "cult-sect-church" sequence. We suggest that *all* forms of RMOs are inherently unstable and experience pressures to move in a *variety* of organizational directions, no matter what the form, not simply toward some sort of workaday pattern.

Loose Coupling and Ambiguity in Analysis. The forms of organization just outlined are defined by the type of action (polite, protest, violent) to which each is partial; yet few engage *exclusively* in their own central class of action. There is considerable cross-over among the classes and such crossing-over may well be on the increase.

Difficulties in recognizing this loose coupling and treating it in its own right continues to befuddle analysts of movements who often use the language of social movement organizations to speak of what are, when examined concretely, interest groups or even workaday organizations. Thus we find such staid interest groups as Common Cause treated as social movements (McCarthy and Zald 1973; McCarthy 1982), a proclivity that robs the concept of social movement organization of whatever analytic bite it might ever develop. On the other hand, we need also to grapple with the fact that the increase of crossing-over blurs the distinction between, especially, interest groups and MOs. The first step in managing this development is clearly to recognize it as a new fact.

Differential Recruitment and Socialization Processes. Processes of recruitment and commitment to citizen organizations differ vastly among the five forms outlined and as a function of the degree of commitment required. As the three studies of conversion comprising part 2 document, investigators continue to struggle with the presumption that there must be some single, overarching process that obtains over vast ranges of all these forms of organization. The emerging and sobering realization is that there is no single social-psychological or social process dynamic. At minimum there are fundamentally different social-psychological patterns of joining both within and between the several forms of citizen organization. Chapter 6, "Conversion Motifs," is Norman Skonovd's and my effort to state what these patterns seem to be.

The studies of conversion presented in the first two chapters (5 and 6) of part 2 should be read in the light of conversion motif analysis presented in chapter 7. Both those chapters focus on recruitment and commitment to a specialized form of citizen organization, the *religious* movement organization that demands intense commitment. Little that is said in those chapters, therefore, can be generalized to workaday, interest group, violent organizations, ad hoc "organizations," or even *political* or *ego* movement organizations (subforms of MOs explained in chapter 7) without exceeding care and caution.

Recruitment and Socialization to Organizations versus Gatherings. In the same vein, recruitment and socialization to a citizen organization is vastly different from recruitment and socialization to a human gathering. While this may seem obvious, the distinction is widely ignored in causal accounts of why and how people come to be involved in social movements. Evidence from studies on one is commonly treated as virtually interchangeable with evidence developed from studies on the other (e.g. Zurcher and Snow 1981; Morris 1981; Wood and Jackson 1982, pt. 2). To do this, however, is to confound enormously varying levels of participant interest and effort. For example, it is surely reckless to equate attendance at a Billy Graham rally with becoming a Moonie, since the two activities are virtually incomparable in the levels of effort and interest required, but exactly this kind of equation is frequently made (see further, Snow and Machalek 1984).

Clear recognition of the distinctions between (1) gatherings and citizen organizations, (2) high- and low-intensity commitment citizen organizations, and (3) MO and interest groups forms of citizen organizations helps in identifying a disjunction of foci between the chapters of parts 2 and 3 of this volume and the chapters of part 4. The former chapters are addressed to aspects of *high-intensity MOs,* while the latter addressed to aspects of *low-intensity interest groups and gatherings* (mainly forms of protest action).

This disjunction has biographical and situational rather than analytic sources, and only reflects the kind of access to what sorts of data I have had in different periods of research, as well as the broadening of my interests over time. As long as these differences are recognized as such, I trust they pose no special problem.

Fully Comparative Analysis of Citizen Organization. The first three chapters of part 3 (chs. 7, 8, 9) and the concept of citizen organizations offered here, are efforts to push forward in the fully comparative analysis of all organizational forms of reacting to and acting toward central institutions and the macrostructure of societies. Considerable lip service is given to the desirability of such a project, but the larger and unfortunate fact is that the study of interest groups, protest organizations, and violent organizations—in particular—are carried on in relative isolation of one another.

The conceptions explained in chapter 7 and 8 are thus efforts to break down barriers even within the category of the protest movement, striving to bring the religious, political, and ego forms under a single framework of analysis. Chapter 15, on interest groups, appears here precisely for the purpose of stressing that class of organization as a primary comparative referent. Still ahead of us is the task of detailed comparative analysis and, even more saliently, the serious incorporation of violent organizations into studies of collective behavior and social movements.

MACROSTRUCTURE

The macrostructural component of the public arena is also commonly termed the social context, macrosituation, society, or macrosocial organization, among other labels for the arrangements, problems, constraints, and opportunities that embrace the entire arena.

Structures. The macrostructure itself divides into those matters that have existed with relative stability for a period, such as the age and social class distribution of the society, level of industrialization, numerical and armory strength of the military, and the like. This is the *standing structure*. This is different from recent changes that are defined as such and as of problematic and indefinite duration. Examples of these include sharp decreases (or increases) in the availability of food, fuel, and other staples of everyday life, attack or invasion by a foreign government, large-scale environmental disasters, and rapid escalation of government belligerence toward foreign governments.

Issues. Analysts of the public arena tend to focus on only one or two of the five components and neglect the others, or at least to look at the others only from the point of view of their favorite component(s). Moreover, they tend, in round-robin fashion, to charge that others neglect their pet force(s) improperly.

What is needed is a stronger conception of how all the components are interdependent and dovetailed. This is easy enough to say but hard to achieve, for there are casts of mind, intellectural styles, and theoretical perspectives also at stake and at work. Lip service to complementarity notwithstanding, scholars disagree on where to start—and where it is *most* important to focus—all the while admitting to the importance of forces other than their own favorites.

This is preamble to admitting that I am guilty as everyone else in having "pets." That my favorites are human gatherings and citizen organizations is clearly communicated by the ordering and emphasis of this introduction. The studies of this volume say relatively little about the macrostructure of the public arena, although depiction of it is not entirely absent. For example, chapter 10 places great (but brief) stress on its importance in the rise of the new religions of the early nineteen seventies, and in chapter 5, on the youth ghetto, both the standing structure and emerging situation of "ghettoization" around large universities is treated in reasonable detail. Still, macrostructure has not been central to these studies, and even in "The Youth Ghetto" piece I do not bother to mention some salient macrostructural facts that importantly help to account for the ferment of the high sixties: the pig in the python age structure that caused youth ghetto expansion, the war in Vietnam, and war-fueled economic affluence.

CENTRAL INSTITUTIONS

The central institutions of the public arena consist of those organizations which claim to exercise (largely successfully) a monopoly over the use of violence in maintaining social order, together with those organizations closely allied with the keepers of such violence. In familiar terms, the central institutions consist of the government, the military, the police, the larger economic organizations, organized labor, the major religious associations, and the educational establishment. Agents of central institutions are the targets of many varieties of citizen organization, human gatherings, and protest actions.

Structures. Classification of types of central institutions is itself a small industry in which political scientists and political sociologists specialize. For the modest purposes at hand, two crude sets of distinctions suffice. First, there is a need to distinguish among the central institutions in terms of the degree and the way in which their agents attempt to penetrate and organizationally to control the citizenry at large, especially its economic activities. Three very large clusters along this dimension are ordinarily labeled something like pluralistic/ democratic regimes, state-socialist regimes, and (statistically infrequent but nonetheless of paramount importance) fascist regimes.

Second, for some purposes—especially concerning democratic/pluralist societies—we must distinguish the numerous component organizations of the central institutions and the satellite citizen organizations that agents of central institutions feel it necessary to take into account. In particular, specific targets of protest must be distinguished from the media, agents of social control, and various on-looking "third parties" who are part of the central institutions (e.g. Turner 1970; Lipsky 1968; Garrow 1978).

Dynamics. Dynamics of central institutions vis-à-vis other components include the following.

Central Institutions Encouraging Protest Action. The facts are far from in, but the most supported formulation at hand is that central institutions against which protest action is most encouraged and effective is "marked by paradox," the phrase used by Peter Eisinger in reference to his comparative study of the incidence of protest in forty-three American cities.

> The paradox of protest is that while on the one hand it appears to be a response to certain closed system characteristics, it only takes place on a

persistent basis in systems in which other characteristics are open. The incidence of protest was associated, for example, with a relatively small managerial work force, with a high crime rate, and with the ambiguous variables of Model Cities and minority uniformed police. The former two are indicative of a restricted opportunity structure, while the latter two potentially signify both open and closed characteristics (Eisinger 1973:26).

Such findings are applicable by extension to scales of central institutions other than cities, as in these generalizations.

Those who pursue protest as an ongoing tactic must in effect gain license from the authorities in the system to do so. That is to say, protest will probably not be used in contemporary American cities where it is suppressed by violence. Violent reactions by the authorities will likely stimulate violence by the potential protest population or will cause withdrawal from aggressively demonstrative politics. Official tolerance, signified by the unwillingness or even inability to suppress protest by force, may serve as the functional equivalent of license to protest. Such license represents an opportunity in the whole structure of opportunities: protest offers a chance to gain a hearing in public councils. The openness of the system, in other words, is conducive to protest.

In a similar way the system which responds to protest is likely by its very responsiveness to encourage protest. Elites who attempt to mobilize people to protest will fail eventually to recruit participants if protests are never successful. Protesters must gain satisfaction through protest on occasion or they will stop using it as an instrumental tactic. . . . Protest . . . feeds on the responsiveness it succeeds in eliciting. System responsiveness is an opportunity in the sense that people are more likely to get what they want in responsive political systems than in unresponsive ones. Protest is more likely to flourish in relatively open systems where it elicits responses (Eisinger 1973:27-28).

We certainly see such processes played out in another arena—the California Capitol—in chapter 15 below, on symbolic sit-ins.

Effects and Effectiveness of Protest Action. Everyone is concerned with the question of whether protest action works—and works how well relative to polite and violent action. I do not offer a comprehensive answer to this question in the chapters that follow, although I do struggle with the imponderables of answering it for the specific cases of the symbolic sit-in (ch. 15) and crowd lobbying (ch. 14). Some kinds of effectiveness can be surmised in both cases, although the effects are not often that the protesters set out specifically to achieve.

Any solidly comprehensive answer to the question of effectiveness will require careful specification of the problem in terms of such distinctions as *what types* of protest actions: carried on for *how long* in how many *places:* involving *how many* people (among other considerations); have *what kinds* of effects, when mounted against central institutions of *what scale* and having *what sorts* of "open" and "closed" characteristics (such as those enumerated above by Eisinger).

Added to this is the even more formidable task of placing protest in the comparative-effectiveness contexts of polite and violent action. It is on this score that we already have the widely debated and ominous findings of Gamson (1975, ch. 6) from *The Strategy of Social Protest* which suggest that violence—or at least involvement in violence—is more effective than polite or protest action. David Garrow's (1978, ch. 7) exhaustive study of the Southern Christian Leadership Conference's protest campaign at Selma, Alabama in the spring of 1965 can be read as telling the same story (public espousal of protest values and action to the contrary norwithstanding).

Role of Third Parties. Pioneered by Michael Lipsky (1968) and brought to excellent case study application and fruition by David Garrow (1978) is the recognition of the critical role of several kinds of "third parties" in determining the outcome of protest actions (as well as polite and violent actions). Even if they do not *require* involvement of third parties, protest objectives are at least facilitated by the "socialization" of conflict—the arousal of third party interest (Garrow 1978:214). The initially relevant and perhaps key type of third party is the news media. In Lipsky's (1968:1151) oft-quoted sentence: "Like the tree falling unheard in the forest, there is no protest unless protest is perceived and projected." Portrayal in the media provides a reality to which additional organized third parties can respond, both directly to the protest organization and indirectly to agents of central institutions. Agents of central institutions who are either the direct or indirect targets of the protest are then themselves in a new situation. They know that third parties of concern to them are aware of the protests and they know that the protests might become topics of concern to the mysterious fifth element of the arena—mass opinion.

A multiparty dynamic thus arises. Some scenarios of that dynamic have been traced by Lipsky (1968), Tarrow (1983), and Garrow (1978), among others. Aspects of yet other scenarios are seen in the several symbolic sit-ins that Michael Fink and I treat in chapter 15.

MASS OPINION

Mass opinion is the grand amorphous and mysterious force of the public arena. Citizen organizations and agents of central institutions alike devote a good deal of their time to discerning its moods, directions, and preferences and to getting or keeping it on "their side." Both forces claim to "speak for it" and citizen protest organizations, especially, often strive to give evidence of "it" being sympathetic to them by using the device of the *large* protest gathering (Tarrow 1983b).

For better or worse, the specialization in "pet elements" of the public arena that I just described has proceeded to the extreme in the case of mass opinion. Historically an integral part of social movement and public realm studies (e.g. Park and Burgess 1924:867-70, Blumer 1969b:89-93, Lang and Lang 1961, ch. 13), specialists in it have in recent decades migrated off into their own domain and social movement scholars have hardly bothered to note their departure. Only one at least relatively recent text (Turner and Killian 1972, pt. 3) continues to treat it. I must admit that I have followed this larger trend. I discuss mass opinion only in chapter 1, the general chapter on collective behavior, and that discussion is confined (following the definition of collective behavior used) to more "aroused" and atypical states. It is further indicative that the volume for which chapter 1 was prepared accorded "public opinion" its own chapter (Lang and Lang 1981), which was not even grouped with the chapters on collective behavior (Lofland 1981) and social movements (Zurcher and Snow 1981).

THE CONCEPT OF SOCIAL MOVEMENT

With the five elements of the public arena before us, we have the conceptual response necessary to formulate a definition of the concept of social movement, a definition that will serve further to specify what the studies of this volume are and *are not* about.

A social movement consists of: 1. a surge of newly and independently founded or rejuvenated protest or violent organizations; 2. a rapid rise in the numbers of (and participants in) planned and unplanned protest and/or violent actions (especially gatherings); 3. an arousal of mass opinion; 4. all of which are directed to agents of central institutions; 5. in response to emerging changes in the macrostructure and/or actions of central institutions.

A social movement involves changes in all the elements of the public arena and, most saliently, exhibit a "surge" or "wave" quality. Operationally, one knows when one is looking at a new (or revived) movement by, most obviously, such simple, quantitative measures as the number of relevant new organizations being formed, the degree of membership increase in existing MOs that are relevant, and the increase in numbers of planned and unplanned protest or violent actions.

Two empirical aspects of these surges merit mention. One, they tend to be relatively short-lived, running perhaps five to eight years. Indices such as those just listed begin to plateau or even decline. The movement still exists, but it has "cooled down" (Mauss 1975:61-70). Two, there are many protest and violent organizations that would like to be a social movement, or at least be part of one as just described. They work hard to little or no avail to create a social movement—or if they have a different theory of the way the world works, they wait patiently for the next shift in the macrostructure (e.g. the next "crisis of capitalism") or the next bout between God and Satan, or both, and the misworkings of central institutions. We think of these as movements in the wings, premovements, or would-be movements.

This definition provides a relatively precise rendering of why the studies in this volume are mostly *not* about such broad social movements. Instead, the foci are organizations, actions, and gatherings of several sorts, especially protest. Nonetheless, two social movements in the broad sense do lurk in these pages. The analysis of the youth ghetto (ch. 3) strives to capture part of the surge and aroused quality of, mainly, (1) the student movement of the late sixties (not to be confused with the antiwar movement with which it is often conflated—Gambrell [1980] sorts this out clearly). The studies of conversion and movement organization in parts 2 and 3 are heavily informed by the (2) new religions movement of the early nineteen seventies, a wave of organizational foundings and celebratory gatherings, aroused mass opinion, reactive central institutions, and shifting macrostructure exemplifying the depiction of social movements provided just above.

In the context of social movements so defined, the Unification Church (UC) in the United States (aspects of which are analyzed in chs. 4, 5, 9, 10) is an interesting phenomenon. On the one hand, UCers definitely conceive of themselves as a social movement and often refer to their enterprise as "the Unification Movement." Moreover, one can point to a dramatic upsurge in protest actions mounted by them, their membership and number of organizations, an arousal of mass opinion with regard to them, demands made on central institutions by them, and relevant shifts in the macrostructure of society to which they respond.

On the other hand, even though there was an upsurge in their membership and a proliferation of organizations sharing their views, both the membership and organization were part of a single, relatively centralized effort coordinated by a circle of UC leaders that involved large membership growth and organizational proliferation relative to the organization's prior state, but which was still quite minuscule relative to the population of the United States. Had the membership growth and organizational proliferation been more "grass-roots" (relatively independent of central funding, coordination, and control) and had the membership size been a larger portion of the society, I would be more comfortable thinking of the UC as a social movement in the broad sense rather than as simply an aspiring or would-be movement.

Nonetheless, the UC was certainly one organization within what was definitely a social movement in the broad sense in the American early seventies—the new religions movement (or cult movement).

Furthermore, it is important to appreciate that the UC aimed to *create the impression* of being a social movement in the broad sense and to *become* such a movement. As Mayer Zald and John McCarthy (1979: 156) observe regarding the analysis I present in chapter 10, we see "how a small . . . movement organization can manufacture the image of itself as a widespread and vital force."

RESTATED OVERVIEW

By means of the conception of the public arena with its five components, I have tried to provide a general scheme within which we can locate the efforts contained in this volume. For readers to whom the foregoing is overly broad, allow me to conclude with a short and streamlined summary that recasts the foregoing.

In simplest formulation, this volume addresses the question of when and how humans undertake protest—collective action aimed at achieving significant social or personal change opposed to central institutions. This overarching question is too abstract and general for a meaningful answer and it must therefore be subdivided to facilitate precision. The chapters of this volume address *four* such subdivided questions (and as we have seen above, there are many other subdivisions):

1. What are the larger contexts and immediate circumstances in which people collectively define a need for concerted action of an oppositional character?
2. In such collective behavior contexts, what are the social processes through which people undergo the sharply discontinuous changes in social and personal identity we call "conversion"?
3. When people form themselves into social movement organizations, what is the range of structural forms for doing this?
4. Considered systematically, what are the organized actions MOs undertake in pursuit of oppositional social change?

Reduced to the simplest captions, these become the four questions of (1) contexts of protest: *collective behavior;* (2) readiness for protest: *conversion;* (3) associating for protest: *movement organiza-*

tion; (4) doing protest: *movement action*—which are the four parts of this volume. Taken together, they may be viewed as forming a temporal sequence or "natural history" of collective protest. The sequence runs from (1) situations of unrest and questioning to (2) personal change, through (3) organizing, and (4) engaging in protest action.

Part One

COLLECTIVE BEHAVIOR: CONTEXTS OF PROTEST

INTRODUCTION

The chapters of part 1 address relations between collective behavior and protest, and collective behavior per se.

COLLECTIVE BEHAVIOR AND PROTEST

Protest as an act, gathering, event, or whatever is a *type* of collective behavior (CB), is facilitated or inhibited by various *contexts* of collective behavior, and is *caused* or prevented by other forms of collective behavior.

PROTEST AS A TYPE OF COLLECTIVE BEHAVIOR

In chapter 1, collective behavior is conceived as a circumstance of collective, emotional arousal and nonroutine action in a situation defined as "something unusual happening" and as a variable, as something that is more or less present in specific instances. Protest, therefore, as a form of collective behavior, varies in the degree to which it is such. One well-known and basic dynamic is the fact that any specific type of protest act, gathering, campaign, etc. that is repeated frequently loses its interest—its features as collective behavior—prompting searches for fresh possibilities—for "additions to the repertoire" (the title of Bert Useem's column in *Critical Mass Bulletin,* 1983:27).

Conceiving collective behavior as variable also alerts us to what is perhaps most unique about protest. At its most effective, it dances on the margin of the routine, taken-for-granted world of predictability and security and the fearsome unpredictability of strongly collective behavior situations, particularly those that are violent. Eisinger (1973:14) captures this uniqueness well by calling attention to protest as *implicitly* threatening, stopping short of the explicit threat of violence:

> The implicit-explicit dividing line is crucial. Protest harnesses aggressive impulses by controlling and, to some extent, masking them, while violence gives free reign to these impulses.
>
> Protest . . . is a device by which groups of people manipulate fear of disorder and violence while at the same time they protect themselves

from paying the potentially extreme costs of acknowledging such a strategy.

COLLECTIVE BEHAVIOR SITUATIONS AS CONTEXTS FOR PROTEST

There are myriad elementary forms or situations of collective behavior, and I strive to inventory many of them in chapters 1 and 2. The term *elementary* needs to be stressed because an array of complex forms into which the elementary ones can be subsumed is not discussed in those two chapters but needs to be recognized. Under some conditions of major macrostructural shifts and changes in central institutions, elementary forms of collective behavior increase in frequency and variety and form waves or cycles to which analysts begin to apply more macrosocial labels. The nomenclature for these concatenations is contested by analysts but includes peasant revolts, rebellions, Jacqueries, uprisings, civil wars, insurgencies, civil disturbances, insurrections, unrest, turmoil, genocide, revolutionary situations, protest movements, and revivalist movements.

Such generalized or widespread collective behavior periods themselves constitute contexts fostering innovations in forms of protest and the adoption of such innovations by segments of the population not previously participants in protest (Tarrow 1983 a, b). Chapter 3, on the youth ghetto, is a case study of one important kind of context of collective behavior (including protest within the yet larger context of the collective behavior wave/cycle that took place in the American sixties). In addition to emerging macrostructural situations fostering collective behavior cycles, these cycles are facilitated by particular kinds of local circumstances of ghettoization, be these based on race, ethnicity, gender, or almost whatever. Chapter 3 suggests how ghettoization can be based on age and how this operated in the ghettoization of youth around large universities in the sixties, thereby creating geographic centers of potential and actual protest, as well as collective behavior of the many other kinds surveyed in chapters 1 and 2.

PROTESTS AS CAUSES OF OTHER COLLECTIVE BEHAVIOR FORMS

Although not addressed in this volume, it needs to be noted that often the effects of protest include diverse forms of responsive collective behavior on the part of new segments of the population "drawn into the action." Among the richer studies of this is David Garrow's (1978) detailed rendering of the various forms of collective behavior flowing from the Southern Christian Leadership Conference's protest campaign in Selma, Alabama in 1965 and their both local and national collective behavior reverberations, including their impact on the passage of the Voting Rights Act of that year.

Most protests likely stimulate collective behavior that is hostile (those are the forms largely documented by Garrow, for example), but we need also to be alert to patterns of collective *joy* (described in chapter 2) that can be both incorporated into protest or follow in its wake. Or, more broadly, there may be senses in which protest waves (or lesser scales of protest) stimulate other—likely joyful collective behavior forms—as competing alternatives to the "contentiousness" of protest involvements.

ANALYZING COLLECTIVE BEHAVIOR

FROM CROWDS TO GATHERINGS IN THE STUDY OF COLLECTIVE BEHAVIOR

Scholars of collective behavior are on the verge of a significant breakthrough in the clarity of their conception of what they are studying and, therefore, in the acuity of their analyses. I like to believe that the materials presented in chapters 1 and 2 contribute to this new understanding even if they do not themselves yet achieve it.

The transition aborning involves sharpening our perception of some basic units of human association or organization, irrespective of, initially, their relevance to collective behavior. A signal crystallizing step in this process is Erving Goffman's (1983) masterful synthesis of his life work titled "The Interaction Order." In it he identifies features and units of "the interaction order" with a clarity not heretofore achieved and decisively opens the way to importing his specifications into the study of collective behavior.

Among other things, he speaks of five basic units of the interaction order: "ambulatory units, contacts, conventional encounters, formal meetings, platform performances, and social occasions" (Goffman 1983:7). The exact features of this formulation are less relevant here than is the step taken by the notion of "collected" behavior. A great part of what we call "collective behavior" is "collected behavior"— the occasion of a number of people being in the same place at the same time acting together under some encompassing definition of the situation. Following Clark McPhail (another architect of this transition, who follows Goffman), these are, generically, *gatherings* (McPhail and Wohlstein 1983:58).

To use the at once obvious and obscure notion of the "gathering" as one key starting point is to achieve several things. One, no distinction between "institutional" and "emergent" behavior or forms is initially drawn. That remains a distinction subsequently to be recognized *within* the domain of study rather than a bifurcation that puts aside "institutional gatherings" and fails seriously to return to them, as has been the debilitating error of collective behavior studies over several decades. Put differently, a critical class of contrast cases—institutionalized/ordinary gatherings—have been improperly excluded from collective behavior analysis.

Two, again following McPhail, the concept of the "crowd" drops out for several reasons. (1) It is too general, abstract, and vague to serve as a unit of human association. (2) It carries too much excess conceptual baggage, such as "the illusion of unanimity" (McPhail and Wohlstein 1983:38). (3) Most important, it is the central concept of the classic "collective behaviorist" tradition descended from LeBon's (1960) *The Crowd,* with all the emotional baggage of irrationality, irritability, excess, fickleness, and violence.

Three, conjoining the definition of collective behavior as a certain kind of variable (discussed in chapter 1) with the concept of human gatherings, facilitates seeing that many conventional and planned gatherings are "conventional collective behavior" in the sense that unusual actions, emotional arousal, and a perception of the extraordinary are planned features of such gatherings. Collective behavior can be not only emergent or extra-institutional behavior (the rough definition with which chapter 1 opens), but part and parcel of institutionalized life. A central question about gatherings becomes, then, to what degree and in what ways are they "collective behavior" and not merely "collected behavior"?

The aborning shift I have described is one of the more recent and technical-scholarly manifestations of the larger and longer-term trend in collective behavior which stresses its similarity to ordinary life along such dimensions as viewing its participants as rational rather than irrational, acting in solidarity rather than in atomized disorganization (a "build-up" versus "break down" stress), obeying (emergent) norms rather than breaking out of the bonds of control, creating new organization rather than reacting to its lack, pursuing goals and policies rather than goalless tension-release and expressive emotionality.

However, the shift to which I call attention here is also different from these others in that it continues to view collective behavior as a distinctive phenomenon, unlike the view taken by some other analysts. The shift from "crowds" to "gatherings" partakes of the larger "similarity trend" only in the special sense of highlighting the ubiquity of collective behavior and its appearance in mild forms in the midst of ordinary life and as an integral part of it.

HAZARDS OF FORECASTING COLLECTIVE BEHAVIOR WAVES: REFLECTIONS ON "THE YOUTH GHETTO"

Chapter 3, on the youth ghetto, is one of several ventures I have made into a variety of "predictive sociology," the effort to be severely analytic about a rapidly changing and current collective behavior circumstance. Five of the analyses in this volume so venture (chs. 3, 10, 13, 14, 15), but only one—the youth ghetto—gets quite so "carried away" with the form.

The underlying structure of the form exhibited by the youth ghetto (and to a lesser degree the other chapters mentioned) is an interweaving of an effort to forecast the direction of a set of social forces with a dispassionate analytic conception of how the forces fit together and operate. In its own way, this is an applied sociology: The best things one can say sociologically are marshalled for a diagnostic and predictive task at hand.

Such efforts have their severe hazards, however, and the youth ghetto shows them starkly. First, immediate diagnosis and prediction requires detailed use of currently available data, and such data "dates" the effort quickly. The youth ghetto analysis thus reeks of 1967—the year of its composition. Because the essay *also* contains a time-transcendent analysis, I was tempted in preparing it for inclusion here to delete or update the time-place "dating" features, but soon decided that such an act was decidedly improper because those time-place framing features are an integral part of the analysis.

Second, many of the predictions I made in the youth ghetto have not come true. Age-grade segregation continues to exist, but has not proceeded as I forecast. Youth ghetto cultural distinctiveness has declined and dramatic age-grade confrontations have vanished. (Anyone can now invoke many plausible factors to account for these shifts, including, especially, the end of the Vietnam War and a broad front of adult efforts to mollify and coopt youth.)

Despite such hazards, there are good reasons to risk being wrong in these fashions. First, efforts to meld transcendent theory and current turmoil do appear to help people achieve helpful distance on turmoil, to foster a calmer frame of mind and therefore more considered action. That was a major reason for writing the article in the first place, as its opening paragraphs indicate. Second, application of general principles to an emerging case constitutes a kind of test of their range and robustness. The general principles at issue in the youth ghetto are a phase of the general theory of social conflict and taken specifically from the work of Gerald Suttles (1968) on inner city slums. I simply extracted salient features of the model Suttles propounds for the ethnic ghetto and tried to see how much of it we also found in the youth ghetto. Conceived more broadly, this was an instance of what Kenneth Burke long ago called "perspective by incongruity," a procedure widely and effectively employed in social science (Burke 1936; Lofland and Lofland 1984, ch. 8). In doing this I was also greatly helped by a knowledge of the work of Max Heirich (1968) on a series of protests at Berkeley.

Although the data and the predictions are "dated," the principles of conflict employed nonetheless hold and remain some of our best and most enduring insights, an assertion I can make with modesty because I only applied those principles to a new setting rather than having originally formulated them. I urge, therefore, that the youth ghetto be read with these *two* vantage points—generic theory versus specific data and predictions—in mind. By so doing one can avoid fruitless embroilment in the particulars and predictions of the late sixties and attend directly to the generic social processes of conflict seen in operation.

1

ELEMENTARY FORMS OF COLLECTIVE BEHAVIOR (1981)

INTRODUCTION

QUESTIONS AND EMPHASIS

As used by sociologists, the term *collective behavior* refers (roughly) to "emergent and extra-institutional social forms and behavior" (the phrasing employed in the bylaws of the American Sociological Association's section on collective behavior and social movements)—panic-stricken, riotous, and ecstatic crowds being among the more dramatic of its myriad expressions.

In a manner logically identical to that in other fields of inquiry, students of this subject seek to isolate *forms* and *causes* of collective behavior; *processes* of its operation; the functions it performs or the *consequences* it has for other social forms and for participants; and *strategies* people employ toward and in the context of it, among other concerns.

Each of these and still other foci are valid and indispensable moments in the full round of analysis in all fields of inquiry. But for reasons we may reserve for the scrutiny of the sociologists of knowledge and science, not all are accorded equal attention by investigators at each point in the history of a specialty, and such an imbalance is particularly noticeable in the field of collective behavior. Specifically, in more recent decades, collective behaviorists have displayed a marked preoccupation with questions of causes and some aspects of questions of process to the relative neglect of other questions, especially the question of form (Marx and Wood 1975; Aguirre and Quarantelli 1980; Marx 1979). This pronounced neglect of forms is having a critically retarding effect on the development of the field of collective behavior, and I attempt in this analysis to begin to redress the imbalance.

One could challenge the assertion that lack of attention to forms critically retards the study of collective behavior. In its favor, let me point to several matters. First, without articulate taxonomy, there is little guidance for cumulating relevant empirical inquiries. Important studies suffer inattention because no scheme, by its logic, directs attention to them. Among other forms described below, I refer, for example, to lynching and the more abstract pattern it exemplifies, one that goes virtually unconsidered in recent treatments of collective behavior. An important mission of this and the following chapter is *generic rescue,* an effort to save the varieties of collective behavior from death by citation neglect in the midst of publication overkill. I try to construct a metaphorical Noah's ark in which to keep the creatures safe in an ocean of informational glut swept by waves of selective attention. Second, without a strong sense of context provided by articulate taxonomy, study of process becomes highly indefinite and prone to loggerheaded and even sterile debate. I fear this has happened, specifically, in debates over the relative merits of the contagion, convergence, emergent norm, and rational calculus views of processes in crowd behavior (Turner 1964; Perry and Pugh 1978; Tierney 1980). The next large step in that debate will take the form of specifying the taxonomical (and temporal) location of the operation of each of those four processes. The traditional topics of *milling* and *rumor* are also likely to advance in that manner. Third, I expect that a more complex and variegated rendering of forms will also have a salubrious effect on the study of causes. Undisciplined by taxonomy, causal statements tend either to be extremely general and virtually vacuous or, on the other side, situationally idiosyncratic ("historistic"). Stronger efforts at mid-range types and causal treatments so geared are likely to stimulate attention to new kinds of variables. I think, in particular, of Albert Bergesen's (1976, 1980) excellent work on "official riots" and his attendant innovations in causal thinking (see below). (It is for such contextualizing purposes that I, in what follows, sometimes depart from a strict form-focus, especially as regards study of process.)

For these reasons, my treatment is selective and somewhat different from most recent efforts. Because it is, I fear that many scholars of collective behavior who have focused on other questions, and who have made outstanding contributions to answering those questions, will be offended by my relative neglect of their achievements. I want to stress that my admitted neglect in this chapter proceeds not from ignorance or cavalier dismissal, but from a belief that expanding initiatives are in order. Expanding initiatives are not necessarily incompatible with existing concerns—at least not in this case—and my larger aim is to enrich the study of collective behavior rather than displace or ignore what exists. My selectivity arises, instead, from the constraints of space and time and an assessment of priorities within such limits.

NATURE OF COLLECTIVE BEHAVIOR

The most basic question of "form" is that of collective behavior itself as a form relative to other social forms. Employing the ideal type or idealization (Lopreato and Alston 1970) strategy of theorizing, it is helpful to conceive the pure case of collective behavior as a limiting instance. Such a case may never (or rarely) be encountered in the empirical world, but the ideal-typical model provides a benchmark in terms of which we can gauge the empirical cases we do see. In ideal-type logic, the features of the model are in fact variables—aspects that are more or less present in specific cases. Five such aspects may be pointed to in providing a definition of collective behavior.

Adhering to the spirit of historic ideas and sensitized by a decade of "reality-constructionist" and related thought, a first component is cognitive and concerns how people are defining a situation. As the phenomenologically inclined have urged us to see, ordinary actors go about their ordinary lives within something these analysts call "the attitude of everyday life" (Berger and Luckmann 1966). Within such an attitude, the emerging events of experience are labeled "nothing unusual is happening" (Emerson 1970). For whatever reasons and with whatever consequences, certain actors at times label an emergent situation as to some degree outside "everyday life." They begin to label a situation as "something *un*usual is happening." The attitude of everyday life is to some degree suspended; the frame of ordinary reality, the taken-for-granted world, is made consciously problematic. A situation is to some extent defined as unordinary, extraordinary, and perhaps as unreal. Such a suspension is the beginning point of the possibility of collective behavior, but it is not yet collective behavior. The attitude of everyday life is probably suspended most frequently by individuals or by very small groups rather than by collectivities of significant size. Episodes of robbery, mugging, interpersonal violence, grave financial loss, illness, and dying are typical situations of suspending the attitude of everyday life, but their private and individual character make of them scenes of deviance, crime, or mere personal crisis rather than of collective behavior. Second, therefore, collective behavior requires suspension of the attitude of everyday life by relatively large numbers of people—by crowds and masses. What is a relatively large number of people? We are speaking of a continuum, and there are, therefore, a set of ambiguous cases between mere personal crises on the one side and full collective behavior on the other. Third, suspension of the attitude of everyday life is accompanied by increased levels of emotional arousal in participants. This level is highly variable in the same individual over time and from individual to individual at the same time and over time. In their strongest form, states of emotional arousal may approach what we ordinarily label panic, rage, or ecstasy. There are also many states that fall short of these. Fourth and completing the ancient trinity of the intellectual, emotional, and physical, in collective behavior episodes the emerging definition and affective arousal is accompanied by action defined by participants and observers as outside the ordinary. The degree to which action is extraordinary is itself a variable and at the extremes we can conceivably point to such behavior as uncontrolled flight, indiscriminate violence, and complete loss of voluntary control during states of exaltation. Finally, the proportion of a collectivity suspending the attitude of everyday life in varying degrees and experiencing emotional arousal in varying degrees differs over time. In the ideal-typical case, the proportion and degree of suspension and arousal are maximum and sustained.

The idealized profile of collective behavior, then, is unanimous, and maximum suspension of the attitude of everyday life in a collectivity combined with uniform and maximal emotional arousal and universally adopted extraordinary activities. This ideal-typical situation rarely, if ever, occurs. It is useful as a domain-marking approach exactly because it is so rare, and, as formulated, turns collective behavior into a variable, something that is measured across participants and is a matter of degree in concrete instances.

In so constitutionally incorporating the idea of diversity within and between collective behavior episodes, one of the major contributions of the emergent norm approach is elevated to a preeminent consideration. As pioneered by Ralph Turner (1964), that approach stresses the lack of unanimity in collective behavior episodes. By stressing that fact at the outset, we are better prepared to develop a more systematic intra- and inter-episode comparative perspective. Although I elect to treat forms, below, in terms of level of dominant emotional arousal, other reasonable directions include scales for measuring the presence of collective behavior that encompass a wider array of relevant indicators (cf. McPhail and Wohlstein 1983).

PRIMARY VARIATIONS

Attuned simultaneously to the received literature in collective behavior (my "generic rescue" concern) and the emerging logic of the field (just treated), three primary variations may be employed as vehicles for preserving the former while hopefully advancing the latter, albeit with some tension between the two.

Dominant Emotion. From among the several basic features of collective behavior just described, I am impressed with the usefulness of employing an episode's dominant emotion as the most basic classifying variation. The notion of dominant emotion refers to the publicly expressed feeling perceived by participants and observers as most prominent in an episode of collective behavior. For an emotion to be publicly most dominant—to have become the reigning definition of the emotional situation—is not to say that an especially large portion of that collectivity feels that emotion. Following the lead of Ralph Turner's (1964) formulation of emergent norm theory, the dominant emotion is almost always far from a matter of uniform, unanimous, or even majority inner feeling. In so referring to what is publicly communicated and socially shared, the idea of dominant emotion has much the same logical status as that of the emergent norm. The shift here is simply away from the cognitive (that is, the notion of norm) to the affective.

If we are to focus on dominant emotion, there is then the question of what emotions are to be employed. There are at least two approaches to deciding this. First, we can scrutinize the accumulated literature on collective behavior, asking what emotions appear dominant. Second, we can ask what emotions theorists of emotions per se would offer us. Happily, there is a reasonable accord between these two rather independently developed bodies of theory and research.

Without anyone making a strongly conscious effort, collective behavior studies have moved—haltingly and inarticulately—toward organization around three fundamental emotions: fear, hostility, and joy. This half-century trend is signaled most clearly in Neil Smelser's (1963) monumental *Theory of Collective Behavior,* which organizes the field in terms of types of "generalized beliefs" and the special topics of the "panic," "hostile outburst," and "craze." Ostensibly about belief, the titles of the forms themselves are also clearly suggestive of dominant emotions. In codifying a vast literature around those three kinds of beliefs, Smelser was being responsive to the long-standing and wide use of something similar to such a trinity in collective behavior studies. Considered the single most important work in collective behavior for many years after its publication in 1963, Smelser's demarcation of the field has persisted, albeit revolving around matters more cognitive than emotive.

Turning to students of emotion per se, we discover several competing schemes of fundamental emotions, but virtually complete agreement that these three are among the most fundamental and even, moreover, transspecific (e.g. Izard 1977; Plutchik 1962). Irrespective of these two sources of wisdom, only a modest amount of reflection on social life is required to recognize that these are ubiquitous and central emotions, and emotions that are especially entailed in collective behavior.

But why these three, and why only three? A fully appropriate answer would require an excursus into the sociology of knowledge, because, for better or worse, the historic concerns of the received literature have run largely along these lines. To the degree that we take the literature seriously, our actions are constrained.

There are, nonetheless, other basic emotions that can become dominant in collective behavior. Among them are grief, disgust, surprise (Plutchik 1962), and shame (Izard 1977). Although there are some studies relevant to these emotions, they are so few that I will not attempt to treat them, save briefly to mention grief as an uneasy variation on fear (see below). One future task is expansion of the basic divisions of collective behavior in terms of other basic and dominant emotions.

Last, there is the question of the use of dominant emotion as a means of classifying forms of collective behavior. Some people would observe that the most recent movement in the field is explicitly away from concern with emotion because such a stress asserts or implies unusual or peculiar psychic states or mechanisms such as "contagion," "circular reaction" (Blumer 1969b:70-71; Turner 1964), cognitive "short-circuits," and "compressed" ways of acting (Smelser 1963:71). Imputations of "crudeness, excess, and eccentricity" arise along with characterizations of collective behavior as "the action of the impatient" (Smelser 1963:72).

I have no quarrel with those who reject such images of collective behavior and fear that they are a consequence of a stress on emotions. My concern is that stress on the cognitive (and behavioral) commits the opposite error, that of reducing the field to exercises in cognitive theory or, even more extremely, to a species of behaviorism in which the study of collective behavior is merely the study of human coordination (e.g. Couch 1970; McPhail and Wohlstein 1983). At bottom, it is probably impossible to decide rationally which course to take, because the longer-term consequences of the cognitive, affective, or behavioral stresses are impossible to assess beforehand and the fruitfulness of each changes as each emergently takes account of the others. In the end, effort to integrate all three must be made.

Organizational Form. Crosscutting each of the dominant emotions are questions of the organizational form in which collective behavior arises. Historically, the field stressed distinctions between the *crowd,* the *mass,* the *public,* and the *social movement.* Over recent decades the latter two have come increasingly to be treated as separate specialties, especially in the case of the public and public opinion. (Virtually alone, Turner and Killian's [1972] text continues to treat public opinion.) It is indicative that the American Sociological Association-sponsored volume in which this analysis originally appeared provided each its own chapter.

In many recent treatments, even the distinction between the crowd and the mass has been deemphasized in favor of addressing collective behavior per se (e.g. Perry and Pugh 1978). Neil Smelser's (1963) grand synthesis appears to have started this trend by defining its main dependent variables—the panic, craze, and hostile outburst—in a way that rendered crowd and mass forms irrelevant.

Nonetheless, the distinction is critical to understanding forms of collective behavior in relation to dominant emotions. A crowd may be thought of as a relatively large number of persons who are in one another's immediate face-to-face presence. A crowd is a special kind of *encounter* as that concept has been developed by Erving Goffman (1961b) and others (Lofland 1976, ch. 8). A crowd is an "overpopulated" encounter in the sense that it presents an exceedingly complex array of mutual monitoring possibilities and constraints. Informed by the new sensitivities that scholars such as Erving Goffman have provided us about encounters, it is to be hoped that we can again begin to take crowds seriously. Features of the mass are less clear than those of the crowd, and it tends to be defined residually, that is, as whatever is left over after we have looked at crowds. More positively, the term refers to a set of people who attend to a common object but who are not in one another's immediate physical vicinity.

The two dimensions of dominant emotion and organizational form provide a framework for organizing detailed types of collective behavior. The intersection of these two dimensions is shown in Figure 1.1, that also provides a synoptic overview of the patterns treated in the sections that follow.

Level/Form. Pursuant to conceiving collective behavior as a variable, more specific forms within each of the six master types (so to speak) ought to be arrayed in terms of level of dominant emotional arousal. And pursuing ideal-type logic, the highest level dominant

FIGURE 1.1
Elementary Forms of Collective Behavior

		Dominant Emotion		
		Fear	Hostility	Joy
Organizational Form — **Crowd**	Panic Terror Dread Horror Dismay		Political C →← I, e.g., mob attacks C →← C, e.g., political clashes C →← E, e.g., protests E →← I, e.g., bourbon lynchings E →← C, e.g., official riots Leisure C →← C, e.g., intrafan violence C →← E, e.g., resort disorders Emergent C →← I, e.g., proletarian lynchings C →← C, e.g., communal riots C →← E, e.g., ghetto riots Captive C →← C, e.g., inmate clashes C →← E, e.g., pre-planned bids	Ecstatic upheavals Ecstatic conventions Ecstatic congregations Euphoric moods Revivalist crowds Reverent crowds Revelous crowds Excited crowds
Organizational Form — **Mass**	True dangers Environmental disasters , e.g., earthquakes Social disasters, e.g., revolutionary situations Environmental trends, e.g., eco-hysteria Social trends, e.g., red scares False dangers Environmental disasters, e.g., industrial hysteria Social disasters, e.g., space invasions Environmental trends Social trends, e.g., crime waves		Mass vilification Mass rioting	Crazes El Dorado rushes & booms Promised land migrations Fashions Lifestyles People Activity systems Events Items Fads Objects Ideas Activity

Abbreviations: C = citizens; I = Individual; E = Establishment; →← = against.

emotions ought to be presented first, moving through successive and lesser degrees of forms of dominant emotions. On the assumption that, overall, crowd situations possess a potential for dominant emotional arousal exceeding those of mass situations, crowd forms need to be treated prior to mass ones.

These principles lead us to envision three pure anchor points to which the paler empirical instances of real-world crowds and masses can be contrasted. These may be labeled, in order, *crowd panic, rage,* and *ecstasy*—terms taken to be, by definition, the highest levels of fear, hostility, and joy, respectively. By bearing the pure possibilities in mind, we will have a clearer conception of how far we are straying from the center in our analytic travels. In accordance with this conception, explication within each of the three main domains will proceed, insofar as the materials make this feasible, from the strongest dominant emotions to the weakest, from forms and behavior that are consensually collective behavior to phenomena that probably ought not be discussed in the context of collective behavior.

The similarity of this "ideal-type anchoring" to certain aspects of Neil Smelser's (1963) formulation may be noted. Smelser's effort to portray (and account for) the panic, hostile outburst, and craze also moves in the direction of ideal-type logic. Throughout, he mentions other and lesser "outcomes" without specifying what these might be. The three that he does treat involve high, or fairly high, levels of dominant emotions (and three that are fairly rare in actual occurrence). I have tried to take that logic further by thinking of maximal levels of dominant emotions and the character of "other and lesser" outcomes.

Having outlined principles from which ideally to proceed, I must now demur and report that the obdurate world of existing materials has not always allowed me to execute these principles. I often need to revert to the prior and more primitive task of simply sorting important forms without judging the level of dominant emotion. This reversion is seen most clearly in the treatment of mass fears and crowd hostilities. When forced to a choice between the dual aims of this chapter (generic rescue and expanding initiative) I have preferred generic rescue. One consequence is that, in order to rescue forms irrespective of dominant emotion, I invoke classificatory principles in an ad hoc fashion. In one instance I even switch from emotion to behavior in ordering forms. In this I subscribe to Erving Goffman's admonition that we treat sociological concepts "with affection," tracing each in its own terms, sensitive to the materials themselves and not merely to logical consistency. As Goffman (1961a:xiv) has put it: "Better, perhaps, different coats to clothe the children well than a single splendid tent in which they all shiver."

COLLECTIVE FEARS

By means of the term *collective fear* I seek to isolate occasions of collective behavior where the dominant emotion is, in dictionary terminology, the "anticipation or experience of pain or great distress." The term *fear* is used because it is the most general and least intensity-specific of a family of terms that are relevant: *dread, fright, alarm, dismay, consternation, panic, terror, horror, trepidation. Fear* seems most accurately to overarch and to capture the spectrum of arousal possibilities.

CROWD FEARS

Crowd fears, as a class, involve by definition a relatively large number of persons in one another's immediate face-to-face presence, each of whom must deal with the fact of mutual presence as a critical contingency entailed in how each can deal with an anticipated or existing pain or significant distress.

Panic. The classic, ideal-typical, and pure level of fearful crowd arousal is the so-called crowd panic. The archetypal illustration is the panic rush from the burning theater and the oft-repeated example is the burning of the Iroquois Theater in 1903 (e.g. Turner and Killian 1957:96-97). A large but older literature addresses the two questions of the nature of the mental state of the panic-stricken person and the conditions under which crowd panic occurs (Smelser 1963, ch. 3).

Although relatively little research has been done on panic in recent years, two directions of work seem particularly important. First, the category of crowd panic is itself probably more heterogeneous than fruitful. A resurrection of older partitionings, such as that between *escape* and *acquisitive* forms (using Roger Brown's [1954:859ff.] terms), might be productive. Further, within escape panic the organizational context of occurrence—the dissolution of a formal organizational effort (as in the collapse of a military attack) versus the flight of unorganized gatherings, such as audiences—seems an important dimension, oft-mentioned but rarely pursued. Second, and more important, the understanding of the psychology of the panic participant may be advanced by a more tenacious pursuit of process explications of the panic situation. The last stab in this direction seems to date from 1938 when LaPiere (1938:445ff.) strove to articulate a three-phase "psychological sequence" in crowd panic, a sequence reported by Roger Brown (1954:859) in an important statement since ignored. Other than that effort, process analysis of crowd panic remains largely at the level of a distinction between what Smelser (1963:154) terms the "real" versus the "derived" phases. The real phase is viewed as a response to the initial definition of danger, but the derived phase is importantly a response to the perception that others in the crowd situation are acting in an agitated, if not panicky, manner.

Terror. Attention to crowd panic has meant a relative lack of attention to lesser levels of dominant crowd fears. Such lesser, dominant arousals are, nonetheless, of interest. I think in particular of crowds taken hostage, especially aboard airliners, by terrorist organizations, thereby creating terrorized crowds even if not crowd panic. Such a trapped terrorized crowd often has a rather long existence which is likely to display its own processes, as distinct from crowd terrors where there is no entrapment and where orderly withdrawal from what is feared or orderly convergence on the feared object for the purpose of subsequent withdrawal is possible.

Dread. At a lower level than crowd terror—which connotes a focused and proximate fear—is the pattern of crowd dread, a persistent and chronic apprehension of a more diffuse danger. I have in mind the situation of a crowd trapped by physical mishap rather than by other human beings who are acting in what may seem to be a capriciously violent manner. Small groups trapped by mine cave-ins, unexpected storms (as with the Donner party), and mechanical failure, are prominent concrete types. Such crowd situations are especially interesting when they are prolonged and thus come to require, not just gestures toward a new social order, but the construction of one. Such new orders do not often seem to evolve along the lines of the *Lord of the Flies* (Golding 1959), but narrower adaptive innovations, such as cannibalism, drinking urine, and novel codes of morals, seem to occur. One of the most exhaustive and careful accounts of such a situation has been produced by Rex Lucas (1969) in his *Men in Crisis: A Study of a Mine Disaster.*

Horror. Crowds are sometimes witness to fearful and dangerous events that are socially and psychologically disruptive but do not significantly and directly endanger members of the crowd. The explosion of the Hindenburg in 1937, a nearby plane crash, an unusually large crack-up during an automobile race, may serve to upset crowds without arousing or endangering them to the extent of the forms previously mentioned. One especially vivid instance occurred at a concert of the Boston Symphony Orchestra on November 22, 1963, when the audience was informed that the president of the United States had been assassinated. As we still lack a careful language for depicting the features and process of such a crowd, it must suffice to say that it begins with a collective astonished and mournful outcry.

Dismay. On the morning of Monday, November 27, 1978, the mayor of San Francisco and a member of the County Board of Supervisors, an avowed homosexual and advocate of civil rights for homosexuals, were assassinated by a disgruntled public official. That night, thousands of San Franciscans, drawn heavily from nearby homosexual bars and residential districts, marched carrying candles to the front of the City Hall where singer Joan Baez and the acting mayor led an emergent memorial ceremony. Wednesday at noon, a similar ceremony was held in the same place and attended by multiple thousands of a diverse public.

In a more refined treatment of collective behavior, episodes such as this would perhaps better be viewed as having a dominant emotion of grief, sorrow, or mourning. Short of the day there is enough material to establish a fourth division, we can allow such patterns to huddle here as mild forms of fearful crowd arousal. Without debating the intricacies of emotions and their expression, it might even be suggested that fear of a sort is involved in the mourning-grief-sorrow complex in the sense that the sudden loss of revered figures renders standing social arrangements problematic and presages the need to reconstruct understandings in order to take account of the abrupt loss. Leaders, especially, are survivors of intricate processes of selection, compromise, and promises. Sudden removal means that the process must begin anew, especially in the context of a high degree of social fragmentation and conflict.

These types and levels of crowd fears are tentative and crude. They *are* things that exist "out there," however, and must in one or another way figure in more refined depictions of their nature and better and more elaborate schemes of scaled types.

MASS FEARS

The bulk of episodes relevant to the dominant emotion of fear seems not to involve crowds. Crowds may coalesce from time to time within a larger mass configuration, but mass fears occur decidedly more frequently, at least judging from the skewing of the literature.

Consistency and ideals of elegance require that mass fears be treated in terms of the same or similar levels of arousal as those of crowd fears.

The materials of mass fears do not, unhappily, yield to such treatment, and other partitioning principles must be employed. Explained at appropriate points, there are three of these.

True Dangers. The first principle is the truth or falsity of the danger identified as fearful, a distinction that will be explained when I address *false dangers*. The second principle is the space-time visibility of that for which a collective alarm occurs, distinguishing sudden space-and-time-circumscribed dangers (labeled *disasters)* from slow, space-and-time-dispersed *trends*. The third principle is the source of the asserted danger, varying for these purposes in terms of being *environmental* in the strict sense or *social-organizational.*

Environmental and Social Disasters. The most intensively worked area of mass fears is that of collective alarm in the situation of environmental disaster, situations where the physical environment has more or less suddenly and momentously gone awry. There are important variations within this category relative to the scale, duration, degree of prior warning, and suddenness of danger. One of the more frequently repeated substructions has been that of L.J. Carr (1932), who distinguishes the instantaneous-total, instantaneous-partial, progressive-diffuse, and progressive-focal patterns. Codifications may in the future take such patterns or some successor to them seriously, as has been attempted by Allan Barton (1969, ch. 2) in *Communities in Disaster* and Russell Dynes (1970, ch. 3) in *Organized Behavior in Disaster.* Such schemes do not seem to be used in organizing data on environmental disasters; they tend to stand, instead, alone in their separate sections as interesting schemes.

Human beings can sometimes produce collective trauma through assault on their own social organization. Among these, what are called "revolutionary situations" rank at or near the top of any scaled list of mass fear arousals. In these situations, a wide array of routine activities is physically disrupted or merely suspended. The high degree of ambiguity about the nature and fate of the social order renders ordinary and mundane activities temporarily meaningless, as documented by Bowden (1977) for certain years in Ireland and Palestine. Rapid increase in violence that is random from the point of view of the ordinary citizen thus provokes widespread fear (save perhaps among the revolutionarily dedicated who, in contrast, may be experiencing ecstatic joy) (Brinton 1957, esp. ch. 7, "Reigns of Terror").

The more diffuse social disarray of revolutionary situations is to be distinguished from sharply focused space-time social events that serve to suspend a sense of "business as usual." In one variety of such sharp jolts, a few days of significant suspension of ordinary life is followed by a quick return to it. The prototypical case might be the sudden loss of a venerated leader. Upon the assassination of President John Kennedy, for example, a great deal of ordinary life simply ceased, and, indeed, one professional sports team that insisted on playing a scheduled game was widely criticized for an "inappropriate attitude" (Sheatsley and Feldman 1964).

Environmental and Social Trends. Environmental and social disasters involve by definition sharply visible and objective changes in natural and/or social arrangements. They can literally be pointed to because they occupy circumscribed space and time. The collective alarm observed is more or less calibrated to the rise of objective danger. As the danger subsides, so does the collective alarm. That pattern needs to be distinguished from situations in which collective alarm is observed in the absence of any sharply visible and highly dangerous event that is responsible for the alarm. Moreover, those alarmed do not assert the existence or portent of any such event. Instead, they claim to discern a trend, a critical cumulation of ominous events that foretell a disastrous future. And less involved observers can assess that there is, in fact, a trend. The alarmed are pointing to something real, something that is enlarging or increasing, as they claim. Such observers may not subscribe to the predictions the alarmed make about the future of a trend, and they may not subscribe to the import, interpretation, or meaning the alarmed read into the objective trend in question, but they can agree on the narrow fact of the trend.

Given that dire trends are often long-term and sometimes subtle, and that alarm about them is highly variable and sporadic, the key sociological question about given alarms becomes: Why *now* that alarm? Why not a decade earlier, or later, or at all, for that matter?

The distinction between *environmental* and *social-organizational* dangers is especially pertinent with regard to trend alarms in modern societies. Environmental deterioration in the wake of industrialization and urbanization in America has been well documented and widely seen and appreciated for several decades, but the complex, fearful clamor about it that has been called "eco-hysteria" did not burst forth until late 1969 and early 1970. Mixed with collective hostility and joy, fear of environmental destruction possessed Americans. One indicator of its collective behavior character was suspension of the ordinary activities of the educational system, from top to bottom, on "Earth Day" (April 22, 1970) and the closing of many governmental units as well as some businesses. Rallies, marches, and dramatic acts were ubiquitous. Public television provided more than six hours of coverage. But the collective clamor waned almost as fast as it waxed, leaving, however, a new complex of laws and organizations in its wake (Downes 1972). Why 1970 and not 1965 or 1975 or some other year? Why at all?

More common are collective alarms over developing aspects of social arrangements, beliefs, or actions. As a class, these quickly shade off into mere matters of routine public debate and public opinion (important matters nonetheless). The most aroused levels of alarm, though, seem to operate in ways that are almost qualitatively different from those found in the ordinary play of public opinion. Perhaps the historical lenses are distorting, but the approximately 18-month episode in American history commonly called "the Red scare" (1919-20), strikes one as providing an almost ideal-typical case against which we can gauge degrees of fearful arousal found in other social trend alarms. Prior to and during part of that period there seemed to be an objective increase in liberal and radical thought and action in American society; that is, the mass fear known as "the Red scare" was responsive to a real, not imaginary, trend. And there seems to have been, in late 1919 and early 1920, a public definition of a national situation requiring extreme and emergency action to deal with that trend. Large segments of the society bracketed liberal and radical thought and action together as equally threatening. Grave countermeasures had to be mounted. These included large-scale raids on, and roundups of, alleged radicals, deportations, and refusal to seat properly elected but publicly suspect legislators. Sedition and Red flag laws proliferated and mob attacks on radicals occurred, most spectacularly in the Centralia Massacre of November 1919 (Murray 1955). If we can trust historians' accounts, the level of fearful arousal documented in the Red scare is rather rare. Certainly the so-called McCarthy era seems not to have approached it. Such fears, though, may occur in specific locales and fail to gain society-wide currency.

The analytic problem for collective behavior is where to draw the line between such mass fear and ordinary public opinion. For the sake of analytic purity, I am inclined to draw it at quite high levels. Thus, the Gallup and other polls regularly ask Americans questions such as: "What do you think is the most important problem facing this country today?" The lists of matters commonly elicited are seemingly routine problems. They provide clues to what might become objects of true alarm, but they are not yet alarms.

False Dangers. The reality-constructionism of much sociology in recent decades has been analytically useful but it also has definite limits. If social analysis is to have any credibility, analysts are in the end forced to make judgments about the degree to which environmental and social dangers are actually "out there" in the empirical world. The disaster and trend fears and their associated alarms just reviewed seem quite real in the sense that we can discover independent evidence of the dangers about which participants are alarmed. In the case of trends, if there is disagreement with participants, it is over the degree of danger rather than the existence of the trend.

Environmental and Social Disasters. This discussion is considerably more than merely theoretical, for, among other reasons, there are a surprisingly large number of episodes that display a pattern of mass (and quasi-crowd) fears of environmental disarray that seem not to be "real," at least not in the terms asserted by participants. The best-known case is perhaps that studied by Kerckhoff and Back (1968) and reported in their book *The June Bug*. In the summer of 1962, within the space of about a week, sixty-two persons employed in a clothing manufacturing plant "suffered what purported to be insect bites" (Kerckhoff, Back, and Miller 1965:3). The physical symptoms were quite real, but government investigators could discover no physical cause for them. Other such episodes in which there was a seemingly phantom physical cause accompanied by observable symptoms of a physical sort have involved merphose (McLeod 1975), "mystery gas" (Stahl and Lebedun 1974), food poisoning (Pfeiffer 1964), and assorted, vague odors (Cohen et al. 1978). The advent of the federal government's National Institute for Occupational Safety and Health has caused an upsurge in the reporting and documentation of such cases in the United States (Colligan and Stockton 1978). Investigators are amazingly in accord that the symptoms observed have a psychological rather than physical origin, and in plant settings refer even to "industrial hysteria" or "assembly-line hysteria." Affected workers are typically those who must perform "under great pressure," have "poor relations with supervisors," little opportunity for expressing grievances and effecting change, and associated problems (Cohen et al. 1978:15). "Having been left with no resource to cope with the situation, an objective physical stressor . . . can serve to provide justification to display somatic symptoms" (Cohen et al. 1978:15).

Scrutinized from a process point of view, false collective perceptions of social disaster differ quite markedly in the focus of their primary or initial phase (Smelser 1963). On the one hand, there is a set of episodes similar to environmental false alarms in that the onset events consist of a sequence of people manifesting unusual physical symptoms that have no easily identifiable physical cause and that seem best viewed as episodes of conversion hysteria. The classic case is the "phantom anesthetist" of Mattoon, Illinois (Johnson 1945), but there are many other such instances of epidemic hysteria (e.g. Knight, Friedman, and Sulianti 1965; Schuler and Parenton 1943; Tan 1963; Rankin and Philip 1963). Their common feature is a rapid spread of hysterical symptoms attributed to some mystery attacker, "mysterious ailment," the sighting of ghosts, or nothing in particular. The affliction is manifested only by a small minority of the community involved and reaches a peak, after which few or no new crises are reported. The social response to this "blip" of unusual behavior is one of excited fearfulness and search for remedy. The atmosphere may be "tense and electric" (Tan 1963:72), provoke "unreasoning rush" (Schuler and Parenton 1943:234), and the disorganized activation and scurrying of authorities (Chaplin 1959:111-17). But because the affliction does not spread, the fear seems to subside quickly and ordinary social life resumes. (All this is also the pattern commonly displayed by the environmental false alarms reviewed above.)

On the other hand, the primary phase of such false alarms may be merely cognitive in the sense of being only a report that some fearful event is happening or about to happen. The most dramatic form is supplied by the media of mass communication, technologies with unique capacities simultaneously to misinform masses of persons. The archetypical episode is Orson Welles's misheard broadcast of the "War of the Worlds" (Cantril 1940). Other documented false media alarms include the "Barseback Panic" (Rosengren et al. 1975) and the "phantom slasher of Taipei" (Jacobs 1965). Analysis of process in such episodes requires accurate descriptions of how many people of given social locations did what, at what point in time, after the alarm. For many years Hadley Cantril's characterization of relatively widespread flight and associated panic behavior in response to the Welles broadcast has been accepted in the literature. Recently, however, studies of a similar incident in Sweden found very little "on-the-ground" citizen response, a finding that has prompted a close rereading of the Cantril reports and a questioning of the characterizations drawn from them (Rosengren et al. 1975). The new reading suggests that a tiny minority of people act in an extraordinary fashion, rumors (false reports) of extraordinary behavior flourish, and local telephone systems overload temporarily, but that is about the extent of immediate reaction. In the view of the Rosengren group, the key feature is, instead, *exaggerated media processing* of the isolated and short-lived panic behavior. Public officials and a variety of policy-conscious persons are drawn in on the basis of the exaggerations, accepting them as accurate. The secondary phase then consists of fault-finding and blame-laying over the then unquestioned "fact" of the alleged panic. Whatever may turn out to be the case, the efforts of the Rosengren group teach us, at minimum, the need to be extremely cautious about media processing of alarms. The pressures under which media people work promote distorted portrayals, which are then taken by media viewers as accurate.

Environmental and Social Trends. The episodes examined above often involve assertion of disaster where there is, in fact, no threat at all. These are *pure* false alarms. In other cases, though, *something* may be happening—as in chain-reaction conversion hysteria—but it is not the threat the participants define it to be, nor is it as threatening as they define it. Both such patterns of false disaster alarms need to be distinguished from cases in which a long-standing feature of a social order, one that has been more or less constant over time, is suddenly fixed on and redefined as a dangerous *trend* that warrants drastic action.

The selectivity of collective social focus and agenda-setting means that only a few trends are at any time defined as meriting such treatment (Cobb and Elder 1972). The interesting obverse of this seemingly banal observation is that at any time there are *also* a multitude of standing conditions that are suppressed from public and collective awareness but about which reasonable numbers of people have significant anxiety. The collection of such conditions form a social ante- or stockroom of matters that, under given conditions, emerge as objects of collective fear. The key point is that the condition itself need not have changed, only the collective assessment of the degree to which it is a threat. The reassessment, however, is likely to be accompanied by the assertion that the condition is not merely stable but exhibits trend features.

The crime wave is one of the best documented and recurrent instances of this process of asserting false trend dangers. It appears there is rarely if ever such a thing as a crime wave (Bell 1961, ch. 8; Sutherland and Cressey 1966, ch. 11). Sporadic collective belief in and alarm over crime waves are a fact, however, and the key sociological question is how a constant comes to be treated as a variable.

An alarm requires an alarmer and in the case of the crime wave the alarmists have been clearly identified as various of the mass media. In his typical forthright fashion, criminologist Donald Cressey has declared "most 'crime waves' are fabrications of the press" (Sutherland and Cressey 1966:259). Following on that idea, Mark Fishman (1978:540) and his associates have made a signal contribution to understanding how media crime waves are precipitated by tracing a "crime wave against the elderly" in the New York media. Working as part of a team of observers in a New York TV station, Fishman observed the unsurprising fact that media people organize news in terms of themes and, more interestingly, newspeople rely heavily on viewing one anothers' productions to decide what themes deserve or require coverage. Further, police try to cooperate with media by organizing and presenting daily reports to them. These reports are constructed to emphasize certain kinds of crimes: crimes in public places, "crimes between strangers and crime specific to age." The intersection of these practices produces a steady stream of stories on "crimes against the elderly." They are "normal" news. Then a media editor decides to feature that steady-state theme as a problem. Other media see the feature, find that there is such a thing, and follow suit to "meet the competition." Enter now public officials who feel they must comment and act. The crime theme has then become a crime wave. The Fishman analysis points up two main questions about such alarms. (1) How is information structured and routed in a way that determines that some rather than other things become objects of alarms? Fishman suggests, for example, that police reporting is structured to conduce alarms only about street crimes. The police "wire" Fishman studied did not, for example, report consumer fraud, environmental pollution, or political bribery. (2) From such a prestructured pool, what are the dynamics of selection and its timing?

COLLECTIVE HOSTILITIES

Hostility is the second emotion often dominant in collective behavior episodes, an emotion ordinarily defined as "antagonism, opposition, or resistance in thought or principle." Associated terms are *animosity* and *enmity* as well as the concept of anger and its family of terms: *wrath, rage, fury, frenzy, ire,* and mere *displeasure*.

The core cases of this broad pattern are well established in the literature under such rubrics as "acting crowd," "hostile outburst," "collective violence," and "riot." These and other such concepts are both too narrow and too abstract as dependent variables. They are frequently too narrow in identifying violence and disorder as the sine qua non of collective hostility when there are many varieties that are neither violent nor disorderly. These concepts are frequently too abstract, even within this narrowness, because quite diverse occurrences of violence and disorder are grouped together, occasions that need to be separated for their best understanding. We need, therefore, to broaden and differentiate the view.

To establish the range of relevant phenomena, three levels of collective hostility may be described. The first and lowest is *symbolic,* the range of ways people speak and act to communicate their displeasure short of physically interfering with the property and bodies of those toward whom they feel hostility. Disregarding the crowd/mass distinction for the moment, varying levels within symbolic hostility may be arrayed from weakest to strongest in this fashion: written declarations, speeches to crowds, protest marches and rallies, mau-mauing (Wolfe 1971), taunting, crowd baiting. Many of these are most often quite marginal as collective behavior, but they may set the stage for collective behavior and, to inexperienced participants, they might *be* collective behavior. In totalitarian countries the symbolic level of collective hostility is definitely collective behavior.

A second level of collective hostility is directed toward real and personal property and ways in which their uses can be hampered and hamstrung: confiscation of objects (for example looting); boycott (of objects or persons); strike; occupation or takeover of a place (for example sitting in, storming); destruction of objects or places (for example firebombing). The third and highest level is directed to the bodies of other human beings, in the direct forms of capture, assault (for example clubbing, torturing), and murder.

CROWD HOSTILITIES

Within the area of crowd hostilities, empirical work has focused heavily on the two higher levels—interference with property and bodies. While clearly important, that focus is too narrow and probably results from the tendency to relegate lower-level episodes to the study of social movements because such episodes are often the creatures of social movement strategy. However, we need only to distinguish between encounters and formal organizations as units of analysis to appreciate the relevance of symbolic hostility to the study of collective behavior.

Unlike the other two domains of collective behavior, literature on crowd hostility yields a number of articulated types. The task is less one of discerning and more one of systematizing. Two basic principles can be employed. (1) Episodes of crowd hostility start from significantly different definitions of the situation of assembly. The careers and consequences of episodes vary as a function of the on-the-scene notion of what the assembly is about and what it is. The four main varieties of such standing definitions of the situation may be labeled the political, leisure, street, and captive. Each is explained at an appropriate point below. (2) Crosscutting these on-the-scene definitions and associated variations in social organization are variations in who is contending. Who is expressing hostility toward whom? In episodes of collective hostility there are three basic parties: a single *individual* (or perhaps a small group); a significant segment or category of the *citizenry;* and the *establishment*—people in positions of political authority and those who associate with such persons. It takes two parties to contend, and the resultant typology provides nine situations of contention, only some of which are collective-behavior relevant (for example, individual-to-individual contentions involving high levels of hostility are labeled "crime" or "deviance," individuals initiating high levels of hostility against citizens or the establishment are coded "mad-dog killer" or some variant thereof). Contentions tend to be initiated and dominated by one party even though both parties claim the other "started it" by reason of long-persisting and nefarious actions or by a recently committed provocative action. Acknowledging such complications, it is still possible to isolate the more initiating and active party in particular episodes.

Political Crowds. Crowds assemble under *political* definitions in the sense that "everyone" understands before and at the assembly that the object is to make a statement of some sort about social arrangements. Common instances are demonstrations, rallies, and marches. More broadly, a political crowd is any assembly that is trying "to get particular other people to do particular things," to quote Charles Tilly (1978:143), whose conception of a collective action is similar to that of a political crowd except that for Tilly (1979) not all collective actions seem to involve crowds. Using Tilly's language, political crowds are assembled to make *claims* where, ordinarily, there is an articulate and pressed conflict of interests as defined by the parties in contention.

Not untypically, members of such crowds are relatively well known to each other or at least leaders are known to one another and people participate as members of cliques. The crowds are clique-composites and are led through predesigned routines by previously evolved leadership. Of the nine logical types of parties in contention, five have been documented at one or more levels of dominant hostility.

Citizens against Individuals (e.g. Mob Attacks). Robert C. Meyers's (1948) well-known case study of an "anti-communist mob action" provides a near-prototype of a high level of dominant crowd arousal where citizens are arrayed against an individual or a small set of them. The 1947 event involved thousands of emotionally worked-up veterans of World War II assembled vocally and physically to comment on three members of the Communist Party scheduled to speak at a Trenton, New Jersey, auditorium. Such high levels of dominant arousal between parties of this sort seem rather more rare in recent decades, although lesser levels in which liberal/radical students harass conservative speakers on college campuses have not been unusual.

Citizens against Citizens (e.g. Political Clashes). Likewise, high-level dominant arousal involving citizens against citizens in political crowds have seemed in decline in Western societies in recent decades, particularly in the United States. Accounts of the Red scare period, for example, suggest frequent and high levels of mob violence between "socialists" and "patriots" in the context of each appearing at the others' political gatherings. One of the most violent was perhaps the famous clash between the Wobblies and an American Legion parade in Centralia, Washington, on Armistice Day (November 11) 1919 (Murray 1955:183-85). The political clash of crowds remains, however, a potent tool, and there are suggestions of its resurgence in encounters between conservative Whites and liberal/radical Blacks.

In a somewhat relaxed conception of political crowds, we might attend to those occasions on which territorial units and groupings come into overt conflict over alleged instances of offensive behavior. For example, in urban slum settings displaying a "segmentary system" (Suttles 1968:31), there are recurrent rumors or acts of interethnic or neighborhood offensiveness in which "more and more people are involved in the anticipated conflict" (Suttles 1968:198). "Frequently this takes the form of a predicted 'gang fight' " (Suttles 1968:201). Infrequently, there is an actual confrontation of two named street-corner groups. In form, it is not unlike the violent conflicts sometimes occurring between youth of rival towns of a bygone rural world (cf. Tilly 1978:145, 1979).

Citizens against Establishments (e.g. Protests). The great "growth industry" among political crowds in recent decades seems to have been in episodes of citizens against the establishment—establishment meaning those citizens who are imputed to control important social units, to make decisions in the name of, or almost in the name of, society, or to be direct agents of such persons. The dominant level of arousal of such crowds has been quite low, or at the first or symbolic level identified above (Etzioni 1970). This level is itself quite compli-cated and one important line of advance is identification of its more detailed forms and levels. A key sourcebook for that effort is Gene Sharp's (1973) monumental *The Politics of Nonviolent Action,* a tour de force of case study compilation. Unfortunately, Sharp's coverage is constrained by his moral preference for nonviolent protest. Ruthlessly empirical inquiry will articulate the full range of what people actually do. Something of the breadth required is suggested by historians such as George Rudé (1964), whose *The Crowd in History* is extremely instructive regarding repertoires of crowd actions in political situations and the complexity of the view of political crowds we will need to develop. As he concludes, the political crowd of early modern Europe was "violent, impulsive, easily stirred by rumor, and quick to panic; but it was not fickle, peculiarly irrational, or generally given to bloody attacks on persons" (Rudé 1964:257).

Establishments against Individuals (e.g. Bourbon Lynchings). The notion of the political crowd calls attention to precrowd scene organization that has a political definition. There is a deliberate and coordinated movement to a physical site for the purpose of making a claim or demand. It is a preplanned expression of hostility aimed at achieving or stopping a change. The level and form of hostile action that ensues is, of course, problematic. The Bourbon lynching is perhaps the most prominent pattern of such a crowd within the more restricted category of the establishment crowd mobilizing against an individual. As developed by Arthur Raper (1933) and treated by Hadley Cantril (1941:94) it is a "relatively exclusive and well-regulated" affair "often engineered by leading citizens with the knowledge of law-enforcement officers." The small crowd is orderly and quiet. Even though it engages in an act of murder, the level of *overt* emotional arousal is reportedly not high.

Establishments against Citizens (e.g. Official Riots). The classic images of crowd hostility depict segments of the downtrodden citizenry and assorted underclasses rising against the powers that be. Closer attention to parties in contention suggests that the powers that be may have been as active in collectively assaulting citizens as being assaulted by them. Collective behavior scholars have simply not turned their attention in this direction albeit the concept of the pogrom does appear, in a minor way, in the literature.

One of the more recent and acute efforts to correct this omission has been provided by Albert Bergesen (1976:9) in his reanalysis of the Detroit and Newark ghetto riots of 1967. He is able to document that violence by officials escalated faster than citizen violence and it became "random, indiscriminate and personal in the clear absence of corresponding civilian violence. There seems to have been an increasing lack of organizational or normative control over the actions of officials, which suggests the presence of an 'official riot.' " That is, there were "two separate riots."

Bergesen (1976) also provides some fresh causal thinking on crowd hostilities in calling attention to the similarities between the French grain riots and the racial disorders of the American 1960s. Both involved the drawing of new categories of citizens into the national state and the concomitant undermining of the authority of local establishments. He isolates three stages of this process in the American case: (1) federal intervention in local politics, actions that "disequilibriated the local states' order"; (2) the onset of status uncertainty that was associated with the rise of Black protest; and (3) the riot of threatened Whites.

Leisure Crowds. A second genus assembles under a definition of its situation as *leisure*. Its object is to witness a sporting or other entertainment, or simply to lounge, as on beaches. Although contentions over social arrangements, decisions, and rights may emerge during assembly, such conflicts are not the predecided objects of the assembly per se, in contrast to the political case just discussed. Here, also, individuals tend to be part of cliques, although somewhat smaller. Leadership is more tenuous, absent, or socially remote (such as mere loudspeaker announcers). In both types, though, members have preplanned their participation.

Following Goffman (1961b), focused may be distinguished from unfocused leisure crowds, a distinction that in the case materials correlates highly with two common patterns of the parties in contention.

Citizens against Citizens (e.g. Fan Violence). Focused crowds assemble to witness some kind of event, most commonly a contest between two sporting teams or persons. In one of its forms of higher dominant arousal, stagers of the event desire and expect the crowd to achieve an overt but orderly level of hostile arousal. Participants apparently also arrive with that expectation and are disappointed if it does not occur. Further, reports on British football, especially, suggest that the organized fan clubs have prepared routines for "whipping" themselves into "frenzied" states of hostile arousal and creating an "electric atmosphere" (Marsh et al. 1978:119). This involves more or less set chants, singing, gestures, and other devices. The mood is sometimes described as one of "fun and excitement" combined with hatred (Smith 1975: 310, 316ff.). Such hostile arousal is channeled by roles, rules, and shared meanings that extend to occasions of violence between fan categories and toward officials and players. "Fights . . . do not start up randomly. They occur in circumstances which fans are able to specify and which are seen as legitimizing their actions" (Marsh et al. 1978:107). (Moreover, the hatred combines with fear when violent encounters are in the offing.)

Citizens against Establishments (e.g. Resort Disorders). Unfocused leisure crowds congregate on a common site without a single and overt object of attention, as on beaches, parks, and certain promenades. The pattern in which such crowds become hostilely aroused against an establishment is most familiarly identified with the mid-sixties phenomenon of hordes of late adolescent youth converging on the beach resort towns of East Coast America. Milling by the thousands, typically on a Saturday night or other major holiday evening such as Labor Day, some provocative event transformed the diffuse search for "action" into focused hostility. Commonly, a police action was the offending event after which an array of violent acts ensued.

In a too neglected analysis, Thomas Smith (1968:177) has documented the process through which the Labor Day adolescent crowds of Ocean City, Maryland, even evolved into yearly occasions of ritualized crowd expression of hostility. After an initiating disorder on Labor Day 1959, in succeeding years

> a crowd would form at Ninth Street; the police would instantly surround and capture it; a few arrests would be made, and the police, in the process of cooling off the crowd, would get "dumped-on" to the delight of on-lookers and retreating participants. The newspapers would feature the story the next day and grind subsequent features out of it for weeks after that. The police would get a slap on the back, and for the following year the teenagers would talk excitedly about what had happened.

Emergent Street Crowds. The third major context of crowd hostility evolves in unplanned street situations where there is no preplanning of participation. The crowd is accidental in the sense that the individual comes upon the matters that begin to occupy his/her attention. There is little prior definition of "what the assembly is about." The hostile meaning, if it occurs, is *emergent*. There is little preexisting internal social networking and preestablished leadership as compared with political and leisure crowds. Leadership, if any, is emergent. The degree of social organization that might be displayed evolves over the course of the situation.

Citizens against Individuals (e.g. Proletarian Lynchings). In one ideal typical pattern of emergent citizen crowds against an individual, the offending act(s) of an identifiable and locatable person becomes the object of face-to-face talk among persons who have congregated without preplan or design in a public place. In the absence of predesignated leaders, talk and associated physical and emotional milling increase feelings of hostility or outrage. The more vocal of the emergent leaders or keynoters speak in voices loud enough to be heard widely and to suggest hostile courses of action. Under certain microecological conditions facilitating crowd growth and stimulated by focusing events, such emotions are translated into acts of an escalating hostile character. In the most extreme case, the offending individual is taken by force from the custody of authorities and subjected to various acts of violence and to murder. Durwood Prudens's (1936) account of the 1930 Leevile, Texas, lynching is no doubt still the most detailed chronicle available on one of the more gruesome trajectories of such events (Cantril 1941, ch. 4).

Citizens against Citizens (e.g. Communal Riots). In the situation of relatively active street life and pedestrian traffic (which is not yet a crowd, but which provides a recruitment flow for one), a few categorically opposed citizens may fall into hostile and perhaps violent exchange. This provides the focus for a crowd to form and for additional clashes to start. The scene may be multinucleated in the sense that several small crowds are engaging in intercategorical violence along with "citizens against individuals." The literature has focused on interracial instances and prompts the label "race riot." Conceived more generically, the term *communal riot* (Janowitz 1968) seems more accurate, because the common background and process of these clashes involves competition of citizen categories for the scarce resources of housing, employment, and recreation.

Conspicuous features of such specifically interracial clashes as reported by Grimshaw (1960) and others include concentration of violence "along borders of contested areas" and "at transportation transfer points" (McCall 1970:346), a relatively high degree of physical violence between the races, and relatively little property damage. Fogelson (1971) has characterized the White-initiated part of the violence as "reactionary" in the sense that it is directed to stopping the movement of Blacks into previously White-controlled housing, jobs, and public accommodations.

Citizens against the Establishment (e.g. the Ghetto Riot). The type of collective behavior that caused so much concern in the American sixties was the hostility of citizens against the establishment. It has been labeled the "ghetto riot," and while Black ghettos were the most obvious instances, at least some of the disorders that took place in university cities can be viewed as emergent street crowd hostilities of the youth ghetto (Lofland 1968; ch. 3 this vol.). One of the better-known episodes is that documented by Quarantelli and Hundley (1975) with regard to emergent crowds of students and their hostility to jaywalking laws in the illustrious youth ghetto of Columbus, Ohio.

The ideal-typical pattern entails disorder and violence *within* the ghetto rather than along its borders, and a relatively small amount of body-directed violence relative to a large amount of property destruction and appropriation. Direct intercategorical clashes are relatively infrequent. The initiating incident is an interchange between an agent of the establishment (almost always the police) rather than between ordinary members of opposed segments of the citizenry (McCall 1970; Quarantelli and Hundley 1975).

Captive Crowds. The three crowd contexts just described have in common the fact that they occur in "civil society," by which I mean that the participants are involved in a more or less space-and-place segregated round of life—they work, sleep, eat, and recreate in separate places. In contrast, the integrated place rounds identified by Erving Goffman (1961a:xiii) as "total institutions" involve "a place of residence and work where a large number of like situated individuals, cut off from the wider society, . . . together lead an enclosed formally administered round of life."

Total institutions create peculiarly tight and alienating situations of life and of associated crowd formation and functioning. Physical and/or social and legal barriers to exit and the hothouse character of social life within them produce a uniquely sensitive, systemic, and socially reverberating structure. Once a social order of some sort has evolved and achieved a working consensus, efforts to change parts of it appear to have severe hostility-provoking consequences. Surveying studies of crowd hostilities in total institutions, Norman Denzin (1968) has classified such disorders as stemming from changes in (1) division of labor, (2) channels of communication, and (3) normative structure. One finds, in particular, the anomaly that reform measures in prisons and mental hospitals are productive of disorders because such innovations upset existing social arrangements, providing new advantages for some inmates while depriving others of previously favored situations.

The citizens-against-citizens/citizens-against-establishments distinctions are equally relevant to the context of captive crowds. The recent history of American prisons can be written in terms of the decline of the latter and the rise of the former. Inmate organization has come increasingly to be based on antagonistic racial categories rather than solidaristic opposition to prison authorities—the establishment (Irwin 1980). (The rise of one has not, however, meant the disappearance of the other.)

It can now be suggested that these four differences in contexts of crowd hostility identify a wide variety of ways in which episodes differ with regard to causes of crowd assembly, participants' definitions of the situation and motivations for participation, triggering events for the escalation of hostility, reactions of authorities, subsequent public perception of and responses to episodes, among many others. One important line of advance will be the specific comparative analysis of episodes with regard to such contexts and their correlates.

MASS HOSTILITIES

Crowd hostilities, especially the higher levels of arousal, have been extensively researched, but mass hostilities have hardly been speculated about, much less probed empirically. Two kinds of effort must suffice to suggest lines along which this area might fruitfully be developed.

The first direction is illustrated by Orrin Klapp's (1971, ch. 10) discussion of the mass villain and the process of vilification in the context of the "urbanized mass," as well as in other contexts. He distinguishes four major phases of vilification in terms of the "symbolic tasks" entailed. First, there is a period from the start of social unrest to emergent definition of a "crisis or problem of a kind calling for a villain" (Klapp 1971:86; Bergesen and Warr 1979 on threat and "boundary crisis"). The second phase is "growth of a demand for a specific villain to fit the moral alarm." Third, action must be organized and carried out, involving debate over the nature of that action. Fourth, there is the "creation of a consummatory dramatic image of the treatment of the villain" (Klapp 1971:87; Bergesen and Warr 1979 on "ritual persecution"). Klapp's formulation is open-ended and needs adaptation and elaboration with empirical cases, as has begun in the work of Albert J. Bergesen (Bergesen and Warr 1979) and James M. Inverarity (1976).

In a second direction, several types of crowd hostilities, especially those involving violence and disorder, seem to occur in "disorder curves." That is, after the first few, there is a rapid spread in place of occurrence and rise in their number, followed by a precipitous decline and virtual cessation. Such was, for example, the curve of both the American race and youth ghetto disorders of the sixties. Similar waves have been documented in the history of American prisons (Irwin 1980) and in the "swastika epidemic" of 1959-60 involving anti-Semitic markings and vandalism (Smelser 1963:257-60). Even though the crowd (or small group) remains the basic "acting unit," there is at minimum a mass-like quality to the manner in which later disorders have the form of earlier ones and follow so close upon them. The mass media are obviously critical in the dissemination of physical images and definitions of the emerging situation. There is some suggestion in the work of Spilerman (1976) and others that, in the case of Black ghetto rioting (and perhaps in other curves), local conditions of disadvantage and deprivation become less predictive of disorder the farther along in the series a given disorder occurs. That is, there is perhaps such a contradictory and seemingly impossible thing as a mass riot in the special sense that mass media make it possible for crowd actions to have quite remote inspiration, inspiration not closely geared to specific and particular circumstances at hand (albeit obviously related to them in a general way). Specifically, "incidents [of Black ghetto disorder] tended to cluster in time following a few dramatic events such as the massive Newark disorder in July 1967 and the assassination of Martin Luther King in April of 1968" (Spilerman 1976:790). Further, Spilerman (1976:790) asserts "there is considerable evidence that skyjackings, prison riots, bomb threats and aggressive crime of other sorts have been spread by television and other mass media."

COLLECTIVE JOYS

We move from the unpleasant and grim matters of fear and hostility to the positive and enthralling matter of joy. By "joy" is meant "the emotion evoked by well-being, success, or good fortune or by the prospect of possessing what one desires." It is a "state of happiness or felicity." Associated terms include *delight, gaiety, pleasure, jubilation, merriment,* and *bliss.*

The joys of interest are collective in either of two senses: the dominant emotion of a face-to-face assembly (a crowd), or a shared emotion among a dispersed set of persons attending to the same object at more or less the same time and who are aware that other people are attending. These foci exclude a host of private, personal, dyadic, and small-group joys such as religious, sexual, and kindred ecstatic states, excitement associated with deviant acts, adventures of risk-taking sports such as parachuting, and drug highs, among others. However, to the degree that any one of these becomes a crowd or mass focus, it becomes relevant to collective behavior analysis. The exclusion of any of these is based on empirical rather than analytic grounds.

CROWD JOYS

Although crowd joys are extremely important, they have been almost totally neglected by scholars in recent decades. In an effort to stimulate interest in them, I have made a special effort to assemble and order fugitive materials relevant to their study. That effort was extensive enough to justify publication apart from this chapter and it incorporated all the materials originally appearing in this section.

Because that separate treatment appears as the next chapter (chapter 2), I will not repeat the brief materials initially appearing in this section that are available in that expanded version.

MASS JOYS

Mass joys vary in three ways; a cross-classification of these ways can assist us in achieving a more systematic apprehension of their most familiar forms: the *craze,* the *fashion,* and the *fad.* First, like crowd joys, they vary in the dominant level of emotional arousal. Second, they vary in the degree of seriousness with which they are invested. Third, there is variation in the scope, duration, and regularity of the participants' involvement. Put differently, the degree of obtrusiveness into participants' ordinary lives differs from the craze, to the fashion, to the fad (cf. LaPiere 1938, ch. 19).

Mass Excitements: Crazes. A *craze* is an exciting mass involvement that is quite serious in nature and consequence and in which people are more or less encompassingly involved for relatively long periods (cf. Brown 1954:868). The word *craze* is one of a family of terms none of which comfortably characterizes the empirical instances ordinarily associated with them. The other terms are: *fever* ("heightened or intense emotion . . . transient enthusiasm . . . unstable condition of mind or society"); *madness* ("extreme folly . . . rashness . . . complete involvement"); and *mania* ("excessive or unreasonable enthusiasm"). *Craze* itself is sometimes defined as a "transient infatuation." Tradition sanctions the use of any of these terms and in the interest of continuity it seems reasonable to continue the usage despite my misgivings that even the mildest of these words—*craze*— denotes a level of arousal and mindless abandon difficult to document in the episodes ordinarily so classified. Following LaPiere (1938), two patterns of craze should be distinguished.

The El Dorado Rush and the Boom. The rush to El Dorado centers on the belief that sudden personal wealth is in the offing if one will only physically or socially "go for it" *now* (LaPiere 1938:495-96). The physical form involves rushing to a specific place to take possession of wealth. The California gold rush of the 1850s is perhaps the most famous instance. The most important recent contribution to our understanding of this form is Gary Hamilton's (1978:1478) "The Structural Sources of Adventurism," an analysis in which the social type of the adventurer is developed and interpreted as an adaptive response to societies stressing "particularistic achievement."

In the social form, certain commodities or investments are defined as sudden sources of wealth and, further, the rush to possess it sets up the well-know "boom dynamic" in which people acquire an object "because they expect others to buy at a higher price; and these others buy at that higher price because they fully expect others to buy from them at a still higher price" (LaPiere 1938:502). A limit is inevitably reached and people shift from buying to selling; they shift, that is, from positive excitement to alarmed escape.

Promised-Land Migrations. LaPiere's brief discussion of what he calls the "mass movement" is one of the few efforts to analyze waves of mass decision making and migration based on the idea that "peace and security" are to be had in a new land. Unlike the fabled departure of the Israelites from Egypt, which had qualities of a social movement, true mass migrations have no central coordination. Individuals and families independently decide to seek a "land of milk and honey," and they do so in large numbers or over a relatively short period of time. In more recent decades, the rural commune migration of the American sixties had the qualities of such a movement.

Mass Pleasures: Fashions. A fashion is a pleasurable mass involvement that participants and observers define as important but not critical, and in which people are variously engaged depending on the particular fashion. The fact that almost all collective behavior treatments include fashion is an anomaly, for one of its most commonly asserted features is that of being a "prevailing or accepted style" "believed to be superior practice" and to have superior merit in some field (Blumer 1969c:286). This means that "fashion has respectability [and] . . . carries the stamp of approval of an elite" (Blumer 1969c:272). A fashion need not be recognized by participants as such. It is often only "from the detached vantage point of later time" that fashions are detected (Blumer 1969c:288). Fashion is associated with moderate levels of dominant emotional arousal, and pleasure mingles with a "careful and discerning" attitude (Blumer 1969c:277). "While people may become excited over a fashion, they respond primarily to its character of propriety and distinction" (Blumer 1969c:277). And even though fashion has serious consequences and is important, such judgments do not reach the critical levels we associate with crazes. Fashion, then, is relatively institutional in character as opposed to collective behavior. However, it must also be acknowledged that its study has no other analytic (or actual) home and it must perforce remain with the collective behaviorists because, although marginal, it has a certain relevance for the reasons stressed by Blumer (1969c) regarding "collective ambiguity" and the merits of "competing models" of practice and belief.

Efforts to specify types or patterns of fashion have mostly pointed to the multiinstitutional occurrence of these types, eschewing the idea that fashion has only or largely to do with matters of personal adornment and household decoration. It is rife in even such sacred areas as physical science, religion, and business as well as in such venal domains as politics, sex, and social science. Taking that point as given, the next step would seem to be the breaking down of the global notion of fashion along more generic lines. I am inclined to do this in terms of the third mode of mass joy variation: scope-duration-regularity. This requires asking several interrelated questions: (1) How broad is the "package of elements" that compose the fashion? (2) How long is the typical involvement in a fashion and the life of the fashion itself? (3) How regular is participation: full time, brief time daily, once a week, occasionally, no special time because of its character? (4) How obtrusive into prefashion life is the new fashion? The concrete fashions of the empirical world vary infinitely along these lines. Simplification is necessary and three patterns may be suggested: lifestyle, activity system, and item.

Lifestyle. Lifestyle fashions entail a relatively rich package or cluster of items in dress, speech, activity, belief, and social relations. The participants define the package as a distinctive and coherent cluster. Participation is constant or, at minimum, many times a week and it requires, at least, a gradual giving up of one's prefashion lifestyle. If there is any doubt about the respectability of the lifestyle, there is also possible the claim of superiority and avant-gardism. Among the most respectable and snobbish of lifestyle fashions, mention may be made of "Marin County trendy" (made famous by Cyra McFadden [1977] in *The Serial),* "posthippie, bourgeois bohemians," and "upper-middle-class trendies." (For these I am indebted to the keen eye and description of John Irwin 1977:64-71.) Although of marginal and controversial respectability, the "hippie style," "surfer scene" (Irwin 1977), "dandy life" (Smith 1974), "singles life," and associated "emerging alternative lifestyles" (Butler and McGinley 1977), all illustrate past and present "posing packages."

Activity System. Activity-system fashions are less encompassing. Participation is likely to be regular but segregated in the individual's round of life. Joining involves devoting interspersed hours during a week or on weekends rather than the holistic assumption of an altered daily round, language style, and clothing pattern. Following Irwin's (1977:27) use of the idea of activity system, conspicuous examples are:

"tennis, . . . car racing, cooking, skate-boarding, transcendental meditation, nudism, skydiving, stamp collecting."

Like lifestyle fashions, these are involvements that participants define as important, but not apocalyptic or critical. Entry and exit from them is relatively private and voluntary, lacking in the kinds of transition trauma we associate with social movement involvements and the mainline institutions of the family, work, and education. While both types of fashion may have a competitive element, sometimes highly competitive, it is not quite the same kind of devastating competition associated with mainline institutions. Fashion may provide, nevertheless, a basis of pride, as in the report that in some parts of America "possession and display of the snowmobile has become a badge of distinction proclaiming that the owner has made it and knows 'where it's at' " (Martin and Berry 1974:109). (Such an attitude is of course the essence of fashion.)

Items. Particular and specific cultural items are the kinds of things that more ordinarily come to mind when using the term *fashion*. The archetypical item is the female dress and, concretely and oddly, its length and breadth. A signal feature of item fashions is their relative lack of obtrusiveness into the participant's life. The concept of the participant becomes less appropriate than that of the user. Participants have to go out of their way to "get into" something, as was said in the American seventies, whereas users import items to "where they are."

Among item fashions, the best known kinds are physical objects, particularly clothing, such as (in recent years) the T-shirt, Levi jeans, and neck chains. Facial hair is also in this class. Beyond these are fashions in items of household decoration, for example houseplants, design (such as two-car garages), food items and preparation (slow cookers, bottled water), consumer "toys" (CB radios), and so forth.

Ideas, like physical objects, are matters of fashion. More elaborated and enduring ideas—philosophies—may be fashionable as long as a decade or so. Most ideas, however, are not as complicated and robust and have far shorter lives, as in such once-fashionable phenomena captured by such concepts as "radical chic" (Wolfe 1971), "environmental salvation" (Downes 1972), and "nostalgic reminiscence" (F. Davis 1979). The narrowest of idea fashions involve mere words and expressions, as in the succession of ways in which American youth has expressed approval: *"swell"* (circa thirties); *"neat"* (fifties); *"right on"* (sixties); *"really"* (seventies).

Discrete forms of activity may be in or out of fashion, interesting instances being regular exercising (Gallup 1977), bicycling (Harmond 1972), genealogical searching, and karate (Gehlen and Doeren 1976).

To the degree an activity is elaborated and associated with public settings of action and contact it "graduates" to being an "activity system" as mentioned above and discussed by Irwin (1977:27-28).

Specific people (or categories of them à la the adorations of radical chic) may be in or out of fashion. In the dead hero category, for a period in the mid-seventies, Harry Truman was fashionable, as evidenced in his more or less simultaneous celebration in a song, bumper sticker, book, play, TV special, and the placement of his dusted-off portrait in the White House cabinet room. The living are, however, more likely the beneficiaries of fashion, especially in the entertainment, sports, and political realms (Klapp 1964).

Finally, for purposes of expanding the conception of fashion, elaborately staged events may be infused with the approving aura of fashion. At a purely mass level, such multievening television happenings as *Roots* (1977) and *Holocaust* (1979) were very much in fashion. Combining mild crowd joy arousals with mass joys, there are the more regularly recurring fashions of the televised Superbowl and *Sun Day*.

Mass Amusements: Fads. A fad is an amusing mass involvement defined as of little or no consequence and in which involvement is brief (cf. Turner and Killian 1972:129; Brown 1954:868). Words often associated with the term include: *madcap, hijinks, antics, lark, silly, funny.* The notion of a "fancy" is not inappropriately connoted, a "liking formed by caprice rather than by reason," something that is "whimsical and irregular." Fad objects have no serious impact on anyone's life (save perhaps to produce a fortune for promoters/manufacturers). Further, fads tend to be shorter-lived than crazes or fashions. They tend both to boom rapidly and die out with equal rapidity.

These features bear on the complexity, elaboration, and organization achieved by, or found among, fads. As seen above, crazes and fashions can become quite complicated. Crazes may entail prolonged and arduous travel, novel equipment, or sequences of investment decisions. Fashions are sometimes almost complete lifestyles or activity systems. Little or none of this is found in fads. From the point of view of the ordinary participant (user), fads are largely confined to the complexity identified among fashions as the item level.

In spite of these guidelines, the notion of a fad is quite slippery and subject to debate when applied in concrete instances. A brief listing of candidate fad items may serve to join the issue of how, more operationally, to define them. Such candidates may be arrayed in terms of the same categories used to array item fashions.

1. Object fads of the seventies included blacklight and drug-extolling posters, message bumper stickers, the round, yellow, smiling face, biolators, pop rocks, the pet rock, and gnomes. Older clothing fads include beer jackets, rope beads, raccoon hats, and hooded blouses (Horn 1968:179).
2. Idea fads of the same period included the rumor of the death of Paul McCartney (Suczek 1973) and the practice of astrology and interest in witches. (Marcello Truzzi [1972:22,26] characterizes interest in the latter two as "highly irreverent, almost playful . . . fun . . . [and] non-serious.")
3. Activity fads have included the oft-mentioned miniature golf, yo-yo playing, telephone booth stuffing, and most spectacularly, streaking (Miller and Evans 1975).
4. Fad people are also spoken of as fad heroes, people who are not quite seriously adored despite the fact that their faces are briefly ubiquitous. An indicator of their unseriousness is their absence from lists of "people most admired" that are generated by public opinion polls. (The people on such lists are fashionable rather than faddish.) Fad heroes of the seventies included the Fonz (actor Henry Winkler), Farrah Fawcett-Majors, and assorted figures grouped under the heading "punk rock."

CONCLUDING REITERATIONS

I would like to conclude by reiterating the aims of this chapter. First and foremost, I have tried to make at least modest progress in the task of delineating forms of collective behavior, an aspect egregiously neglected. In pressing that task, I may well have produced, as critics would have it, a "mere catalogue of cryptic accounts" based on an assortment of unrelated principles of classification. But even so, there is a fundamental mission of generic rescue to be performed, and I am satisfied that I have at least begun that work. A decent portion of the relevant array has been minimally displayed.

Second, and less centrally, I have tried to bring emotions back into the study of collective behavior by using their substance and "dominant level of arousal" as principles of classification. It is to be hoped that such an approach is compatible with the more common cognitive and behavioral conceptions popular in the field at present.

I want to urge, finally, that these two tasks ought not be confused with my specific modes of addressing them. As is often and rightly observed, care must be taken not to throw a baby out with its bathwater. Regardless of the usefulness of the present effort to specify elementary forms and reintroduce an emotive component, those two tasks abide. It is from its own ashes that the phoenix arises in youthful freshness.

NOTE

Several scholars have been exceedingly generous of their time in criticizing an earlier version of this analysis. I have profited greatly from their suggestions, but (for better or worse) have not accepted a great deal of their good advice. I therefore absolve them from guilt by association and express my deep appreciation for having made an effort to save me from errors: Richard Gambrell, Lyn H. Lofland, Enrico Quarantelli, Morris Rosenberg, Neil Smelser, Ralph Turner, and several anonymous reviewers. Most of all, I am indebted and grateful to Lyn H. Lofland.

2

CROWD JOYS (1982)

Historically, sociological scholars of collective behavior addressed crowd and mass phenomena that were dominated by one or another of three kinds of intense emotional arousal: fear, hostility, and joy. Initially, all three received something approaching "equal time" in general discussions of the field. But as the decades have gone by, the third element of this trinity—joy—has been gradually dropped out. Matters of crowd and mass fear and hostility have increasingly occupied the attention of scholars and the old, classic categories have come to sound almost quaint. Who now seriously speaks of "ecstatic crowds," "social epidemics," "manias," "fevers," "religious hysterias," "passionate enthusiasms," "frantic and disheveled dances," or even of "expressive crowds" (Ross 1908; Park and Burgess 1924; Blumer 1969b)? A small amount of work on mass joys—fashions, crazes, and fads—persists, but only as languishing and marginal concerns. The eclipse is so complete that some more recent treatments say little or nothing of these matters and do so without apology or explanation (e.g. Genevie 1978; Perry and Pugh 1978). For better or worse, I propose that we bring joy back into the study of collective behavior and elevate it once again to a prominent place.

COLLECTIVE JOY

Joy as a general term refers to "the emotion evoked by well-being, success, or good fortune or by the prospect of possessing what one desires." It is a "state of happiness or felicity." Associated terms include *delight, gaiety, pleasure, jubilation, merriment,* and *bliss.*

The joys of concern to us as social scientists are collective in either of two senses: the dominant emotion of face-to-face assembly (a crowd) or a shared emotion among a dispersed set of persons attending to the same object at more or less the same time and who are aware that other people are also attending (a mass).

71

I will here treat only crowd joy, setting aside the mass form as a special domain worthy of treatment in its own right and consisting of crazes (mass excitements of which the El Dorado Rush, the boom, and the promised land migration are the main forms); fashions (mass pleasures, of which lifestyles and activity systems and items are the main kinds); and fads (mass amusements) (see ch. 1, this vol.).

LEVELS OF AROUSAL

Joy is a variable, and one prime task is the identification of an ordered and orderly set of dominant "levels of arousal." With regard to crowd joys, we may point to five dimensions of variation, the several values of which can serve to provide profiles of arousal. The higher a crowd is on each of the five, the higher is its dominant level of joyous arousal.

First, temporarily ignoring the number or proportion of the crowd displaying a given behavior, there is variation in the amount of overt motor activity combined with display of emotion socially defined as joyous. A modest level of arousal is suggested by such acts as hand clapping, dancing, singing, foot stomping, and cheering. Higher levels are suggested by unintelligible screaming, body shaking, glazed eyes, tranced demeanor, and fainting with indications of strong emotion and signs of ecstatic states. The greater the frequency of such acts, the higher the state of crowd arousal.

Second, crowds vary in the proportion of members displaying varying levels of these acts. At lower levels, only leaders and performers display them to a silent audience. At the highest levels, the audience/performer "polarization" (Brown 1954:843) disappears and the behavior becomes generalized.

Third, the social definition of the nature, meaning, and import of the arousal varies. At higher levels, the psychophysical features of the first dimension are defined as sacred, profound, and of supreme existential or religious consequence. They are viewed as the special and unique communications of a divine realm, and the joyous situation at hand is viewed as warrant for suspending ordinary routines of life or even of abandoning one's previous way of life. At more modest levels, such definitions are evoked, but conclusions requiring personal or social upheaval are not drawn. And at the lowest levels, the psychophysical manifestations are viewed as merely fun, leisure, or recreation.

Fourth, occasions of crowd joy differ in the degree to which they are institutionalized in the sense of being predesigned, planned, and regular in their occurrence. At the highest levels, they are a surprise to all involved—participants, onlookers, investigators, and others. They are in that sense "pure" collective behavior. At more modest levels—and more marginally collective behavior—"everyone" knows more or less what will happen when the crowd assembles, and it more or less does in fact happen.

Fifth, crowd joys vary in the duration of a single occasion of arousal and in the degree to which they are or are not linked to a rapid series of occasions of arousal. The highest levels involve long occasions— perhaps eight or more hours—that are spaced "back-to-back" over an unbroken series of days, or, if the series is more broken, it may extend over weeks or months.

These five dimensions only *tend* to increase and decrease in a uniform fashion. It is likely most common for occasions to be high on one or two and relatively low on the others. To be high on all five, is to have achieved the ultimate in crowd joy—the pure instance of ecstatic collective behavior. It is also likely that no human crowd has ever achieved (or fallen into or regressed to) maximal arousal on all five dimensions. Maximal arousal is unlikely, indeed impossible, entailing as it does an emergent and totally tranced ecstatic crowd sustaining such states day after day. Even if it somehow did emerge, outsiders would likely intervene. Instead, empirical cases are merely approximations.

SACRED CROWD JOYS

For purposes of explicating levels of joyful crowd arousal, it is helpful to employ the third variation, the definition of the import of the arousal, as an initial classifying device. Several forms of arousal imputed to be sacred will be isolated, followed by reference to arousals that are felt to be merely profane.

ECSTATIC UPHEAVALS

Among crowds most closely approaching maximal arousal, let me first point to a pattern that has no established label but which might be called the "ecstatic upheaval." Unfortunately, the crowd aspect of this pattern gets obscured by scholars who view it as an aspect of a social movement, applying such labels as "crisis cult" and "revitalization movement." Social movements may or may not rise out of ecstatic upheavals, but at the start they are emergent, joyous crowds. Perhaps the most famous instance is the late 1919 episode starting near the village of Vailala, in the then British territory of Papua (New Guinea), and known as the Vailala Madness (Williams 1923). Numerous other instances have been reported, with Felicitas Goodman's (1974) account of a "trace-based upheaval in the Yucatan" among the more recent and closely documented.

The Vailala Madness displayed a sequence in which several members of a given village began to behave in a hysterical or ecstatic manner, often characterized as a sense of one's head "going around." There might be agitated twisting of the body, "bending . . ., gesticulating erratically, . . . muttering [of] unintelligible exclamations" (Goodman 1974:232), and "falling to the ground." Twenty or more persons of a village might be so affected in rapid succession. These and other unusual behaviors were defined as meaning that the ancestors of the villagers were about to return in cargo-laden ships. A second phase of more generalized excitement among the nonphysically affected ensued. Ordinary village routines were suspended, and agitated preparations for ancestral return began. The village atmosphere during such a period was described by one British colonialist as a "ferment of excitement for weeks and in some villages even for months" (Williams 1923:71-72). A large portion of the time people simply sat quietly, but much time was also spent singing, dancing, receiving spirit world messages, and, among varying portions of different villages, displaying a variety of trance, agitated, and dissociated states. Within a few months, however, village life was resumed, and life returned to something like its former way.

The Yucatan upheaval reported by Goodman centered on the congregation of a small Apostolic church, a group whose new minister encouraged glossolalia, the crowd practice of which escalated and encompassed a large portion of the membership. In an episode extending about a month in the summer of 1970, emergent leaders received visions of the imminence of the Second Coming. The congregation accepted this prediction and such gatherings became frequent and intense. The church was frequently crowded and "the pulsing noise level, the rhythmic pounding of the many glossolalia utterances [boosted] . . . everyone's trance level. This effect appeared to be quite uncontrollable for the individual participant, assuming an autonomous aspect" (Goodman 1974:306). Ordinary routines of life were suspended, a few people went to preach the Second Coming to nearby villages, and several messages mandating throwing out of Bibles, the elimination of all colored objects, and other unusual acts were received and variously acted on. The beginning of the end started when one of the more faithful was accused by the others of being unfaithful. Shocked, she called in a regional church authority who informed the congregation it had been possessed by demons. The status quo ante was quickly reinstated.

I sketch these two cases to call the attention of sociologists to their sheer existence, to note their neglect, and to point up the need to develop models of crowd and group process for their understanding. At present, the anthropologists who are analyzing these sorts of materials resort to macrosocial notions that stress "cultural distortion" and "revitalization," to mention two ideas in the much-used model of Anthony Wallace (Goodman 1974:349). Or, there is descent to individual psychology and even linguistic analysis to elucidate the intricacies of such things as "trance behavior" (Goodman 1974:361). But clearly there is a need to elaborate the interactional level that falls between the micro and the macro.

Summarized in terms of the five dimensions of variation, ecstatic upheavals tend to: a high level of psychobiological involvement; a large minority to majority of the crowd involved displaying medium to high levels of such involvement; the arousal being defined as of ultimate significance, requiring suspension of ordinary life; and the episode being emergent and of relatively long duration.

ECSTATIC CONVENTIONS

Some societies and other social organizations have apparently harnessed ecstatic crowd energy into regularized and multiday occasions of crowd ecstasy. The dominant level of arousal is quite high, but it is planned, and it is defined as profound but less than reason to throw over the existing social order. The existing order is, rather, suspended for a time. The most familiar, but oddly neglected depiction of the ecstatic convention appears under the caption of social "effervescence" in Durkheim's (1915:214ff.) *Elementary Forms of the Religious Life*. Drawing on several reports, he (1915:215-16) uses terms such as the following to characterize them:

> Crying . . . shrieking, rolling in the dust, brandishing . . . arms in a furious manner . . . a sort of electricity . . . extraordinary degree of exaltation . . . violent gestures, cries, veritable howls and deafening noises of every sort. . . . The sexes unite contrarily to the rules governing sexual relations . . . violent super-excitation [and they] finally fall . . . exhausted.

Durkheim also calls attention to several devices for stimulating crowd ecstasy which include special costuming, "singing without pause," swaying of bodies, piercing cries, chanting, circular dancing, leaping and prancing, and night-time staging amidst flaming torches. The reports he quotes claim that one ecstatic convention was an "altogether . . . genuinely wild and savage scene of which it is impossible to convey any adequate idea in words," the latter declaration being a statement one encounters frequently in these contexts (Durkheim 1915:218).

Durkheim stresses the degree to which such multiday ecstatic conventions are defined by participants as apart from—radically different from—ordinary life. People "set themselves outside of and above their ordinary morals" (Durkheim 1915:216). Participants are left with the "conviction that there really exists two heterogeneous and mutually incomparable worlds." In one, "his daily life drags wearily along." But the person gains access to the other by "entering into relations . . . that excite him to the point of frenzy" (Durkheim 1915:218).

Durkheim focused on certain simple societies of Australia, but ecstatic conventions are reported elsewhere, including the early phases of the American Indian Ghost Dance and the American pioneer Camp Meeting (Davenport 1905:38ff; Pratt 1920; LaPiere 1938:476). Observers of them, too, were prone to comment "no pencil can describe the result" but also to report chanting, marching, wailing, moaning, shrieking, dancing, and a wide variety of muscle twitchings, quiverings, and final exhaustions.

ECSTATIC CONGREGATIONS

Several degrees below ecstatic upheavals and conventions, there is the relatively routine and repetitive assembly of circles of believers for the purpose of expressing devotion to and emotional involvement in a religious purpose. Such assemblies last less than a day and mostly for a few hours only. Unlike upheavals and conventions, ecstatic congregations may be viewed directly by interested observers almost anywhere in the world.

Weston LaBarre's (1962:6-9) description of services at Zion Tabernacle may be taken as prototypical. The participants know one another, they have a leader, hold services, and have a specific and preformed sense of "what a service is." In outline, it involves a minister speaking and reading from their Bible, guitar playing, and the gradual escalation of enthusiastic hand clapping and singing. As these build, "shaking reactions" begin to occur and some members begin "jerking their heads and bodies around wildly." Several stand up and "perform a vivacious dance." "The minister begins to speak in unknown tongues, as do others." In some services of this particular group, poisonous snakes are brought out and handled. A "mood of general excitement" prevails. People are "shaking violently . . . dancing around . . . sobbing, shouting and singing," and there is a laying on of hands in healing.

These three patterns invite comparison with Blumer's (1969b:85) classic category of the "expressive" crowd, an entity identified as having "no goal or objective" and as being "spontaneous." "Their form and structure are not traceable to any body of culture or set of rules." None of these features seem to obtain in the three patterns described. In the examples above, there is goal orientation: to receive messages from the beyond, to prepare for the Second Coming, and to be in contact with the sacred. Many are obviously quite planned and not spontaneous. Ecstatic congregations, at least, are units of churches and have easily identifiable bodies of culture and rules. Of course, one can *define* expressive crowds as the absence of such features. To do so, however, is likely to create a category of which there are no empirical instances. That might be theoretically interesting, but it does not direct our attention to actual patterns.

On causal aspects of ecstatic crowds, there is a tendency to view them as escapes from or sublimated revolts against social oppression. Ecstatic upheavals of the "cargo cult" sort have been depicted as deflected and inward-turning rebellions against colonialism; ecstatic congregations have been viewed as escapist behavior on the part of persons of disadvantaged class standing and meager education. There is surely merit to such lines of causal reasoning, but they do not cover all the relevant cases, namely, ecstatic conventions in simple societies where social class, colonialism, and other evils of modernity—such as urbanism—are not present. In such cases we need perhaps to look for causal explanations rooted more directly in the human condition, or perhaps even in nature, for events akin to ecstatic conventions have been observed among other species (Armstrong 1965, ch. 15).

It is possible that the frequency and prevalence of ecstatic crowds has, in the long sweep of history, been declining. If so, social class, colonialism, and the like may be their dampeners rather than their stimulants.

It is with some hesitation that I have used the term *ecstasy* to label the three patterns above. The term is perhaps too strong for the reality, but the reality is headed in that direction and the term does suggest the proper order of experience. By *ecstasy* is meant a state that is "beyond reason and self-control," associated with "overwhelming emotion, especially rapturous delight" and "intense emotional excitement." Other aspects include "a state of exaltation" and "a trance state in which intense absorption in divine or cosmic matters is accompanied by loss of sense perception and voluntary control." A portion of the crowds described above appears to approach such states, but a large portion also clearly does not; hence my misgivings.

These three forms of the ecstatic crowd are set apart from the next three in terms of their sheer intensity or frenzy. The three forms to be considered now involved emotional arousal, but it is not displayed with as much physical abandon. All six are alike, however, in defining the crowd occasion as having a cosmic and ultimate existential meaning.

EUPHORIC MOODS

The euphoric mood is outwardly mild or even invisible, but inwardly of deep and intense significance. As reported by Benjamin Zablocki (1971:188) with regard to the Bruderhoff settlement he studied, new waves of the euphoric mood in that community are occasioned by "success in the decision-making process." The brotherhood's decisions must be unanimous and inwardly accepted by everyone. This requires long and repeated meetings in which there is an air of crisis but also of slow building euphoria as the community approaches consensus. When consensus is achieved, ordinarily late of an evening, "there is a feeling of exultation in the air. Perhaps some stirring communal songs are sung" (Zablocki 1971:189). But they do not spend the night in "joyous celebration." Rather, they retire, but the days that follow are permeated with "fresh remembrances of their common euphoria. Each member throws himself into his work with new vigor" (Zablocki 1971:189). According to Zablocki (1971:191), Bruderhoff life is importantly characterized by a "crisis-euphoria" cycle in which crises are expected and "more important [they] expect the joyful end of all crises, even when this is nowhere in sight."

In Zablocki's (1971:189) view, the Bruderhoff have adroitly built "the collective behavior experience" into their way of life by muting the intensity of its expression at a given moment and spreading it "out instead as a glow over life." He contrasts this with more common social arrangements into which the collective behavior experience does not fit and "merely erupts" (as in ecstatic upheavals) or is confined to special, institutional occasions such as those I have described above. Such an integration and permeation is not easily achieved. It requires a variety of conducive social arrangements, the detailed features of which Zablocki brilliantly presents in chapter 4 of his report *The Joyful Community*. It will suffice here to say that these arrangements involve the thoroughgoing subjection of self to the collective and deep immersion in a totalistic religious system.

Much paler, but not dissimilar, sorts of euphoric arousals appear also to be found in the encounter groups movement (Marx and Elison 1975:448); the pentecostal movement in the Catholic Church (Harrison 1974:394-97); and in the emergent small-crowd form LaPiere (1938:473) has identified as the "confessional."

REVIVALIST CONGREGATIONS

The revivalist crowd is the most commonly occurring—and garden variety or weed if one prefers—crowd joy with a claim to existential import. It is associated with such famous evangelists as Dwight Moody, Aimee Semple MacPherson, Billy Sunday, and Billy Graham. Careful and sophisticated planning goes into its staging, and the assembled crowds are emotionally aroused in an orderly and constrained manner. There is some audience participation in the form of singing and perhaps some clapping, but there is little or none of the abandon associated with the ecstatic congregation. A strong polarization of performer and audience is maintained. The strongest form of audience participation is the "calling forth" of sinners and/or the sick to be saved and/or healed.

James Pratt's (1920:177ff.) characterization of the revivalist crowd continues to be one of the best, calling attention as it does to the use of hymns that are joyful but not gay and tunes that are "catchy," as in Billy Sunday's favorite, "Brighten the Corner." The revivalist's address tends classically to play on many emotions—humor, pathos, and sorrow among them—but most centrally on fear and love: fear of damnation and love of the divine (Pratt 1920:178). Unlike the crowd forms already examined, the revivalist him- or herself is critical to the crowd process. It is a situation of a star performing as much or more than mutual crowd facilitation. McLoughlin (1978, 1959:240) has thus observed of Dwight Moody: "The rapidity with which he jerked audiences from tears to laughter to solemnity and anxiety was the essence of his pulpit technique."

In the context of the revival, I want to mention a form of crowd joy that does not clearly display the patterns we have seen, yet is not dissimilar enough to justify separate classification. It combines features of the ecstatic congregation, the euphoric mood, and the revival. I refer to the crowd joys staged at the "conversion camps" of the Unification Church (the so-called Moonies), especially those in Northern California (and by a few other of the so-called new religions).

Through the seventies, Moonies each day encountered young adults on San Francisco Bay Area city streets, invited them to dinner and then to a weekend "retreat." Each Friday evening, perhaps fifty to seventy young people, accompanied by a like number of church members, traveled by bus and van to the remote camp. During the 3-hour trip, there was incessant group and solo singing of rousing songs and enthusiastic chanting and cheering. That set the tone of the coming two days of constant group activity one participant characterized as "one long rousing camp song." The more than 100 participants were divided into groups of eight to ten, half seasoned members and half newcomers. Further, each newcomer was paired to a specific member—a "host"—who stayed with the prospect at all times, often held his/her hand, and otherwise proferred emotional interest, support, and the display of what could be perceived as love.

The weekend activities cycled back and forth between assemblies of everyone and directed discussions in the small groups. In the large assemblies, sometimes formed as a large circle, there was arm linking, singing, chanting, and praying. In lecture periods, church members enthusiastically cheered points made by the lecturers. Lectures were preceded and followed by drum- and guitar-accompanied singing/ shouting of spirited songs and were interspersed with exercises and games, especially a frenzied form of dodgeball in which there was nonstop shouting of the "team" chant (e.g. "smash with love").

The more jaded or knowing, such as sociologist David Taylor (1978), who underwent the weekend several times, were impressed with its staged and theatrical quality, an aspect Taylor likened to being on stage during a boisterous Broadway musical such as *West Side Story*. But as with a musical, the fact of its staging did *not* destroy an "aura of excitement." "The constant flow of ritualized cheers, chants, singing and applause envelops all participants" nonetheless (Taylor 1978:86). There was a marked "transition from a relatively mundane world to a dynamic environment of ecstatic youth" (1978:107). And, of critical import: "failure to join in . . . places one in the role of the maverick, subject to embarrassment" (1978:104).

Two days of this loving, rousing, and encompassing crowd were sufficient to entice about half of the "guests" to stay on for a week-long "seminar," each day of which was much of the same round of lectures, games, singing, hugging, and so forth. "As various activities are repeated throughout the week, new people require fewer and fewer behavioral clues" (Taylor 1978:115). About half of a week-long group would stay on and become members of the Unification Church.

In grappling with the type of emotional crowd climate, David Taylor (1978:154), as have his predecessors, complains that "it is difficult to find words suitable for the phenomenon described." He elects "enthrallment" as the best single term, a term he had heard used by an ex-Moonie to describe the emotional experience.

> All aspects of the training session blend together with exhilarating momentum. The Family's [i.e. the church's] enthusiasm requires prospects to invest their entire beings into the participatory events. Jumping up to sing tumultuous songs; running from place to place hand in hand

with a buddy; and cheering, chanting, and clapping in unison with dozens of other inevitably makes a deep impression on prospective members.

Even the most reticent participants finds it difficult to resist being swept into this performance of continual consensus. One may remain intellectually unsympathetic to the Family's beliefs and goals, but he or she will be in some way moved by the intense revelry. Possibly no participant escapes feeling excitement, even if he or she regards the performance as inauthentic [Taylor 1978:153-54].

The Moonie crowd joy and similar ones created by other new religions have an unusual relation to the urban, educated youth who both undergo and stage them. One important reason for their remarkable impact seems to be sheer novelty. Having little or no experience with the "collective behavior experience," as Zablocki (1971) has termed it, secular youth are suddenly and unexpectedly immersed in a joyful collective behavior situation and discover entirely new types and levels of emotion in themselves. Having little or no preformed way to define and act toward those emotions, they are especially susceptible to definitions offered by the stagers, who construe the joyous experience as evidence of the validity of the new religion being proferred. In the absence of alternative understandings and of experiences with the profound emotions of such crowd situations, that linking is rather easily convincing. (Clearly, however, crowd joy has its own enormous power that is independent of its novelty.) The contemporary rarity of crowd joys and our underdeveloped understanding of them also help explain the appeal of "brainwashing," "programming," and "snapping" notions of affiliation with new religions. Erroneous ideas of that kind flow in to fill a conceptual void, a circumstance of behavior change not adequately accounted for by sociological models stressing role behavior and emotional bonds to members or by psychological models featuring predisposing attitudes and personality problems.

REVERENT CONGREGATIONS

Least overtly agitated, but aroused nonetheless, is the pattern of crowd joy associated with *reverence*— the quiet, worshipful coming together of people to give homage to what is defined as the cosmic and to make requests thereof. The more purely collective behavior versions of this are emergent in the sense that some new reverable object is declared and people are drawn from diverse points to a new place in order to give homage. What Tumin and Feldman (1955) call "the miracle at Sábana Grande" is the classic episode—a gathering of over 100,000 people at Rincón, Puerto Rico, May 25, 1953 to see the reappearance of a virgin saint. The saint elected not to materialize, but that day and subsequent days were apparently quite moving crowd events involving much prayer, singing, and chanting.

Less well-attended, emergent episodes of a similarly reverent kind have involved crowds gathering to see the image of Christ appearing on a schoolhouse wall (Associated Press 1975), the viewing of a woman going into ecstasy "before a statue of the Blessed Virgin and serving as a voice for the Mother of Jesus" (Carney 1975:19), and a 16-year-old girl strapping herself publicly to a cross for three days to exorcise demons (United Press International 1978).

More institutional, and therefore more marginal as collective behavior, are the yearly reverent gatherings staged by organized religions. The most massive and impressive of these appears to be the Hindu Kumbh Mela festival, a gathering during which, in recent years, 10 million pilgrims bathe in the sacred Ganges River at its confluence with the Jamuna River. Reported to be the "largest mass gathering in the world" (Associated Press 1977), its dominant emotion is a "quiet fervent spirit." It is marked by the "quiet play of chanted prayers, splashing water and bare feet in mud." The specific time and place of the bathing is defined as "the most significant ritual a Hindu can perform in his search for salvation," a definition of cosmic proportions indeed.

More generally, humans have long constructed gatherings directed toward reverential propitiation of the cosmic, or more particularly the seasonal cycle of "breeding and hunting seasons, or seed-time and harvest" (James 1961:11). James's (1961) *Seasonal Feasts and Festivals* is a catalog of these for a portion of Western history.

Reverence as a mode and level of cosmic crowd arousal is transferable to the political realm, a transportation effected most successfully in modern times by the German Nazi party under Adolf Hitler. Despite having an ersatz quality to outsiders, Nazi rallies and festivals were designed to be and were experienced by many as much more than mere political demonstrations. They brought their multitudes, in the words of Hitler, "under the spell of a deep prayer" (Sinclair 1938:583). A "mystic effect" was intended and achieved. The scale of devices for achieving such an effect remain mind-boggling to this day: huge public spaces and gigantic symbols (especially flags and banners); massed choirs and drum corps; adroit use of lighting; hundreds of thousands of people deployed in precise marching and singing movements carrying perhaps 25,000 flags. The rallies at Nuremberg were reportedly most stunning and for a week each fall in the late 1930s "nearly every other event [in Germany] went into obscurity" (Sinclair 1938:582).

Such crowd stagings derived from the Nazi theory of the necessity for a direct relation between political leaders and the masses, a theory of long development in Germany according to George Mosse (1975), who speaks of it as "the nationalization of the masses." Under the Nazi "law of festivals," a broad and complicated schedule of large-scale crowd arousals was built into daily routine. The goal and slogan was "no spectators, only actors" (1975:205). The nation was to be swept up into "processions . . ., speaking choruses, silent marches, confessions of faith [and] choruses of movement," all aimed at "creation of an atmosphere of shared worship [and] . . . active participation" (1975:205).

Analysis of Nazi Germany from the point of view of "crowd joys" ought to be very enlightening. Only rarely are discernments of principles of crowd joy revealed so clearly and executed so explicitly.

The foregoing six varieties of joyful crowds define their emotional arousal as having an existential, religious, sacred, or cosmic meaning. Variations in such meanings include seeing the joy as caused by the cosmic, as a manifestation of the cosmic, as a direct communication with the cosmic, and/or as an act of soliciting the help of the cosmic.

PROFANE CROWD JOYS

We now make a transition to a cluster of joyfully aroused crowds in which the joy is not defined in such a grandiose way. Words such as *ecstatic, reverent,* and *awed* are less appropriate than *amused, delighted, excited, revelous,* and merely *happy.*

REVELOUS CROWDS

The highest level of collective arousal among "noncosmic" crowds seems best labeled "revelous," a term denoting a "wild party or celebration" and connoting abandon. The prototypical revelous scene is one in which thousands of people are dancing and otherwise cavorting in the public streets hour after hour, day after day. Richard Critchfield (1978:53) reports something of the sort to occur for six days each spring in Salvador, Brazil, a period when "an entire city of a million people goes mad dancing up and down the main street day into night." Critchfield (1978:53,57) strives to represent that "carnival" using words and phrases such as "shrill shouts . . . rhythm pulsates from the drums . . . flashing lights . . . sparks fly . . . mists of confetti drift . . . thunder rising from the pavement . . . eyes flashing, faces filled with laughter . . . ear splitting, all-obliterating din." Critchfield (1978:57) characterizes carnival arousal as fun in the sense of a "bodily and mental experience that occurs completely independent of your rational self. With an intense physical and emotional realness, you are scarcely aware of your own presence and movement . . . it is compulsive and it is marvelous."

Revelous crowds as a type are to be distinguished from "audiences," polarized or focused crowds where there is a single object of attention. Revelous crowds are unfocused or at most multifocused in the sense that there is continuing arousal in copresence, but this is not geared to an overall plan or program as is the case with the "excited" crowds to which we will come below.

Revelous crowds may be distinguished among themselves in terms of the degree to which they are planned or emergent. The carnival just referred to and occasions of its kind, including the saturnalia, are built into yearly or other rounds of social organization. They may even be labeled as some sort of a "festival," as described by LaPiere (1938:471-73). At levels of social organization below the community, certain establishments may be more or less regular—perhaps weekly or nightly—scenes of revelous crowds. LaPiere calls attention to the "participant audience" in such a light, making reference to the old-fashioned melodrama, amateur night, and certain vaudeville scenes. Less focused is the "old-time beer hall" and its singing, boisterous crowd. More recently something of the sort is seen in the phenomenon of the "Rocky Horror Show," a motion picture gathering in which the revelous audience is as much its own object as the motion picture being seen. Institutionalized on a mass scale is the dance hall, whose crowds may occasionally achieve revelous arousal. In the history of the United States there appear to be ebbs and flows in the degree to which dancing occasions are regularly revelous (Skolnick 1978). Thus, the dance crowds of the fifties and much of the sixties seemed on the whole much less routinely revelous than those of the disco-dominated seventies, the latter being reminiscent of the Salvador carnival mentioned above.

Revelous dancing is a strikingly neglected topic and its neglect is likely related to its apparent decline in modern life, along with the decline in several forms of the ecstatic crowds that have been outlined. One valuable source for a revived interest remains the article by A.E. Crawley (1918) "Processions and Dances," especially his discussions of dance autointoxication and ecstasy, and of war, agricultural, magical, and courtship dancing.

Of a distinctively modern cast are the somewhat revelous crowds of college youth that form each spring in and around Fort Lauderdale, Florida. In an era of cheap and easy travel, they became successors to the previous and more community-bound spring occasions of revelous release.

Emergent revelous crowds vary in scale, the smallest of which is the *spree,* aptly identified by LaPiere (1938:473-74). They are not uncommon among small groups of male workers whose occupations isolate them from ordinary and ongoing occasions of leisure. Such occupations have included "soldiers, sailors, lumberjacks and oil field workers" (LaPiere 1938:474). They can also develop in other contexts, as at parties, after-game dances, "celebrations of a football game," and victory gatherings on election nights (LaPiere 1938:474; McPhail and Miller 1973). Student dormitory settings during the tensions of spring and nubility are also observed to give rise to such revelous occasions as waterfights and panty raids.

On a larger scale, what have started out to be stagings of hostile crowds can grow into revelous festivity. Such is reported of a 1977 1-day general strike in France that came off "closer to that of a national holiday than a national crisis" *(Los Angeles Times* 1977). One protest march was a kind of "folk-fest with the strikers linking arms, dancing and singing ribald songs and chants." And, of course, there is the well-known "carnival glee" or "Roman Holiday" phase of ghetto rioting (Firestone 1972).

EXCITED CROWDS

The excited crowd is among the most constrained and ordinary of aroused crowds, a pattern of arousal so constrained and orderly that it barely merits mention in the context of collective behavior. The garden variety instance of the excited crowd cheers, sings, chants, and otherwise expresses itself in favor of a person, team, or other contestant. The ordinary excited crowd, that is, is responding to a *staged contest* in which there is a "simple but dramatic form of conflict" (LaPiere 1938:477). The conflict is socially related to the spectators in such a way that they become "vicarious participants," especially when the contestants are symbolic representations of the social identities of the spectators (LaPiere 1938:477). The collective behavior aspect enters more clearly when the spectators begin to take the conflict literally rather than vicariously or symbolically, either in celebrating revelry or hostile attack, as reported of fan violence.

The level of excitement itself is critically a function of the level of indeterminancy of the outcome of the contest and of the several subphases leading up to an outcome. In a ground-breaking article on cheering at stockcar races, Richard Gambrell (1979:10) has documented how levels of excitement (measured by frequency, duration, and "shape" of cheering) are associated with emergent "trouble" between cars on the track and with the final burst of intense driving competition with which each race ends. In its indeterminancy and intensity, the final burst has a "captivating" quality. Peter Adler (1981) has tried to elucidate this "captivating" aspect for sports more generally in his discussion of the nature of "momentum" and factors that enlarge, diminish, or destroy it.

Crowd excitement, however, seems to involve more than simple indeterminancy of outcome. Events as such have their own "aura" that does not derive purely or merely from their contest aspects. Thus when thousands of runners and more thousands of spectators assemble for the San Francisco Bay to Breakers Race, it is perhaps less the contest than the event per se that is "magical." As one of the runners has written: "It's hard to explain the high degree of excitement in the air . . . it's like the air is . . . crackling with static electricity. . . . [There is a] party atmosphere." A similar, albeit more boisterous or revelous atmosphere, has been reported of crowds at classic public executions (Bleackley and Lofland 1977:296-99).

OTHER PROFANE CROWD JOYS

Several other dominant emotions in joyfully aroused crowds may be mentioned briefly. First, there are focused crowds whose excitement is single-minded *adoration*. Sally Quinn (1975) reports of a crowd greeting entertainer Lana Turner: "They just died over her. They gave her a standing ovation, whistled and cheered, jumped up and down, cried out in ecstasy 'you are the most beautiful woman in the world.' " More extreme adoration is available in the record, including episodes in which competing and grasping fans pull off the adored's clothing and handfuls of hair. Second, Dorothy Peven (1968:101) has documented what can be called the *ersatz revival* pattern, a type of gathering staged by the famous plastic bowl company that peddles its wares by means of the "home-party plan." Having to rely on a dispersed, relatively uncommitted and unsupervised workforce (housewives), the company strives to build commitment and morale by means of periodic rallies that present the plastic bowl as a "sacred" object and instill "team spirit." At the rallies there is much singing, pageantry, ceremonial, handshaking and clapping, and other devices calculated to foster a "common mood of camaraderie, anticipation, and excitement."

Third, one special kind of crowd is excited in a purely lighthearted and *comic* manner. Its dominant activity is laughter. One of the most charming instances of such crowds is seen at the dachshund races staged each year during the University of California at Davis Picnic Day. Hundreds of people congregate on bleachers and laugh uproariously while watching seven races, in each of which four dachshunds erratically chase a lure pulled in front of them. Last, I would be remiss not to at least mention that creature of the late sixties, the "mellow, laid back, passive, stoned" crowd. The high point was, of course, the Woodstock Festival held near White Lake, New York, on a weekend in August 1969.

CONTEXT AND PROSPECT

Several key theoretical decisions are presumed by or at least involved in the foregoing, and I want now to state them. First, for more than a decade, the dominant approach to crowd behavior has been *cognitive*. Collective behaviorists have stressed the reasoned, orderly and (emergent) normative features of action in crowd circumstances (e.g. Turner 1964; Couch 1968; Berk 1974; Tilly 1978). More recently, a vigorous behaviorist approach takes the achievement of bodily coordination in crowds as the preeminent problem in their study (e.g. Couch 1970; McPhail 1978). Both approaches seem suffused with the fear that discussion of emotion—the classic and a third approach—inevitably drags us back to the likes of Gustave Le Bon (1960), Sigmund Freud (1922), or even Herbert Blumer (1969b) and imputations of assorted irrationalities and "group mind" perspectives. We encounter among contemporary collective behaviorists that what seems to be a conspicuous feature of the topic—aroused emotions—is at the same time one that is most suppressed from explicit consideration. This chapter and the larger effort of which it is a part (chapter 1 of this volume) is in this way rather heretical.

Second, it must be acknowledged that the cognitivists and behaviorists are correct in their concern that a focus on emotions has tended to be associated with unjustified imputations of "contagion," "circular reaction," cognitive "short-circuits," and overgeneralized portrayals of "crudeness, excess and eccentricity" (Smelser 1963:71-72). We must be careful, however, not to read the mere preferences of classic theorists as logical necessity. Here, as elsewhere, the baby is not the bathwater, and we can surely throw out one without the other. It is in this spirit that I have carefully employed the term *dominant emotion* when characterizing crowds. This concept refers to the publicly expressed feeling perceived by participants and observers as most prominent in an episode of collective behavior. For an emotion to be publicly most dominant (to have become the reigning definition of the emotional situation) is not to say that an especially large portion of that collectivity necessarily feels that emotion. Following the lead of Ralph Turner's (1964) formulation of emergent norm theory, the dominant emotion is almost always far from a matter of uniform, unanimous, or even majority inner feeling. In so referring to what is publicly communicated and socially shared, the idea of dominant emotion has much the same logical status as that of the emergent norm. The shift here is simply away from the cognitive (the notion of norm) to the affective.

It is in that spirit that variation in the proportion of crowds engaging in diverse sorts of actions has been stressed. This also follows Turner's (1964) lead in underscoring the lack of unanimity in collective behavior episodes. By stressing that fact at the outset, we are better prepared to develop a more systematic intra- and interepisode perspective, and one that is not overly prone to indiscriminate imputations of "contagion" and "convergence" (Turner 1964) characterizations of what we observe.

Third, in reintroducing emotion in this manner, I do not seek to displace or demean the cognitive of behavioral perspectives. Rather, I desire to expand the array of aspects we scrutinize. The three are complementary rather than competitive.

Regarding the next steps or prospects, the taxonomic approach employed here may well not be the most productive way in which to think about "levels of dominant emotional arousal." Taxonomy serves the important, provisional purpose of displaying important patterns that have been neglected, but it might best give way to quantitative scales of joyful crowd arousal. Second, I have only addressed some questions of the nature of the dependent variable. A host of causal, processual, functional, participant-strategic, and other aspects need to be introduced into the study of each type and/or into some scaled scheme of crowd arousals. Finally, it must frankly be observed that the long-standing neglect of collective joy by sociologists does not bode well for change. I suppose, though, that this ought not surprise us, because this neglect is only one instance on a much longer list of positive things that are neglected, a list that includes such topics as love, friendship, loyalty, heroism, saintliness, and the sociology of art, literature, and music. Sociologists are preoccupied with much more weighty matters of fear and hostility and seem unlikely to shift their attention.

3

THE YOUTH GHETTO: AGE SEGREGATION AND CONFLICT IN THE AMERICAN SIXTIES (1968)

Given all the current clamor over youth, teenagers, and the like, it is with considerable hesitation that I add yet another statement to the confusing caldron of polemics. At the same time, I feel it necessary to do so, for I have become a bit disturbed by the emotional stance taken by those people who talk about youth. Commentators, and even researchers on the topic, seem to feel so strongly about it, to be so close to it, that they have been unable to achieve the emotional and social distance necessary for adequate understanding. It seems that those things most in need of discussion come often to be the most confused and least understood. There may even be a tendency to talk about important topics so much that we become saturated, baffled, and bored—and finally give up.

Despite my concern over the way in which otherwise dispassionate scholars can be exercised about the topic of youth, I want to try to approach the subject from the point of view of a bemused and intrigued, outsider to the debate. From such a distance it is hopefully possible to argue that the issue of youth is only an empirical instance of some very general social processes that have to do with far more than merely youth or even age. From such a distance one can try to surmount the idiosyncracies that arise from thinking in terms of popular labels, and one can perhaps raise general considerations relevant to, but far more general than, the topic. By so doing I hope to show again the merit of the famous platitude that the longest way around may be the shortest way home.

In order most effectively to achieve, first distance and finally closeness, it will be necessary, first, to introduce some very abstract and remote or seemingly irrelevant topics. These apparently remote conceptions involve an understanding of the notions of social categories, of categorical clusterings, and of pivotal categories. Approaching somewhat closer, I will discuss, second, age as a social dimension and the characteristics of age categories—in particular, the categories of child, teenager, youth, and early, middle, and late adult. Finally, I will, from the distance so developed, focus directly upon what might be called "the youth ghetto," and discuss adult conceptions of and practices toward it, conduct within it, and interaction between it and categories of adults.

SOCIAL CATEGORIES: DISTINCTIONS, CLUSTERS, PIVOTS

In describing social categories, we may begin with the observation that there exists a most peculiar species of animal whose most distinctive characteristics include, among other things, the following: it walks on its hind legs, uses symbols, and is extraordinarily sensitive to what the other animals of its kind think and feel about it. This animal is further distinguished by, and very peculiar in, the assiduousness with which it feels a need linguistically to designate objects in the world. So it is that this creature has a category with which it designates its general kind of object and which serves to set it off from all other objects in the world. The more esoterically inclined of these animals label the general category "homo sapiens," while the more mundane dub the category merely "mankind," "human beings," "people," or that vestige of male supremacy, "man."

DISTINCTIONS

This animal is not satisfied, however, with simply setting itself off from all the other kinds of objects in the world. Nor is it satisfied with the enterprise of making fine distinctions among all the objects that fall outside its own general category. No, this animal, which calls itself "man," or humankind, engages also in making distinctions within the category of its most general kind.

One of the more popular subdivisions is based on differential place in what is identified as the reproductive cycle. The dimension of sex is thus divined and there arises a division between the categories of male and female. A second very widespread division identifies the amount of time human objects have existed and divides humankind on the dimension of age. There are thus categories such as "child," "adolescent," "adult," and so forth, the specific terms depending on who is doing the discriminating and designating.

Because it is possible for selected combinations of people to produce other people and to cooperate in managing their joint young products, and, moreover, to cooperate in the task of sheer survival, there exists yet another basis for further division of humankind, this time along the dimension of their biological relationships to one another. There are thus categories of family or kin position. Many units of kin occupying adjacent ground may come to see that particular territory as reasonably and legitimately theirs, setting it off (at least symbolically) from all other pieces of ground on the planet. As some kin groups come to dominate others, the claimed area may grow quite large relative to total space on the planet. Or it may be quite small, yet be seen as equally crucial, as for example with units such as neighborhoods or even city blocks. Our animal may even get to feel that the location of one's residence on the planet is a crucially important dimension along which to distinguish categories of territorial habitation.

Such a territorial category of humans, settled in a place for a long period of time, may even come to feel that it has some special way of life that distinguishes "his kind of people" from all the rest of the people in the world. There can thus arise a dimension called "culture" with its own various categories.

In moving around on the planet, differences in specific definitions of sex, age, kinship, and territory may be seen as associated with differences in the color or form of the surface casing of the animal; and so another dimension along which to divide kinds of people in the world appears, sometimes called "race" or "ethnicity."

The process of extracting sustenance from the surface of the planet (or from other people) may place these two-legged animals in relation to one another such that it is felt reasonable to divide the general category yet again, this time along the dimension of how the materials necessary for physical survival are assembled. Such designations may be called "jobs" or "occupations" and in some societies may run into thousands upon thousands of distinctive categories. Such categories, themselves, have differential capacity to assemble resources. Some seem able to command the obedience of many of the other animals. Thus there can grow up a dimension of difference designated by this animal with categories such as the more wealthy and the less wealthy, or the rich and the poor.

This species of animal, then, is that kind of creature that is constantly dividing itself into categories of "kinds of people" along dimensions such as sex, age, kin, territory, culture, race, work, and material resources.

CLUSTERS

Having complicated its world by discriminating all these and other dimensions and designating numerous categories along them, this peculiar animal then tries to simplify its world again through the process of clustering selected categories of some of the dimensions. So it is that a significant proportion of the species feels, for example, that animals of a certain category of the dimension "race" should reside in certain categories of the dimension "territory" and should assemble sustenance by occupying themselves with certain categories of the dimension "work." More particularly, some of the species feel that "Whites" should reside in "nice" neighborhoods and make a living from some of the "cleaner" kinds of work; and correspondingly, other categories of "race" have their appropriate other places and other categories of work.

Some of the species may feel that certain categories of age are most appropriately clustered with certain kinship and occupational categories. When these presumed proprieties of clustering are breached, comment and perhaps punishment are undertaken as a means of forcing these erroneously clustered instances of the species back into a proper or acceptable cluster of displayed categories. We see such a concern on those occasions when newspapers, for example, deem as newsworthy the fact that two married 16-year-olds are publisher-editors of a town newspaper *(Detroit Free Press,* March 15, 1965, p. 1). Or, when it is deemed newsworthy—even to the extent of requiring an accompanying picture—when a 16-year-old girl marries a 62-year-old man, thereby becoming "stepmother to five, grandmother to another five and a great-grandmother" *(Detroit Free Press,* July 21, 1965, p. 2).

These and numerous other occurrences are seen as worthy and in need of reporting and comment because they violate shared conceptions of appropriate categorical clustering. Such cluster violations are also objects of many kinds of punishment—the reason, I suspect, that the 62-year-old husband just mentioned felt it necessary to tell reporters, "We'll make a go of it if they leave us alone." While these age-kinship examples are, in a sense, trivial, they illustrate the fundamental principle of categorical clustering.

If categories are clustered, we can conceive the possibility that a large number of categories along the most fundamental dimensions can pile upon one another, creating a new or derived class of the species "humankind" out of the coincidence of categories. Thus in an exaggerated case, the human animals in the category "immigrant" (on the dimension "nativity") can be almost exclusively of a particular category of race or ethnicity and also almost exclusively of low education. They can be also almost exclusively those who occupy certain territories (say, inner-city areas); almost exclusively those who work in low-paid, unskilled jobs and who are unemployed; and almost exclusively those who practice a given category of religion or culture.

Such a situation is empirically rare, but in that territory called "America," this extreme of categorical clustering has sometimes been approximated (cf. Suttles 1968, pt. 1).

PIVOTAL CATEGORIES

When the categories of a set of dimensions begin, empirically, to pile upon one another—to cluster—this peculiar animal not only perceives and comes to expect the clustering but introduces a further simplification. One of the categories of the dimensions so piled up is singled out and treated publicly as their most important and significant feature. It defines the character of those animals whose categories are so clustered. That is, there comes to be a pivotal category that defines "who those people are," socially speaking. Indeed, as we shall see, the singled out pivotal category may have ascribed to it a causal force; it may be seen as responsible for "making" the animals the way they are relative to their other clustered categories.

Through time and across societies, what particular categories have piled upon one another or have clustered seems to have varied considerably; and, therefore, so have the particular categories singled out as pivotally defining human animals to one another.

What category is defined as pivotal is a function of specific, defined situations and the social-organizational units of reference within which human animals are encountering one another. A person momentarily situated within a work setting may be pivotally defined as a worker. The same person, shifted to a family, political, or religious setting, may, in them, be pivotally defined, respectively, as a father, politician, or believer. In these examples, the social-organizational units of reference are organizations and the categories attributed as pivotal derive from the designative framework of the corresponding setting.

Under some conditions the unit of reference with which a large proportion of the population defines one another in specific encounters comes to be the society at large. Thus in contemporary America, if the male just mentioned is, say, Black, and in a racially mixed work setting, others are not likely to pivotally define him as a worker but as a Black who happens incidentally to be a worker as well.

Those pivotal categories which permeate a wide variety of concrete settings (are used by a very high proportion of the population as a basis upon which they pivotally identify) and which are in conflict with one another are nationally dividing dimensions and pivotal categories.

Pivotal categories which are activated as a basis for organizing action and conflict in only a few settings and are dropped in others, or permeate a variety of kinds of settings only in some confined part of the population, are localized pivotal categories.

In the short history of America there has already been a succession of different nationalized dimensions and pivotal categories around which division and conflict have been organized. Going back only to the middle of the last century, we see, in succession, the nationalized dimension of territory and its nationalized pivotal categories—Northerner and Southerner; the nationalized dimension of income or work and its nationalized pivotal categories—capitalist and worker; the nationalized dimension of nativity and its nationalized pivotal categories—immigrant and native-born; the nationalized dimension of sex and its nationalized pivotal categories—suffragette (female) and male; the nationalized dimension (more recently) of race and its nationalized pivotal categories—White and Black.

Although a variety of nationalized dimensions of categorical conflict may be taking place at any given time, it would seem, from these examples, that one or another nationalized dimension becomes more or less primary in a given period and a variety of other dimensions of conflict are assimilated to the prime nationalized dimensions. That is, alliances are formed for the purpose of a single basis of conflict. Thus in the Northerner/Southerner case—the agricultural/industrial, slaver/nonslaver, states' rights/federalism categories became assimilated to a dimension of territory and its categories.

If one or another nationalized set of pivotal categories is likely to be a primary basis of conflict during a given period, there is raised the question of how one or another specific set comes to have this primacy. One can assume there is always some prime dimension of conflict—some prime, nationalized, pivotal categories—and inquire into the conditions under which a particular dimension comes to the forefront.

While this is the most general question to pose, it is not my purpose here to explore a generalized answer. It is my purpose, rather, to take the question and its conceptual context as a framework within which to view some contemporary trends on the basis of which tentatively to project what might be the next nationalized dimension whose pivotal categories are, for Americans, the foremost bases of conflict.

AGE AS A PIVOTAL CATEGORY

The current piling up of categorical sharing strongly suggests that the dimension of age (and the categories it provides) is becoming our next identity and conflict equivalent of Southerner and Northerner, capitalist and worker, immigrant and native-born, suffragette and male, White and Black.

YOUTH

Let me point to some of the ways in which this new kind of piling up is occurring, referring first to the age category of youth.

If a dimension is to provide pivotal identities, it is highly facilitating to have it pile upon or coincide with territory. While territory itself may become the dimension of pivotal identification—as with Northerner/Southerner, United States/Soviet Union—very often the sharing of territory will facilitate the public articulation of some other category that happens to coincide with a particular territory. One wonders, for example, whether the categories capitalist/worker, immigrant/native-born, Black/White, would have been so nationally pivotal if they had not also been founded upon each opposing category having its own territory. In these terms, one might suggest, also, that the suffragettes, in contrast with the groups mentioned above, were never able to escalate sex categories as pivotal identities and bases of conflict to the extent that they might have wished because every major piece of territory they occupied was massively infiltrated by males.

Relative to age in American technological society, the coincidence between it and territory is proceeding apace and is most spectacular in the host communities of the ever-expanding multiversities. Into many of these communities in recent years there have thronged literally tens of thousands of youth—human animals ranging in age from late teens to middle twenties. Because the political powers have opted for the model of a few large educational institutions, rather than many small ones, "cities of youth" are being created. The populations of some of them now approach or surpass 40,000 and the end is not yet in sight. Apparently some institutions even project enrollment figures of 50,000-75,000 within the not-too-distant future. Already, for example, 30 percent of the population of Ann Arbor, Michigan, is composed of youth, or more precisely, students at the University of Michigan. They are not, however, distributed evenly throughout the city but are concentrated at its center, around the university. As the current high rate of apartment construction continues and as the university expands by about 1,000 students a year, one can envision the day when the entire city of Ann Arbor will be composed almost exclusively of human beings in their late teens to middle twenties. This trend is fostered in no small measure by the enormous rental rates in the center city which are likely to continue to rise and which force other age categories into the suburbs.

Thrust upon communities typically unprepared for their arrival, a significant proportion of the youth in these territories live crowded in inadequate housing or equally crowded in new but rent-gouging apartment buildings. Current circumstances of student living conditions—high density, crowding, bad housing, and rent gouging—remind one of the living conditions and exploitation of the immigrants in New York and Chicago in the early part of the century and of the Blacks in those (and other) cities somewhat later. Ghetto landowners come to think the ghetto area, as one owner of apartment buildings in Ann Arbor has put it, "a real estate paradise."

Also similar to early immigrants and later Blacks, the youth piled into these territories have low incomes, a fact which further serves to differentiate them from the surrounding population. Lacking the considerable amount of excess resources necessary to paint and fix-up their dwellings, youth, as did immigrants and as do impoverished Blacks, come to have publicly identifiable—that is, "sloppy and shoddy"—places of habitation. And, like other low-income peoples, past and present, they can only rent rather than buy dwelling space.

Faced with uncertain employment and residence futures—actually a certainty that they will have to move—youth in these territories do not develop identification with local social institutions that precede their arrival—the preexisting local political organizations, churches, business organizations, and so forth. As was said of the earlier ghetto dwellers, they "stay with their own kind" and participate in informal and formal social organization dominated by others of their own category.

Such piling up of categories makes for the possibility of ghettos very similar to those that the dominant population worried about in connection with Italian, Irish, and Polish immigrants some forty or more years ago and the kind that we still worry about today in connection with Blacks.

Only now, instead of Italian, Irish, Polish, or Black ghettos, the dominant sectors of the population may well become concerned about youth ghettos and all the social processes that surround concern over ghetto areas are likely to begin. Indeed, they have begun, as I shall suggest in a moment.

OTHER AGE CATEGORIES

First we must pursue the obvious implication that categories piling up in one kind of territory means that other kinds of categories are likely to be piling up in yet other territories. If youth are being territorially segregated, they cannot be in some other places. These other places are of equal interest, for in them reside the sectors of the population who will be engaging in concern over youth ghettos.

Concomitant with the rise of youth ghettos has been a growth of rather age-homogeneous bands of territory ringing American cities. These are the well-known suburban tracts, many neighborhoods of which have a peculiar character. In some of them one finds a population composed almost exclusively of early adults (ranging in age from late twenties to late thirties) and children. Middle adults (in their early forties to late fifties), and late adults (in their sixties and older), and teenagers are in a decided minority; in many cases they are hardly present at all.

Piled upon this age category of early adult and its coincidence with a territory, one finds the employment and financial state known as "struggling" or "being on the way up." The neat row houses of early adults market in the $15,000 to $25,000 range. Deep in installment debt, their lives are centered on the family unit. They are concerned that politicians treat them kindly, that is, that taxes be kept down. And they are likely to have voted for Goldwater.

In other suburban tracts, one finds a population composed almost exclusively of middle adults (forties and fifties) and teenagers. The neighborhood is largely "undisgraced" by the presence of children, early adults, or late adults, and the neat row houses market in the $25,000 to $50,000 and up range. In large measure the middle adults have passed their "struggling." They have, in some sense, arrived.

There would seem to be evolving a pattern wherein an age-sex unit of early adults establishes itself in an early-adult neighborhood, its members spawn their offspring and then, at the appropriate age, move to a middle-adult territory. In this way, age-sex units are always able to be with their "own kind," territorially protected from the contamination of contact with many other age categories. Teenagers, especially, are usually able to be with their corresponding age category mates. They can be uncompromised by entanglements with children, early adults, or late adults.

Although all this is only a tendency at present, it would seem to be a growing one which assumes additional significance in light of the already more pronounced territorial segregation of late adults. Persons of sixty and over—often described with polite euphemisms such as "senior citizens"—have begun to assemble in special buildings in cities, in special neighborhoods within suburbs, and in special areas of the nation. Significant portions of Florida, Arizona, and Southern

California are becoming something like the states of late adulthood. Piled upon these categories of age and territory are others, such as the marginal or unemployed state, often called "retirement." Special kinds of legislation have developed for this age group, defining their monetary rights and duties and relating even to the possibility of their marrying one another.

Among these six categories of age, two—youth and late adulthood—are already proceeding toward highly pronounced territorial segregation with the concomitant clustering of yet other categorical sharings around their respective ages and territories. The remaining four are already splitting into two sets of two each. Early adults are still territorially linked to children, and middle adults are still territorially linked to teenagers.

However, the territorial link between middle adults and teenagers show signs of weakening, given the absorption that teenagers have in the culture that centers on the high school. While teenagers must still share a household with middle adults and face school and other specialized keepers of teenagers, they are achieving a well-defined and dominated set of territories spread throughout communities. These include the school itself, drive-ins, and the like (Coleman 1961). This separation is limited in a way similar to that in which the territorial integrity of the suffragettes was limited. While both had or have special territories, there were or are not large areas from which persons of other categories could or can be, at least formally, excluded.

Nonetheless, this partial territorial segregation exists and is deepening. Combined with the propensity of early adults to send their children to school at ever earlier ages, one can wonder if these remaining two sets of two categories (early adults and children; middle adults and teenagers) will not themselves territorially divide.

Perhaps it is not entirely unrealistic, fanciful, or whimsical to suggest that there may come a day when children are almost entirely segregated under the supervision of child-rearing specialists. Perhaps parts of, say, Nevada, Utah, Wyoming, or Montana could be given over to the task and designated as Children's States. Under such circumstances, early adults could devote themselves exclusively to the struggle of making it to the next neighborhood. The increasing numbers of college-educated, female early adults who now mourn the disuse of their talents and the incompatibility of children and career, would be free more actively to participate with their male partners in the climb up.

Likewise, the separation of teenagers into teen cities, very much like the developing youth ghettos, would free their middle-adult parents to participate more intensively in the social and political machinations of the occupations in which they have now come to power.

Segregation has its attractions as well as its limitations. Given the already strong tendency of children and teenagers (indeed, of all age categories) to group together and prefer one another's company, these youngest categories may well, in the future, come to demand the same kinds of territorial rights now enjoyed by youth and late adults. At present, they are still dominated by their respective age superiors in territories run by, and fundamentally belonging to, these superiors. Equal justice for all might well be construed in the future to mean that each age category, including children and teenagers, has a right to its own piece of ground.

At such a future time, arguments are also likely to arise for the efficiency and effectiveness of specialized age territories for children and teenagers. In the same way that the family-oriented cottage industry and the "putting-out system" of industrial manufacture collapsed in the face of competition by the superior effectiveness of a centralized, industrial process, so too, the last remaining cottage industry—that of producing persons—might well falter in the face of harsh criticism of its inefficiency, its widely variable standards of production, and its excessive rate of rejects. Although phrased in different terms, many educators are already making these criticisms.

LIMITS

Any consideration of divisive forces must at the same time consider forces that limit the division. There is, after all, a strong ideology that adults should love their children, teenagers, or youth and that they should devote personal attention to them. Persons in the various age categories are still highly linked, despite geographic separation. Even youth still have parents and know that they will one day move into the older age categories.

It is nonetheless too easy to overemphasize the importance of such linkages, for youth in particular, as the slogan "don't trust anyone over thirty" forcefully suggests. Parents may be linked to and love their youth but they are still capable of suspicion, rejection, and distrust of them. They can feel defamed and betrayed by them. As age-category segregation deepens, as more youth go to live in youth ghettos and come under the influence of the special kind of life carried on there, we should expect an increasing proportion of parents to feel that all the effort they put into Johnny or Mary was for naught and to ask themselves, "What did I do wrong?" Of course, they did nothing wrong, unless one counts as wrong their willingness to send their youths to college and allow them to reside in youth ghettos.

SOURCES OF AGE SEGREGATION

To understand the social sources or causes of age-category segregation, a detailed analysis of at least the last seventy years of American history would be required. Systematic comparisons with similar and different developments in other societies would be indispensable. I will only suggest some very gross and proximate forces promoting age-category segregation.

First, there is the peculiarly American guiding conception that the least expensive and most efficient technological alternative in projecting action is the "best." It seems to be cheaper and more efficient to expand universities and create giant new ones than it would be to construct and staff a multitude of small ones. It seems to be cheaper and more efficient to build tracts of similarly priced houses on an assembly line basis than to intermix variously priced houses on a custom basis. It is believed to be cheaper and more efficient to bring late adults together into special housing adapted to their "needs"—likewise built on an assembly line basis—than to do otherwise. Specialized organizations and occupations are most cheaply and efficiently provided for these age categories if each is massed together in a single area. Professors are more easily provided for youth; schools are more easily provided for children and teenagers; and medical specialties are more easily provided for late adults.

Second, there are the requirements, or rather lack of them, of a technological economic system. Despite all the demand for technical personnel existing in some sectors of the economy, the larger fact seems to be that there are simply not enough occupational slots in that economy to absorb any significant proportion of the hordes of youth and late adults in the population. In terms of economic necessity, youth and late adults (as well as teenagers and children) are surplus population. A basic condition permitting them to congregate in their own grounds is that the vast bulk of them are not needed, anyplace, to perform economic functions.

One way, in particular, to manage youth is to develop the conception that they require advanced training or education if they are to participate eventually in the technological economy. This conception is given teeth by requiring education as a condition of employment, a condition which propels an ever-increasing proportion of these youth—some 40 percent of them, or about 6 million at present—into colleges, and a proportion into youth ghettos.

The surplus is eased out at the other end through the development of the conception that people are not really very good workers after about sixty or so, and should, for their own good and enjoyment, give up useful employment.

If age-category segregation is induced by forces such as these and many others, once begun it comes to have a dynamic of its own. Seeing less and less of one another, it becomes more difficult to know how to interact comfortably across age-category divisions. Having less practice and experience in it, early and middle adults, for example, come to be more uncomfortable about interacting with those late adults they do encounter. The same is true of interactional relations among the other age categories. Such difficulties, in turn, provoke more mutual avoidance and an increasing constriction of topics about which they might have common interest. Segregation having begun, a process of spiraling or increasing isolation across the age grades is set up.

THE YOUTH GHETTO

Let me shift, finally, to a direct focus on the youth ghetto. I will discuss, in order, relations of adults to this territory, conduct within it, and some aspects of interaction between the two. These topics are appropriately conceived in terms that we might use in discussing other, more familiar, kinds of ghettos. The more familiar ones have historically been based on religion, ethnicity, or race. However, certain kinds of social processes seem relatively common to almost all ghettos, age-category ones included.

ADULT IMPUTATIONS AND CONTROL

A condition of territorial segregation wherein a variety of additional categories are piled up promotes a situation of low information flow from the ghetto to the surrounding territories. When low information flow occurs in the context of a measure of suspicion, fear, and distrust, the information most likely to be noticed, remembered, and circulated by persons in extraghetto territories is that which is discrediting or defaming. Adopting the point of view of suspicious, fearful, and distrustful persons, it is altogether reasonable for them to be attuned to discrediting information from the ghetto; such information serves to put them further on guard to protect themselves.

One type of defamation takes the form of imputing to the pivotal category in question a wide range of personal failings, often felt to be caused by the pivotal category itself. Non-ghetto dwellers build up in their minds an imputed "personality" of sorts that is believed to be characteristic of the particular ghetto dwellers, the particular pivotal category (Suttles 1968).

In recent years we have begun to see the development of the rudiments of an imputed ghetto personality of youth, or, more narrowly, of students. Adults, the superordinate category in this case, seem to have begun the process of noticing, remembering, and relating a variety of kinds of imputed personal features of this latest stigmatized category.

One hears it commented that "they" are boisterous, they have no respect for property, they work irregularly, and drive recklessly. They throw garbage out of their windows and break bottles in the streets and on the sidewalks. They lounge in unseemly fashion on balconies, dangle out of windows, and congregate in public thoroughfares. They accost strangers on the street with arcane propositions. They gamble all night, fail to pay shopkeepers and landlords, shoplift, and engage in riotous drinking sprees. They hang around on the streets, jaywalk, talk in a loud and crude fashion in public places, and live in disorder and filth. They let their dwellings run down, living like "animals," crowded six and seven together in small apartments. They have loose sexual behavior and fail to keep their bodies and clothes properly scrubbed and ordered. They engage in crime. The women have no shame but dress scantily and recline suggestively on lawns or around buildings. They are residentially unstable, always moving, frequently leaving the landlord or even their own kind in the lurch. Establishments which cater to their peculiar tastes are dimly lit and outfitted in outlandish decor. Obscene slogans and writings and pictures are likely to be found in the stores they frequent, especially the book shops.

While yet scattered and relatively uncrystallized as a personality portrait of youth ghetto residents, there would seem to be here already the elements of the classic portrait of failings attributed to ghetto dwellers throughout American history. This portrait has typically included—as it does here—the elements of laziness, irresponsibility, hedonism, lack of pride in property or personal appearance, promiscuousness, deviousness, and family and employment instability. We are currently most familiar with this portrait of imputations relative to Black and Hispanic ghetto dwellers, but the same kinds of imputations were once made of, for example, the Italians and the Irish before their ghettos disintegrated. Where ghettos based on these latter pivotal categories persist, the process still goes on (Suttles 1968). Such failings were imputed also to "laborers," or workingmen, during the struggle for unions in America. (A similar kind of imputation of personal failings also takes place between regions of nations and nations themselves that are in conflict.)

The similarity between the imputations now beginning to be made of residents of youth ghettos and those made at one or another time of residents of Irish, Italian, Black, and Hispanic ghettos suggest considerable continuity in the portrait of imputed failings in American society. While the particular category that bears the brunt of these imputations has changed, the imputations themselves continue to be with us.

Such continuity, despite change in the particular pivotal category that is the object of the imputations, could be taken to suggest the social necessity of a stratum believed to embody all the failings so feared by the dominant sectors of society. Such an embodiment of what most people should not be seems always to be there, a vivid and living object-lesson in the difference between good and evil. If everyone is good, how are participants in a society to know the difference between good and evil? It is perhaps through the dramatization of evil, achieved by assigning some sector of society the task of "acting it out," that the remainder of society more easily finds it possible to be good. The repository category of evil provides "good citizens" with the empirical materials needed in making a meaningful contrast and in gauging the appropriateness of conduct.

In addition to becoming objects of defaming imputations, ghetto dwellers find themselves, as well, the objects of specialized processes of social control and recognition. Such efforts are specialized because, while they are sometimes described as though they applied to the entire population, they are directed at the ghetto dwellers in particular.

Although they are relatively rudimentary as yet, we already see such specialized control and recognition efforts in, for example, the University of Michigan's attempt to regulate student operation of automobiles anywhere in an entire county without special registration. New laws regarding mufflers on motor vehicles have been adopted, and aimed, according to the public discussion, at the motorcycles of youth. (They are, it is said, terribly noisy.)

Within the context of ghettoization, existing controls aimed at youth take on new significance. The military draft, which falls with special force on youth, comes to be defined as a special burden. Because of the uncertainty over whether any of them is twenty-one years of age, the purchase of alcoholic beverages becomes, typically, an occasion for an ID shakedown. In much the same way that Blacks in some parts of the country even today have to worry about obtaining public service, youth have to be concerned over producing a sufficient amount of "ID" even to ratify their minimal standing as persons. The treatment they receive at the hands of bartenders and liquor store clerks communicates their special pivotal identity and others' assumption that youth are "likely to be liars." So, too, their credit may be a matter for suspicion and the obtaining of a telephone may require a special "security deposit," serving organizationally to impute to them an untrustworthy personal character.

Also parallel to Blacks, employers are willing to offer many youth only menial unskilled jobs and reluctant to offer employment with career or developmental possibilities. Employers discriminate against youth in terms of whether they have made some kind of settlement with the military. If none has been made, reasonable employment is difficult to obtain. While employers may be entirely rational in this, it constitutes, from the point of view of youth, a form of discrimination.

Youth become, too, objects of special recognition in the name of nondiscrimination. A few radio stations, for example, have demonstrated their democratic virtues not only by having ethnic and racial radio programs but by setting aside hours or even days for youth programs. Radio stations in Ann Arbor recognize that area's special German past with "old country" shows, and at least one station gives over Saturday to student "ethnic radio." The youthful announcer for that day refers to Ann Arbor as "Student City." (Like the separate entrances for Whites and Blacks in Southern states, Ann Arbor, Michigan's, YM-YWCA has a special side door neatly lettered with the sign "Youth Entrance."

Eventually most ghettos rouse the moral sentiments of the dominant population to the point that a special corps of helping and rehabilitative personnel is recruited and deployed into the areas. Their mission is to reduce the number of horrendous things that go on there and make the residents straighten up and be good citizens.

While this kind of missionary activity, on any significant scale, may lie far in the future in relation to youth ghettos, one can discern its beginnings in such enterprises as the "campus ministry" and in the expansion of psychological counseling for student youth.

If and when there comes to be a "war on youth ghettos," and even federal programs for such, these missionaries will no doubt follow the classic pattern of previous ghetto forays. They are likely to be more concerned with adjusting people to their lot within the existing structure than with considering alternative modes of social organization.

Informational inaccessibility and fear and suspicion of ghettos promote, in addition to defaming stereotypes of imputed personal features and specialized control, a special revelationary literature. This literature is centrally oriented to the question: "What are X (the pivotal category) *really* like?" Whether the "X" has been Southerners, workers, suffragettes, immigrants, or of late, Blacks, the popular press has frenzied itself with efforts to "inform" the dominant sectors of society what is "really" going on, what, of late, is "happening." Such popular revelations promise us an "inside view" of the innermost sections and horrendous events of the ghetto. Complete with the most grim or bizarre photographs and drawings, such revelations often lead the reader to believe that not only are the worst suspicions true but things are even worse.

While we are most familiar with these popular revelations, historically, in connection with immigrants and Blacks, a similar kind of presentation is now being made about youth. One of the most recent, put out by *Look,* the contemporary master of popular revelation, is called *Youth Quake* (Fox 1967). Retailing for one dollar, its cover features a blurred psychedelic-like photograph of youth on a dance floor in "wildly" colored dress, presumably writhing under the sounds emitted by a musical group. The front page text promises to tell us "What's Happening" in these terms: "Turned on and tuned in . . . teeny-boppers, hippies . . . Sunset Strip to Washington Square . . . conversations parents never hear—sex, drugs, God, morality, success—mod and mini . . . psychedelic lights . . . and much much more."

Popular revelations of ghetto life are not entirely negative. While there is a large element of indignation and "tut-tutting," these revelations contain a mixture of horror and romantic fascination with "people who live that way." Evil, after all, must have its attractions—to be natural—otherwise it would not be so popular. Nor would the dominant categories of a society have to put so much energy into eliminating or holding it in check. (These are long-noted features of "evil," but they were most forcefully brought to my attention by Gerald Suttles in conversation.)

It is in part such romantic fascination that, in the past, made Harlem such a lure for White Manhattan residents and tourists. Historically, a variety of kinds of ghettos have come to service the vice needs of the population at large. Youth ghettos will perhaps also come to service the demand for vice.

Parallel to the growth of popular revelations and lagging behind them somewhat, there begins to be produced about ghettos a much less titillating but probably more accurate body of scholarly revelations. In historical succession, sociologists, for example, produced an enormous body of material on immigrants (now no longer read by much of anyone but historians of the field) and on Blacks, under the rubric "race relations." They are now "getting hip" to the "youth thing," and the scholarly outpouring has begun. Originally called "juvenile delinquency" in the fifties (when there were large amounts of money to be had for research on that), the caption has been expanded to "youth." Highly indicative is a recent well-received collection of writings called *Handbook of Modern Sociology,* which has a special chapter by David Matza (1964), "Position and Behavior Patterns of Youth," without a corresponding chapter on any other age category.

The theoretical debate common to the sociological literature on immigrants, Blacks, *and* youth is the question of the degree to which they are "really" different or similar to the rest of society. In all three bodies of materials, some people argue that "they" are significantly different in some fundamental fashion. This position is opposed by theorists who choose to emphasize different facts in the direction of saying that the category is fundamentally similar. The debate has focused on whether the ghettoized category has a distinctive culture.

The urge to produce such revelations inevitably gives rise to the phenomenon of ghetto spies, persons who either are permitted openly to hang around in the ghetto or who actually pass as "one," whatever the "one" in question may be. The spies of popular revelations are often reporters on assignment, but quite often, also, free-lancers, as was apparently the case with race-ghetto spy John Griffin, author of *Black Like Me* (1961). Paul Goodman (1956) is perhaps the leading youth-ghetto spy among a wide range of persons who have tried to get in on this new kind of "act." Perhaps the ultimate in age-category spying has already been achieved by that 33-year-old lady who claimed, "I Passed as a Teenager" (Tonabene 1967). As always, the scholarly revealers have lagged behind in getting out their own spies, but they are beginning to catch up.

And, as has occurred with respect to previous ghettos, some members of the dominant pivotal category defect to "the other side." In the same way that some of the economic elite, in Marxian terms, are said to see the "true" direction of history and defect to the workers, or that some Whites defect to and take up the Black cause, we are now beginning to have age-category defectors. Edgar Friedenberg (1965) is perhaps the leading exemplar of such defection.

INTERNAL DYNAMICS

In attempting briefly to characterize what happens within ghettos, we must keep in mind two previously discussed points. First, the piling up or clustering of devalued categories in a given territory is taking place. Second, this factual clustering is perceived (however dimly) by the surrounding populace and becomes a basis upon which all manner of additional failings are imputed. Taken together, factual clustering and the additional imputations form the situation of the ghettoite.

Two significant features of the situation of the ghettoite are: (1) extraordinary exposure to others of one's "own kind," and correspondingly limited exposure to persons of "other kinds"; and (2) limited objective possibilities for establishing a stable lifestyle, primarily because of low income, which is, in turn, a function of the imputations and practices of disreputability made of "his/her kind" by the surrounding populace.

The situation of the ghettoite is conducive to or "ready-made for" familiar strategic lines of adaptation or response. I will mention two well-known strategies of adaptation appearing frequently in all ghettos which are now appearing in youth ghettos.

First, it is possible, and rather reasonable, for the ghettoite to accept the just-mentioned facts of her/his situation and accommodate to them. He/she can come to believe that the imputations made and treatment accorded to the category by the dominant sectors of society are in a significant measure true, reasonable, and justified. While viewing these as sad facts, they are nonetheless accepted as valid. The imputations of the ways in which he/she displays personal failings become then a basis upon which actual and new items of "personal failure" are predicated. (The irony is that such new personal failings are perceived by the dominant categories and become the basis upon which they, in turn, predicate more intensive imputations and discriminatory practices. That treatment, in turn, feeds back to the ghettoite, and so it goes on.)

Under conditions of low income and almost exclusive exposure to one's "own" stigmatized kind and an uncertain residential future, and indeed, an uncertain future generally, it becomes reasonable to relax one's efforts at a conventional personal appearance and to relax one's efforts, as well, to maintain a conventionally clean, well-kept, and orderly household.

We are familiar with the relaxation of personal and household standards in ghettos based on ethnic or racial pivotal categories. And we are familiar, too, with the imputations sometimes made as to why these standards are relaxed. Among the most popular has been the notion of a special "lower-class personality" which causes personal and household disorder and dirt.

However, exactly the same pattern of relaxation occurs in youth ghettos. The youth found to display this pattern are drawn largely from middle- and upper-middle-class backgrounds, a setting which presumably trained them in high standards of personal and household order and cleanliness. In the youth ghetto, we find a portion of them living in a fashion very similar to that in which people in other ghettos live. (I refer here to the garden-variety, run-of-the-mill youth in such ghettos, not simply the more spectacular patterns embodied in youthful radicals or hippies.) Presumably when they depart from the ghetto for early adult neighborhoods, they will maintain the very particular style of cleanliness and order so characteristic of those neighborhoods.

The youth ghetto pattern of personal and household disorder and dirt is a very important "control" or contrast case which tells us that it is not ghetto people's deep-lying personality patterns that conduce to this relaxation, but rather the ghetto situation. The ghetto situation is one of high exposure to one's own kind, low income, and uncertainty of residential and general future. Exposure almost exclusively to one's own kind reduces the felt need for "respectable" presentation. Low income makes respectable presentation extremely difficult to accomplish. Middle-class people are insufficiently appreciative of the very high total costs of the tools and machines, paint, repair materials, and furnishings necessary to the rehabilitation and maintenance of a "respectable" household. This is especially the case where one is attempting this in what is already a ghetto dwelling. And, of course, an uncertain residential and general future renders the entire effort unreasonable in the first place. If we are to understand this pattern of ghetto living, we are better advised to scrutinize the characteristics of the ghetto situation rather than the personal characteristics of whatever category of people happen to be found there.

Second, while the majority of ghetto residents seem to "take it" and a proportion drift into the first pattern, a minority refuse to accept their situation and project a more active strategy of response. Comingling in the intensive fashion now made possible and necessary, some ghetto dwellers begin to crystallize new and unusual ideologies which purport to explain and interpret their particular situation and, typically, also to describe and explain all the rest of the world. Those who live in the ghetto situation seem particularly likely to spawn and be attracted to new and unusual ideologies characterized by members of the dominant society as radical, bizarre, peculiar, or fantastic. Ghettoites are particularly likely to so occupy themselves because of a lack of exposure to the more moderate and modulating categories of persons who might convince them of other realities; because of the stigmatizing imputations they face; and because of the objective deprivation and social exclusion under which they labor.

The general class of active ideological response to the ghetto situation itself divides into two types of directions, which sometimes even compete with one another for adherents. One type, the political response, defines the ghetto situation and other sectors of society in terms of relatively immediate measures that can be undertaken to better the lot of ghettoites and perhaps even the life of the entire society. We are familiar with this in regard to Black ghettos and the variety of civil rights organizations seeking to make a given change in the social order. The suggestion here is that we can also understand the New Left—meaning, most prominently, Students for a Democratic Society—as a movement arising out of the youth ghetto in the same way political movements have, historically, risen out of other kinds of ghettos.

If the ghettoization of youth continues, we should expect to see the rise of a variety of kinds of other political responses, many of them more limited and moderate than Students for a Democratic Society. Already there are attempts to organize renters and register student voters to increase their political power. There may come a day when some cities will find that their politics revolve around the voting strength of various age-category ghettos, in the same way that Chicago politics has long revolved around ethnic and racial enclaves.

The other type of more active ideological response is considerably more sweeping in the scope of its projected change in the social order, but ironically more passive in the degree to which it seeks to make changes in that order. I refer to the various retreating and utopian—not untypically, religious—responses which involve withdrawing into highly distinctive residential enclaves, often within the ghetto, and living out therein a life that is considered perfect and ideal. The outside world is seen as sinful, demented, deluded, decadent, or otherwise in need of revolutionary change. Except for perhaps some efforts at making individual converts, such utopians do not directly attack the social order. The most famous instance of this type of response in connection with Black ghettos has been Father Divine's Heavens (Harris 1953). We are witnessing an analytically identical strategy of response in the "hippies" who have appropriated certain dwellings in youth ghettos as their utopian communities and who have even moved out to create their own ghettos, as in the Haight-Ashbury district of San Francisco. Although yet lacking a widely acknowledged messianic leader (Leary is apparently "out"), their ideology is remarkably similar to that espoused by followers of Father Divine, especially in the emphasis on love, goodwill, and the decadence of the larger society.

One other pattern of response should be mentioned, although it has not as yet appeared in the youth ghetto, at least not in organized form. This is the militant revolutionary pattern, exemplified by the Black nationalists, or at least those among the Black nationalists who advocate guerrilla warfare and violent subversion. But perhaps this still lies in the future and will only appear if youth ghettoization becomes very extreme.

The possibility and viability of the militant revolutionary pattern, and all the other patterns of response are crucially undercut by a fundamental feature peculiar to age. While people who are identified in terms of racial and ethnic pivotal categories will remain instances of those categories all their lives, youth as a category is transitorily occupied. It would seem very difficult to predicate any kind of enduring collective action on a population of participants that is continually leaving the category while others are continually arriving. In the end, that feature must be recognized as fundamentally debilitating to organized age-category conflict.

YOUTH GHETTO-ADULT CONFRONTATION

Nonetheless, conflicts between the age categories of a more limited but highly spectacular character are still possible, and even likely, under conditions of youth ghettoization.

The prime meaning of ghettoization is the piling up of all manner of categories of dimensions that are different from those of the rest of society. A prime effect of this piling up of categories shared within a territory and little shared across territories, is the decline of routine, trustful relationships with individuals and organizations in extraghetto territories. Ghettoites are intensively and routinely exposed to other ghettoites, but only fractionally exposed in a routine fashion to non-ghettoites.

Such a situation of separation of categories of people serves to create distance, in both the physical and social senses and, therefore, to engender relative ignorance or lack of information as to the intentions, plans, motives, and good or ill will of the other pivotal category.

If there comes to be an absence of cross-categorical interaction, joint problem solving, routine negotiation, and the like, there is created within both pivotal categories a condition of distrust and fear of the opposite category. This situation of separation and therefore distrust and fear spawned by ignorance is to be contrasted with the kinds of relations between social categories that create trust and confidence and therefore social stability. Cross-categorical trust and confidence are most likely to prevail where there is a high rate of relatively free interaction, relatively large numbers of communication channels, and prompt attention to grievances which can easily be brought to the attention of persons who will act to settle disputes in a just manner. A large number of communication links between categories allows each reasonably to present its point of view, its motives, its plans, its intentions. While each category may not agree with the other on such matters, each side is at least relatively accurately informed and there is little or no necessity for making all manner of surmises, guesses, and imputations of the motives and plans of its opposite number. Equally important, in preparing such cross-category revelations of its plans and intentions, each is induced to modify its perspective to make it more acceptable to the opposite category. Concomitant with such exchanges are personal friendships, informal ties, personalistic advantages and payoffs, and other more diffuse intercategorical modes of compromising the involvements of persons in their own category. A tradition of exchange of views and negotiated settlements makes it more likely that any action initiated by one side will be received in an atmosphere of trust. All these practices make it less likely that any action by either category will be defined as threatening.

We find precisely the opposite obtaining between ghettos and the host society. The absence of effective communication, cooptation, and compromise breeds fear, suspicion, and distrust. Such a situation is fertile ground for the spread of all manner of fearful and cynical rumors as to what "the other side" is "really" up to. In the absence of reasonable information, the most gross of cynical motives can be and are imputed. (I refer you again to the slogan "don't trust anyone over thirty.") It is in the situation of separation, fear, distrust, and negative imputations between categories that an action initiated by one category can be defined as threatening to the basic interest of the opposite category.

If an action is defined as a threat, then it is reasonable to respond to this threat with a swift, decisive, strong defense. Of course, the opposite category which is the recipient of this defense thereupon feels itself grossly threatened. The recipient category, to protect its now felt-to-be-threatened fundamental interests, reciprocates with its own swift, decisive, strong defense. The opposite category is consequently even more threatened and responds in kind. We thus have an escalation of conflict, a process that is the joint product of the two parties and that seems always to have an ambiguous beginning point, unless one traces the history of the relation all the way back to the beginnings of the original categorical separation. (Excellent documentation and conceptualization of these situations and processes are presented in Suttles [1968] and Heirich [1968]. The process sketched in the foregoing passages may well be among the few found at all levels of social organization.)

Where the swift, decisive, strong defense involves large numbers of ghetto persons acting in a nonroutine manner in public places, it is popularly labeled a demonstration, riot, or collective outburst. (When such defensive action involves merely individuals or small groups, it is labeled crime, delinquency, or deviance. When it involves nations it is war. Such differences in popular labels should not detract attention from the essential similarity of the social processes.) We have seen a number of these in connection with Black ghettos. It is in the same terms of ghettoization—the terms of separation, fear, distrust, and high probability of threat—that we can also best understand similar events occurring on college campuses, that is, in youth ghettos.

If youth ghettos have already fired their shot heard around the world, it was probably the Berkeley "demonstrations," "disturbances," "revolt," or "revolution" of 1964-65. (Pick a label according to the preference of your age category.)

The well-known events at Berkeley were only a spectacular episode in the long history of decreasing categorical sharing and the growth of a relatively enclosed youth ghetto along the southern edge of the Berkeley campus. The relations between the two categories—university and youth—came finally to a confrontation where each category saw itself enormously threatened by the other. Each category saw itself as rightly defending itself against the threats posed by the other. It is ironic that the growth of Berkeley's academic eminence in America closely corresponds to the growth of the conditions of separation between youth and the university. Berkeley's scholarly and research eminence was purchased at the price of relative indifference to, and separation from, its almost 28,000 charges. And, as the university learned, the price was much higher than it had been originally calculated. Although allowing at least one-quarter of the tenured faculty in many departments to be on leave for research (and a large "in residence" proportion on psychological leave) and a large proportion of the teaching to be performed by youth called "teaching assistants" is conducive to a worldwide reputation for scholarship, these practices, when combined with a wide variety of other kinds of indifference and separation, are incompatible with linking the category of youth to the social order. (My characterization of the Berkeley events is drawn from Heirich's [1968] definitive study, especially chapter 1, "Structuring the Conflict.")

Even more ironic, where there has been little communication, cooptation, and compromise between categories, it becomes all the more difficult to initiate them. Under conditions of separation, fear, threat, and defense, each category comes rather fiercely to pronounce its refusal to compromise what are now well-articulated and ideologized principles. The existing separation tends to deepen and solidify into principled intercategorical opposition. Universities that embark on the Berkeley quest for eminence in the same manner, might be apprised of the possibility that there may be a youth ghetto like Berkeley's in their future.

I have suggested the possibility that we may be embarking upon a period in the American experience when age will become a nationalized pivotal dimension around which categories of persons are differentiated. A new kind of segregation may be afoot. I am mindful of all those oft-printed remarks, running back at least to ancient Greece, which tell us that almost every generation has thought that new and unprecedented (and most often terrible) things were taking place among its youth. Such reprinted expressions of alarm are intended to tell us that the perception of the unprecedented—typically the decadent—is simply a generational illusion spawned by the fears of older persons. While I will make no judgment as to whether younger generations were or are decadent, one can say that very frequently there has in fact been an enormous change in generational views and practices, a change enshrined most recently in the transformation of Western societies into advanced, industrial, technological social orders.

We should be prepared to expect that the coming of this newest kind of social order might itself create a wide variety of likewise new types of categorical segregations, while yet other segregations disintegrate. So far as I have been able to determine, the current scale of the clustering of persons into territories on the basis of age is a new phenomenon.

While the emerging primacy of the age dimension and its categories seems to be new, the social processes it follows, and that follows from it, are very old and universal. While we may have to come to grips with a new content and substance of social conflict, we need not despair, because we do know something about the character of the formal and analytic processes involved and the concepts and propositions appropriate to an understanding of it. The primary question becomes—will the human animal use such understanding in coping with this new and emerging basis of conflict, or will it stumble through in the same gruesome manner it has done in the past, and play out, yet again, the painful drama of blind hostility?

NOTE

I would like to express my indebtedness to the works of, and conversations with, Lyn H. Lofland, Jerry Suttles, and Max Heirich. The seemingly unconnected but actually parallel and complementary work of Suttles (1968) on an inner-city slum and of Heirich (1968) on campus demonstrations have provided, in part, the data, concepts, and propositions upon which I will attempt a more generalized statement with particular reference to youth. While these people are responsible for what follows in the sense of making it more possible, they are not to be held accountable for the direction taken or conclusions reached. This article is a revision of an address given at Kalamazoo College, July 13, 1967, in a series on The Moral Revolution of Our Time. Much more than other articles in this volume, "The Youth Ghetto" is decisively framed by the time and place in which I wrote it (Ann Arbor, Michigan, 1967). It weaves back and forth between the prophetic-participant and transcendent-analyst points of view and is most profitably read with these two clearly in mind. I explain the difference between these vantage points (and the difference they make) in the introduction to part 1 of this volume and I urge a reading of those introductory remarks prior to reading "The Youth Ghetto."

Part Two

CONVERSION: READINESS FOR PROTEST

INTRODUCTION

The three studies of conversion presented in this part relate to protest in ways explained just below. The better to provide perspective, in the next section I outline the distinctive history of conversion studies within which the three studies were written.

Data on the Unification Church—the so-called Moonies—are integral to all three chapters. A number of questions concerning the relations of researcher and researched have arised concerning these data and I want to discuss two of these as an additional form of introduction. I shall address (1) the question of according anonymity to groups and (2) the reasons for researching a seemingly trivial and unimportant organization.

CONVERSION AND PROTEST

The diverse units of social organization to which the concept of protest can refer, alert us to the complexity of the question of participation in protest. Because of the diversity of the units in which a person can participate, it is almost meaningless to ask: What are the causes of participation in protest? At least, the answer to the question so posed will massively sacrifice precision and complexity for the sake of generality. More fruitfully, we need to inquire into units of protest: isolated acts, gatherings, events, campaigns, waves, cycles, organizations, movements. It is likely that we need to make many more such distinctions, especially highlighting differences between planned and unplanned protests and forms of citizen organizations.

These considerations provide context for understanding the specialized focus of the three chapters comprising part 2. All three are addressed only to recruitment to *organizations* of a protest character. (However, we also see how *gatherings,* especially of a celebratory nature, figure in many important kinds of organizational recruitment, a feature that is still not to be confused with the study of gatherings per se.)

The three are further specialized in that protest organizations exhibiting crucial features are emphasized. That is, these chapters deal mostly with those protest organizations which display a *religious* worldview that is highly absorbing and that fosters *high-intensity commitments*. Recruitment of "political" or "ego" movement organizations (distinctions explained in chapter 7) and/or to organizations that are low in commitment intensity probably exhibit features other than those stressed in chapters 4 and 5, especially. This is a central message of chapter 6, on diverse "conversion motifs."

PERIODS IN THE HISTORY OF CONVERSION STUDIES

"Becoming a World-Saver" (chapter 4) was written with Rodney Stark in the very early sixties before that decade became The Sixties and the object of so much nostalgia in the early eighties. The formulation in that report was well received during the sixties (although it "caught on" still more in the seventies, for reasons to which I will come). In summary the "becoming a world-saver" argument went:

> For conversion a person must: (1) experience enduring acutely felt tensions; (2) within a religious problem-solving perspective; (3) which leads to defining her/himself as a religious seeker; (4) encountering the new group at a turning point in life; (5) wherein an affective bond is formed (or preexists) with one or more converts; (6) where extracult attachments are absent or neutralized; (7) and where, if the person is to become a deployable agent, he/she is exposed to intensive interaction [Lofland and Stark 1965:874, slightly edited].

My surmises about the bases of responsiveness to this formulation are of several sorts. First, the sort of "qualitative process analysis" (a phrase discussed in chapter 5) it represented was simultaneously much in vogue as an idea in that era but infrequently applied in concrete research. Howard Becker's (1953) process account of marijuana use and Neil Smelser's (1963) value-added depiction of collective behavior were dominant and widely praised examples of such thinking and Stark and I quite directly and self-consciously emulated the logic they employed. (I first studied Smelser's famous model in 1961 in the form of a faint carbon copy of a typed manuscript on noncirculating reserve in the University of California at Berkeley library). Odd though it may now seem, the very notion of a series of explicit, time-ordered series of stages had, in itself, a peculiar resonance at the time.

"Becoming a World-Saver" also had a second, more latent, and less savory, appeal. In the heyday of political protest and movements, the data of the paper depicted social movement members as decided losers, for the case studies dwell on converts' past failures and discontents. I am *not* saying that the converts are depicted incorrectly in the report. Rather, the concrete specifics document the association of discontent and personal failure in a way certain to appeal to the conventional persons who dominate social science (who may view themselves as liberals or radicals, but who are fundamentally conservative) (cf. Freeman's [1983:xvii] comments on the "distaste . . . for movements" of the period). The report inadvertently caters to the "activist as incompetent" myth promoted by such writers as Eric Hoffer (1951) in a way that I, on recent readings, can now recognize and find unsettling. On my own behalf, however, the report also contains a muted rejection of this drift. Notably, it ends with the declaration that there need not be "extensive characterological conjunction between participant and pattern of participation."

Sixties political protest faded and was replaced by the early and midseventies blossoming of new religions in America and other countries. Numerous social scientists scurried out to study them and especially to study processes of affiliation. As one of only a handful of previous treatments of conversion, the "world-saver model," as it was labeled, became one reference point for this new spate of conversion researchers (e.g. Snow and Phillips 1980). Never having believed that what Stark and I said was universally applicable to all conversion events, I became increasingly perturbed by efforts to test the truth of the model on other religious and political groups. Even though it was usually faulted in only minor ways (it is so abstract as to be virtually unfalsifiable, as explained in chapter 5), the question to me was not the validity of the model per se but specifying the range of its applicability. The difference in conception is not merely semantic. In the former, to find that one's new data fails to fit a model is to reject the model because it failed "the test." In the latter, disjunction between data and model is taken as the starting point for exploring conditions under which a particular pattern is or is not found—does or does not occur. This and allied concerns are major burdens of the second chapter of this part (chapter 5), that revisits the world-saver model a decade later.

The "revisit" chapter also looks back at the original report in a second and different way. The millenarian group I studied in the early sixties—now often called the "Moonies" (the name itself being a topic I will treat shortly) catapulted from obscurity to worldwide fame and infamy in the mid-seventies. This change was amazing to me and in 1976 I undertook to understand how and why it happened. Chapter 5 focuses on changes in recruiting organization and is one part of a comprehensive treatment that appears as the epilogue in the 1977 republication of my 1966 monograph on the group titled *Doomsday*

Cult. (A brief summary of the organizational development aspects of that epilogue is provided as chapter 9, "White-Hot Mobilization," of this volume.)

As both these reports detail, the pool of persons from which the Unification Church recruited shifted dramatically in the seventies, as did its recruitment practices. In particular, the UC began to convert young people who could not easily be construed as "losers." Indeed, the new Moonies were fearsome winners, a most ominous turn of events in the eyes of many.

The seventies flowering of new religions and scholarship on such groups created a new wave of conversion studies in the late seventies. Inevitably, investigators quarreled over the relative importance of one or another factor, approach, or stress in accounting for conversion. In the same way I have regarded tests of the world-saver model as pseudotests, disputes about the relative merits of the diverse approaches to conversion that also emerged struck me as pseudodisputes that arose from a continuing persistence of the presumption that if a pattern is found in some cases it must be found in all. This is the presumption that Norman Skonovd and I have striven to rebut in the third chapter (6) of this part, a review of the conversion literature in which we try to specify major and diverse patterns of conversion experience. These we lable the: (1) intellectual, (2) mystical, (3) experimental, (4) affectional, (5) revivalist, and (6) coercive. Not "this *or* that" but "this *and* that."

FROM "DPs" TO MOONIES

It is common and even ethically enjoined in social science to protect the anonymity of people studied, especially of people not in the public eye. The group I studied in the early sixties was quite obscure, and as a matter of course I changed the names of the participants and even of the group itself. For a decade or so no one gave thought to this mundane fact. But in the mid-seventies people began frequently to guess or assert that the "DPs" were the newly famous Moonies. One scholar even devoted an article to documenting the assertion that the "two" groups were but one, and reflecting on the meaning of this fact for the development of social science (Lynch 1977). Against numerous scholarly and media solicitations in the middle and late seventies to breach the "cover" I had given the group, I continued my disguises, as seen in all the articles of this part and in the 1979 article appearing as chapter 9 in this volume.

However, the situation was becoming ever more awkward, and in late seventies publications I felt constrained to couch my disguises with such phrases as "my pseudonyms are now somewhat labored" (Lofland 1977:345). Into the early eighties the "secret" had become absurdly obvious, so obvious that continuing the "cover" seemed pointless.

In 1983, I therefore asked the president of the American branch of the UC to release me from the agreement I had made with the person occupying the equivalent of his office in March 1962. The president granted my request and agreed, further, that only the organization and its founder required reference by their actual names. All other participants would be identified only in terms of their movement positions. (In this I follow the practice I have used in publications of my research on lobbying and protesting—see part 4 of this volume—a practice that is widespread in scholarly research on organizations oriented to the public realm.)

This change is founded on more than convenient escape from the awkward transparency of my disguises in view of the UC's worldwide fame. The code of ethics of the American Sociological Association (the professional organization of my discipline) accords stronger rights of biographical anonymity to small and private human actions and associations than to large and public collectivities and persons in the public eye. The latter are held as "not entitled automatically to privacy and need not be extended routinely guarantees of privacy and confidentiality" (American Sociological Association 1982). Beyond the mere impossibility of disguise, there are ethical principles of accountability and the likelihood of possessing power to protect one's interests.

The UC has moved itself from the private to public categories of collectivity and has become subject to a different ethic of research anonymity. It is critical, nonetheless, that the UC formally released me from my initial agreement, for the ASA code also holds that if privacy and confidentiality guarantees are extended to groups, regardless of size and public/private status, "they must be honored unless there are clear and compelling reasons not to do so" (American Sociological Association 1982).

SCHOLARLY MILIEU AND OBSCURE RELIGIONS

In recent years people have quizzed me on how it was that I had the "amazing" foresight to know that the UC would become so famous and had therefore decided to study them. Some people have attributed to me a kind of mystical prescience or at least some unusual ability to predict the development of social groups. Why, apart from such foresight, would one elect to study such an obscure and unimportant group?

These queries and imputations are basically misconceived and I think it is important to understand how I came to study the Moonies. I did not (and do not) have special powers to predict the careers of organizations or other social matters, as my foray in chapter 3, "The Youth Ghetto" amply illustrates. When the UC "made good" I, as a person who knew something about them, was more surprised than the less informed.

The bases on which I came to have an active interest in groups like the Moonies, to encounter them, and then to select them for study are prosaic and display for us once again some conventional and omnipresent processes of social organization, mainly processes of encouraging scholarly activity in mainline educational institutions.

The most central fact was that I was living in a social milieu in which the study of groups like the UC was legitimate and encouraged. When I became a graduate student in the Department of Sociology at the University of California, Berkeley, in the fall of 1960, having only a general interest in radical religions, I came to associate with four members of that faculty who were supportive of that interest: Herbert Blumer, Charles Glock, Erving Goffman, and Neil Smelser. It is salient to recall that the famous *When Prophecy Fails* by Festinger, Riecken, and Schachter, was a recent (1956) publication that elicited considerable interest. Those social psychologists of stature lent legitimacy to the idea of studying radical religions (and to studying them in natural settings).

The nature and strength of the support given by several members of the faculty at Berkeley is displayed in the following anecdote. Late in the fall of 1961, a San Francisco newspaper front-paged a report from Cleater, Arizona, where a group was gathering to wait for the imminent end of the world. Three of us with an interest in such matters—sociology graduate students Fred Templeton, Rodney Stark, and I—decided that a trip there was in order and we approached Blumer, Glock, Goffman, and Smelser with a request for funding to support the venture. Financing was arranged within hours. Erving Goffman even met me at his bank and handed me a several-hundred-dollar cash advance out of his personal checking account against the university funds which were going to take longer to have in hand than we dared wait before departing for Cleator. These faculty also gave us crash courses in "what to look for." Needing to begin the trip as soon as possibie, Neil Smelser tutored us some two hours early on a Sunday morning, the day of our departure.

Also suggestive of a wider interest in radical religions, we arrived in the small and remote Arizona town in the mountains south of Flagstaff at virtually the same time as three graduate students in psychology from Stanford—who were working with Leon Festinger, of course!

The point is that I lived in a scholarly milieu where relevant and supportive interests were part and parcel of "the scene." The real question is "Why pick the Moonies?" rather than "why did you study a radical religion?" The answer to the former involves circumstance and chance.

Members of fringe religions tend to gravitate toward one another and to form a "milieu" (Lofland 1977: 69-72). I and a few other students in sociology at Berkeley moved in that milieu. Over time, one became acquainted with the array of groups and figures that populated it. In this sense, it was only a matter of time until I, or anyone in the milieu, encountered members of the UC, for they "worked" it in search of converts. The first Moonie I met approached *me*—rather than vice versa—while I was browsing through a book display at a flying saucer convention taking place in Berkeley's Claremont Hotel.

But once encountered, why select the UC from among the array of alternatives? The orginial decision to study them was taken by three of us—Templeton, Stark, and me—and we did so because, in the context of the time and place (in the context of the groups with which we were familiar), the Moonies stood out as markedly different in a number of ways. One, fitting the "when prophecy fails" theme mentioned, they forecast apocalyptic social change and the millennium *soon*. Two, they had a Messiah who was the "Second Christ." Three, their members lived collectively and gave all their earnings to their missionary leader. Four, members spent all their nonemployed time (and even some of their employed time) trying to "spread the word" and make converts. Or as I described our response in the methodological appendix to *Doomsday Cult*: The DP "was not just so much peculiar rhetoric, but a living, radical faith. . . . Unlike the ideological permissiveness of the occult milieu, the DP was a sharply defined, intense microcosm markedly out of step with its environment" (Lofland 1977:270). Again, the context of the time—the San Francisco Bay Area in early 1962—is critical. A decade later, in that area and now around the world, groups with the features just listed peppered the social landscape. They were not at all common in early 1962—or at least this was the first one we encountered (or saw at all) in that era.

It is therefore inaccurate to surmise that I or anyone else had some special foresight in electing to study the early UC. I was simply a member of a scholarly circle in which groups such as the UC were defined as relevant objects of research.

All this leads us to the question of why study such an irrelevant group. Some faculty at Berkeley were critical of my decision to study the UC, asserting that the group was trivial and unimportant. Assessed in terms of membership and political power in the early sixties this judgment was true. But membership size and political power were not, for my scholarly circle, the features that rendered groups relevant or irrelevant for study. Instead, we were interested in answering a number of generic questions about social life and organization, among them: How do people come to believe in obscure and wildly implausible (in their time and place) ideologies? How do people go about inducting others into such cognitive systems? And, how, once committed, is faith sustained? These are the three questions around which my monograph on the UC, *Doomsday Cult,* is organized. (Chapter 4 of this volume, the world-saver model, is the separately published answer to the first question.)

Stated differently, we were pursuing some basic sociological questions rather than the study of specific groups for their own sake or for their political significance. In an important sense, therefore, I did not study the early UC. Instead, I studied three basic questions for which I employed data from the UC to generate answers.

This is yet another reason why I cannot be said to have had any unusual perception of the dramatic UC future. The particular questions I asked directed my attention away from rather than toward concern with their organizational development in the long term. My private sense was that they were likely to go out of existence while still obscure and I did not anticipate what has come to pass—for the UC, America, or world society, of which UC development is intimately a function (see ch. 9, below; Lofland 1977:315-16; Bromley and Shupe 1979, ch. 3).

4

BECOMING A WORLD-SAVER: A THEORY OF CONVERSION TO A DEVIANT PERSPECTIVE (1965)

With Rodney Stark

All humans and all human groups have ultimate values, a worldview, or a perspective furnishing them a more or less orderly and comprehensible picture of the world. Clyde Kluckhohn (1962:409) remarked that no matter how primitive and crude it may be, there is a "philosophy behind the way of life of every individual and of every relatively homogeneous group at any given point in their histories." When a person gives up one such perspective or ordered view of the world for another we refer to this process as *conversion*.[1]

Frequently such conversions are between popular and widely held perspectives—from Catholicism to communism, or from the worldview of an underdeveloped or primitive culture to that of a technically more advanced society, as from the Peyote cult of the Southwest Indians to Christianity. The continual emergence of tiny cults and sects in Western industrial nations makes it clear, however, that sometimes persons relinquish a more widely held perspective for an unknown, obscure, and often socially devalued one.

In this chapter we shall outline a model of the conversion process through which a group of people came to see the world in terms set by the doctrines of one such obscure and devalued perspective—a small millenarian religious cult. Although it is based on only a single group, we think the model suggests some rudiments of a general account of conversion to deviant perspectives. But the degree to which this scheme applies to shifts between widely held perspectives must, for now, remain problematic.

BACKGROUND

Our discussion is based on observation of a small millenarian cult headquartered in Bay City,[2] a major urban center on the West Coast.

This movement constitutes the American following of a self-proclaimed "Lord of the Second Advent," a Mr. Chang, who has attracted more than 5,000 converts in Korea since 1954. The Divine Precepts, the doctrine Chang claims was revealed to him by God, concerns a complete "Restoration of the World" to the conditions of the Garden of Eden by 1967. The message was brought to this country by Miss Yoon-Sook Lee, a graduate of Methodist seminaries, and a former professor of social welfare at a large, church-supported, women's college in Seoul.

In 1959 Miss Lee arrived in a university town (here called Northwest Town) in the Pacific Northwest, and, in two years gained five totally committed converts to the Divine Precepts (hereafter referred to as the DP). In December 1960, after difficulties with local clergymen and public opinion, largely touched off when two female converts deserted their husbands and children, the group moved to Bay City.

By mid-1963, fifteen more converts had been gained and by the end of 1964 the cult numbered more than 150 adherents. Converts were expected to devote their lives to spreading "God's New Revelation" and preparing for the New Age theocracy which God and a host of active spirits were expected to create on earth shortly. Typically the converts lived communally in a series of houses and flats, contributed their salaries from menial jobs to the common treasury, thus supporting Miss Lee as a full-time leader, and gave all their spare time to witnessing and otherwise proselytizing.

In this brief report, analysis will be limited to the single problem of conversion. Under what conditions and through what mechanisms did persons come to share the DP view of the world, and, conversely, who rejected this perspective? The logical and methodological structure of the analysis is based on a "value-added" conception (cf. Smelser 1963:12-21; Turner 1953:604-11). We shall offer a series of seven more or less successively accumulating factors, which in their total combination seem to account for conversion to the DP. All seven factors seem necessary for conversion, and together they appear to be sufficient conditions.

The sequential arrangement of the seven conditions may be conceived in the imagery of a funnel; as a structure that systematically reduces the number of persons who can be considered available for recruitment, and also increasingly specifies who is available. At least theoretically, since the mission of the cult was to "convert America," all Americans are potential recruits. Each condition narrows the range of clientele: ultimately, only a handful of persons responded to the DP call.

Typically, and perhaps ideally, the conditions develop as presented here, but the temporal order may vary. The ordering principle is *activation,* rather than temporal occurrence alone: The time of activation is the same whether a condition exists for a considerable time prior to its becoming relevant to DP conversion or only develops in time to accomplish conversion.

Data were gathered through participant observation in the cult from early 1962 to mid-1963. Further information was obtained from interviews with converts, their acquaintances, families, and workmates; with persons who took some interest in the DP but were not converts; and with a variety of clergymen, officials, neighbors, employers, and others in contact with the adherents. A less intensive observation was conducted through mid-1964.

Although complete data pertinent to all seven steps of the conversion model were not obtainable for all twenty-one persons classified as converts by mid-1963, full information on all seven factors was available for fifteen converts. All the available data conform to the model. In presenting biographical information to explicate and document the model, we shall focus on the most central of the early converts, drawing on material from less central and later converts for illustrations. The converts were primarily White, Protestant, and young (typically below thirty-five); some had college training, and most were Americans of lower-middle-class and small-town origins.

CONVERSION OPERATIONALLY DEFINED

How does one determine when a person has "really" taken up a different perspective? The most obvious evidence is his own declaration. This frequently takes the form of a tale of regeneration, about how terrible life was before and how wonderful it is now.[3] But verbal claims are easily made and simple to falsify. Several persons who professed belief in the DP were regarded as insincere by all core members. A display of loyalty and commitment, such as giving time, energy, and money to the DP enterprise, invariably brought ratification of the conversion from all core members, but to require such a display as evidence of actual conversion overlooks four persons who made only verbal professions but were universally regarded as converts by core members. To avoid this difficulty two classes or degrees of conversion may be distinguished: *verbal converts,* or fellow-travelers and followers who professed belief and were accepted by core members as sincere, but took no active role in the DP enterprise; and *total converts,* who exhibited their commitment through deeds as well as words.

Up to a point, the same factors that account for total conversion also account for verbal conversion and initially we shall discuss the two groups together. Later we shall attempt to show that verbal conversion is transformed into total conversion only when the last stage in the conversion sequence develops.

A MODEL OF CONVERSION

To account for the process by which persons came to be world-savers for the DP, we shall investigate two genres of conditions or factors. The first, *predisposing conditions,* comprises attributes of persons *prior* to their contact with the cult. These are background factors, the conjunction of which forms a pool of potential DP converts. Unfortunately, it has become conventional in sociology to treat demographic characteristics, structural or personal frustrations, and the like, as completely responsible for "pushing" persons into collectivities dedicated to protest against the prevailing social order. These factors are not unimportant, but a model composed entirely of them is woefully incomplete. The character of their incompleteness is expressed by a Meadian paraphrase of T.S. Eliot: "Between the impulse and the act falls the shadow." The second genre of conditions is this shadowed area, the situational contingencies.

Situational contingencies are conditions that lead to the successful recruitment of persons predisposed to the DP enterprise. These conditions arise from the confrontation and interaction between the potential convert and DP members. Many persons who qualified for conversion on the basis of predisposing factors entered interpersonal relations with DP members, but because the proper situational conditions were not met, they did not become converts. With these two classes of factors in mind, we may turn to a discussion of the first and most general of predisposing conditions.

TENSION

No model of human conduct entirely lacks a conception of tension, strain, frustration, deprivation, or other version of the hedonic calculus. Even the most cursory examination of the life situations of converts before they embraced the DP reveals what they at least *perceived* as considerable tension.[4]

This tension is best characterized as a felt discrepancy between some imaginary, ideal state of affairs and the circumstances in which these people saw themselves caught up. Acutely felt tension is a necessary, but far from sufficient, condition for conversion. That is, it creates some disposition to act. But tension may be resolved in a number of ways (or remain unresolved). Hence, that these people are in a tension situation does not indicate *what* action they may take.

Just as tension can have myriad consequences, its sources can also be exceedingly disparate. Some concrete varieties we discovered were: longing for unrealized wealth, knowledge, fame, and prestige; hallucinatory activity for which the person lacked any successful definition; frustrated sexual and marital relations; homosexual guilt; acute fear of face-to-face interaction; disabling and disfiguring physical conditions; and—perhaps of a slightly different order—a frustrated desire for a significant, even heroic, religious status, to "know the mind of God intimately," and to be a famous agent for his divine purposes. (It is currently fashionable to reduce this last to more mundane "real" causes, but it is not necessary here to prejudge the phenomenology.)

Brief life histories of a few central believers will indicate concretely what bothered them as preconverts. The case of "Miss Lee," the "Messiah's" emissary in America, illustrates the aspiration to be an important religious figure.

Miss Lee was born and raised in Korea and converted to Chang's cult in 1954 when she was 39. During her early teens she was subject to fits of depression and used to sit on a secluded hilltop and seek spirit contacts. Shortly she began receiving visions and hearing voices—a hallucinatory pattern she was to maintain thereafter. Her adolescent mystical experience convinced her she had a special mission to perform for God, and at the age of nineteen she entered a Methodist seminary in Japan. She was immediately disenchanted by the "worldly concerns" of the seminarians and the training she received, although she stuck out the 5-year course. Prior to entering the seminary she had become engrossed in the Spiritualistic writings of Emmanuel Swedenborg, who soon began to appear to her in visions. Her estrangement from conventional religious roles was so great that upon graduating from seminary she, alone among her classmates, refused ordination. She returned to Korea at the start of World War II, and by 1945 was professor of social welfare at a denominational university in Seoul. In 1949 the Methodist Board of Missions sent her to a Canadian university for further theological training. There she wrote her thesis on Swedenborg, who continued to visit her in spirit form. In Canada, as in Japan, she was bitterly disappointed by the "neglect of things of the spirit," caused concern among the faculty by constantly hiding to pray and seek visions, and occasionally stole away to Swedenborgian services. Her spirits continued to tell her that she was a religious figure of great importance. Returning to her academic life in Korea she fell ill with chronic diarrhea and eventually nephritis, both of which resisted all medical treatment. After two years of this, her health was broken and she was completely bed-ridden. At this time her servant took her to see Chang.

Thus is summarized a portrait of a desperately estranged maiden lady, with secret convictions of grandeur, frequent "heterodox" hallucinations, and failing health, who felt herself badly entangled in the mundane affairs of modern religious bureaucracy. Although the cultural context is rather different, the cases of "Bertha" and "Lester" follow lines similar to Miss Lee's, but include an important sexual theme.

Bertha, twenty-nine at conversion, was the daughter of German immigrants and was raised in a suburban town. After high school she attended a modeling school, the kind operated in large cities for naive, fame-hungry girls, regardless of suitability. She returned to marry a local boy who was employed as a stereotyper in a printing plant. On her wedding night she spent two hours locked in their hotel bathroom, and subsequently did not improve her evaluation of sexual intercourse. Later the couple separated briefly, reunited, and after five years of marriage had their first child (1955). The second came in 1957, and they moved to the West Coast. There Bertha began having private religious hallucinations, including "sanctification"—being made holy and free of all sin. She went to various ministers to tell of her marvelous experiences, but was not warmly received; most advised psychiatric help. She then began to tell her husband that one day she would be very important in the service of the Lord. Following a homosexual episode with a neighbor woman, Bertha demanded to be taken elsewhere and the family went to Northwest Town in April 1959. There they settled in rural Elm Knoll, a collection of half a dozen houses about seven miles from town. This was soon to be the scene of the initial formation of the cult group, and here she came to know two neighbors, "Minne Mae" and "Alice." These young housewives drew the attention of other neighbors by spending many hours hanging around the nearby general store, sometimes drinking beer and often complaining a good deal about their husbands. During this period Bertha attended churches of various denominations and continued to have frequent ecstatic religious experiences, mostly while sitting alone in a clump of bushes near the house, where she was also reported to have spent a good deal of time crying and moaning.

Like Miss Lee, "Lester" (twenty-five at conversion) went to a seminary (Lutheran) after a series of hallucinatory, spiritualistic experiences and aroused a good deal of curiosity and opposition among his fellows and the faculty. He left after an abortive part-time year to take up full-time graduate work in linguistics at a large state university in the same Bay City as the seminary. He remained convinced he was destined to be a one-man revitalization movement in the church. He took an extremely active role in campus student religious programs, meanwhile increasing his preoccupation with spiritualism and his own psychic experiences. For his first full-time year of graduate school he was awarded a Woodrow Wilson fellowship. But he was much more concerned about his religious life, and a new interest: He went to live with a young Hungarian ex-aristocrat, well known in the area as a practicing homosexual. The young Hungarian led Lester to organized Spiritualism, where his religious preoccupation and hallucinations were greatly reinforced and increased, but Lester found these groups wanting. They contented themselves with very mundane affairs and seemed uninterested in speculations on larger theological matters. In addition, Lester was very ambivalent about his homosexuality, unable to explain it, unable to accept it, and unable to quit it. Then he met Miss Lee.

Bertha's friend, "Minnie Mae," did not aspire to significant status, religious or otherwise. She pined, rather, for the more modest goal of marital satisfaction.

Minnie Mae (twenty-seven at conversion) was born in Possum Trot, Arkansas, of hillbilly farmers. She was one of eleven children, began dating at twelve, and married at fifteen, having completed only rural elementary school. She and her young husband left Arkansas for lack of jobs and settled in Northwest Town. Her husband took a job as a laborer in a plywood factory. Although the young couple did not join the church, they came from a religious background (Minnie Mae's mother was a Pentecostal lay preacher), and they began attending tent meetings near Northwest Town. During one of these Minnie Mae began speaking in "tongues" and fell into a several-hour trance. After this her husband discouraged church activities. The couple had three children at roughly 2-year intervals, and until 1960 Minnie Mae seems to have spent most of her time caring for these children and watching television. She reported tuning in a local channel when she got up in the morning and keeping it on until sign-off at night. In 1958 the couple built a small house in Elm Knoll. Here, in her behavior and conversations with neighbors, she began to reveal severe dissatisfactions in her marriage. She repeatedly complained that her husband had intercourse with her about once a month, but she also reported being very afraid of getting pregnant again. Furthermore, she wanted to get and have some fun, go dancing, etc., but her husband only wanted to watch television and fish. She wondered if she had let life pass her by because she had been married too young. And she often complained about her husband's opposition to fundamentalist religious activities.

"Merwin" and "Alice" followed quite a different pattern. Theirs was not an intensely religious concern, indeed their grandiose ambitions were for fortune.

Merwin (twenty-nine at conversion) was raised in a Kansas hamlet where his father was the railroad depot agent. After high school he tried a small Kansas junior college for a year, did poorly, and joined the marines. Discharged in 1952, he spent one year at the University of Kansas majoring in architecture, and did well, so he transferred to what he felt was a better school in Northwest Town. Here he did not do well and adopted a pattern of frequently dropping out, then going back. Estranged and alone, he bought a few acres in Elm Knoll with a small ramshackle cottage and took up a recluse's existence—he rarely shaved or washed, brewed his own beer, and dabbled in health foods, left-wing political writings, and occult publications, while supporting himself by working in a plywood plant. Next door, about twenty yards away, lived Alice, her two children and her husband, also a plywood plant worker. Alice's husband worked a swing shift, while Merwin worked days. The result was that Alice filed for divorce and moved over to Merwin's. The husband departed without undue resistance. After their marriage, Merwin began to put his plans for financial empires into action. He considered a housing development, a junk-yard, and finally bought a large frame house in Northwest Town to convert into a boarding house for students. After he had bought furniture and made other investments in the property, the city condemned it. Merwin filed bankruptcy and returned to Elm Knoll to lick his wounds and contemplate his next business venture. Merwin had long been disaffected with the established religions, had considered himself an agnostic, but was also interested in the occult. These interests were developed by his work partner, "Elmer," whom we shall meet in a moment.

Alice, also a small town girl, had traded for what she felt was a better man, one who was "going places," but these hopes seemed to be fading after the bankruptcy. She still bragged to Minnie Mae and Bertha that Merwin would be a big man someday, but there was little evidence to support her.

"Elmer" 's case illustrates yet another kind of frustrated ambition, that of attaining status as a man of knowledge and invention.

Elmer was born on a farm in North Dakota but his parents fled the drought and depression for the West Coast during the late thirties and settled on a farm near Northwest Town. Elmer, twenty-six at the time of his conversion, was of slight build with something of a vacant stare. After high school, he flunked out of the university after one semester and spent the next two years in the army where he flunked medical technician school. After the army he enrolled in a nearby state college and again lasted only one semester. He then returned to his parents' farm and took a job in the plywood factory. Elmer conceived of himself as an intellectual and aspired to be a learned man. He undertook to educate himself, and collected a large library toward this end. Unfortunately, he was virtually illiterate. In addition to more conventional books (including much of the Random House Modern Library), he subscribed to occult periodicals such as *Fate, Flying Saucers, Search,* etc. He also viewed himself as a practical man of invention, a young Thomas Edison, and dreamed of constructing revolutionary gadgets. He actually began assembling materials for a tiny helicopter (to use for herding cattle) and a huge TV antenna to bring in stations hundreds of miles away. On top of all this, Elmer was unable to speak to others above a whisper and looked constantly at his feet while talking. He had great difficulty sustaining a conversation, often appearing to forget what he was talking about. But despite his objective failures at intellectual accomplishment, Elmer clung to a belief in his own potential. The consequences of failure were largely to make him withdraw, to protect his self-image from his inability to demonstrate it.

These case histories provide a concrete notion of the kinds of things that bothered preconverts. These problems apparently are not qualitatively different from those presumably experienced by a significant, albeit unknown, proportion of the general population. Their peculiarity, if any, appears to be that preconverts felt their problems were acute, and they experienced high levels of tension concerning them over long periods.

From the point of view of an outside observer, their circumstances were not extraordinarily oppressive; in the general population, many persons labor under tensions considerably more acute and prolonged. Perhaps the strongest qualitative generalization supported by the data is that preconverts felt themselves frustrated in their rather diverse aspirations. Most people probably have some type of frustrated aspiration, but preconverts *experienced* the tension rather more acutely and over longer periods than most people do.

Explanation cannot rest here, for such tensions could have resulted in any number of other resolutions, and in fact they usually do. Thus, these unresolved problems in living are part of the necessary scenery for the stage, but the rest of the props, the stage itself, and the drama of conversion remain to be constructed.

TYPES OF PROBLEM-SOLVING PERSPECTIVES

Since conversion to the DP is hardly the only thing people can do about their problems, it becomes important to ask what else these particular people could have done, and why they did not. Because people have a number of conventional and readily available alternative definitions for, and means of coping with, their problems, there were, in the end, very few converts to the DP. An alternative solution is a perspective or rhetoric defining the nature and sources of problems in living and offering some program for their resolution. Many such alternative solutions exist in modern society. Briefly, three particular genres of solution are relevant here: *psychiatric, political,* and *religious*. In the first, the origin of problems is typically traced to the psyche, and manipulation of the self is advocated as a solution. Political solutions, mainly radical, locate the sources of problems in the social structure and advocate reorganization of the system as a solution. The religious perspective tends to see both sources and solutions as emanating from an unseen and, in principle, unseeable realm.

The first two secular rhetorics bear the major weight of usage in contemporary society. No longer is it considered appropriate to regard recalcitrant and aberrant actors as possessed of devils. Indeed, modern religious institutions tend to offer a secular, frequently psychiatric, rhetoric concerning problems in living. The prevalence of secular definitions of tension is a major reason for the scarcity of DP converts. Several persons, whose circumstances met other conditions of the model, had adopted a psychiatric definition of their tensions and failed to become converts. In one exaggerated instance, an ex-GI literally alternated residence between the DP headquarters and the psychiatric ward of the veterans' hospital, never able to make a final decision as to which rhetoric he should adopt.

All preconverts were surprisingly uninformed about conventional psychiatric and political perspectives for defining their problems. Perhaps those from small towns and rural communities in particular had long been accustomed to define the world in religious terms. Although all preconverts had discarded conventional religious outlooks as inadequate, "spiritless," "dead," etc., prior to contact with the DP, they retained a *general propensity to impose religious meaning on events.*

Even with these restrictions on the solutions available for acutely felt problems, a number of alternative responses still remain. First, people can persist in stressful situations with little or no relief. Second, persons often take specifically problem-directed action to change troublesome portions of their lives, without adopting a different world-view to interpret them. Bertha and Minnie Mae might have simply divorced their husbands, for instance, and presumably, Lester could have embraced homosexuality. Many preconverts attempted such action (Merwin *did* start a boarding house, Elmer *did* attend college, etc.) but none found a successful direct solution to his/her difficulties.

Third, a number of maneuvers exist to "put the problem out of mind." In general these are compensations for or distractions from problems in living: addictive consumption of the mass media, preoccupation with childrearing, immersion in work. More spectacular examples include alcoholism, suicide, promiscuity, and so on. Recall, for example, that Minnie Mae, Alice, and Bertha hung around the general store during the day getting high on beer during the summer of 1959. Had they done this in a more urban setting, in bars with strange men available, their subsequent lives might have been different.

In any event, we may assume that many persons with tensions not only explore these possible strategies, but succeed in some cases in "making it," and hence are no longer potential DP recruits.[5]

SEEKERSHIP

Whatever the reasons, preconverts failed to find a way out of their difficulties through any of the strategies outlined above. Their need for solutions persisted, and their problem-solving perspective was restricted to a religious outlook, but all preconverts found conventional religious institutions inadequate as a source of solutions. Subsequently, each came to define her/himself as a religious seeker, a person searching for some satisfactory system of religious meaning to interpret and resolve this discontent, and each had taken some action to achieve this end.

Some hopped from church to church and prayer group to prayer group, pursuing their religious search through relatively conventional institutions. A male convert in his early twenties recounted: "My religious training consisted of various denominations such as Baptist, Methodist, Congregationalist, Jehovah's Witnesses, and Catholicism. Through all my experiences, I refused to accept . . . religious dogma . . . because it was Truth I was seeking, and not a limited belief or concept."

Others began to explore the occult milieu, reading the voluminous literature of the strange, the mystical, and the spiritual, and tentatively trying a series of such occult groups as Rosicrucians, Spiritualists, and the various divine sciences.

> In April 1960, my wife and I . . . [began] to seek a church connection. [We] began an association with Yokefellow, a spiritual growth organization in our local church. My whole religious outlook took on a new meaning and a broader version. I grew emotionally and spiritually during the next two and a half years.

> However, as I grew, many spiritual things remained unanswered and new questions came up demanding answers with Yokefellow and the church seemed not to even begin to touch upon. . . . My wife and I became interested in the revelation of Edgar Cayce and the idea of reincarnation which seemed to answer so much, we read searchingly about the Dead Sea scrolls, we decided to pursue Rosicrucianism, we read books on the secret disclosures to be gained from Yogi-type meditation. The more we searched the more questions seemed to come up. Through Emmet Fox's writings I thought I had discovered a path through metaphysics which through study would give me the breakthrough I longed for.

Or the seeker might display some amalgam of conventional and unusual religious conceptions, as illustrated by a male convert's sad tale:

> I was reared in a Pentecostal church and as a child was a very ardent follower of Christianity. Because of family situations, I began to fall away and search for other meanings in life. This began . . . when I was about twelve years old. From that time on, my life was most of the time an odious existence, with a great deal of mental anguish. These last two years have brought me from church to church trying to find some fusion among them. I ended up going to Religious Science in the morning and fundamentalist in the evening.

Floundering about among religions was accompanied by two fundamental postulates that define more specifically the ideological components of the religion-seeking pattern. Although concrete preconvert beliefs varied a good deal, all espoused these postulates about the nature of ultimate reality.

First, they believed that spirits of some variety came from an active supernatural realm to intervene in the material world. Such entities could, at least sometimes, break through from the beyond and impart information, cause "experiences," or take a hand in the course of events.

Second, their conception of the universe was teleogical, in the sense that beyond all appearances in the sensate world exists a purpose for which every object or event is created and exists. The earth is as it is to meet the needs of humans, for example, and humans manifest the physical structure they do in order to do the things they do. More important, humans as a phenomenon must be on earth because somewhere, sometime, somehow, it was decided that homo sapiens should fulfill a purpose. Accordingly, each person must have been put on earth for some reason, with some sort of job to perform.

Beliefs were typically no more specific than this. Religion seeking itself was in terms of finding some more detailed formulation of these problematically vague existential axes.

A few words on the general question of the importance of prior beliefs in affecting conversion are necessary at this point. A number of discussions of conversion have emphasized congruence between previous ideology and a given group's appeal (e.g. Brown 1943; Almond 1954), while others treat the degree of congruence as unimportant so long as the ideology is seen as embodied in what appears to be a successful movement (e.g. Hoffer 1951:10). Both views seem extreme (Blumer 1957:147-48).

Our data suggest that only the two gross kinds of congruence that make up the ideology of religious seekership are necessary for conversion to the DP. Presumptively important items, such as fundamentalist Christianity, millenarian expectations, and hallucinatory experience were far from universal among preconverts. Most believed in a vaguely defined New Age that would appear gradually, but they *became* apocalyptic premillenarian only upon conversion.

The role of these gross points of congruence is suggested in the substantive DP appeals to preconverts. Active spirits were rampant in their view of reality. Converts lived with an immediate sense of unseen forces operating on the physical order (e.g. the weather) and intervening in human affairs—in relations among nations, in the latest national disaster, and in their own moment-to-moment lives. Nothing occurred that was not related to the intentions of God's or Satan's spirits. For persons holding a teleological conception of reality, the DP doctrine had the virtue of offering a minute and lawful explanation of the whole of human history. It systematically defined and revealed the hidden meaning of individual lives that had lacked coherence and purpose, and of course, it explained all hallucinatory behavior in terms of spirit manifestations. These spirits had been preparing the preconvert to see the truth of the DP.

Although acute and enduring tensions in the form of frustrated aspirations is not an ideological component, in the sense of being a more abstract postulate about the nature of reality—in relation to the matter of congruence the DP also offered a proximate and major solution. Converts were assured of being virtual demigods for all eternity, beginning with a rule over the restored and reformed earth in the immediate future. By 1967 God was to impose the millennium upon earth, and those who converted early, before the truth of this message became self-evident, would occupy the most favored positions in the divine hegemony. Converts particularly stressed this advantage of conversion in their proselytization: "Those who get in early," as one member often put it, "will be in on the ground floor of something big."

Religious seekership emerges as another part of the path through the maze of life contingencies leading to DP conversion. It is a floundering among religious alternatives, an openness to a variety of religious views, frequently esoteric, combined with failure to embrace the specific ideology and fellowship of some set of believers.[6] Seekership provided the minimal points of ideological congruence to make these people available for DP conversion.

THE TURNING POINT

The necessary attributes of preconverts stated thus far had all persisted for some time before the preconverts encountered the DP; they can be considered background factors or predispositions. Although they apparently arose and were active in the order specified, they are important here as accumulated and simultaneously active factors during the development of succeeding conditions.

We now turn to situational factors in which timing becomes much more significant. The first of these is the rather striking circumstance that *shortly* before, and *concurrently* with their encounter with the DP, all preconverts had reached or were about to reach what they perceived as a turning point in their lives. Each had come to a moment when old lines of action were complete, had failed or been disrupted, or were about to be so, and when they faced the opportunity (or necessity), and possibly the burden, of doing something different with their lives. (Cf. Hughes 1958, ch. 1; Strauss 1958; and the often-noted "cultural dislocation" and migration pattern found in the background of converts to many groups, especially cults.) Thus Miss Lee's academic career had been disrupted by long illness from which she recovered upon meeting Chang; Bertha was newly arrived in a strange town; Lester was disaffected from graduate studies after having quit the seminary; Minnie Mae no longer had a preschool child at home to care for; Merwin had just failed in business after dropping out of school; and Elmer had returned to his parents' farm after failing in college for the second time.

Turning points in general derived from recent migration; loss of employment (a business failure in Merwin's case); and completion, failure, or withdrawal from school. Perhaps because most converts were young adults, turning points involving educational institutions were relatively frequent. Illustrations in addition to the cases described above are a graduate student who had just failed his Ph.D. qualifying examinations, two second semester college seniors who had vague and unsatisfying plans for the future, and a 17-year-old who had just graduated from high school. Recovery from or the onset of illness, marital dissolution, and other changes, extant or imminent, such as Minnie Mae's new freedom, were relatively infrequent. The significance of these various turning points is that they increased the preconvert's awareness of and desire to take some action about his/her problems, *at the same time giving him/her a new opportunity to do so.* Turning points were situations in which old obligations and lines of action were diminished and new involvements became desirable and possible.

CULT AFFECTIVE BONDS

We come now to the contact between a potential recruit and the DP. If persons who go through all four of the previous steps are to be further drawn down the road to full conversion, an affective bond must develop, if it does not already exist, between the potential recruit and one or more of the DP members. The development or presence of some positive, emotional, interpersonal response seems necessary to bridge the gap between first exposure to the DP message and accepting its truth. That is, persons developed affective ties with the group or some of its members while they still regarded the DP perspective as problematic, or even "way out." In a manner of speaking, final conversion was coming to accept the opinions of one's friend (Cf. Shibutani 1961:523-32, 588-92). (Schein [1961:277] reports that "the most potent source of influence in coercive persuasion was the identification which arose between a prisoner and his more reformed cellmate." See also Alan Kerckhoff, Kurt Back, and Norman Miller 1965:2-15).

Miss Lee's recollections of her conversion provide a graphic illustration:

> In addition to this change [her recovery from illness] I felt very good spiritually. I felt as if I had come to life from a numb state and there was spiritual *liveliness and vitality within me by being among this group.* As one feels when he comes from a closed stuffy room into the fresh air, or the goodness and warmth after freezing coldness was how my spirit witnessed its happiness. *Although I could not agree with the message intellectually I found myself one with it spiritually.* I reserved my conclusions and waited for guidance from God [italics added].

Miss Lee further revealed she was particularly attracted to Mr. Chang and resided in his dwelling to enjoy the pleasure of his company, until, finally, she decided his message was true. Her statement that she "could not agree with the message intellectually" is particularly significant. Other converts reported and were observed to experience similar reservations as they nevertheless developed strong bonds with members of the group. Thus, for example, Lester, the most highly intellectual of the converts, displayed an extremely strong attachment to the middle-aged Miss Lee and manifested the "intellect problem" for some weeks after he had turned his life over to her. At one point late in this period he could still reflectively comment to an observer: "I have not entirely reconciled [the DP world view] with my intellect, but [Miss Lee] keeps answering more and more questions that are in my mind so I am beginning to close the holes I have found in it."

Conversions frequently moved through *preexisting* friendship pairs or nets. In the formation of the original core group, an affective bond first developed between Miss Lee and Bertha (the first to meet Miss Lee and begin to espouse her views). Once that had happened, the rest of the original conversions were supported by prior friendships. Bertha was part of the housewife trio of Minnie Mae and Alice; Merwin was Alice's husband, and Elmer was Merwin's friend and workmate. Subsequent conversions also followed friendship paths, or friendships developed between the preconvert and the converts, prior to conversion.

Bonds that were unsupported by previous friendships with a new convert often took the form of a sense of instant and powerful rapport with a believer. Consider, for example, a young housewife's account of her first view of Lester while attending an Edgar Cayce Foundation retreat:[7]

> I went to [one of the] Bible class[es] and saw [Lester] in our class—I had seen him for the first time the night before and had felt such love for him—he was my brother, yet I had not met him. He looked as if he were luminous! After the class I wanted to talk to him—but our project group had a discipline that day—complete silence—I did not want to break it, yet I felt such a need to talk to him. I prayed and asked God what He would have me do—I received such a positive feeling—I took this as an answer and sought out [Lester]. When I found him, I did not have anything to say—I just mumbled something—but he seemed to understand and took me to the beach where he told me: "He is on earth!" Oh, what joy I felt! My whole body was filled with electricity.

The less-than-latent sexual overtones of this encounter appeared in a number of other heterosexual attachments that led to conversion (and quite a few that did not). Even after four years of cult membership Elmer could hardly hide his feelings in this testimonial: "Early in 1960, after a desperate prayer, which was nothing more than the words, 'Father, if there is any truth in this world, please reveal it to me,' I met [Miss Lee]. This day I desire to never forget. Although I didn't fully understand yet, I desired to unite with her."

Although a potential convert might have some initial difficulty in taking up the DP perspective, given the four previous conditions *and* an affective tie, he/she began seriously to consider the DP and to accept it as his/her personal construction of reality.

EXTRACULT AFFECTIVE BONDS

One might suppose that non-DP associates of a convert-in-process would not be entirely neutral to the now immediate possibility that he/she would join the DP group. We must inquire, then, into the conditions under which extracult controls are activated through emotional attachments and how they restrain or fail to restrain persons from DP conversion.

Recent migration, disaffection with geographically distant families and spouses, and very few nearby acquaintances made a few converts "social atoms"; for them extracult attachments were irrelevant. More typically, converts were acquainted with nearby persons, but none was intimate enough to be aware that a conversion was in progress or to feel that the mutual attachment was sufficient to justify intervention. Thus, for example, Lester's social round was built primarily around participation in religious groups. Although he was well known and appreciated for his contributions, he was not included in any local circles of intimacy. Many people knew him, but no one was a *personal* friend. Further, Lester's relations with both parents and step-parents manifested considerable strain and ambivalence, and his homosexual liaison was shot through with strain.

In many cases, positive attachments outside the cult were to other religious seekers, who, even though not yet budding converts themselves, encouraged continued "investigation" or entertainment of the DP rather than exercising a countervailing force. Such an extracult person might be only slightly behind his/her friend in the conversion process.

In the relatively few cases where positive attachments existed between conventional extracult persons and a convert-in-process, control was minimal or absent, because of geographic distance or intentional avoidance of communication about the topic while the convert was solidifying his/her faith. Thus, for example, a German immigrant in his early thirties failed to inform his mother in Germany, to whom he was strongly attached, during his period of entertainment, and only wrote her about the DP months after his firm acceptance. (She disowned him.)

During the period of tentative acceptance and afterwards, converts possessed a rhetoric that helped to neutralize affective conflicts. An account by a newly converted soldier in Oklahoma conveys the powerful (and classic) content of this facilitating and justifying rhetoric:

> I wrote my family a very long, detailed, but yet very plain letter about our movement and exactly what I received in spiritual ways plus the fact that Jesus had come to me himself. The weeks passed and I heard nothing but I waited with deep trust in God.
>
> This morning I received a letter from my mother. She . . . surmised that I was working with a group other than those with the "stamp of approval by man." She . . . called me a fanatic, and went on to say: "My fervent constant prayer is that time will show you the fruitlessness of the way you have chosen before it consumes you entirely. A real true religion is deep in the heart and shines through your countenance for all to see. One need not shout it to the house tops either."
>
> At first it was the deepest hurt I had ever experienced. But, I remember what others in [the DP] family have given up and how they too experienced a similar rejection. But so truly, I can now know a little of the rejection that our beloved Master experienced. I can now begin to understand his deep grief for the Father as he sat peering out of a window singing love songs to Him because he knew that the Father would feel such grief. I can now begin to feel the pain that our Father in heaven felt for 6,000 years. I can now begin to see that to come into the Kingdom of heaven is not as easy as formerly thought. I can now see why many are called but few are chosen. I began to understand why men will be separated, yes, even from their families. I begin to see the shallowness of human concern for God as a Father and their true blindness. Oh my heart cries out to Our Father in greatful [sic] praise and love for what He has given.
>
> [In the words of Miss Lee:] "As we get close to the Father the road shall become more difficult"; "only by truly suffering, can we know the Leader and the heart of the Father"; "you shall be tested." "He will come with a double-edged blade." Only now am I beginning to realize the deep significance of these words. Only now am I beginning to know the heart of the Father and the great suffering in our Lord.

When there were emotional attachments to outsiders who were physically present and cognizant of the incipient transformation, conversion became a "nip-and-tuck" affair. Pulled about by competing emotional loyalties and discordant versions of reality, such persons were subjected to intense emotional strain. A particularly poignant instance of this involved a newly wed senior at the local state university. He began tentatively to espouse the DP as he developed strong ties with Lester and Miss Lee. His young wife struggled to accept, but she did not meet a number of the conditions leading to conversion, and in the end seemed nervous, embarrassed, and even ashamed to be at DP gatherings. One night, just before the group began a prayer meeting, he rushed in and tearfully announced that he would have nothing further to do with the DP, though he still thought the message was probably true. Torn between affective bonds, he opted for his young bride, but it was only months later that he finally lost all belief in the DP.

When extracult bonds withstood the strain of affective and ideological flirtation with the DP, conversion was not consummated. Most converts, however, lacked external affiliations close enough to permit informal control over belief. Affectively, they were so unintegrated that they could simply fall out of relatively conventional society unnoticed, taking their coseeker friends, if any, with them.

INTENSIVE INTERACTION

In combination, the six previous factors suffice to bring a person to *verbal conversion* to the DP but one more contingency must be met if he/she is to become a "deployable agent"[8] or what we have termed a "total convert." Most, but not all, verbal converts ultimately put their lives at the disposal of the cult. Such transformations in commitment took place as a result of intensive interaction with DP members, and failed to result when such interaction was absent.

Intensive interaction means concrete, daily, and even hourly accessibility to DP members, which implies physical proximity to total converts. Intensive exposure offers an opportunity to reinforce and elaborate an initial, tentative assent to the DP worldview, and in prolonged association the perspective "comes alive" as a device for interpreting the moment-to-moment events in the convert's life.

The DP doctrine has a variety of resources for explicating the most minor everyday events in terms of a cosmic battle between good and evil spirits, in a way that placed the convert at the center of this war. Since all DP interpretations pointed to the imminence of the end, to participate in these explications of daily life was to come increasingly to see the necessity of one's personal participation as a totally committed agent in this cosmic struggle (cf. Schein 1961:136-39, 280-82).

Reminders and discussion of the need to make other converts and the necessity of supporting the cause in every way were the main themes of verbal exchanges among the tentatively accepting and the total converts, and, indeed, among the total converts themselves. Away from this close association with those already totally committed, one failed to appreciate the need for one's transformation into a total convert.

In recognition of this fact, the DP members gave highest priority to attempts to persuade verbal converts (even the merely interested) to move into the cult's communal dwellings. During her early efforts in Northwest Town, Miss Lee gained verbal conversions from Bertha, Minnie Mae, Alice, Merwin, and Elmer, many months before she was able to turn them into total converts. This transformation did not occur until Miss Lee moved into Alice and Merwin's home (along with Elmer), placing her within a few dozen yards of the homes of Minnie Mae and Bertha. The resulting daily exposure of the verbal converts to Miss Lee's total conversion increasingly engrossed them in DP activities, until they came to give it all their personal and material resources.[9] Recalling this period, Minnie Mae reported a process that occurred during other verbal converts' periods of intensive interaction. When one of them began to waver in his faith, unwavering believers were fortunately present to carry him through this "attack of Satan."

Most verbally assenting converts were induced out of this tenuous state, through contrived or spontaneous intensive interaction, within a few weeks, or more typically, a few months. In a few instances the interval between assent and total commitment spanned a year or more. When the unmarried older sister of the German immigrant mentioned above came to entertain the DP perspective, some eleven months of subtle and less subtle pressures were required to get her to leave her private apartment and move into the communal dwelling. Within two months she went from rather lukewarm belief to total dedication and subsequent return to Germany as a DP missionary. The following ecstatic testimonial given during her second month of cult residence contrasts sharply with her previously reserved and inhibited statements:

> In the beginning of May I moved into our center in [Bay City]. A complete new life started for me. Why had I not cut off my self-centered life earlier! Here under [Miss Lee's] care and guidance I felt God's power and love tremendously and very soon it became my only desire to whole-heartedly serve our Father. How fortunate I am being a child and student of our beloved mother and teacher, [Miss Lee]. She reflects in all her gestures, words and works the love and wisdom of our Lord and Master.

Verbal conversion and even a resolution to reorganize one's life for the DP is not automatically translated into total conversion. One must be intensively exposed to the group supporting these new standards of conduct. DP members did not find proselytizing, the primary task of total converts, very easy, but in the presence of persons who reciprocally supported each other, such a transformation of one's life became possible. Persons who accepted the truth of the doctrine but lacked intensive interaction with the core group, remained partisan spectators, who played no active part in the battle to usher in God's kingdom.

SUMMARY

We have presented a model of the accumulating conditions that appear to describe and account for conversion to an obscure millenarian perspective. These necessary and constellationally sufficient conditions may be summarized as follows. For conversion a person must: (1) experience enduring, acutely felt tensions; (2) within a religious problem-solving perspective; (3) which leads to defining him/herself as a religious seeker; (4) encountering the DP at a turning point in life; (5) wherein an affective bond is formed (or preexists) with one or more converts; (6) where extracult attachments are absent or neutralized; (7) and, where, if the person is to become a deployable agent, he/she is exposed to intensive interaction.

Because this model was developed from the study of a small set of converts to a minor millenarian doctrine, it may possess few generalizable features. We suggest, however, that its terms are general enough, and its elements articulated in such a way as to provide a reasonable starting point for the study of conversion to other types of groups and perspectives.

A closing caveat. The DP had few competitive advantages, if any, over other unusual religious groups, in terms of the potential converts' predispositions. In terms of situational conditions the DP advantage was simply that they were on the scene and able to make their "pitch," develop affective bonds, and induce intensive interaction. We hope our effort will help dispel the tendency to assume some deep, almost mystical, connection between worldviews and their careers. Like conceptions holding that criminals and delinquents must be "really different," our thinking about other deviants has too often assumed some extensive characterological conjunction between participant and pattern of participation.

NOTES

This investigation was supported in part by a Public Health Service fellowship to the senior author from the National Institute of Mental Health (MPM-16,661; Fl MH-16,661-02).

1. The meaning of this term has been muddled by the inconsistent usage of Christian religious writers. Often they have used "conversion" to refer to an aroused concern among persons who already accept the essential truth of the ideological system. Yet in keeping with the earliest Christian examples of conversion, such as that of St. Paul, they have also used the word to describe changes from one such system to another. These are very different events and ought to be indicated by different words.
2. All names that might compromise converts' anonymity have been changed.
3. Peter Berger has given us a delightful characterization of the reconstructive functions of such tales. See his *Invitation to Sociology* (1963, ch. 3).
4. We conceive this tension as subjective to avoid judgments about how tension-producing the "objective" circumstances actually were, attending instead to the way these circumstances were experienced.
5. Our analysis is confined to isolating the elements of the conversion sequence. Extended analysis would refer to the factors that *in turn* bring each conversion condition into existence. That is, it would be necessary to develop a theory for each of the seven elements, specifying the conditions under which each appears. On the form such theory would probably take, see Ralph Turner's (1953:609-11) discussion of "the intrusive factor."
6. For further suggestive materials on seekers and seeking see H.T. Dohrman (1958), Leon Festinger, Henry Riecken, and Stanley Schacter (1956), and Sanctus De Santis (1927:260-61). For discussion of a generically similar phenomenon in a different context see Edgar H. Schein (1961:120-36, 270-77).
7. Lester was at this retreat precisely for the purpose of meeting potential converts. Attendance at religious gatherings in the masquerade of a religious seeker was a primary DP mode of recruiting.
8. On the concept of the "deployable agent" or "deployable personnel" in social movements see Philip Selznick (1960:18-29).
9. Although a number of our illustrative cases are drawn from the period of the group's formation, the process of cult formation itself should not be confused with the analytically distinct process of conversion. The two are merely empirically compounded. Cult formation occurs when a network of friends who meet the first four conditions develop affective bonds with a worldview carrier and collectively develop the last two conditions, except that condition seven, intensive interaction, requires exposure *to each other* in addition to the worldview carrer. For a different conception of a subculture formation see Cohen (1955, ch. 3).

5

BECOMING A WORLD-SAVER
REVISITED (1977)

More than a decade ago, Rodney Stark and I observed a small number of then obscure millenarians go about what was to them the desperate and enormously difficult task of making converts. We witnessed techniques employed to foster conversion and observed the evolution of several people into converts. We strove to make some summarizing generalizations about those conversions in our report "Becoming a World-Saver" (Lofland and Stark 1965 and ch. 4 of this vol.), a report that has received a gratifying amount of attention over the years. I want here to offer some new data on the conversion efforts of the same millenarian movement as it operates a decade later, to assess the new data's implications for the initial world-saver model, and to share some broader reflections on the model itself.

DP CONVERSION ORGANIZATION REVISITED

The conversion efforts witnessed by Rodney Stark and myself in the early sixties were in many respects weak, haphazard, and bumbling. The gaining of a convert seemed often even to be an accident, a lucky conjunction of some rather random flailing (Lofland 1966, pt. 2). Starting about 1972, however, all that was radically changed and transformed. The DPs, as I continue to call them,[1] initiated what might eventually prove to be one of the most ingenious, sophisticated, and effective conversion organizations ever devised. I will describe its main phases and elements as it operated at and out of "State U City" and "Bay City," the same two West Coast places where the action centered in *Doomsday Cult* (Lofland 1966).

DPs of the early sixties and seventies alike believed that their ideology was so "mind blowing" to unprepared citizens that they could not expect simply to announce its principal assertions and make converts at the same time. As documented throughout *Doomsday*

Cult, effort was made to hold back the conclusions and only reveal them in a progressive and logical manner to prospective converts. They were dogged by a dilemma: They had to tell their beliefs to make converts, but the more they told the less likely was conversion.

They dealt with this dilemma by a carefully progressive set of revelations of their beliefs and aims, starting from complete muting or denial of the religious and millenarian aspects and ending with rather more disclosure. This process may be conceived as consisting of five quasi-temporal phases: picking up, hooking, encapsulating, loving, and committing.

PICKING UP

Reports of people closely involved with the movement suggest that the multi-million-dollar media blitzes and evangelical campaigns that made DPs famous and virtual household words in the seventies were not significant ways in which people began DP conversion involvement. Perhaps most commonly, it began with a casual contact in a public place, a "pickup." DPs spent time almost daily giving hitchhikers rides and approaching young men and women in public places. Display card tables for front organizations[2] were regularly staffed in the public areas of many campuses as a way to pick up people.

The contact commonly involved an invitation to a dinner, a lecture, or both. Religious aspects would be muted or denied. As described in *Doomsday Cult* (Lofland 1966, ch. 6), this strategy of covert presentations was employed in the early sixties with but small success. It became enormously more successful in the early seventies due to several larger-scale shifts in American society. First, the residue of the late sixties' rebellion of youth still provided a point of instant solidarity and trust among youth, especially in places like State U City, a major locale of public place pickups. Second, even though the number of drifting and alienated youth was declining from the late sixties, there were still plenty of them. They tended to be drawn to certain West Coast college towns and urban districts. DPs concentrated their pickups in such areas, with success.

While of major importance, pickups were not the sole strategy. Some minor and rudimentary infiltrations of religious gatherings continued (cf. Lofland 1966:90-106), and one center specialized in sending "voluptuous and attractive" women to visit "professors at area colleges and persuade them to come to meetings under the guise of Unified Science" (Bookin 1973).

This shift in the strategy of first contact and shifts in the large trends of American society (see Lofland 1977 and ch. 9, this vol.) resulted in a decisive shift in the recruitment pool of the movement. Converts I studied in the early sixties were decidedly marginal and rather "crippled" people, drawn from the less than advantaged and more religiously inclined sectors of the social order. Hence, I quoted the apostle Paul on the choosing of "mere nothings to overthrow the existing order" (Lofland 1966:29). As it became fashionable in the late sixties and early seventies for privileged and secular youth of the higher social classes to be alienated from their society and its political and economic institutions, a portion of such youth encountered the DPs. Some converted. Some of them were offspring of the American upper class, a fact that has caused the organization considerable trouble. What is signal here is that the major pattern of prior religious seeking I reported seemed to fade in significance. People with strong prior political perspectives and involvements (e.g. Eugene McCarthy workers) started converting. (Such changes must also be considered in conjunction with a growing political element within the DP itself.)

HOOKING

By whatever device, a prospect was brought into DP territory. Treatment varied at this point. In mid-1974 Chang himself was still experimenting in the New York City Center with Elmer's ancient notion of playing tape-recorded lectures to people (Lofland 1966:125-29). Fortunately for recruitment to the movement, other centers went in different directions. The most successful hooked into their dinner and lecture guests with more intensive and elaborate versions of the promotion tactics I originally described in *Doomsday Cult* (Lofland 1966, ch. 9). As practiced at the West Coast State U. City Center—the most convert-productive center in the country—these went as follows.

The prospect arrived for dinner to find fifty or more smiling, talkative young people going about various chores. The place exuded friendliness and solicitude. He/she was assigned a "buddy" who was always by one's side. During the meal, as phrased in one report, "various people stopped by my table, introduced themselves and chatted. They seemed to be circulating like sorority members during rush." Members were instructed to learn all they could about the prospect's background and opinions and to show personal interest. In one training document, members were told to ask: " 'What do you feel most excited about . . .'. *Write down* their hooks so that the whole center knows in follow up." The prospect's "buddy" and others continually complimented him: "you have a happy or intelligent face"; "I knew I would meet someone great like you today"; "your shoes are nice"; "your sweater is beautiful"; and so forth (cf. Lofland 1966:175-77). The feeling, as one ex-member put it, was likely to be: "It certainly felt wonderful to be served, given such attention, and made to feel important." DPs had learned to start conversion at the emotional rather than the cognitive level, an aspect they did not thoroughly appreciate in the early sixties (Lofland 1966:189).

It is on this foundation of positive affect that they slowly began to lay out their cognitive structure. That same first evening this took the form of a general, uncontroversial, and entertaining lecture on the principles that bound their Family group. Key concepts include sharing, loving one another, working for the good of humankind, and community activity (Taylor 1975). Chang and his movement were never mentioned. At State U City (and several other places with the facilities), prospects were invited to a weekend workshop. This was conducted at The Farm in the State U City case I am following here, a several-hundred-acre country retreat some fifty miles north of Bay City. A slide show presented the attractions of The Farm. During the three years of most aggressive growth (1972-74), probably several thousand people did a weekend at The Farm. Hundreds of others had kindred experiences elsewhere.

ENCAPSULATING

The weekend workshop (and longer subsequent periods) provided a solution to two former and major problems. First, by effectively encapsulating[3] prospects, the ideology could be progressively unfolded in a controlled setting where doubts and hesitations could be surfaced and rebutted. Second, affective bonds could be elaborated without interference from outsiders. Focusing specifically on The Farm, the encapsulation of prospects moved along five fundamentally facilitating lines.

Absorption of Attention. All waking moments were preplanned to absorb the participant's attention. The schedule was filled from 7:30 a.m. to 11:00 p.m. Even trips to the bathroom were escorted by one's assigned DP "buddy," the shadow who watched over his/her "spiritual child."

Collective Focus. A maximum of collective activities crowded the waking hours: group eating, exercises, garden work, lectures, games, chantings, cheers, dancing, prayer, singing, and so forth. In such ways attention was focused outward and toward the group as an entity.

Exclusive Input. Prospects were not physically restrained, but leaving was strongly discouraged, and there were no newspapers, radios, televisions, or an easily accessible telephone. The Farm itself was miles from any settlement. Half of the fifty or so workshop participants were always DPs, and they dominated selection of topics for talk and what was said about them.

Fatigue. There were lectures a few hours each day, but the physical and social pace was otherwise quite intense. Gardening might be speeded up by staging contests, and games such as dodgeball were run at a frantic pitch. Saturday evening was likely to end with exhaustion, as in this report of interminable square dancing.

> It went on for a very long time—I remember the beat of the music and the night air and thinking I would collapse and finding out I could go on and on. The feeling of doing that was really good—thinking I'd reached my limit and then pushing past it. [At the end, the leader] sang "Climb Every Mountain" in a beautiful, heartbreaking voice. Then we all had hot chocolate and went to bed.

A mild level of sexual excitement was maintained by frequent patting and hugging across the sexes. Food was spartan and sleep periods were controlled.

Logical, Comprehensive Cognitions. In this context, the DP ideology was systematically and carefully unfolded, from the basic and relatively bland principles (e.g. "give and take"; Lofland 1966:15-16) to the numerologically complex, from the Garden of Eden to the present day, following the pattern I reported in chapter 2 of *Doomsday Cult*. If one accepted the premises from which it began, and were not bothered by several ad hoc devices, the system could seem exquisitely logical. The comprehensiveness combined with simplicity were apparently quite impressive to reasonable numbers of people who viewed it in The Farm context. The "inescapable" and "utterly logical" conclusion that the Messiah was at hand could hit hard: "It's so amazing, its so *scientific* and explains *everything*." The encapsulating and engrossing quality of these weekends was summed up well by one almost-convert:

> The whole weekend had the quality of a cheer—like one long rousing camp song. What guests were expected (and subtly persuaded) to do was participate . . . completely. That was stressed over and over: "give your whole self and you'll get a lot back," "the only way for this to be the most wonderful experience of your life is if you really put everything you have into it," etc.

LOVING

The core element of this process was deeper and more profound than any of the foregoing. Everything mentioned so far only in part moved a person toward a position in which they were open to what was the crux: the feeling of being loved and the desire to "melt together" (a movement concept) into the loving, enveloping embrace of the collective. (We learn again from looking at the DPs that love can be the most coercive and cruel power of all.)

The psychodynamic of it is so familiar as to be hackneyed: "People need to belong, to feel loved," as it is often put. People who want to "belong" and do not, or who harbor guilt over their reservations about giving themselves over to collectivities, are perhaps the most vulnerable to loving overtures toward belonging. The pattern has been stated with freshness and insight by a young, recently-Christian woman who did a Farm weekend, not then knowing she was involved with the DPs:

> When I did hold back in some small way, and received a look of sorrowful, benevolent concern, I felt guilt and the desire to please as though it were God Himself whom I had offended. What may really have been wisdom on my part (trying to preserve my own boundaries in a dangerous and potentially overwhelming situation) was treated as symptomic of alienation and fear; and a withholding of God's light. Those things are sometimes true of me, and I am unsure enough of my own openness in groups that I tended to believe they were right. Once, when [the workshop leader] spoke to us after a lecture, I began to cry. She'd said something about giving, and it had touched on a deep longing in me to do that, and the pain of that wall around my heart when I feel closed off in a group of people. I wanted to break through that badly enough that right then it almost didn't matter what they believed—if only I could really share myself with them. I think that moment may be exactly the point at which many people decide to join [the DPs].

The conscious strategy of these encapsulating weekend camps was to drench prospects in approval and love—to "love bomb" them, as DPs termed it. The cognitive hesitations and emotional reservations of prospects could then be drowned in calls to loving solidarity:

> Whenever I would raise a theological question, the leaders of my group would look very impressed and pleased, seem to agree with me, and then give me a large dose of love—and perhaps say something about unity and God's love being most important. I would have an odd, disjointed sort of feeling—not knowing if I'd really been heard or not, yet aware of the attentive look and the smiling approval. My intellectual objection had been undercut by means of emotional seduction.

Sometimes the group would burst into song: "We love you, Julie; oh, yes we do; we don't love anyone as much as you. I read it this way: we *could* love you if you weren't so naughty." And, of course, they *would* love her. This incredibly intense encapsulating and loving did not simply "happen." DPs trained specifically for it and held morale and strategy sessions among themselves during the workshops:

> On Sunday morning, when I woke really early, I walked by the building where some of the Family members had slept. They were up and apparently having a meeting. I heard a cheer: "Gonna meet all their needs." And that did seem to be what they tried to do. Whatever I wanted—except privacy or any deviation from the schedule—would be gotten for me immediately and with great concern. I was continually smiled at, hugged, patted. And I was made to feel very special and very much wanted.

As characterized by investigative reporter Andrew Ross (1975), people were "picked up from an emotional floor and taken care of." "The appeal is love—blissed out harmony and unity." Ross and his coworkers discovered some converts who had been in the movement four to six months who truly seemed to have attended to little or nothing regarding Chang and his larger movement. They were simply part of a loving commune. Some, on being pressed explicitly with Chang's beliefs and aims, declared they did not care: their loyalty was to the family commune. Such, as Stark and I discussed with regard to "affective bonds," is an important meaning of love (Lofland and Stark 1965:871-72 and ch. 4, this vol.).

COMMITTING

It is one thing to get "blissed out" on a group over a weekend, but it is quite another to give one's life over to it. And the DPs did not seem immediately to ask that one give over one's life. Instead, the blissed-out prospect was invited to stay on at The Farm for a week-long workshop. And if that worked out, one stayed for an even longer period. The prospect was drawn gradually—but in an encapsulated setting—into full working, street peddling, and believing participation.

Doubts expressed as time went on were defined as "acts of Satan" (Lofland 1966:193-98), and the dire consequence of then leaving the movement would be pointed out (Lofland 1966:185-88). A large portion of new converts seemed not to have had extramovement ties to worry about, but those who did—such as having concerned parents—seemed mostly to be encouraged to minimize the impact of their DP involvement to such outsiders and thereby minimize the threat it might pose to them.

A part of the process of commitment seemed to involve a felt cognitive dislocation arising from the intense encapsulating and loving.

One prospect, an almost-convert who broke off from his "buddy" after a weekend, reported: "As soon as I left Suzie, I had a chance to think, to analyze what had happened and how everything was controlled. I felt free and alive again—it was like a spell was broken."

Another, on being sent out to sell flowers after three weeks at The Farm, had this experience:

> Being out in the world again was a shock; a cultural shock in which I was unable to deal with reality. My isolation by the church had been so successful that everyday sights such as hamburger stands and TVs, even the people, looked foreign, of another world. I had been reduced to a dependent being! The church had seen to it that my three weeks with them made me so vulnerable and so unable to cope with the real world, that I was compelled to stay with them.

This "spell," "trance," or "shock" experience is not as foreign, strange, or unique as it might, at first viewing, appear. People exiting any highly charged involvement—be it a more ordinary love affair, raft trip, 2-week military camp, jail term, or whatever—are likely to experience what students of these matters have called "the reentry problem" (Irwin 1970, ch. 5). Reentry to any world after absence is in many circumstances painful, and a desire to escape from that pain increases the attractiveness of returning to the just-prior world. Especially because the DP situation involved a supercharged love and support experience, we ought to expect people to have reentry unreality, to experience enormous discontinuity and a desire to flee back. DPs created their own attractive kind of "high"—of transcending experience—to which people could perhaps be drawn back in much the same way Lindesmith (1968) has argued people employ certain drugs to avoid withdrawal (reentry pains?) as well as exploiting them for their own inherently positive effects (Lofland and Lofland 1969:104-16).

THE WORLD-SAVER MODEL REVISITED

A first and prime question is: What are the implications of the above for the world-saver model that Stark and I evolved from an earlier era of DP conversion organization? As summarized in the report's abstract, the model propounds:

> For conversion a person must experience, within a religious problem-solving perspective, enduring, acutely-felt tensions that lead to defining her/himself as a religious seeker; the person must encounter the cult at a turning point in life; within the cult an affective bond must be formed (or pre-exist) and any extra-cult attachments, neutralized; and there he/she

must be exposed to intensive interaction to become a "deployable agent" [Lofland and Stark 1965:862].

My impression is that the situational elements of the model, at least, are so general and abstract that they can, with no difficulty, also accurately (but grossly) characterize the newer DP efforts. They are general and abstract to the point of not being especially telling, perhaps reflecting the rather pallid data with which Stark and I had to work. The play of movement and external "affective bonds" and "intensive interaction" continues, certainly, but the new DP efforts now permit much more refined and sophisticated analysis, a level of refinement and sophistication at which I have only been able to hint in my descriptions of "encapsulating" and "loving." Close study of the two major DP conversion camps could result in a quantum step in our understanding of conversion, for the DPs have elaborated some incredible nuances.

Relative to the more "background" elements, the concept of the turning point is troublesome because everyone can be seen as in one or more important ways at a turning point at every moment of their lives. Like concepts of tension, it is true and interesting but not very cutting. There seems to have been a definite broadening of the range of people who get into the DP. The pattern of prior and universal religious seeking, at least in its narrow form, became far less than universal. People not previously religious at all have joined in noticeable numbers. Only further study can sort out the contexts and meanings underlying the diverse new patterns. Further study ought to address the possibility that an entire generation of youth became, broadly speaking, religious seekers in the early seventies and frenzied themselves with a fashion of "seeker chic," a sibling of Wolfe's (1976) aptly identified "funky chic." Last, there seems no reason to modify our polymorphic characterization of tension, which remains a virtually universal feature in the human population.

Be all that as it may, let me now step back and view the world-saver model as an instance of *qualitative process theorizing*. I have been impressed that, although there have been efforts to give the model a quantitative testing, to employ it in organizing materials on conversion to other groups, and to state the correlates of conversion, almost no one has tried their own hand at qualitative process models of conversion. The world-saver model was intended as much as an analytic description of a sequence of experiences as it was a causal theory, and it was very much informed by Turner's (1953:609-11) too-neglected formulation of the distinction between "closed systems" and "intrusive factors." That kind of logic has not caught on, despite the oddity that much lip service is given to it, and the world-saver model provides an example of it, as do the widely known and generically identical models of Becker (1953) on marihuana use, Cressey (1972) on trust violation, and Smelser (1963) on collective behavior. Indeed, and I think now in error, my own effort to generalize the world-saver model to all deviant identities lapsed into the mere causal-factorial approach in providing eleven social-organizational variations that affect the likelihood of assuming a deviant identity and reversing it (Lofland with Lofland 1969:pts. 2, 3). Such an approach is fine and necessary, but it is a retreat from the study of process, signaled in my all too abstract, brief, and shakily founded depiction of "escalating interaction" (Lofland with Lofland, 1969:146-54).

I would have hoped that by now we might have at least half a dozen qualitative process models of conversion, each valid for the range and kind of event it addressed, and each offering insights, even if not the most sophisticated account that might be given. We then could be well on our way to talking about types of conversion and types of qualitative conversion processes. Instead, some investigators get "hung up" in trying to determine whether the world-saver model is right as regards the group they have studied. Such investigators would advance us better by looking at the conversion process directly and reporting what they saw. Stark and I did not feel it necessary to wear anyone's specific model when we went to look at conversion. People ought not to compulsively wear the tinted spectacles wrought by Lofland and Stark when they go to look at conversion. I would urge a knowledge of the logic of a qualitative process point of view, but an eschewing of harassing oneself to look at the world through a specific application of that logic (Lofland 1976, pt. 1).

Stepping back yet further, I have since come to appreciate that the world-saver model embodies a thoroughly passive actor—a conception of humans as a "neutral medium through which social forces operate," as Herbert Blumer (1969a) has so often put it. The world-saver model is antiinteractionist, or at least against the interactionism frequently identified with people such as Blumer.

It is with such a realization that I have lately encouraged students of conversion to turn the process on its head and scrutinize how people go about converting themselves. Assume that the person is active rather than merely passive (Lofland 1976, ch. 5). Straus's (1976) "Changing Oneself: Seekers and the Creative Transformation of Life Experience" is an important initial effort to lay down new pathways of analysis within such an activist-interactionist perspective. I hope there will soon be many efforts of its kind.

Looking back from the perspective of a decade, students of conversion have ample reason for celebration and optimism. Stark and I had very few models and theoretical and substantive material to guide us. Limitations aside, there is now a solid and rich body of reasonably specific ideas and data bits that can guide investigators. We now know more about conversion than we did a decade ago, and I have every confidence that we will know enormously more in a decade.

NOTES

1. Because of DP fame, my pseudonyms are now somewhat labored, but I must continue to protect the anonymity of the movement for the reasons indicated in Lofland 1977, n. 1. The main phases of the development of the DP movement from 1959 through 1976 are chronicled in my epilogue to the Irvington edition of *Doomsday Cult* (Lofland 1977) and in chapter 9 of this volume. Transformations in membership size and composition, modes of operation, funding, and other aspects are as startling as the changes in conversion organization I report here. My account is drawn from the diverse sources described in Lofland (1977, n. 2), save here again to acknowledge the indispensable help of Andrew Ross, Michael Greany, David Taylor, and Hedy Bookin.
2. DPs evolved dozens of front organizations from behind which they carried on an amazing variety of movement-promoting activities (see Lofland 1977, phase two, sec. 4, "Missionizing"; ch. 9 of this vol.).
3. I use the concept of encapsulation here in a related but not identical manner to that introduced in analysis of the deviant act (Lofland with Lofland 1969:39-60).

6

CONVERSION MOTIFS (1981)

With Norman Skonovd

The study of religious conversion has undergone a research renaissance in recent years. In the wake of the worldwide wave of "new religions" and the resurgence of traditional ones, social-scientific and journalistic inquiry into this phenomenon has blossomed. As is to be expected, investigators have stressed different aspects of the conversion process. Focusing on how organized group activities can induce conversion, some employ such concepts as "affective bonds," "programming," or even "mind control." Others highlight the individual convert's subjective life and what is seen as the "self-guiding" and "self-induced" side of conversion. Yet others attempt to encompass all these aspects and point to various additional facets. The literature on the topic is becoming so rich and diverse in these and other ways (Rambo 1982) that a pause and provisional stock taking is now in order.

ORIENTING CONCEPTIONS

Such stock taking is prompted by a sense, moreover, that the differences among conversion experiences which investigators are reporting with increasing frequency are not simply a matter of the "theoretical goggles" worn by the researchers—or, in a pejorative view, their conceptual blinders. Rather, such differences are inherent in the central or key features of conversions themselves. Therefore, we explore the usefulness of the analytic supposition that there are several major types of conversions or even "conversion careers." Given this assumption, our yet more restricted aim is to isolate what we think of as key, critical, orienting, defining, or "motif" experiences as they vary across conversions. The notion of a motif experience in conversion is, on one side, an effort to attend to accounts of conversion which describe the subjective perceptions of the convert. What converts stress in their accounts varies markedly, and we suspect that the differences are not simply artifacts of the accounting process (Beckford 1978), biases elicited by researchers, or the result of selective perception in the construction of conversion accounts. Instead, we are suggesting that holistic, subjective conversions vary in a number of acute, qualitatively different ways best differentiated by their respective motif experiences. Motif experiences, then, are those aspects of a conversion which are most memorable and orienting to the person effecting or undergoing personal transformation—aspects that provide a tone to the event, its pointedness in time, its positive or negative affective content, and the like.

However, in so attuning to the convert's subjective experience we do not elect to be entirely bound by it. We want also—on the other side—to "bracket" that subjective experience in longer, temporal terms and in broader ways than the convert might be prone to do. We need particularly to look at the objective ways in which the social-organizational aspects of the process differ. Our approach strives to blend phenomenological fidelity with some distance on the perspective to which we are faithful. Both sides together—salient thematic elements and key experiences combined with objective situations—may be thought of as making up the motif of a conversion.

By such an approach we hope both to incorporate and go beyond the kind of problems James Beckford (1978) poses in his seminal thoughts on accounting for conversion. Beckford (1978:254) points out that among Jehovah's Witnesses, at least, there is a rather formal, public, or even official conception of appropriate features of the conversion experience. The organization provides a paradigm which converts use to pattern their conversion accounts; some aspects are stressed, others deemphasized or deleted altogether. In the case of Jehovah's Witnesses, conversion is expected to be slow, progressive, extremely cognitive, and something one achieves. Experiences "which smack of sudden or idiosyncratic illumination/revelation [are not] reconcilable" with Witness theory.

Some investigators take such molding to pose an insurmountable problem confining us forever to the study only of molds. We, however, do not consider such molding or structuring a problem. Instead, we recognize that the conversion experience itself is partly molded by expectations of what conversion is about or "is like," that there is therefore the probability of a relatively good fit between the real experiences and paradigmatic accounts. Because it is probable that they reflect "raw reality" (the *first level* of social reality), it is our intention here, in part, to delineate the variety of conversion accounts (the *second level* of social reality).

The efforts of analysts may be thought of as a *third level* of social reality—one that tries to keep pace, often unsuccessfully, with the ever-changing character of the first two levels.

Following tradition, we use the term *conversion* to refer to, in the oft-quoted words of Richard Travisano (1970:594), "a radical reorganization of identity, meaning, life." Or, in Max Heirich's (1977:674) felicitous rendering, conversion is "the process of changing a sense of root reality" or "a conscious shift in one's sense of grounding."

CONVERSION MOTIFS

It is worthwhile to distinguish six motifs of conversion. These and the major variations that distinguish them are depicted in Figure 6.1. The five major dimensions along which they vary should not be construed as exhaustive profiles of features of each type. Instead, they are only *major* aspects that serve to locate each in a very large field of possibilities.

The five major variations that appear most salient in the raw reality of conversions, in the conversion accounts, and in our bracketing of those accounts, encompass the traditional trinity of the intellectual, physical, and emotional. The first variation is quite physical in asking the degree to which the actor is subjected to and experiences external social pressure to convert. The second is also physical in inquiring into the subjective and objective duration of the conversion experience. The third and fourth focus on affect, the former seeking to gauge the degree of emotional arousal accompanying the experience, the latter concerned with its content. The fifth dimension seeks to determine the sequential order in which individuals adopt a religion's cognitive framework and participate in its ritual and organizational activities. As Figure 6.1 illustrates, it appears rather common for people to participate actively in their new roles as converts in advance of their cognitive assent to its theological implications. This is a conscious, conspicuous, and significant aspect of some conversion motifs.

INTELLECTUAL

The first motif we want to single out is as yet relatively uncommon, though we expect it to become increasingly important. The intellectual mode of conversion commences with individual, private investigation of possible new grounds of being, alternate theodicies, personal fulfillment, etc. by reading books, watching television, attending lectures, and other impersonal or "disembodied" ways in which it is increasingly possible sans social involvement to become acquainted with

FIGURE 6.1
Conversion Motifs

Conversion Motifs					
	1. Intellectual	**2. Mystical**	**3. Experimental**	**4. Affectional**	**5. Revivalist**	**6. Coercive**
1. Degree of Social Pressure	low or none	none or little	low	medium	high	high
2. Temporal Duration	medium	short	long	long	short	long
3. Level of Affective Arousal	medium	high	low	medium	high	high
4. Affective Content	illumination	awe love, fear	curiosity	affection	love (& fear)	fear (& love)
5. Belief-Participation Sequence	belief-participation	belief-participation	participation-belief	participation-belief	participation-belief	participation-belief

alternative ideologies and ways of life. In the course of such reconnaissance, some individuals convert themselves in isolation from any interaction with devotees of the respective religion. A prototypical case is that of sociologist Roger Straus (1979a:7) who, while an undergraduate, substantially converted himself to Scientology through extensive reading. His first contact with a Scientologist was for the predetermined purpose of attaining full membership: "Although I was highly suspicious of any organized group, after several months I concluded that the only way to check the whole thing out was to take the plunge: I walked into New York Org and asked the receptionist what I had to do to 'go Clear' and become an auditor."

In the literature, this pattern is spoken of as the "activist" model of conversion (Lofland 1977; this vol. ch. 5; Straus 1976, 1979b; Richardson 1979). In terms of the major variations mentioned, there is little or no external social pressure; the events defined as making up the conversion appear to be drawn out over a number of weeks or months—a period we might characterize as "medium" in length. The convert-in-process is affectively aroused, but the emotional level is far from ecstatic. The emotional tone of the experience seems best characterized as one of "illumination." Furthermore and most importantly, a reasonably high level of belief occurs prior to participation in the religion's ritual and organizational activities.

The intellectual or self-conversion motif is largely a new mode of entry into a religious community or movement. Its incidence as a conversion mode is probably on the increase due to the "privatized" (Luckmann 1967) nature of religion in Western society, the smorgasboard assortment of religion's competing for members, and the ever-increasing presence of disembodied modes of religious communication: books, magazines, specialized newspapers, movies, television, video and audio cassettes, etc. The so-called electronic church—the TV-production-oriented Christian Fundamentalist groups whose congregations are essentially TV viewers—is a particularly good example of this current trend. It has become very easy for people privately to control their own decisions about religious beliefs, organizations, and even ways of life quite apart from any physically embodied social contact, support, or inducement of an affect-laden sort. In such a situation people in search of "truth," community, identity, salvation, etc. can calmly and privately elect to "go for it," as people in the late seventies often expressed their adoption of a new "trip."

MYSTICAL

Historically speaking, the best known conversion motif is probably the one we here lable "mystical"—a term not entirely accurate but better than its alternatives such as "Damascus Road," "Pauline," "evangelical," and "born again." The term *mystical* at least has the virtue of signaling the common feeling among converts that "the experiences cannot be expressed in logical and coherent terms,"—that "clear characterizations . . . miss its depth" (Jules-Rosette 1975:62). The prototypical instance within the Christian tradition is the conversion of St. Paul in a dramatic incident on the Damascus Road in the first century A.D. St. Paul's conversion, as recorded in Acts 9 and elsewhere in the New Testament, has in a sense functioned as the ideal of what conversion should be in the Western world.

The earliest scholars of conversion—William James (1902), Edwin Starbuck (1911) and E. T. Clark (1929)—focused heavily on mystical conversion. The reason for this may have been its more widespread incidence in late-nineteenth- and early-twentieth-century America. It seems to have attracted less interest among converts and scholars (who simply follow converts) in the middle third of the twentieth century, save as a minor topic within psychoanalysis. Our contemporary definitions of mystical conversion are provided by psychoanalytically oriented scholars such as Carl Christensen (1963:207), who describes it as "an acute hallucinatory episode occurring within the framework of religious belief and characterized by its subjective intensity, apparent suddenness of onset, brief duration, auditory and, sometimes, visual hallucinations, and an observable change in the subsequent behavior of the convert." It is characterized, further, by seeming "not to be wrought by the subject but upon him" (Coe 1916:152, quoted in Christensen 1963). This "feeling of submission—of giving up or giving to" is preceded by "withdrawal from others with a sense of estrangement and often in feelings of unreality," and the outcome is "a sense of sudden understanding accompanied by a feeling of elation and by an auditory and sometimes visual hallucination. . . . There is a feeling of change within the self . . . associated with a sense of presence" (Christensen 1963:214).

In terms of our "major variations," there is little or no social pressure, the convert is even likely alone at the time of the event. What the convert defines as the most critical period of the conversion is quite brief—perhaps on the order of minutes or hours—although a period of stress preceding the critical event may stretch back some days or weeks. Its very brevity functions, indeed, to heighten meaning. As stated by an anthropologist who was converted to an African Apostolic church: "In my case the initial shift from one set of interpretations to another was dramatic, resulting in a moment of shock in which even the physical terms of existence seemed to alter" (Jules-Rosette 1975:62-63). The level of emotional arousal is extremely high—sometimes involving theophanic ecstasis, awe, love, or even fear. And the event signals the onset—or active intensification—of belief which is then followed by participation in the ritual and organizational activities of the religion with which the conversion experience is associated.

EXPERIMENTAL

As observers of social life we are prone to commit the *fallacy of the uniformly profound*. If someone makes a dramatic change of life orientation ("a radical reorganization of identity, meaning, life," as Travisano puts it), we are likely to feel that equally dramatic, deep, and strong forces must have brought it about. In the eyes of analysts, one strong event must be balanced, as it were, by some other strong event or events. Accounts of mystical conversion, for example, often display such a balancing of cause and effect in the reports of both convert and analyst—as in the crescendo of personal guilt which culminates in the mystical experience.

The imagery often seems to fit the first and second levels of reality we have mentioned—but not always, thus we have the fallacy of the uniformly profound. Recent research is uncovering the surprising degree to which—and frequently with which—a transformation of religious identity, behavior, and worldview can occur quite tentatively and slowly and yet be identified by the convert-in-process as happening in that manner. This motif has been scrutinized most closely by Robert Balch and his associate David Taylor (1977:5). Studying followers of the Process—a group in which one gives up all possessions and becomes an itinerant—they have found a "pragmatic 'show me' attitude, ready to give the Process a try, but withholding judgment" for a considerable length of time after taking up the lifestyle of the fully committed participant and making significant sacrifices. Attuned to similar themes proposed by Bromley and Shupe (1979) and Straus (1976), Balch (1980:142) concludes: "The first step in conversion . . . is learning to *act* like a convert. . . . Genuine conviction develops later . . . after intense involvement.

The research that has revealed this conversion motif has focused on "new age," metaphysical types of groups. However, experimental conversions do not appear to be confined to them. Groups that might appear to be poles apart in their authoritarianism and organizational structure, such as Jehovah's Witnesses and Scientology, typically insist that the prospective convert take an experimental attitude toward—and *participate* in—the group's ritual and organizational activities. This is clearly brought out in James Beckford's (1978:253, 255, 257) analysis of Jehovah's Witnesses' talk about conversion. He outlines four characteristics of conversion which are central in conversations among Witnesses concerning their conversions: (1) it is thought to involve a "progression of mental states"; (2) it is considered to be "predominantly cognitive" in nature; (3) it is "framed as something they *achieved*"; and (4) it follows a policy immediately to involve the neophyte "in practical work alongside more mature Witnesses" (see also Straus 1979a:9).

In terms of our list of major variations, experimental conversions involve relatively low degrees of social pressure to participate, since the recruit takes on a "try-it-out" posture. The transformation of identity, behavior, and worldview commonly called "conversion" takes place over a relatively prolonged period—often months or even years—and does not appear to be accompanied by high levels of emotional arousal in most instances. The affective content of the experience appears to be that of curiosity.

This motiff of change is not unique to religious or other highly ideologized contexts. It resembles the ubiquitous manner in which people learn new social roles and are more ordinarily assimilated into groups. The social mechanisms of such socialization processes have long ago been identified by Howard Becker (1964) as "situational adjustment"—commitment being the end result of increasing adaptation and the making of side-bets. The notion of situational adjustment provides for us a "picture of a person trying to meet the expectations he encounters in immediate face-to-face situations," thus encouraging us to "look to the character of the [micro and immediate] situation for the explanation of why people change as they do. We ask what there is in the situation that requires the person to act in a certain way or to hold certain beliefs" (Becker 1964:44). Once we assume that, for whatever reasons, a person wants to continue in a given situation, subsequent behavior can be understood in terms of ordinary situational requirements.

It is in such terms that we can hope to shed new light on the consistent finding that "intensive interaction" is a significant feature of many conversion experiences. One recent study of Nichiren Shoshu asserts that intensive interaction is "the key to . . . transformation" (Snow and Phillips 1980:444). Reformulated, "intensive interaction" is an abstract and rather gross way in which to talk about opportunities for progressive situational adjustments and the consequent development of committing side-bets in Becker's (1964) terms.

AFFECTIONAL

As alluded to at the outset, a continuing interplay of three levels of reality occurs in the study of conversion. At the first level—that of raw reality—the conversion process involves actual, "out there" occurrences or situations. That level is, however, ambiguously and imperfectly available to us. The second level—that of the convert's experience and interpretation—is structured by the first level and by any particular paradigm found useful to the convert to interpret the former. The third level—that of analytic interpretations—provides, in its own right, a screen through which we attempt to perceive the social-psychological reality of the transformation. However, we must keep in mind that the prominence of any particular conversion motif is likely to vary over time and geography, partly as a function of shifting fashions at the second level, but mostly as a consequence of more weighty factors such as the prevalence and content of mass communications. And, of course, the third level changes in order to keep up with the first two.

We reiterate these ideas because they are especially pertinent in understanding the dominance of the "affectional conversion" motif over the last two decades in social science theory and research. The identification of this motif dates back to John Lofland and Rodney Stark's (1965) analysis of positive affective bonds in the conversion process. The notion was widely adopted and rapidly documented during subsequent years (see e.g. the literature reviewed in Gerlach and Hine 1970, ch. 4; Richardson 1978; Hierich 1977; Robbins, Anthony, and Richardson 1978; Snow and Phillips 1980). By 1980, the motif was formulated in such phrases as "interpersonal bonds are the fundamental support for recruitment" (Stark and Bainbridge 1980b:1389)—a more formal rewording of the original phrase that becoming "one" was "coming to accept the opinions of one's friends" (Lofland and Stark 1965:871). Critical causal efficacy implied here aside, the motif thesis is that personal attachments or strong liking for practicing believers is central to the conversion process. Such sentiment has the same defining importance or central significance in the process of affectional conversion as intellectual illumination, mystical encounter, or experimental immersion do in the motifs already described.

We would like to believe that the fashionableness of the affectional motif in social science in recent years has been more than mere intellectual fadishness. Rather, during that period, investigators were uncovering—however fitfully and imperfectly—a new central meaning in conversion—one that was both there in raw reality (our first level) and to a reasonable extent in the convert's own perceptions and accounts (the second level).

As a motif, the cognitive element is deemphasized (in decided contrast to intellectual conversion). Reflecting the reality-constructionism of the sixties (itself a reflection of a broader relativism of the time), there is stress on the strong degree to which all systems of social knowledge and beliefs are sustained by an underlying "sentimental order" (Shibutani 1961; Berger and Luckmann 1967). Truth is a function of what is defined as such in the individual's social and emotional milieu. Social pressure is certainly present but exists and functions more as support and attraction than as inducement to convert. Analysts are somewhat vague on the point, but one gets the impression that the process is relatively prolonged—a matter of at least several weeks. Even if the central experience is affection, the ordinary level of emotional arousal seems more in the range of medium intensity rather than the more extreme states we find in the revivalist or mystical motifs. As in experimental conversion, belief arises out of participation.

REVIVALIST

In several studies since World War II, the phenomenon of revivalist conversion has been debunked by the finding that the most famous of revivalist preachers and their organizations appear merely to simulate or stage mild conversions rather than bring about the kind of dramatic occurrences asserted to have been common in the eighteenth and nineteenth centuries (e.g. Lang and Lang 1960; Altheide and Johnson 1977). We have become cynical about the existence of true revivalist conversions, and the abundant literature documenting their occurrence in earlier centuries has been ignored or neglected. However, that neglect is combined with the probability of decline in the incidence of revivalist conversions in modern societies—or at least a decline in the incidence of their more extreme versions, representing a decline of experiential acuteness at what we have called the "first level of reality."

It is particularly incumbent on those of us who work at "level three" of reality to keep alive in human consciousness the broad spectrum of possibilities in all areas of social life, including that of conversion. Even though it appears to be in decline in contemporary industrialized societies, conversion whose central feature consists of profound experiences which occur within the context of an emotionally aroused crowd is far from absent in most societies throughout the world. Probably owing to a rationalist tendency to retreat from emotionalism, however, scholars of crowd behavior—or collective behavior—have generally lost sight of the fact that crowds *can* be brought to ecstatic arousals, having a critically transforming effect on some people. Social pressure and "contagion"—albeit brief—can produce fear, guilt, and joy of such intensity that individuals may obediently go through the outward and inward methodology of a fundamentalist or evangelical conversion (Lofland 1982b; this vol., ch. 2).

There are apparent revivalist waves of recurrence in spite of the long-term decline of this conversion motif in Western societies (McLoughlin 1978). Some people have even argued that we witnessed a relatively mild wave of revivalist conversions during the early seventies concommitant with the coming of the "new religions." The Unification Church appears to have resurrected the revivalist experience in highly effective modern garb. Prospective converts recruited literally off the streets are taken on weekend retreats which involve a whirlwind round of singing, chanting, hand-holding, preaching, and diffuse, loving comaraderie. In the apt terminology of its closest participant observer, David Taylor (1978:107), the effect is "enthralling" for many. There is a marked "transition from a relatively mundane world to a dynamic environment of ecstatic youth."

> Events and activities have an exciting quality. Participants experience emotional heights without suffering subsequent letdowns. The exceptional nature of collective joy lies in . . . members' ability to create events [that] have natural endings, yet the stimulation produced is seemingly inexhaustible. There is the promise of more—the next event, the next day, the coming week.
>
> All aspects of the training session blend together with exhilarating momentum. [The members'] enthusiasm requires prospects to invest their entire beings in the participatory events. Jumping up to sing tumultuous songs; running from place to place hand in hand with a buddy; and cheering, chanting, and clapping in unison with dozens of others inevitably makes a deep impression on prospective members.
>
> Even the most reticent . . . find it difficult to resist being swept into this performance of continual consensus. One may remain intellectually unsympathetic to [the members'] . . . beliefs and goals, but he [or she] will be in some way moved by the intense revelry. Possibly no participant escapes feeling intense excitement, even if he regards the performance as inauthentic [Taylor 1978:153-54].

COERCIVE

We come, finally, to a conversion motif that takes place only in extremely rare and special circumstances but which has been alleged by some to be rampant among the new religions of the Western world. Our reference is to what has been variously labeled "brainwashing," "programming," "mind control," "coercive persuasion," "thought reform," and "menticide," among others.

The accusations surrounding this topic make it especially important to form a clear conception of the nature of the "beast" under discussion—a step that seems noticeably neglected in the leading literature (e.g. Delgado 1977). Toward that clarification, we draw on the best and most accurate summary of brainwashing. It appears under that title in the *International Encyclopedia of the Social Sciences* (1968) and was written by Albert Somit. An extremely cogent treatment remaining inexplicably unattended, Somit's vision may have been clear because we wrote *after* the fifties' fears of communist brainwashing and *before* the seventies' fears of "cult mind control."

The two key features of brainwashing—or as we prefer, coercive persuasion (Schein 1961)—are (1) the *compulsion* of an individual and (2) *sincerely* to confess guilt or embrace an ideological system. The process of brainwashing individuals was independently invented in the early twentieth century by European Communists extracting simple confessions of guilt and by Chinese Communists striving for systematic ideological conformity.

While practices differed somewhat in Europe and China, Somit delineates seven "measures" which characterize both traditions: (1) *total control* of the prisoner's round of life "down to the most intimate needs"; (2) *uncertainty* of the charges against one and one's entire future; (3) *isolation* from the outside world; (4) *torture* in the form of "mental and physical torment"; (5) *physical debilitation and exhaustion* achieved by a "diet . . . planned to ensure rapid loss of weight, strength, and stamina" and induced by the "constant interrogation, tension, and terror" associated with the other measures; (6) *personal humiliation* associated with denial of "any previous claim to personal dignity or status"; and (7) *certainty of the captive's guilt*—"the unyielding assumption that he will confess and change"—which, when displayed by the captors, "justifies even in the prisoner's mind the stringency of the measure applied." Although these are the fundamental, social-interactional aspects of brainwashing, the process is not entirely negative. As the subject begins to capitulate—or to "see the light"—"living conditions improve . . . [and] even . . . interrogators become more friendly and less impersonal" (Somit 1968:139-40).

As a strategy, however, coercive conversion has two serious problems which limit its usefulness even by ideologues who hold state power. First, if allowed to return to a more or less open society, subjects "backslide"; "the results achieved are not permanent" (Somit 1968:142). Something similar to this may have happened to Patricia Hearst who, after having been converted to the radical Marxist doctrine of the Symbionese Liberation Army, appeared to return to her earlier sociopolitical beliefs relatively easily and quickly once she was removed from the influence and control of her abductors. Second, an inordinant amount of personnel, space, time, and other resources are required to achieve sincere ideological change. At best, a relatively large staff must be marshalled to "process" a single person or, at most, a small group. Compared to other motifs, this is likely the "most expensive and uneconomical" of possibilities (Somit 1968:142).

We appreciate it is currently common to summarize chapter 22, titled "Ideological Totalism" of Robert Lifton's (1961) *Thought Reform and the Psychology of Totalism* in characterizing brainwashing. The eight "psychological themes" he so skillfully evokes have become a kind of litany on the topic. We also think it is a litany that is off the mark even though it is *also* likely accurate as a characterization of certain abstract features of certain ideologies. *By definition,* ideological totalism is constructed of the eight items he enumerates: milieu control, mystical manipulation, the demand for purity, a cult of confession, a sacred science, loading the language, doctrine over person, and dispensing of existence. Such features are surely found in brainwashing settings but *not confined to or definitive of them.* Instead, we must go on to *add* the kinds of considerations Albert Somit makes so explicit (above) but which are muted in Lifton's treatment. And we must appreciate how we can find totalistic settings (in the sense they display Lifton's eight features) which are *not* brainwashing settings (in the sense they do not have Somit's seven features), as for example the Bruderhof as reported by Zablocki (1971).

The possibility of *social-psychological* coercion cannot, nevertheless, be ignored; interactional affective pressures and fears resulting from theological precepts could conceivably function as coercively on some individuals as physical restraints and threats. For example, some evidence of such pressures is apparent in Taylor's (1978:153-54) description of revivalism quoted in our discussion of revivalist conversion. Future treatments will have to deal with the crossovers between revivalist and coercive conversion as well as the question of what "legitimately" constitutes coercion.

Summarized in terms of our five major variations, coercive conversion entails an extremely high degree of external pressure over a relatively long period of time, during which there is intense arousal of fear and uncertainty, culminating in empathetic identification and even love. Belief, of course, follows participation.

IMPLICATIONS

We want to conclude by pointing out two classes of implications of this kind of endeavor. The first concerns the social psychology of conversion per se. Differentiating motifs, careers, or styles should allow us to sharpen our understanding of the phenomenon of conversion. Irrespective of the merits of the present formulation, we feel that efforts of this kind are very much in order, and we urge others interested in the subject to join us in improving on schemes of conversion types. The present effort is quite narrow in the specific sense that it adduces types but does not go on to delineate steps, phases, or processes within each type. In future refined schemes that render this one obsolete, we hope this specification of process will receive prominent attention.

A second class of implications is sociohistorical and organizational. We suspect conversion motifs differ significantly from one historical epoch to another, across societal boundaries, and even across subcultures within a single society. There are probably trends and subtrends in the prevalence of particular conversion motifs and in the social conditions with which such trends are correlated. Among other possibilities, we have suggested that in the media-drenched ("advanced") societies, intellectual and experimental conversions are on the increase, and revivalist ones in relative decline. A wide variety of other conjunctions of social circumstances and conversion motifs are likely discernible. Certain religious ideologies and organizations may have an affinity with some, rather than other, conversion motifs. The classification of religious systems is itself a complex and contention-ridden task. Nevertheless, one recurrent dimension of difference appears to be the degree to which a religion absorbs and reorders an adherent's round of life. We might expect, for example, those religious systems least affecting an individual's life to be characterized by the least arousing conversions (intellectual and experimental ones), while those most affecting an individual's life to be characterized by more dramatic (revivalist) conversions. The picture is far from simple, partly due to the fact the converts to any single religion do not all experience the same kind of conversion, and the dominant motif of any one religion (if there is one) sometimes changes over time (e.g. the Unification Church's moving from affectional to revivalist conversions, as reported by Bromley and Shupe [1979]).

In any event, the topic of religious conversion is among the most active, challenging, and exciting in social science today, and we invite others to try their hand at increasing our understanding of this complex and evolving body of materials.

Part Three

MOVEMENT ORGANIZATION: ASSOCIATING FOR PROTEST

INTRODUCTION

Between the impulse of collective behavior and the action of protest falls the shadow of organization. Collective behavior and conversion (parts 1 and 2) provide energy for action, but action itself is facilitated by organization. Such organization is the focus of the five chapters in part 3.

MOVEMENT ORGANIZATION AND PROTEST

Protest is a type of organization as well as a style of action. In recent jargon, such protest organizations are called "social movement organizations," "SMOs," or "MOs." Their distinctive features include principled and sustained objection to some or all aspects of the current social order of things combined with at least a proclivity to protest action.

The classification of protest organizations set forth in this part is more detailed, refined, and *set within* the classification of citizen organizations offered in the general introduction. The latter depiction strives to capture the entire gamut, while here in part 3 we deal only with those of a protest character, setting aside the vast domain of workaday, interest group, and violent organization (although aspects of some of these do figure in minor ways, especially in chapter 8).

ANALYZING MOVEMENT ORGANIZATION

The five chapters in this part wrestle with the problem of formulating a powerfully fruitful and generic specification of types of social movement organization—while discerning a set of organizational forms whose knowledge also communicates nonobvious generalizations about their respective causes, likely careers, coalition behavior, distinctive weaknesses, proclivities for action, strengths, and so on (cf. Freeman 1983). Each chapter explores a part of this general problem, striving to make a contribution to its solution rather than attempting a single, grand or general solution. These efforts are themselves focused in three kinds of ways.

GENERIC STRUCTURE AND DYNAMICS

The first focus, seen in chapters 7 and 8, is the effort to conceptualize a limited range of fundamental forms. In chapter 7 this is pursued for the *religious* movement organizations (RMOs), setting this apart from political and ego forms. RMOs are themselves broken down into the yet more generic forms out of which we find them composed. This is done in terms of how such elementary forms vary in "corporateness," the degree to which a set of persons actively promotes and participates in a shared and collective life. Arrayed in order of increasing corporateness, five basic forms are isolated: the clinic, congregation, collective, corps, and colony. Many RMOs are complex concatenations and sequences of these forms and several principles of such dynamics are propounded.

Chapter 8 tries to push beyond the religious-political-ego distinctions to specifying fully generic forms at the level of the MO *local,* the small and operating ends of an MO. Focusing yet more tightly on voluntary MOs, the effort is to get at their distinctive microdynamics by asking: What is the "modal member" of the local actually doing most of the time and what portion of her/his round of life is organized by it? Within what is likely the simplest form of local—the association modally sustained by volunteers—we find a series of distinctive forms: the study group, fellowship, congregation, sect, and cell.

MOVEMENT CULTURE

The second kind of focus involves recognition that although movement organization is key, our conceptualization of it can become too severely formal, "structural," and generic, a liability to which all organizational and movement analysis has tended (cf. Deal and Kennedy 1982). Generic severity must somehow be constrained and counterbalanced, and chapter 9 attempts to do this by introducing the idea of "movement culture," a phenomenon that is itself treated as a variable (as something that differs markedly from MO to MO in terms of the degree of its richness or poverty). Detailed features of the three major components of richness—elaboration, expressiveness, and compassion—are explained with particular reference to the Unification Church, a contemporary movement organization that has developed a relatively rich culture. Among other matters, this analysis raises the question of the negativity of protest culture. Protest as objection fosters a focus on what one does not like. For several reasons, this can create a stark and bleak atmosphere or "culture" in an MO—an impoverished culture. The question can then become: What are the conditions under which a stress on protest action can avoid such cultural poverty and be combined with positive joys and the kinds of cultural richness detailed in chapter 2, and the other kinds of cultural richness described in chapter 9?

CASE DYNAMICS

Chapters 10 and 11 offer a third type of focus, the detailed case study of an organizational form and its career dynamics. The first, on "white-hot mobilization," provides an abbreviated and analytic account of how, in the nomenclature of chapters 7 and 8, the Unification Church was transformed from a loosely-strung set of fellowships, congregations, and sect locals into a highly mobilized van-going corps-collective composite for a period of years before settling down to a complex conglomerate that is dominantly a collective and colony. The distinctive strengths—and especially weaknesses—of the state of white-hot mobilization are set out. The other short study—"Mankind United" in chapter 11—chronicles the successive stages of collectivizing through which that movement went over its brief history, playing through forms explained in chapters 7 and 8, moving, specifically, from study group, to sect, to disparaged and retreating colony.

7

RELIGIOUS MOVEMENT ORGANIZATIONS: ELEMENTARY FORMS AND DYNAMICS (1984)

With James T. Richardson

The analytically fruitful and empirically viable classification of basic types of religious organizations has been a central preoccupation of sociological scholars of religion from the very founding of the enterprise (e.g. Troeltsch 1931). But, like justice and freedom, achievement of a scheme with collectively compelling features has been so far impossible, such that many students have given up the quest and the topic itself has gone out of fashion.

The importance of the task abides, nonetheless, and we seek here once more to tackle a part of the question of what are the most fundamental and generic forms of religious organization.

Our perception of a need to come back to this seemingly intractable problem does not arise from abstract contemplation of the field, but rather from the specific turmoils in a particular area of the sociology of religion, namely, our involvement in studying the worldwide wave of new religions of the 1970s. Much of the effort to depict and generalize about these new religions is critically deficient because it lacks a clear conception of how these bodies vary among themselves in some fundamental ways and form diverse "packages" of features, so to speak, that must be explicated and taken into account in formulating, limiting, and specifying generalizations. We acknowledge that there are a few purposes for which "new religions of the 1970s" is a useful category, but there are many other tasks for which it is an entirely specious construct whose use creates enormous theoretical as well as "applied" mischief (e.g. Delgado 1977).

RELIGIOUS MOVEMENT ORGANIZATION (RMOs)

The need to be more precise about referents of generalizations concerning the most recent new religions brings us back to the general question of religious organization, but we cannot allow these new religions to confine our view. They are themselves a subset of a larger category we may call "religious movement organizations," and it is to that larger category that we direct our attention.

Each of the three terms comprising the category's title requires specification. The term *organization* refers to a plurality of persons who view themselves as a corporate social entity that has consciously conceived goals and a program for achieving them. Such entities ordinarily have a formal name, a leader or leadership, and a membership that is coordinated in differentiated activities.

The term *movement* refers to any organization (and to other forms of collectivity not here relevant) that opposes the dominant institutional order and proposes alternative structural arrangements. Or, in the too narrow but useful phraseology of Stark and Bainbridge (1979:124), an organization "whose primary goal is to cause or prevent social change" (italics deleted).

The term *religious* refers to belief systems that overtly and significantly define and sanction action by reference to a super- or extra-natural realm of thought and action. In the terms used by Stark and Bainbridge (1980a:123), its "compensators" are significantly supernatural. The religious is to be distinguished from at least two other major classes of belief systems, the political and the ego. In the former, root reality is natural rather than supernatural and the sources of remedies of human problems reside in arrangements of human power. The latter also stresses the natural but locates the causes and cures of human woes in the person (cf. Westley 1978; Peterson 1971).

The intersection of these three categories isolates the distinctive phenomenon of the "religious movement organization" (or RMO for brevity's sake and elaborating on the terminology introduced by Zald and Ash [1966] and used by Zald and McCarthy [1979]). The conjunction *also* directs our attention to some important neighbors toward whom we need to be looking as we move forward on the comparative-analytic road. We have in mind, in particular, the political movement organization (PMO); the ego movement organization (EMO) (e.g. Peterson 1971; Roberts and Kloss 1979, ch. 4); and the religious conventional (as distinct from movement) organization (RCO).

We have approached the question of specifying a generic set of types of RMOs in a quasi-inductive fashion. Surveying major statements in the literature we (1) compiled a list of features or characteristics researchers have attributed to particular RMOs and converted those to dimensions in terms of how RMOs vary; and (2) simply extracted such dimensions if they were already spoken of as variables. Further, since we are dealing with organizations, we studied ways in which they vary per se (e.g. Aldrich 1979; Hall 1972). These variations were coordinated with a list of what we felt to be "dramatically" contrasting cases of RMOs, an array of what seemed "obviously" diverse enterprises even though it was not precisely clear to us exactly *how* they were diverse.

We have been guided by a list of intuitively diverse cases but we have not felt bound or confined to it. Instead, we have tried to draw out and state the *logic* of organizational forms suggested by cases even if they do not fully embody the logical implications. In this we follow the historic light of Max Weber on ideal types and the modern light of Joyce Rothschild-Whitt (1979) in analyzing "collectivist-democratic organizations." One important implication of our use of ideal-type logic is that when we mention a specific RMO we are *not* saying that it or an element of it is necessarily *fully* that type, only that it *tends toward the type*.

DECOMPOSING RMOs: ELEMENTARY FORMS

Proceeding in this fashion we were forced to an unanticipated realization: Many RMOs were not very easily either summed up as or reduced to any single organizational form. Instead, most of any size are themselves concatenations of strikingly different forms that seemed reasonably termed "elementary units." With this recognition, our overall task was divided in two: articulation of the elementary units versus specification of concatenations of units.

The elementary units lay along a complex, master dimension that we may think of as the *degree* of respective *corporateness* of each, the degree to which a set of persons actively promotes and participates in a shared, positively valued, and collective life.

As a matter of degree at the level of structure, corporateness refers to variations in the provisions made for maintenance of the full round of activities necessary to participant well-being. Viewed from the "full-round" end of the spectrum, the most elaborate degree of corporateness involves: (1) income or other sustenance-producing work; (2) shelter or residence; (3) food provision and eating organization; (4) family or other emotional support circles; (5) collective promulgation of cognitive orientation; and (6) a belief that the organization itself is ideal.

The first four are self-explanatory, but (5) and (6) require introductory definition. The fifth, "collective promulgation of cognitive orientation," refers to the extent to which and the ways in which members assemble as crowds or audiences for purposes of learning, discussing, expounding, and celebrating the faith they share. The pure form of this is the worship service, but many other assemblies not so defined serve the same promulgation functions.

Irrespective of the degree of structural corporateness, the sixth key variation is the degree to which the arrangement is defined by participants as ideal and long-term versus merely temporary, expedient, and utilitarian.

CLINICS

Varying combinations of these six dimensions identify five key elementary units among RMOs. As shown in Figure 7.1, the most elementary of elementary forms seems to be the clinic. To qualify for discussion here, even clinics are *organizations* as previously defined. Clinics are most elementary in the sense of fielding a limited array of provisions for members; namely, they confine themselves to the systematic distribution of cognitive orientation. However, they are in this way at least one step above, organizationally, what Stark and Bainbridge (1979:126) term "audience cults" and seem much the same, formally, as what they call "client cults" and, indeed, the term *client* appropriately denotes the participant component of the organizational concept of clinic.

Clinics center on an organized flow of religious, cognitive orientation but, as coded in Figure 7.1, do not sponsor much collective or crowd dissemination of that flow or the affirmation and celebration of a corporate way of life of the sort associated with the more elaborate organizational forms. As Stark and Bainbridge (1979:126) indicate, the key relationships of clinics often "closely resemble the relationship between therapist and patient, or between consultant and client . . . [and] clients remain little organized." Commonly, the phrase "fee for service" accurately characterizes the financial aspect of the arrangement.

Prominent illustrations of RMOs with important clinic elements include the Rosicrucians (AMORC), ECKANDKAR, transcendental meditation (TM) in its "marketed" phase (the term used by Johnston 1980) and Christian Science and Scientology at several times and places (Wilson 1961, chs. 8, 16; Wallis 1977).

In its marketed phase TM has been perhaps one of the most sophisticated of clinic RMOs. According to Johnston (1980:346-47), the flow of cognitive orientation it provided was worked into something of a "product package" in which recruitment resembled a "sales transaction" beyond which clients became "targets for follow-up [, . . .] such

FIGURE 7.1
Elementary Forms of Religious Movement Organization

	1. Clinic	2. Congregation	3. Collective — Work	3. Collective — Household	4. Corps	5. Colony
1. work/income generated?	−	−	+	−	+	+
2. residence organized?	−	−	−	+	+	+
3. organized provision of food and eating?	−	−	−	+	+	+
4. family/support circles organized?	−	−	−	+	+	+
5. collective dissemination of cognitive orientation?	−	+		+	+	+
6. arrangement viewed as ideal?	+	+		+	−	+

as periodic 'checking' of their mantras, free advanced lectures, and videotape programs." Continued involvement was in the form of "packages of advanced participation" (see also Bryan Wilson's [1961:330-34] remarkably similar characterization of relevant aspects of Christian Science).

In some urban areas, RMO clinics gravitate toward one another and coalesce into cultic milieux (Campbell 1972) or "esoteric communities" (using the term *community* here as only an imprecise metaphor). Jorgensen (1982) reports that one Southwestern metropolis of about a million residents has such a milieu composed of some 100 clinic RMOs. (Perhaps providing the RMO clinic equivalent of the PMO coalitional demonstration, these groups regularly come together in "psychic fairs" [Jorgensen 1982:390-92].)

In broader and comparative terms, the more familiar and conventional form of clinic provides a flow of psychosecular cognitive orientations that are heavily psychiatric and academic-psychological in origin and nature. Beyond them and having the same relation to such conventional clinics as cults to mainstream religions, there are numerous *ego movement organization clinics* such as portions of EST, Silva Mind Control, and the many encounter group EMO clinics that have centered on or emanated from such places as Bethal, Maine, and Big Sur, California (Back 1978; Peterson 1971; Westley 1978).

In the PMO realm, we may note the various "educational" centers in which several PMOs cooperate to offer a political, cognitive flow of orientation. Likewise, as mentioned by Johnston (1980:351), PMOs such as the Cousteau Society and Common Cause have many clinic elements.

Clinics of all sorts have distinctive strengths and weaknesses, or, more neutrally, correlative tendencies. Among RMOs, their *ideologies* tend to be what is variously termed monistic, mystical, or psychic. A bland, calm, inward-turning, optimistic, and privatized state of mind and being is sponsored. This is congruent with the organizational narrowness of clinic organization (cf. Nelson 1969, ch. 14).

Such congruence of ideology and organization makes recruitment more easy—since relatively little is asked of the potential participant—but, in turn, defection rates are high (Bird and Reimer 1982; Johnston 1980:347).

CONGREGATIONS

Like clinics, congregation RMOs do not venture transformingly into the work, residence, eating, or family lives of participants. But unlike clinics, a complex and rich collective life is sponsored and participants are integral parts of it.

The centerpiece, physical feature of the congregation is a place— ordinarily a building—where congregants assemble. Called a church, shrine, temple, center, or whatever, it is the physical embodiment of the body of believers, the focal point of collective activities therein, and the location in which extracenter activities are organized and from which they embark.

Even though carrying on what is socially defined as an "ordinary" round of life in terms of working, residing, eating—the "familizing," members of congregational RMOs tend to have a sense of "communal solidarity" and "emotional bonding" that is very much associated with the "cognitive-constituting powers of collective ritual" (Lynch 1979:29). An ordinary dictionary captures this clearly in defining a congregation as "a body of persons who habitually meet for the worship of God." That is, a *body of persons* who *habitually* meet for *worship* forms a systemic trinity of collective life features. As Bryan Wilson (1961:333) refers approvingly to C.E. Hudson's discussion of the psychology of public worship, "it is difficult to over-estimate the influence exerted on the mind by the mere sight of other people at prayer" (cf. Durkheim 1915).

In congregations, participation is expected to be sustained and is, in theory, lifetime rather than packaged, dispensed, or episodic (as with clinics). This continuity is associated with expectations of uninter- rupted contributions of funds (as in "tithing") to sustain the congrega- tion.

The activities constituting worship are themselves diverse and or- dered in terms of their degree of sacredness—some gatherings promis- ing much closer approach to the supernatural than others. The diver- sity and frequency of congregational gatherings give the appearance of being a "busy round of activities" (Lynch 1979:9). Such activities sometimes include sharing meals and a heavy emphasis on family- centered activities. The sense of positive, communal solidarity both fosters and supports relatively extensive mutual home visiting and other informal association among members (e.g. Damrell 1977, ch. 6).

This profile of features can also be found among many conventional religious organizations (RCOs). This is a key matter to appreciate when scrutinizing RMOs because attention merely to ideology obscures the potent and organizational fact that a great many RMOs are only (or mostly) movements *ideologically* rather than organizationally (cf. Toch 1965:18). At the level of organization and members moving through a round of everyday life, we discover only the most prosaic and conven- tional of generic structure. Thus, when looked at closely we find such diverse and superficially bizarre groups as Jehovah's Witnesses (Beck- ford 1975a), Self-Realization Fellowship and Vedanta (Damrell, 1977),

Meher Baba (Anthony and Robbins 1982), and Church of Magic (Lynch 1979) are virtually identical to each other in fundamental organization, which in turn differs little if at all from many ordinary churches.

Members of clinics and congregations alike tend to view their social arrangement as ideal in the limited sense of the best they can hope for themselves within the framework of the human world in "this age." However, among clinics, the sense of the ideal may often be somewhat stronger than this since the goals of most participants are so private and self-improvement-oriented. Congregational RMOs which, by definition, envision a vastly improved future human state, may on this account be prepared to settle for rather flawed organization that is ideal only in being the best one can expect in a corrupt world. It is an attitude of pessimistic idealism concerning organizational form.

In broader comparative perspective, congregations seem, moreover, to have many generic similarities to the organizational structures of many leisure worlds and their constituent (ego movement) organizations (Irwin 1977) and political movement organizations (e.g. O'Toole 1977).

COLLECTIVES

Clinic and congregation RMOs are fundamentally conservative in organization no matter how radical they may be in ideology. The three units we will consider next, in contrast, are fundamentally radical in organization, irrespective of their ideological content. With them, we cross the great divide between merely talking a good religious game and seriously acting on it (or even furtively playing at organizational innovation as part of arcane and deviant congregational ceremonies, as reported for example by Lynch [1979]).

That great divide is crossed by beginning to make systematic, organizational, and collective revisions in one or more of the four main aspects of everyday functioning: work, residence, eating, and family/personal support circles. At the extreme, all four are brought under a comprehensive plan and efforts are made to implement an ideal scheme of each one's respective functioning and mutual relations.

But short of this and of first relevance are the numerous ways in which only one or a few of these four may be revised. In one salient form, partial revision leaves ordinary work roles intact and confines revision to matters of residence, food, and family. Members retain a conventional relation to the economic order of the host society and elaborate their RMO only in those aspects making up the private sphere. Certain types of Father Divine's heavens seem organized in this fashion (Kephart 1982, ch. 4), as do most of what are labeled "urban communes" of the seventies (Kanter 1979; Erickson 1973). Insofar as there is sufficient information provided to make a judgment, most if not nearly all of the 120 communes studied by Zablocki (1980) seem confined to such matters. As a subtype, these may be referred to as *household collectives*.

Conversely, RMO organizing energy may focus on work with little or no attention paid to residence, eating, and family life. It is here that we most commonly come upon the term *collective,* a subtype properly termed "work" (e.g. Infield 1973; Case and Taylor 1979; Grant 1981). In more recent America the most common movement organizations of this sort have been political (or merely secular) rather than religious in ideology and, as a class, termed "alternative institutions." They "have been created in many service domains—e.g. free medical clinics, free schools, legal collectives, [and] research collectives. . . . Grass-roots cooperative businesses [form] . . . especially in fields with relatively low capitalization needs such as restaurants, bookstores, clothing manufacture and retail auto repair, housing construction, alternative energy installation, [and] newspapers" (Rothschild-Whitt 1979:510).

Members of collectives also cross a second kind of great divide, one relating to the optimism of their idealism about their organizational form. In household or work form, there is an effort to make human life function *organizationally* and *now* in ways that are qualitatively more positive, far-reaching, and demanding than clinics and congregations. Put figuratively, *the future is now* in a central way that it is not for clinics and congregations. In household collectives, for example, the "now future" is commonly the "achievement of community" (Zablocki 1980:7).

When placed in comparative SMO perspective, it appears that there are fewer RMO collectives as a class in recent decades relative to political or ego movement organizations (e.g. Zablocki 1980:207). More specifically, also in recent decades there seem to be many more EMO than RMO *household* collectives (Kanter 1979) and, as just mentioned, many more PMO than RMO work collectives (Rothschild-Whitt 1979; Case and Taylor 1979).

Such apparent variations in relative frequencies are perhaps understood as both cause and consequence of the profound differences among religious, political, and ego ideologies. Religious ideologies may both encourage and legitimize more corporate organizations than do political and ego ideologies (cf. Glock 1964).

Confining our comparisons to collectives, EMO ideologies, in focusing on the person, encourage and legitimize private sphere innovations, while political ideologies direct attention to the public sphere which then involves economic organization. Further, and irrespective of frequency, observers have been impressed that, ironically, RMO household collectives, once founded, seem more stable and long-lived than those founded on ego, political, or no articulate ideology (Kanter 1979: 32; Berger, Hackett, and Millar 1973; Kephart 1974:134).

CORPS

Interposed between the partial revisions of the life round represented by collectives and the full revisions we will call "colonies," is an elementary form often confused with both these neighbors but which is in fact radically different from them. Taking a cue from the military metaphor that their members sometimes employ, we refer to this unit as a "corps," meaning a highly mobile, tactical unit and a "body of persons having a common activity or occupation." Ancillary concepts such as *corps d'élite* (a "body of picked troops") and *corps bruder* ("a close comrade") appropriately connote the social psychology of participation often associated with RMO corps.

As in ordinary military corps, especially those at war, the full round of life activities is organized or at least controlled in the interest of furthering the mission at hand. One of the most dramatic and controversial of such RMO corps among modern religions has been the Mobile Fundraising Teams (MFTs) deployed by the Unification Church with spectacular financial results. In initial form, MFTs were "composed of two vans with five or six persons to a van." Using local movement residences as "crash pads" and also living out of the vans, such teams roamed regions raising money by various public solicitation devices (Bromley and Shupe 1979:120-24). Like military corps, "the usual distractions of domestic/sexual/recreational/occupational responsibilities and options" were managed by suppression and sublimation of energy rather than by positive provision (Bromley and Shupe 1979:122). Even though fragile, this is nonetheless one potent way to revise the entire life round. (For additional ethnographies of corps, see Festinger, Reicken, and Schachter 1956: Balch 1980.)

A critical feature differentiating the corps from other organizational forms is its definition as temporary. Revision of the life-round is made and justified as having a short-term and more or less emergency character. It is perhaps only on such a definition that people can be induced into and sustained through the obvious hardships entailed. Quite unlike other forms, the corps is *not* the "new world in embryo." Instead, it is a stage through which the believer must pass to get to the new and qualitatively better world.

A few entities are hybrids of corps and household collectives in that they view themselves as temporary organizations and establish household collectives, but these households are not viewed as budding, ideal forms of a new world. Like corps, they are expedient and not "prefigurative." The early American centers of the Unification Church were such hybrids (Lofland 1977). For these reasons it is especially inaccurate to describe them as "communes," as some observers have done.

COLONIES

Last and most broadly and elaborately organized is the colony, the RMO arrangement in which *ideal* revision of the total round of human life is undertaken. There is an integration of life and work that is optimistic rather than pessimistic, the best of all possible worlds rather than the best of all feasible worlds. Drawing from Kanter (1972, ch. 2), the idealism centers on such themes as human perfectibility, order, brotherhood, and unity of mind and body.

The preeminent place accorded this idealism legitimizes the totality of the organizational order undertaken. The features of this totality are captured nicely by Rosabeth Kanter (1972:241) in defining a category of relevant units in analyzing nineteenth-century "communes."

> Utopian communities in the past resembled total social orders in that for the most part their members never needed to go outside the boundaries of the community for the necessities of life; the organizational structure took into account practically all of the social roles members played, such as their economic, religious, sexual, familial, and political functions. . . . [The] . . . communities were often demarcated spatially, in terms of their functioning as a centrally planned and controlled residential unit, which explicitly organized living, sleeping, and eating patterns.

The work/income aspects of colonies divide in two main ways. Historically, "comprehensive villages" or economic "generalists" were the vogue in seeking to produce the entire range of goods the participants needed (Kanter 1973:223). Specialization of production processes and consumer items in the twentieth century has led more recent colonies to their own such specialization, as with, for example, the Bruderhof who manufacture a line of children's toys (Kanter 1973:223; Zablocki 1971).

We are aware that the term *commune* is sometimes employed in speaking of RMOs with collective and colony features. Its absence from our nomenclature therefore requires explanation. First, in the literature the term *commune* is applied indiscriminately to collectives, corps, and colonies, and we think it is imprecise to use the word for all three of these very different patterns. Thus, Zablocki's (1980) monumental and excellent study of communes is actually almost entirely about household collectives; Kanter's (1972) classic work on nineteenth-century utopian efforts deals almost totally with colonies. Second, taking all the relevant literature as a whole, a world count would likely show that the term *colony* is used as much or more than the term *commune* (Fogarty 1980). The latter is, indeed, of quite recent vogue. Third, historically, *participants* in this pattern used the term very frequently, as in, for example, Rugby Colony and dozens of others (Fogarty 1980:160). The Children of God furnish a contemporary example (Davis and Richardson 1976). Fourth, participant use is not accidental or capricious. Instead, it captures something central to the social psychology and vision of RMO colonies. As, by definition, the agents of a supernatural and cosmic scheme, RMO colonies are beachheads of perfection in the war to wrest the world from evil. RMO colonies are imperialism without apology, the proud (but humble) carriers and exemplars of a superior way of life, coming to save the heathens.

These, then, are the five main elementary forms of RMOs. In making this assertion, two qualifications are necessary. One, actual world arrangements are often not as crisp as we represent them here; a variety of complications arise when classifying cases, such as the existence of hybrids of the sort we mention above in connection with corps. Two, to depict main forms is also to leave out secondary ones. For example, in a fuller treatment we would need to discuss the distinctive phenomenon of the RMO *camp,* the short-term gathering of members and varying categories of outsiders for the purpose of intensive attention to and propagation of the RMO as well as sheer celebration of its ideology. Such camps are a quite old practice, as seen in the revival camp meetings of the last century (Lofland 1982b). Camps also play an important role in more contemporary settings. The First Annual World Celebration of the Rajneesh Bagwan group held in Oregon in 1982 was perhaps one of the most "media-flaked" camps of all time. The Divine Light Mission's "Millennium 1973" held at the Houston Astrodome was a major international media event. Its failure to attract as many participants as planned was also an important episode in the life of that organization, which went $600,000 in debt because of it. However, since that time the DLM has continued to use smaller festivals as a primary source of funds for the organization. These events require a sizable entrance fee of all followers who come to hear and see the Guru (Richardson 1983). The Unification Church has developed very novel camplike methods that are part of a sophisticated recruitment process (Lofland 1982b; Bromley and Shupe 1979). In comparative perspective, PMOs also field camps as an important even if temporary organizational form. Among these is the yearly one staged by the Western Socialist Organizing Committee and held close to the geographic locations of several other groups of interest to this analysis, in the Sierra Nevada foothills, and known to its aficionados as "commie camp."

What is the larger point of a breakdown such as we propose? Key purposes include: (1) a more sophisticated and articulate *recomposition* in order better to comprehend RMO structure and dynamics; (2) comparative analysis of the decomposed forms per se; and (3) comparisons of RMOs and EMOs and PMOs. We address the first two in the next section and discuss the third in our concluding remarks.

RECOMPOSING RMOs: DYNAMICS AND COMPARATIVE ANALYSIS

Scrutinized in elementary form perspective, a number of what we might think of as principles of RMO dynamics suggest themelves.

INHERENT INTERNAL PRESSURES TO CHANGE AND ELABORATE

Almost irrespective of which form is the initiating or first form, each, by the logic of its respective internal operation and development is under mounting pressure either to shift to another form or to elaborate additional ones. The nature and sources of this internally generated pressure to change is different for each of the several elementary forms, but the result is the same. Overarching, however, is the accretionary process of creating strata or pockets of members whose interests are not served by the form dominant at the outset.

The creation of such strata is especially well documented among clinic RMOs which, operating over several years, produce a pool of aficionados who want more—corporately—than the clinic offers and who tend to organize congregations and household collective within the containing and dominant clinic setting. This pressure is particularly strong where these "advanced clients" are otherwise socially marginal and lacking in significant social ties aside from the clinic. Thus, Christian Science was able to forestall significantly increased corporateness at the relevant juncture in its history because of the integration of its members in ordinary society (Wilson 1961, ch. 16), whereas Scientology, a similar clinic, was not (Wallis 1977). At the other end of the corporateness spectrum, the "decorporatizing" propensities of colonies over time, brought on by the development of families, are legendary and illustrated recently by the emergence of a congregational strata in Hare Krishna (Rochford 1982:181ff.) (among other new religions).

Added to this sheer internal logic of operation is the likelihood that at least some styles of leaders have intense and empire-building ambitions. Irrespective of the organizational form with which they begin, they seek to elaborate at every auspicious (or even inauspicious) turn (see Bainbridge and Stark [1979] on such entrepreneur aspects of RMO leadership).

FORM STABILITY REQUIRES SPECIAL EFFORT

Some few RMOs, however, do stabilize or nearly so in their initial form. We view this as an "unnatural" occurrence that requires scrutiny and explanation. For, quite special and self-conscious effort appears to be required to achieve it continuously (to borrow an ethnomethodological phrasing). In the case of Christian Science, for example, the founder apparently had to lay down very rigid rules mandating the clinic form forever and in minute detail *and* even grudgingly to make a concession and allow congregations, albeit she managed to stunt them and hold them rather close to clinic-like operation (Wilson 1961, ch. 16).

A few RMO ideologies may lend themselves to such initial form stability. Thus, Nelson (1969) argues that spiritualist beliefs in democratic access to the supernatural mitigates organizational pressures to forms more corporate than local and weak congregations. He therefore terms such groups "permanent cults." Conversely, some highly dualistic and authoritarian versions of Christianity have been argued to be especially supportive of colony organization (e.g. Zablocki 1971; Kephart 1974:134).

FORM ELABORATION FACILITATES SURVIVAL AND GROWTH

Initial form stability and, therefore, organizational simplicity seems a marginal and even "deviant" pattern, one that is very likely to increase the likelihood of RMO demise. For, to change form, which ordinarily means to *elaborate* forms, is to increase capacity to adapt to shifting environmental constraints and to exploit opportunities. Only the most sociohistorically fortunate of RMOs is likely able to survive forced form stability and simplicity.

RMO CORPORATENESS IS STIMULATED BY PERCEIVED REPRESSION

Within limits, the more benign and accepting the RMO host society, the less corporate most RMOs are likely to be and become. Conversely, and as illustrated by such varied RMOs as the Puritans of the Massachusetts Bay Colony, the Mormons of the Utah Salt Lake, and the People's Temple of the Guyana jungle, negative sanctions and rejections—repressions—spur colony formation among RMOs.

This relationship is well known and therefore of small interest except when conjoined with the also well known tendency of colonies to dissolve corporateness over time and, especially, to disband (Kanter 1972; Kephart 1974). The relative infrequency and special instability of colonies in all times and places may well have as much relation to environmental openness as to their own internal difficulties.

NONCONGREGATIONAL RMOs MOVE TOWARD CONGREGATION

In societies where there is a high degree of institutional differentiation (a separation of economics, politics, family, etc.) and a reasonable degree of freedom of association, initially noncongregational RMOs tend to drift toward the congregation as either an important component form or as even the dominant or lead organizational arrangement.

The context of institutional differentiation is key to understanding this drift. The congregation as a form is distinctive in providing the most religion a person can have without critically interfering with participation in the major aspects of the larger society. It is the way in which one can have the cake of the major institutions and still eat the reasonably rich cake of a going religion. In contrast, the forms on either side of the congregation (in Figure 7.1) either interfere with participation in the larger society (the collective, corps, and colony) or provide gruel rather than cake (the clinic).

As is well appreciated in sect-church theory, the upshot of this drift, continued over sufficient time, is the redefinition of the RMO into an RCO, a religious organization that no longer advocates or resists significant social change and does not envision alternative social arrangements. This principle restates in organizational terms the well-worn observation that cults and sects sometimes evolve into denominations or churches.

RMO HISTORIES ARE COMPLEX ELABORATIONS AND SEQUENCES OF ORGANIZATIONAL FORMS

The principles so far stated underrepresent the actual and enormous complexity of the organizational histories of a great many RMOs. One mandate of the organizational perspective on RMOs is the specification of what elemental forms are elaborated or disbanded at various periods in their histories.

Such a study is likely to discover that while dozens of profiles of organizational forms and sequences are *logically possible,* only a relative few are found in reality, and some occur much more frequently than others. Thus, it is logically possible for RMOs to transform themselves through four, five, or more major periods in which the primary or lead organizational form is changed. A few have displayed such long and transforming chains of change, but most do not. Or, a few RMOs elaborate *all* the forms; others a few; and some only one. And, taken over time, some RMOs create and disband many kinds of elementary forms.

The principle, then, is that RMOs histories may be conceived as complex elaborations of concatenations and sequences of elaborations of organizational forms. These varied histories likely form generic patterns that we have yet to recognize and therefore to take as topics requiring explanation.

Looking forward to such analysis, we want to provide an example of one not uncommon pattern of organizational elaboration and sequencing. The case is that of the Christian Communal Organization (CCO—a pseudonym) studied by James Richardson, Robert Simmonds, and Mary Steward (1978, 1979). Initiated by a street "youth pastor" in the clinic-like Jesus Movement milieu of Los Angeles in the late sixties, a number of the youthful members of that pastor's church congregation organized themselves into a household collective. The collective was somewhat parasitic the first year or so, living off contributions of nonmembers and members alike. Residence, food, and emotional support were provided; religious services and street witnessing were carried on; and members viewed their arrangement as a form of primitive communism modeled on New Testament references to the communal existence of the early Christians.

As membership increased, several such household collectives were formed in Southern California and were often "coed," with special provisions to keep unmarried members separate within the household. Membership grew further and single-sex household collectives were organized. In this initial period of multiplying household collectives, a leadership cadre made up of house heads emerged, a circle that included the pastor who had organized the original collective.

Out of a felt need to stabilize economic support, the leaders decided to establish a colony. To raise the necessary funds, members first began to work at low-skill labor of various kinds in the Los Angeles area and the income generated was turned over to CCO. The finances accumulated enabled most of them then to relocate as a colony in an agricultural area of a Northwestern state. Their major goal was to raise their own food and otherwise to become economically self-sufficient.

However, not all members were deployed to and lived at the new colony. Many were organized into corps, in this case special work crews geared to agricultural seasons and evangelism. Thus, teams were developed to work at fruit picking, tree planting, and other labor-intensive employment. Some of these teams had more than 100 members who traveled and lived together while doing their jobs. Later, after the relevant skills were developed, traveling construction teams were organized and gained income for CCO by means of remodeling and construction work. Other corps provided janitorial services in the local areas of the colony.

Their enterprises came to include a berry farm, cannery, goat dairy, sheep farm, and orchards. A special group managed the CCO center and coordinated what was rapidly becoming a nationwide organization with over 1,000 members. There was now also a child-care program, a new-member training school, and large kitchen staff at the main colony.

The use of corps combined with the colony in this RMO is especially significant. A corps, as we have indicated, is an expedient rather than ideal arrangement. In CCO, participants acknowledged that apple-picking teams traveling from state to state and other such deployments were not ideal ways of living. Instead, they were practical necessities to raise funds for other organizational activities that were more ideal and even more necessary, such as evangelism.

One class of corps in CCO was organized around evangelism and much money and energies were invested in training and supporting them, for they were the source of CCO's rapid growth. Such teams were trained in evangelism and job skills for several months at the colony and "field-tested" to see whether members got along before being sent to a new area to witness to itinerant youth. After deployment, these teams functioned as hybrids of corps and household collectives in that they were not self-supporting and defined their social arrangement as only practical and temporary. But if the team developed according to plan, they soon became self-supporting, and those that were most successful were encouraged to elaborate their organization into a satellite colony or at least to become self-sufficient as household and work collectives.

CCO also developed clinics, especially in the form of Bible schools for young children in neighborhoods where their evangelism teams cum work collectives/satellite colonies were located, and in counseling activities in prisons.

This elaborate conjunction of organizational forms turned out to be amazingly short-lived. In the late seventies, CCO began very rapidly to shift to congregations as its dominant form of organization. Members had begun earlier to marry one another, to have children, and then to establish single-family households. Partially as a result of this "domestication" process the activities of the main and satellite colonies and household collectives were curtailed, sold, or disbanded although the work team corps were mostly continued but shifted to more ordinary business form. In addition to CCO's growing affluence making this expensive change (organized by the leadership) possible, it was also plainly easier for members to live in collectives and colonies when most were single and young. But, as more and more married and had children, pressure developed to leave the various "communalisms" and live "normally."

The new congregational organization centered on what they called "fellowship halls," a name consciously selected in preference to the term *church,* even though these were places of worship as well as fellowship. In structure they quickly came to resemble ordinary churches in terms of full-time pastors, meeting times for services, and the like.

Finally, and even more striking, in the early eighties almost all these new congregations reaffiliated with the original church out of which CCO had been organized only some fifteen years before. A drastically reduced CCO retained the headquarters and a few other colonies. The headquarters colony now serves as a training center for like-minded religious groups in the region, and almost all CCO members live in ordinary congregational fashion.

Thus we see in CCO a fast-motion playing through of a not uncommon but more temporally drawn-out pattern in Western religious history. Over only about fifteen years it was, in dominant organizational form: milieu clinic, tenuous congregational circle, household collective, colony with complex corps, and finally, congregation with corps that were evolving into ordinary businesses. Such a classic pattern invites us to compare it with other concatenations and sequences of organizational forms and then to inquire into how and why they happen.

SECULAR CONGLOMERATES ENCOURAGE RMO CONGLOMERATES

One of the more spectacular developments of recent decades is large-scale formal organization of all kinds. The so-called multinational corporation is, indeed, only one of the most conspicuous of the big organizations burgeoning on almost all fronts.

Given the competitive advantages that seem to accrue to large-scale organizations, we ought to expect social movement organizations to take this fact into account and, if only in defense, strive to scale-up their organizational efforts in order better to "match the enemy."

As one variant of SMO, we ought to expect RMOs to respond in this fashion. In the same way we are seeing the growth of multinational economic conglomerates, we may well see the growth of RMO conglomerates, RMOs that deploy many and diverse organizational forms of the kind we have been discussing and utilize, moreover, modern techniques of organizational design and control, especially computerized collection and analysis of information. Some observers have suggested that the Unification Church may be a prototype of such RMO conglomerates of the future (Bromley and Shupe 1979).

IMPLICATIONS

We would like to conclude by drawing out some of the larger and longer-term implications of bringing an organizational perspective to the study of religious movements.

SIMPLICITY

The characteristics of RMO organizational forms we have singled out are studiously bald, stark, and even simple. We are quite aware that many lush and colorful variations are here pushed into the background. These include such aspects as styles of leadership, degree of centralization and arrogation of decision making, degree of equalitarianism and "all things in common," distinctiveness of garb and grooming, and a host of other matters.

The simplicity we propose involves the decision that some things are basic and fundamental and some are not. Those that are fundamental set central patterns that reverberate through other aspects of organization and social life; others do not. In this we subscribe to the recent admonitions of Stark and Bainbridge (1979:122) regarding "unideal types" in which one must decide what are defining *attributes* as distinct from empirically problematic *correlates*. All nondefining variations remain relevant, nonetheless; they are now simply treated as matters of empirical investigation or relative frequency among defined attribute classes.

ORGANIZATIONAL AND OTHER PERSPECTIVES

In the study of religious movements it is traditional to stress the content of meaning systems and how they function as solutions to life problems or as adaptive adjustments to stressful environments. Thus the ideology of the Baba movement may be interpreted as a response to "the radical disjunction between private and public realms in modern America" (Anthony and Robbins 1982: 229). Without per se faulting this level of analysis, we would enter the demur that much more than belief is involved; namely, there is also a *pattern of collective action*— a form or organization—offered. What are people *doing* in RMOs irrespective of vast differences in belief systems? A focus on organizational form is one way to get at "member doing" and thus approach questions of motivation for joining from a new direction. Or, with regard to such questions as why some RMOs are treated much more hostilely by their host societies than others, we might look to organization as much or more than to beliefs. In the words of James Beckford (1975b:83), "the cultural appropriateness of a religious movement may have as much to do with its form of organization as with its set of teachings. The medium is certainly an important part of the message."

Among the unfortunate consequences of failing to keep basic differences of organizational form in the forefront of analytic consciousness is the ease with which investigators come to make a great deal out of what are interesting but very minor differences among fundamentally similar RMOs. For example, recent analyses of new RMOs have focused on such variations as "relationship of followers to . . . the sacred power they revere" (devotees, disciples, or apprentices) (Bird 1979:336) and variations in "ways to handle the tension between [the] sacred [and] the profane" (the illumination, instrumental, and service-oriented cult) (Campbell 1978:233). Without at all questioning the validity of such foci or the veracity of the distinctions discerned, we are nonetheless disquieted by the insensitivity to corporate and collective life that is inadvertently sponsored. Indeed, when the groups said to illustrate such patterns are scrutinized organizationally, we find they consist largely of clinics and congregations (with a few collectives mixed in).

CULTS, SECTS, AND RMOs

In the same way that there can and should be reservations about neglecting the concept of communes, scholars can well wonder what has happened to the time-honored categories of cult and sect. There have been important efforts to expand ways of applying these and related concepts (e.g. Wallis 1974; Richardson 1979; Stark and Bainbridge 1979), but we now propose these ideas be treated in a more specific, lean, and organizational manner. Similar to the approach of Stark and Bainbridge (1979), for example, we have simplified the basic conceptions and have pushed forward to a more precise rendering than theirs by recognizing six rather than only "three degrees of organization" (Stark and Bainbridge 1979:126). Therefore, like the concept of commune, the received notions of cult and sect are too general and imprecise in their usual applications.

COMPARATIVE ANALYSIS OF SMOs

But there is a second and more important reason we deemphasize the labels "cult" and "sect." We are trying to look ahead to the full, comparative analysis of social movement organizations, to a breaking down of the accidental barriers of intellectual history that have resulted in distinct and isolated traditions of social movement analysis (Turner 1981; Zald and McCarthy 1979). Such comprehensive, comparative work requires that the existing separate traditions give up or at least mute their pet terms in the interest of a new interdenominationalism. *Cult* and *sect* are among such terms. While we are not adverse to allowing them to hover—especially as data, as words used by lay people—it is time to formulate a broader framework of terms that is also less pejorative.

In the spirit of such consolidation and cumulation, we conclude by adding to the comparative generalizations mentioned above and recalling some intriguing and established ones about classes of organizations to which RMOs need to be compared. Most basically and classically: Consistent repression of PMOs (or the discrediting of politics) is often a backdrop to waves of new (and more corporate) RMOs (Worsely 1957; Smelser 1963; Glock 1964). More abstractly, RMOs compete most successfully with PMOs in situations of great political turmoil combined with high repression. RMOs must also relate to the world of religious *conventional* organizations (RCOs). One generalization of special note is the tendency of RMOs to flourish where RCOs have most weakened by adopting "increasingly vague and inactive conceptions of the supernatural" (Stark and Bainbridge 1981:372; Wuthnow 1978). Another in this vein is that when RCOs encounter difficulties recruiting and retaining adherents in times of successful RMO development, RCOs will often exhibit a tendency to mimic and emulate successful RMOs in an effort to compete for membership by establishing "shadow" organizations. The establishment of many "Christian coffeehouses" and "religious rock groups" (which resemble corps) by mainline churches during the rise of the Jesus Movement are cases in point. And, as Stark and Bainbridge (1979:127) have stressed, EMO clinics have a persistent and remarkable tendency to change into several forms of RMO.

Set in the context of analyzing religious movement organizations, we hope that we have begun to show the likely fruitfulness of wrestling all types of social movements into a single arena of discourse in which new levels of insight can be achieved.

NOTE

We gratefully acknowledge and thank the following colleagues for providing us with valuable criticism of an earlier formulation of this analysis: Eileen Barker, Bruce Hackett, Gary Hamilton, Louis Kriesberg, Ron Lawson, Lyn H. Lofland, John McCarthy, Roger O'Toole, and several anonymous reviewers. Portions were presented at the Tenth World Congress of Sociology, Mexico City, August 16, 1982.

8

SOCIAL MOVEMENT LOCALS: MODAL MEMBER STRUCTURES (1984)

With Michael Jamison

Students of religious and political movement organizations (RMOs and PMOs, in the current jargon) are making notable progress in understanding a number of important questions about them, including why and how people join and leave them, how resources are aggregated or mobilized by them, and how environmental factors shape their founding, proliferation, and decline. (Recent surveys of the literature on these and other key questions include Jenkins [1983], Wood and Jackson [1982], and Zurcher and Snow [1981].)

MOVEMENT ORGANIZATIONS AS STRUCTURES

As important as these and many other matters are, they neglect a central fact about movement organizations (MOs), one that was (and is) keenly appreciated by Lenin and his associates (and successors) but now oddly neglected: MOs are holistic organizational structures. As a type of formal organization, MOs exhibit structure in the sense that members are consciously arranged into a differentiated and coordinated pattern of collective action for the pursuit of social, political, religious, or personal change of an oppositional character. As Lenin preached, these holistic structures differ markedly in their systemic constitution (cf. Curtis and Zurcher 1974).

Movement structures of any size—more than a few people organized in a single locale—exhibit complexity along three lines. One, the principles of organization observed differ between (a) a localized organization and (b) the organization that ties the local units together. Many MOs are at least two-tiered, meaning that in the perception of the participants and in fact there are two or more basic levels of organization. Two, the "lower" level units of translocal MOs do not always themselves exhibit the same principle of organization. The locals may be, instead, highly diverse. Three, the patterns of relations between the "locals" and the "centrals" vary enormously. These three levels may be taken as three interrelated but nonetheless distinct lines of inquiry. The rounded analysis of the structures of MOs necessarily entails specification of the forms appearing at all three levels.

Here we seek to improve our perception of movement organizations at the "lowest" (local) level. Called chapters, cells, units, clubs, circles, locals, or whatever, these are the ongoing and operating ends of movements. In focusing at this level, our search is informed by the interactionist admonition to move in close to salient features of ongoing social life (cf. Blumer 1969a, ch. 1). We want especially to be attuned to what people are *doing* in movement locals.

STRUCTURE AND THE MODAL MEMBER

This interactionist approach to MO locals as holistic structures prompts us to try to cut through the infinity of variations they display by asking these questions: (1) What is the modal member (MM) in the MO local for the most part *doing?* (2) What portion of her/his total daily and longer-term round of life is the MO organizing and absorbing?

Both words in the phrase *modal member* require elucidation. The term *modal* is used partly in the statistical sense of the numerically most frequent category of member. However, we hope for a use stronger than the barely most frequent. We look instead for the category of member that is conspicuously or even overwhelmingly most frequent and therefore dominant. The term *member* is much more elusive than the notion of modality and is likely the unseen and unidentified shoal on which many discussions of social movements have floundered. For purposes of advancing discussion and joining issues, we propose a restrictive definition of MO membership. Overall, to be counted as a member, a person should pass all these "tests."

1. People regarded in an MO as having authority to speak for it (and who occupy formal offices in it) must say the person is a member.
2. The member in question regards her/himself as a member.
3. The member in question is personally acquainted with at least two people who meet all these criteria for membership. By "personally acquainted" we mean that the at least two members and the member in question know one another's names, can identify one another on sight, and are able with reasonable interactional comfort to chat

about the matters of the day and/or of the movement for at least a few minutes.

4. The member in question regularly supplies labor or other bodily presence to the MO, either compensated or donated. By "regularly" we mean that at least the equivalent of one 8-hour a day a year is given.

5. The member in question donates the equivalent of at least one hour of her/his "wages" to the MO in a year.

A large portion of what many people in a variety of MOs (as well as scholars of them) would call "members," does not pass these tests (cf. Fichter 1954, ch. 2). The implications of this fact will become clear as we proceed.

MODAL MEMBER MO VARIATIONS

Focusing on the modal member directs our attention to organizational variations that are most salient to a person's round of the day, week, and longer. Considered quite common-sensically, anyone, not just MO members, needs (or at least typically wants) economic resources, sustenance, residence, socializing, familial relations of some kind, and a definition of what one, two, or all these matters are about. Movements vary markedly in the *degree* to which and the *ways* in which they involve themselves in—the degree and manner they *organize*—these six fundamental aspects of living.

Because these are the six inescapable and irreducible features of all living—features to which MOs are *most especially* sensitive—we adopt them as primary points to profile in drawing pictures of MO locals. Slightly expanded and articulated to draw out modal member aspects, these "points to profile" may be listed as a set of questions.

1. Is economic support provided the MM? If no, how is the MM supported? (a) Job in the dominant society? (b) Other? If yes, from where do the revenues come? (a) Work organized by the MO: manufacturing, retail, fee for services, combination, other? (b) Contributions from organizations (including grants)? (c) Contributions from individuals, including "checkbook memberships"? (d) Illegal seizures (robbery, etc.)?

2. What are sources of economic support for the organization, excluding MMs? (a) Member donations from their ordinary jobs? (b) Member donations from work for the MO, manufacturing, retail, fee for services, combination, other? (c) Donations from other organizations? (d) Donations from individuals? (e) Illegal seizures?

3. Is sustenance for the MMs organized by the local?

4. Is residence for MMs organized by the local?
5. Is socializing for MMs organized by the local?
6. Are familial relations organized by the local?
7. What is the dominant definition of the MO's and the local's situation?
8. What is the dominant definition of the MMs' main duties?
9. What are terms typically employed to describe the form of the local's organization or the place where the local operates?
10. What terms are typically used to describe MMs?

SIX STRUCTURES OF MO LOCALS

Comparative scrutiny of MO locals prompt us tentatively to isolate six main structural or modal member patterns of them. Because we want to focus in some detail on the first and most basic of the six, we list but do not discuss the entire set. Apropos of our modal member perspective, each organizational form of MO local has a corresponding *modal member role*. The forms of organization and modal membership are: (1) associations sustained by volunteers; (2) bureaus employing staffers; (3) troups deploying soldiers; (4) communes composed of householders; (5) collectives consisting of workers; (6) utopias populated by utopians.

The structures are themselves ordered, overall, in terms of their increasing *scope*, to borrow a term used to excellent effect by Amitai Etzioni (1961:160). Scope refers to "the number of activities in which . . . participants are jointly involved" in an organization. For our purposes, "number of activities" is operationally defined as the number of six basic aspects of living (work, sustenance, residence, socializing, family, cognitively orienting) the MO in some manner and to some degree organizes. This variation has otherwise been termed the "degree of corporateness," the degree to which "a set of persons actively promotes and participates in a shared, positively valued, and collective life" (Lofland and Richardson 1984; ch. 7 above).

By way of further orientation, the first three types of MO local may be distinguished in a general way from the last three in terms of, to use Paul Starr's (1979:246) labels, their tendency to be *adversary* versus *exemplary*.

> An adversary institution, such as a political party, a union, or a reform group, is primarily concerned with altering the prevailing social order. Oriented toward conflict, it may not exhibit in its own organization all the values that its supporters hope eventually to realize. Whereas the members of an exemplary organization typically regard its activities as intrinsically valuable, the participants in an adversary organization

regard its activities primarily as a means toward an end. For exemplary organization, the goals mainly involve changes in internal structure, while for adversary organization, the goals involve changes outside. The exemplary institution invests its energies in building up a model of what its organizers would like the world to be; the adversary organization expends its resources against the larger world of power.

We now restrict our focus quite markedly and consider the first pattern just listed above—associations sustained by volunteers.

ASSOCIATION LOCALS WITH VOLUNTEER MEMBERS

The MO structure of narrowest scope may be termed the "association," a term that is too general and therefore ambiguous, but for which there also seems to be no better alternative. In its favor, however, is the very rich tradition of studies on voluntary associations (Knoke and Prensky 1982) and it is the specific linking of the ideas of "association" and "volunteer" that we adopt here. Many MOs are simply a species of the larger class of voluntary associations in the sense that their modal members donate their labor to the MO and largely live a round of employment, sustenance, residence, and social and familial life apart from the association.

In these ways, the degree of MM subordination to and/or absorption in the MO is quite low. There is obviously also, however, variation in subordination/absorption *among* MO associations (to which we will come shortly), but even at the maximum of subordination and absorption, employment, sustenance, residence, and social and family relations remain basically outside the MO even if competitive pressures are intense.

The MO organizational apparatus subsists on member contributions of a regular, ad hoc, or "angeling" sort. Dominant definitions of the MO's situation and the MM's main duties vary widely but are constrained by the centrality of the fact that the MMs are volunteers. While varying among MOs in how much of what is asked, the key duty of a volunteer is to make some kind of regular contribution of bodily presence and/or productive work or other activity.

Volunteer dominance frames the basic strengths and weaknesses of association locals, but such structures still have considerable degrees of "formation freedom," as it were, even within this parameter. The degrees of freedom move along these lines: (1) the exact amount and frequency of "discretionary time" that volunteers contribute to the local; (2) the degree of psychic, political, or cosmic significance collectively imputed to the local itself and the duties of the MM; (3) the nature of the furtive or more aggressive claims the locals make on other aspects of the members' lives; (4) the frequency and intensity with which some pointed—even dangerous—collective action (directed either internally to the MO or externally) is undertaken.

Among association MO locals, these four variations tend to increase together and to exhibit stable but distinctively different *levels of normal mobilization* of locals. At least five such levels are identifiable and, more important, worth identifying.

STUDY GROUP LOCALS WITH STUDENT MEMBERS

The most fragile of MO locals consists of people meeting with some regularity, commonly in someone's home, for the purpose of discussing, studying, and otherwise *only* talking about social, religious, political, or personal change of an oppositional character. The religious version is perhaps most discussed in the scholarly literature where, taken as a class, this formation is referred to as a "cult" and taken collectively, the "cultic milieu" (Campbell 1972; Wallis 1977:13ff.) or "esoteric community." The modal member is commonly called a "seeker." Jorgensen (1982:398) profiles one pattern of such groups in these words:

> The *spiritual* segment of the [esoteric] community is composed primarily of religious and quasireligious collectivities. The word "spiritual" denotes an emphasis on the moral condition of humanity and matters pertinent to the supernatural. The people involved in these networks tend to be concerned with salvation, liberation, and enlightenment. They see their mission as service to human-kind and stand opposed to the perceived "materialism" of people in the psychic segment.
>
> Membership in spiritual groups is relatively small (5-50 per group), transitory, and lower-middle-class. Spiritual groups commonly are organized around a charismatic leader or several dynamic personalities. Female leadership is common. . . . The elements of toleration, flexibility, and change inherent in esoteric thought support deviation from and experimentation with socially dominant patterns of all sorts, from sexuality and sex roles to medical practice, psychic science, and cosmic relations. The continued existence of spiritual groups is dependent on regular contributions from members and visitors (seekers).

In the political realm, many of the groups that have become famous under the rubric "consciousness raising" exhibit essentially the same pattern. Their incidence and importance vary from social movement to social movement. They do not occur in some movements but seem to constitute quite a sizable portion of others. Thus, Jo Freeman's (1975, ch. 4) account of the women's liberation movement gives the impression that what she calls "the small groups"—consciousness-raising groups—were a major portion of that movement at its peak.

In the ego-movement (EMO) realm (MOs focused on psychic rather than social or supernatural sources of human suffering and remedy for it), study groups, under such names as "encounter groups" and "sensitivity-training groups," appear to have been *the* dominant type of MO local of the human potential movement (Back 1978).

As this lowest level of MO "voluntary association" local, study groups of the cultic variety need themselves be distinguished from what Stark and Bainbridge (1979:126) have called "audience cults" that include people gathering to hear a lecture but consists modally of individual "consumer activity," such as reading certain magazines. Lecture audiences and lone consumption may form the "structure of preferences" backdrop out of which study groups are organized, but they are not the same as them. Nor are study groups to be confused with Stark and Bainbridge's "second degree of organization," client cults. These are staff organizations and offer services for a fee to clients. Strictly speaking, client cults are not voluntary associations. Instead, they are bureaus (our second main type listed above) with staffs that sell something in the way that retail stores cater to customers. In the same sense that customers are not members of the stores at which they shop, clients are not members of the clinics from which they purchase services.

Study groups are fluid MO locals and for this reason they are frequent recruiting grounds for agents of more highly mobilized MOs (see Wallis [1977] on Scientology and Lofland [1977, p. 2] on a millenarian sect recruiting in cultic milieu study groups). Highly mobilized MOs sometimes organize *front* study groups to attract students/ seekers in the hope of subsequently leading them into quite another MO local, one whose existence is initially kept secret (Lofland 1977, ch. 7, Epilogue).

To facilitate further analysis of study groups, other terms employed for them may be rostered so that their meanings can be teased out in later treatments. These include the notion of "circle" and the member label "associate."

FELLOWSHIP LOCALS WITH ADHERENT MEMBERS

For want of more precise terms, we may refer to the next, more organized, level of MO local as the fellowship and their members as adherents. While it is important in the larger perspective of social movement analysis to isolate study groups as a level of organization (as consciousness-raising groups in the women's liberation movement forcefully illustrates), study groups lack the ideological crystallization and capacity for collective action that we find in the fellowship (and at higher levels). Nonetheless, fellowships are by definition relatively demobilized most of the time, even though capable of broad-scope and intensive bursts of collective action.

Sensitized by the resource mobilization proposition that "new organization rises out of old organization" in several ways, we need to observe that one key variety of fellowship is intimately intertwined with preexisting and movement-separate human association and sometimes represents only a renaming of a preexisting structure as an MO local. This is especially reported for the fellowship locals called "affinity groups" in the antinuclear movement. Often members of such groups have an interest and involvement in common beyond, and at least technically independent of, their antinuclear sentiments and activities. These include job location, dietary or sexual preference, and ideological accord (Widmer 1979:12; Barkan 1979). However, their relation to one another *as* an affinity group is distinct in members' minds. Most of the time, such affinity group locals are in repose, meaning that they meet with some regularity and look forward to the setting of a date and place for the next protest event or plan for participation in an event whose date and place has been settled. As such, the formal scope of affinity group activity is quite narrow despite the fact that it expands radically and organizes (or suspends) all the fundamental aspects of living during a protest occupation.

Spotty evidence suggests that similarly intertwined structures may occur in other MO locals. We have in mind, especially, local chapters of the antiabortion movement which appear to have the same intertwined relation to independently existing groups within local churches that affinity groups have to independently existing occupational and other associations (McCarthy [1982:4] speaks of these as "thick infrastructures" as opposed to "thin infrastructures" or "infrastructure deficits").

Slightly less intertwined with pre- and independently existing local organization are the basic building blocks of the "Alinsky-style" or community organization, the *block club*. Block clubs are a major, if not *the* major, component of community, umbrella organizations and have much the same relation to their local umbrella organization as many MO chapters in local areas have to their MO "nationals" or "centrals." Robert Bailey (1974:54-55) provides this profile of modal member involvement in the block clubs of Chicago's Organization for a Better Austin:

Residents often form clubs as a defense mechanism to prevent deterioration of the neighborhood. The block clubs serve as a vehicle through
which neighbors can exert pressure on public officials. Club members
frequently visit the alderman to demand improved garbage pickup or
street maintenance. They ask school officials to stop truant children from
loitering in the streets. The police are requested to expedite the removal
of abandoned vehicles, or the dog-catcher may be called. Individually,
these activities appear trivial; cumulatively, they have a serious impact
on the quality of neighborhood life. Failing to cope with such problems
could cause the community to begin to deteriorate into a slum.

Through block clubs, neighborhood opinion is mobilized for the purpose
of social control. Block club members make known to other residents
their disapproval of excessive noise. Members of one South Austin block
club visited another resident because his son was shooting a gun from the
porch late at night. Other clubs have complained to neighbors about
using the street as a place to repair cars.

Reformist in ideology but protest-prone, members of block clubs focus
on correcting problems of their neighborhood, giving themselves such
modest names as "Quincy Housing Committee," and "Geneva Towers
Tenants Association."

One especially prevalent and potent version of the block club as a
generic structure is comprised of tenants who live in a single building.
In fact, such local MOs may well be *the* statistically more common and
proliferating form of MO local in the contemporary United States. Also
referred to as "building organizations" and "tenant unions" (Miller
1979), they are especially notable in Northeastern American cities,
New York in particular (Lawson 1980).

And, showing the least overlap with extra-MO organization are
fellowship locals of RMO and EMO ideology that are devoted in a
narrow-scope way to cosmic or consciousness manipulation, such as
found in the Meher Baba movement: "Local Baba groups are more or
less autonomous. Most of them are fairly egalitarian and 'anti-struc-
tural' [and] . . . most . . . meet one or two times a week to read and
discuss Baba's writings, see movies of Baba, or listen to talks by older
or better-known Baba Lovers" (Anthony 1978:5).

To put the case on the analytic agenda we want at this point to
provide Inge Bell's (1968:90-91) description of the workings of a
Congress of Racial Equality chapter during the heyday of the civil
rights movement. The MO local she describes seems to us rather more
than a fellowship but considerably less than a congregation, sect, or
cell, forms with which we will deal momentarily. But, also, it does not
seem distinct enough to merit identifying as a separate type.

Its internal structure [Southern City CORE] was a cross between a political organization and a college friendship clique or neighborhood gang. On the formal side, there were five elected officers, an executive committee, and several operating committees. There were also regular weekly membership meetings, where all the members were entitled to discuss and vote on the group's business. The attendance at these meetings usually numbered around twenty people. However, the real work and day-to-day decision making was carried on by the active nucleus of officers plus a few other active members, all close personal friends who saw each other almost daily. Most active members reported that all their closest friends were in CORE, and although personal friendship was an important factor in binding the group together, it was the CORE bond, rather than any other common interest, that undergirded the relationships and loyalties of the group.

When CORE members got together, CORE business—past, present, and future—was virtually the only topic of conversation. CORE activities were so time consuming that most of the purely social activities occurred as by-products of CORE business: coffee after meetings, supper to discuss the newsletter, a party after a direct action project, or dropping over to discuss an impending action.

The active nucleus was a true primary group. Most members were emotionally "available" for such close ties because they were becoming independent of their parental households but had not yet established families of their own. More important, perhaps, the nature of direct action invariably bound the participants in close emotional ties. In the words of one CORE member: "We feel we are one family. We have the closeness of a family. We ran from the same things together. We've been implicated in the same things—we're constantly in touch with each other."

In terms of time spent in the group, then, to its active members CORE was truly a total-involvement organization. All those I queried said that they spent at least ten or fifteen hours a week on CORE activities. Some said that they spent almost every hour of their nonworking or nonstudying time in CORE. This is probably no exaggeration if we include the sociability interwoven with CORE activities.

Beyond mere time commitment, it appeared that under the pressure of Southern conditions CORE usually became an overriding obsession with its members. One student who quit CORE to catch up on his graduate work reported: "It wasn't so much the time it took as the emotional involvement. I just couldn't stop thinking about it and start thinking about something else. We were having so much trouble organizing the community effectively that I would find myself always thinking of evolving strategy."

We want also to roster the hypothesis that many ordinary worker union locals in their earliest stages display the fellowship pattern.

As we did with study groups, other sensitizing labels relevant to fellowships may be listed. For the form of organization: club, committee, center, group, circle of friends. For modal members: followers, companions, helpers.

CONGREGATIONAL LOCALS WITH PARISHIONER MEMBERS

Study groups and fellowships maintain a relatively narrow and sharp focus on the matters of social and personal change at much discussed issue and desire. Even well within the parameters set by the dominance of volunteers as members, however, such a narrow and sharp focus can be considerably broadened and softened. This broadening and softening moves along several lines. To the degree that a local moves along these lines, we rise to a mobilization level that may be labeled *congregational* and in which the modal member is a *parishioner* (cf. Fichter 1954).

1. The sheer *number* of collective MO activities can be increased. Study groups and fellowships are, in their ordinary operation, not especially demanding of the time and other resources of the MMs. For study groups, the time demand may be simply one night a week or so and for fellowships the demand may be a couple of nights a week and a day or so on the weekends each month. But much more than this is available from typical volunteers: seven nights a week, two days on weekends, and other times off from employment. The modal member of congregations furnishes times moving further toward this maximum than in study groups and fellowships.
2. As time furnished increases, the diversity or variety of organization and activities staged can and does broaden. In study groups and fellowships, specific topics of personal and social change dominate occasions of collective talk and action. Occasions of this sort continue in congregations, but the social forms diversify and specialize. First, and sometimes peculiar to the RMOs, are *worship services*. Second, member organization and occasions of member assembly specialize along family status, sex, and age lines. Family organization and occasions are differentiated, in particular, from child and youth organization and occasions. Of signal importance, *youth wings* are organized. Third, a distinction between more formal and instrumental as opposed to social gatherings develops. Fourth, various and *regular* forms of *day-tripping* and other travel occur. In addition to collective travel that is overtly and "merely" social, trips to demonstrations, conferences, and conventions are of instrumental importance.
3. In the well-developed congregation, there is at least one MO owned (or rented) place of assembly called a center, headquarters, house, temple, church, fellowship hall, etc. The several sorts of activities

outlined just above take place in and around it, are organized out of it, and depart from it.

4. Such organizationally polymorphic and mobilized MO locals with less sharply and tightly focused ideologies define their situation as requiring long-term action on a broad range of fronts. In some PMOs this may be captured in the recently fashionable phrase "the long march through the institutions." Coalitions with "all progressive forces" may be frequently advocated.

5. The central implications for the duties of the MM are also long-term, even lifetime. Membership is expected to be steady and loyal.

As indicated at the outset, many movement organizations consist of a variety of local forms and cannot accurately be characterized as exhibiting a single type of local. This point is especially salient with regard to congregations, which commonly coexist in a single MO with a number of other types of locals. We find this, for example, in Meher Baba (Anthony 1978), Vedanta (Damrell 1977), and the Unification Church (Bromley and Shupe 1979). In all these examples, however, congregations are conspicuous.

We may tentatively venture the generalization that congregations are more frequent among RMOs than among PMOs and EMOs, particularly among RMOs of a monistic ideology (Anthony and Robbins 1982). At least, available accounts of RMOs feature congregations more often than do accounts of PMOs and EMOs. It is this imbalance that fosters our use of the notion of congregation rather than such an alternative as "party." There are, nonetheless, PMO and EMO locals of the congregational variety. Among them, cooperative grocery stores that require all members to perform a minimum number of hours of work per month, and not to be mere shareholders, are salient instances.

Congregational locals, especially of the RMO variety, exhibit a type of gathering and group feeling to which we must draw particular attention. In the eyes of MMs, all MO activities are not equal in importance. Especially in RMOs, a selected few are thought to draw the member closer to the cosmic or supernatural (or its equivalent in the EMOs and PMOs). These are typically termed "worship services" and frequently feature forms of prayer.

Worship services and prayer are associated, further, with an emotional tenor that is difficult to capture but gotten hold of in part with such terms as "communal solidarity" and "emotional bonding" (Lynch 1979:29). It is an emotional context in which role names for modal members, such as "brother" and "sister" are encountered.

Having sketched fellowships and congregations, we need now to recognize that any number of MO locals hover uncertainly and waveringly between the levels of stable and ongoing mobilization we have conceptually frozen with these two labels. This seems especially the case for such PMOs as the John Birch Society, the Campaign for Economic Democracy, and a variety of women's and gay-political MO locals. Often they lack a central, MO-owned or -controlled place, but nonetheless sustain an impressive array of activities out of an ad hoc concatenation of member homes, local college campus facilities, and church-owned buildings and centers.

SECT LOCALS WITH SECTARIAN MEMBERS

Up one level from the congregation is the famous (or infamous?) phenomenon of the sect, the perhaps best recognized and most studied of the MO voluntary associations. Its stable level of modal member mobilization, at the sheerly physical level, is relatively the same as the congregation. The frequency of collective activity may be somewhat greater and the variety of it may be a bit wider, but these differences are not as pronounced as they are between study groups and fellowships, on the one hand, and congregations on the other. Roger O'Toole (1977:29-30) thus describes a PMO sect, the League for Socialist Action (LSA), in this way:

> LSA members are tempted rather than compelled to spend the whole of their lives within the sect. When they are not proselytizing, demonstrating, or improving themselves intellectually and politically at internal meetings, Vanguard Forums or study classes, they have available not only informal companionship during day-to-day activities but also a full and varied social life. LSA members do not live by politics alone, but participate in a continuous program of films, dances, parties, poetry-readings, theatricals, visits, and summer camps. With such opportunities for recreation, amusement and companionship, strong affective relationships are likely to develop among sect members. Wherever possible, the LSA tries to infuse its social activities with symbolic and practical content. Some work activities, such as leafletting, preparation of flags and placards for demonstrations, and poster-handing, are incorporated into parties with food, dancing and entertainment. Other recreational activities are given a symbolic celebratory theme (for example, Lenin's birthday or the anniversary of the Tet offensive) and traditional celebrations such as Halloween are given a lighthearted political slant. Other activities combine recreation and political education; many of the films shown and plays visited by members as a group have political themes. An LSA member commented: "In the League you soak in the political atmosphere. You take part in *intense* political discussion *all* the time, formal and informal."

Even though frequency and diversity of collective action may well distinguish congregations from sects, students of the latter have been as much or more impressed, instead, with the distinctiveness of the way in which sect MOs define their situation. Among RMO sects, such cognitive distinctiveness is pin-pointed with phrases like "self-conception [as an] . . . elect, a gathered remnant, possessing special enlightenment" (Wilson 1959:4) and "epistemological authoritarianism" in which a claim to "unique and privileged access to truth or salvation" is laid (Wallis 1977:17). While congregations see themselves as one among many legitimate MOs ("pluralistically legitimate"), sects see themselves as "uniquely legitimate" (Wallis 1977:13).

As formulated by Roy Wallis (1977:16), this central and differentiating feature of sect MOs and their MMs has three correlative features: exclusiveness of membership, totalitarianism of MO organization and outlook, and "hostility towards, or separation from, the state or society."

The third correlative feature—hostility to outsiders—is especially salient as an empirical (if not logical) matter because of its relation to the dualistic belief system of the sect. All reality is radically divided by a hidden but historically central conflict between good and evil, most commonly conceptualized more specifically as the battle between God and Satan or Capitalism and Communism. (Ordinarily a sect espouses only one of these two couplets and denigrates the reality of the other; only occasionally does one—such as the Unification Church—venture to incorporate both into a single grand dualism!) Reality thus conceived, sectarians are, in the felicitous phrase of Daniel Bell (1952:22), locked in "mimetic combat on the plains of destiny" (quoted in O'Toole 1977:5). Dualism is heady—even intoxicating—stuff. Declared one young Unification Church member: "Can you imagine just to know the truth? To know exactly why you're here? To know the purpose of everything?" (Skonovd 1981:iv).

Ideological dualism forms (in part) the cognitive cocoon energizing the high and stable level of mobilization seen in sects (and higher levels not discussed in this chapter). With it, *unbounded* demands are legitimized. As Lenin (1970:14) put it in the passage made famous by Benjamin Gitlow (1965): "We must train men and women who will devote to the revolution, not merely their spare evenings, but the whole of their lives." Relative to the entire spectrum of MOs, "the whole of their lives" is an exaggeration for sects, of course, but the phrase does capture the social psychology of the sectarian commitment, if not its behavioral scope.

Nonetheless, the sect does push at the boundaries of the possibilities for mobilization among MOs whose modal members are volunteers. As the quote from O'Toole, above, illustrates, socializing and familizing are affected by this high level of MM mobilization. If these cannot be absorbed or suppressed, competition and conflict are likely consequences.

One clue to the larger social reception of the sectarians as a type of modal member and even personal style is the relative richness of the terms available for making reference to them. In addition to the famous phrase "the true believer" (Hoffer 1951), we encounter: agitator, apostle, comrade, devotee, disciple, extremist, fanatic, radical, vanguardist, zealot.

CELL LOCALS WITH CONSPIRATOR MEMBERS

The several forms of MO locals we have described are carried on in a relatively public way and experience only low-level or sporadic harassment or repression—or merely a living fear of it. Actual, imagined, or anticipated repression is a backdrop to secret MO locals that involve a high level of mobilization (especially *emotional* mobilization), but, because of the need for secrecy, are organized around a narrower range of activities than found in congregational and sect MOs.

Also for reasons of secrecy, such *cell* MO locals are commonly quite small, usually consisting of no more than twelve members and often less (Gross 1974:92ff.). Among RMOs, the early Christians are reported to have used a cell structure, as have covens of witches and Satanic practitioners. Among EMOs, circles devoted to various unconventional sexual practices such as the early "swingers" among married couples, have been cell-oriented.

The most famous of cell MOs occur among PMOs. *Fifth columns* are a version in which underground groups carry on subversion to help foreign invading armies. Elements of terrorist groups in contemporary European countries are so organized. Indeed, one mid-1980s operation in West Germany is even called the Revolutionary Cells or simply Cells, and consists of "small gangs of two to five people." Tellingly, they are also called "spare-time terrorists" because, aside from bombings, kidnappings, and bank robberies, they "lead otherwise normal lives" (Staudinger 1982).

But the most conspicuous and frequent use of cells in the current world is as units which clandestinely support guerrilla armies and revolution in developing nations. Such armies consist of full-time soldiers in platoon formations, supported by villages of otherwise based secret citizen cells. For example, Rolando Morán (1982), commander-in-chief of Guatemala's Guerrilla Army of the Poor, describes such cells, composited into "mass organization," in that country.

> The revolutionary mass organization is a clandestine organization with its own structure and without relation to the legal and open entities. . . . The leadership . . . is secret. [One part of the organization forms secret committees in communities] . . . developing educational work until they win over a majority of the population and have them join our work. . . . In some communities . . . self-defense groups are organized by local clandestine committees. . . . They watch over the security of the community, of the local committees, of the leaders and the families of the guerrillas.

It is likely true that situations of repression are most often associated with cell MO locals that either engage in violence or are systematically supporting people who are carrying out violence. For better or worse, there are some heroic exceptions. The banished Polish union Solidarity of the early 1980s has been the most notable recent instance, a once congregational-style MO forced to become a cell MO that nonetheless eschewed violence.

PURPOSES AND DIRECTIONS

We conclude by reiterating and elaborating the purposes of our efforts and pointing out some directions in which we think it is reasonable to proceed.

VOCABULARY AND PERCEPTION

Foremost, we have tried to depict in generic, structural perspective the contours of the holistic activities in which movement members are modally engaged. In the vocabulary of an optical metaphor, we are striving to increase the resolution of the lens we train on movements; specifically, the lens we aim at movement organization locals. Or, in an interactionist vocabulary, we aim to elucidate for movement locals that elusive but real thing that Erving Goffman (1961:x) has termed "the tissue and fabric of . . . life."

Put less metaphorically and interactionally, an adequate vocabulary or nomenclature is required to perceive and subsequently to analyze anything. No such nomenclature yet exists for the analysis of MOs as structures—local or otherwise—and our task here has been that of forging one from diverse streams of research and theory.

LABELS AND REALITY

So directed, we want also to stress that we are not attached to any of the labels we have employed. We even dislike a number of them, but have been forced to their use by the even lesser aptness of alternatives.

It is the *empirical pattern,* instead, to which we want to draw attention, and *not* the specific labels. We urge readers, therefore, to look *beyond* captions they may not like and *to* what is being described. We fear there is too strong a tendency for people to reject a reality simply because they object to or reject a particular word, a case of the famous baby and its bathwater. Both analytic progress and safe, clean babies are achieved by an unwavering recognition of the difference between the two.

ANALYTIC DIRECTIONS

Beyond this general mandate, why should we, specifically in the case of social movement organizations, seek to improve our perception? Several kinds of answers may be suggested. First, taking into explicit account the character of the local to which people belong sharpens our ability to ask and answer the traditional kinds of questions we mentioned at the outset. We have in mind, especially, the much asked and answered question of affiliation: How and why do people become involved in social movements? Ordinarily, MOs are treated as more or less interchangeable or identical for purposes of answering this question. Explanatory attention focuses, instead, on how people themselves, their situations, and particular recruitment efforts differ. (For recent and comprehensive reviews of this literature, see Zurcher and Snow [1981]; Snow, Zurcher, and Eckland-Olson [1980]; Lofland and Skonovd [1981]). Our suggestion is that variation in what is being offered—in the modal member sense—must also be factored into answers to questions of affiliation. The same point applies to other of the puzzles prominent in social movement analysis. To take a second example, conceptions of "resource mobilization" are vague on the matter of exactly what constitutes what kind of "mobilization" (cf. Zald and McCarthy 1979). The kind of organizational concern we broach permits a much more precise operationalization of resource mobilization as a dependent variable.

Second, a conception of an array of differentially mobilized MO locals invites us to perform comparative analysis of the dynamics of these units per se. Each has distinctive strengths and weaknesses qua system and different propensities to stability and change, be such changes transformations or elaborations. For example (and as elaborated in chapter 7), there is a tendency for many types of MO locals to move toward the congregational form, up from lower levels of stable mobilization, or down from higher levels. This generalization is founded on the broader proposition that all MO locals are inherently unstable in the sense that there are processes both distinctive and internal to each form that create pressures to change or elaborate forms (see ch. 7; Lofland and Richardson 1984).

Third and from an activist perspective, organizers of movements—be they citizen-amateurs or professionals—can direct their energies more effectively if they have clear conceptions of what sort of modal member pattern(s) they are striving to create. Further, refined conceptions of the possible forms of MO locals allow us to consider more clearly the contexts or circumstances that both retard or facilitate the formation and maintenance of each form. Such analysis has both a scholarly and an activist significance. Scholars seek to answer this question as part of the more general effort to depict and explain careers of social movements. And, information on conditions favorable or unfavorable to given forms of MO locals assists activists in deciding what form of MO local to promote. Some may be patently impossible or at least extraordinarily difficult to create in view of conditions that scholars have identified. They may therefore be avoided, and vice versa.

We want to close by indicating that we do not regard our formulation of modal members as an approach, the six "levels" of MO locals, or the five levels of voluntary association MOs as definitive. They are animated by the matters of purpose and direction just discussed, but there may well be better ways of pursuing these purposes and directions.

NOTE

We are grateful to Lyn H. Lofland, Pam Oliver, and several anonymous reviewers for many helpful suggestions on an earlier formulation of this report. An abbreviated version was presented at the annual meetings of the American Sociological Association, Detroit, Michigan, August 30, 1983.

9

SOCIAL MOVEMENT CULTURE (1985)

Students of social movements are accustomed to distinguish among them in terms of the radicalness of their goals, the features of their leadership, the corporateness of their organization, the inclusiveness/exclusiveness of their membership, and in myriad other useful terms. As important as such traditionally identified variations are, singly and in complex combinations, they leave me groping for a way to grasp qualities evoked by such old-fashioned terms as spirit, atmosphere, character, or ambience. At least conceptually independent (and perhaps empirically independent) of the traditional movement variations, are variations in the emotional tenor, presence, affective climate, or demeanor enacted and communicated by movement organizations (MOs).

This nebulous quality varies across MOs in likewise nebulous ways such as rich versus impoverished, elevating versus constricting, compassionate versus spiteful, generous versus hard-eyed, humorous versus humorless, complex versus simple, flexible versus rigid. Aware of the hazards of doing so, I want to label this elusive feature of social movements *culture*, the package of collective ways of approved and fostered member emotions, beliefs, and actions.

My purpose is to explore how MOs differ in the character and complexity of the culture they create, elaborate, and sustain. Contemplating MOs in comparative perspective, I have been struck with how a few seem to create vibrant, multihued, up-beat, complex, outward-extending cultural lives that imbue their members with liveliness and vibrancy. Others, by contrast, display stunted, simple, and emotionally narrowing cultures. And again, although variation in culture may be correlated with variations in substantive ideology, form of organization, and the like, cultural variation is not the same as these other variations.

I propose to employ the strategy of "key-case comparison" in pursuing this puzzling topic of culture and its variations. I will focus on a specific MO that appears to furnish some instructive contrasts when set in comparative perspective. This strategy is to be distinguished from "full-array comparison" where all the relevant types, or at least instances of all the key types of cases, are systematically compared point for point. The key case I will use is that of the Unification Church (UC).

Before MO cultures can be compared, I need first to justify the very notion that MOs have culture. I begin with Gary Fine's (1979:733) observation that "the concept of culture generally has not proven useful as a significant variable in sociology because of difficulties associated with specifying its content and the population serving as its referent. One speaks glibly of the culture of a particular group with the expectation that one's audience will have a common-sense understanding of what is meant." We have not yet learned how to treat culture as something other than "an amorphous, indescribable mist which swirls around society members" (Fine 1979:733).

Following Fine, one way to advance analysis is through focusing on culture as something that specified interacting units sustain and that is to some extent unique to each interacting unit. Fine (1979:734) strives to capture such uniqueness with the term *idioculture*, the "system of knowledge, beliefs, behaviors, and customs shared by members of an interacting group to which members can refer and employ as the basis of further interaction." In this coinage and focus Fine (1979:736) is resurrecting and himself following an older but lapsed tradition in which analysts spoke of "group culture," "variant culture," "small-group culture," and even "laboratory microculture." Such notions and that of idioculture sponsor the "development of a cultural anthropology of small groups" by means of "microethnology."

If it makes sense to speak of smaller units of social organization as possessing cultures, including therefore formal organizations in general and MOs in particular, we can then conceive the possibility that MO culture is a variable. Some microsocial units develop cultures that are in a variety of analytic and not just substantive ways different from others. Such a comparison requires a scheme in terms of which to compare. My effort here is to sketch such a scheme. I will do so in terms of three master clusters of culture variation: elaboration, expressiveness, and compassion.

CULTURAL ELABORATION

Heuristically, we may envision what we would expect to find in a macrosocial unit with the most quantitatively elaborate of cultures. In rudimentary Guttman fashion, the classes of these things may be

ordered from those found in the least elaborate microunit (a specification of "minimum culture"), moving through and up to the least
empirically frequent items found in the empirically less frequent but
most elaborate MO cultures.

DISTINCTIVE COGNITIVE ORIENTATION

Even the simplest microculture has some sort of cognitive categories
by means of which it is set off from other social units, if only its very
name. Beyond that are distinctive goals, approved behavior (norms),
and named roles. Up from these are what get labeled ideology, theory,
analysis, theology, ontology, science, and the like.

MO cultures vary in terms of the sheer number and systematic
interrelation of the cognitive categories making up what we commonly
label "ideology." Despite the fact that classic writers on social movements imply otherwise, most MOs possess quite simple ideological
systems, so rudimentary that the very word *system* is too grandiose. I
think, in particular, of the simplicity of the cognitive screens of the
classic MOs making up much of the civil rights (e.g. Bell 1968),
community protest (e.g. Bailey 1974), commune (e.g. Zablocki 1980),
and many other movements. Only MOs of the ultra-Left, among
political movements, begin to rival our key case, the Unification
Church, in the complexity and range of cognitive categories. In some
ways Blumer (1969b:110) led us astray in his famous formulation of the
"twofold character" of movement ideology, the "erudite and scholarly" versus the popular. The former "is developed by the intellectuals
of the movement [and] . . . is likely to consist of elaborate treatises of
an abstract and highly logical character." In actuality, almost no MOs
generate such a twofold ideology, as do very few movements. It is the
exception rather than the rule, which does not exclude the UC which I
think we must mark down as perhaps the most assiduous of ideological
elaborators among contemporary MOs. In large numbers of publications it undertakes, for example, to apply its principles to ever-new
topics and to elaborate and reformulate its thought on topics it has
already addressed.

COGNITIVE ELABORATORS

One important vehicle for the elaboration of cognition is a strata of
intellectuals charged with exactly that job. Again almost singularly
among MOs (and most especially among those of comparable age and
membership size), the UC has created a large (proportionate to its total
membership) intellectual class whose job is culture creation of a "high
culture" character in that it, to use the words of Blumer (1969b:110),

"seeks to gain for its tenets a respectable and defensible position in [the] world of higher learning and higher intellectual values." The cognitive systems of dominant elites are studied for the purpose of taking account of their claims, formulating UC principles in response to them, and developing UC arguments that can counter cultural elites. All of this has the broader aim of creating an ideology that intellectual and other elites of mainstream society must take seriously. No other current MO barely begins to compete with the UC in such terms. Democratic socialist intellectual Stanley Aronowitz (1983b:18-20) has lamented that the MOs of the American Left not only fail to develop effective theory counter to the "ideological hegemony enjoyed by instrumentalist and positivist paradigms in American intellectual life," but also have a "profound contempt for and fear of theoretical work" associated with a fear of "elitism."

CULTURAL DRAMATIZATION

Macro- and microcultures alike vary in the degrees to which they physically dramatize their cultures.

Salient forms of dramatization include dancing, singing, and playing musical instruments. MOs differ markedly in the degree to which they do these things. Most seem to engage in them relatively little and to reserve such performances for special occasions, such as rallies and marches, and often also to call upon specialized and freelance performers who are not MO members. The UC strides a different road. First, it has an array of its own singing, dancing, and musically performing troups, among them: The New Hope Singers International, Sun Burst, the New World Players, the New York City Symphony, and the Little Angels. Unlike many MOs it does not shy away from professionalism and excellence in cultural performance. Second, musical and other performances by ordinary members in ordinary settings are encouraged, as is collective singing and dancing.

As a broader and comparative generalization, it seems to be the case that religious more than political or ego movements (defined in chapter 7) foster music, dance, and song. In this light, the UC is much like other religious movements, only more so.

MOs differ in the degree to which they engage in expressive, collective assemblies and the adroitness and artfulness of the design and consummation of such assemblies. In my travels through diverse movement worlds I have been impressed by the relative poverty of most MO expressive assemblies. Especially political MOs—being quite "instrumental"—seem almost embarrassed by suggestions that some of their gatherings might be more than, or other than, tightly focused intellectual analyses of the latest atrocities in the world (save for the practice of giving "parties" that are virtually identical in form and function to middle-class cocktail gatherings).

The UC, in contrast, mounts expressive assemblies frequently, elaborately, and diversely. First and most obvious are their religious worship services. Second, there are a series of sheer celebrations in their complex set of "Days." Third, openings of new installations call forth initiating celebrations. Fourth, conclusions of programs require farewell celebrations. The farewell banquets of some of their more elaborate conferences, such as those given for the International Conference on the Unity of the Sciences, are particularly impressive. They consist of a variety of musical performances by church members and guests and culminate in church members' spiritedly singing one of their stirring anthems. And the UC is of course both famous and infamous for the weekend, almost nonstop expressive assemblies it puts on for potential recruits at locations in Northern California (ch. 2).

It is almost absurd even to mention painting, sculpture, musical composition, and literature in the context of movement organizations. Even the UC does little about such matters, but some nonetheless.

CULTURAL DISSEMINATION

Almost all MOs have at least some primitive means of disseminating their views. Most commonly this is a newsletter—the primordial artifact of MO culture. The UC is unusual in striving to cover the gamut of ways in which it is possible to disseminate views: newspapers of several sorts, periodicals, videotapes, pamphlets, posters, books, and more. Most other MOs look anemic alongside the UC in this area. It has even formed a motion picture production company, and fielded one major movie. One supposes that TV shows and records are next.

INTERCULTURAL CONTACT AND PROMOTION

Historically, human cultures were generated in relative or virtually complete isolation from one another. Occasions of initial intercultural contact were quite traumatic. A single person of a different culture coming onto an isolated culture was likely to be either venerated as a god or treated as subhuman. A human, nonmember of one's culture was a difficult or impossible-to-conceive possibility (L. Lofland 1973). As time went on and cultures were increasingly in contact, such touchings were occasions for war and conquest. Only slowly have some humans come to accept the idea that cultures other than one's own can be tolerated and perhaps appreciated and treated with respect rather than dominated and obliterated. Within current nation-states diverse cultures still mostly accommodate by mutual avoidance (between nation-states they of course still seek domination and obliteration).

In a global system of ever-accelerating intercultural contact, variation in the character of such contact becomes itself a topic of signal significance. Such culture as practiced by social movements, because they are promoters of social change, is ever more important. And to the point at this moment, the quantitative elaboration of contact is a key variable.

Sadly, most MOs are not exceptions to the generalizations I have just made about intercultural contacts historically and still dominant in the world today. Like other cultural groups, most MOs tend to look out over the social landscape with suspicion, fear, and hostility, and quantitatively to restrict their contact with people unlike themselves, most particularly with people who are only in small ways unlike themselves. This is marvelously ironic in the case of movement organizations because as movements they are, by definition, in the business of trying to convince other people of the wisdom of certain social changes. The irony is that MO members preach heavily to the converted, except on specially staged occasions, which are commonly marches and rallies, where the speech is public but the persons immediately present are the already believing. Occasions of face-to-face contact with the unbelieving, rare as they are, tend to have an intemperate quality, one extreme form of which has been frozen and displayed for our inspection in the concept of "mau-mauing" (Wolfe 1971).

Both quantitatively and qualitatively, the UC furnishes us dramatic contrasts with this more common MO pattern. Confining our attention for the moment to the quantitative, like many religious MOs, the UC is conversionist and proselytizing. A significant portion of member energy is invested in making contacts with potential members and in presenting the UC point of view to other nonbelieving audiences. Member-for-member it may be the most intensively proselytizing of MOs today. Combined with its wide range of other intercultural contacts, members likely spend much less time, proportionately, in contact with their "own kind" than do members of other MOs.

Beyond efforts to encounter individuals in public places and to entice people to attend revivalist-like assemblies (as mobile teams of their International One World Crusade were doing across the United States in 1983), there are the large-scale, long-running, and unique efforts to make face-to-face contact with various categories of intellectuals and other leaders in societies around the world. Holding aside the moral objections some people have to these efforts, we need only view them from a comparative MO perspective to appreciate their astonishing quantitative and qualitative nature. Imagine the National Organization for Women staging conferences to which they invite the editors of *Hustler* and *Playboy,* and vice versa; imagine the Southern Christian Leadership Conference staging conferences to which they invite members of the Ku Klux Klan, and vice versa; imagine the Campaign for Nuclear Disarmament staging conferences to which they invite the U.S. Joint Chiefs of Staff, and vice versa. The face-to-face contacts of diverse perspectives contrived and achieved by the UC are not quite as dramatic as these but they move in that direction and would move further if the people they invited who are in sharp contrast to UC views did not so frequently decline their invitations.

Whatever objections one may have to the UC, and they have serious faults to which I will come, such objections ought not be allowed to obscure the singular project of intercultural contact in which they have been engaged. In the early eighties they were staging several dozen such conferences each year, involving several thousand intellectuals and others in locations around the world, and on which they have been spending several millions of dollars each year.

But beyond such episodes of interaction with outsiders (which themselves lead to relationships with outsiders), the UC has created numerous specialized organizations they view as implementing their views and to which they recruit persons supportive of the specialized aims of the particular organizations. Similar to broad Left and popular front umbrella organizations for which some political MOs have a penchant, the UC creations address diverse matters: civil rights in the Minority Alliance International; social services for poor communities in the National Council for Church and Social Action; food distribution in Project Volunteer; unity of the sciences in the International Cultural Foundation; conservative student politics in the Collegiate Association for the Research of Principles; world peace in the Professors' Academy for World Peace—among many others that now exist or are in their initial or planning phases. Among this last are organizations geared to staging a religious leader world summit meeting, and religious world fairs associated with a religious olympics.

Even beyond this are the intercultural contacts generated by UC programs in which only UC members are members, but the nature of the task brings members into daily contact with outsiders, as in the Home Church program and their worldwide missionary teams (now claimed to be present in 133 countries) and in their medical teams.

The bulk of MOs restrict their cultural lives to the five classes of matters I have now mentioned: cognition, specialized creators of cognition, dramatization, dissemination, and intercultural contact and promotion. Even within these categories, most MOs tend not to be especially elaborate in their efforts. The UC stands out in its assiduousness at all these levels.

CULTURAL ECONOMICS

The great divide between culturally primitive MOs and those that are truly elaborate is between economic activity necessary to field and sustain activities of the types I have just listed and economic activities that go beyond them. As I have just suggested, very few MOs cross this divide. The UC is of special interest for, among other reasons, it does venture across and into what we may call "cultural economics" (and into an even higher level). It seems to be striving to establish much the same array of economic institutions that we find in total, advanced societies, for they have already become involved in such areas as manufacturing, real estate, agriculture, banking, restaurants, travel agencies, hospitals, newspapers, printing, and office services.

DOMESTIC CULTURE

Finally, highest and most venturesome for MOs, efforts may be made to propound detailed cultural practices for the domestic lives of members. Perhaps because of the sheer intimacy of this "private sphere," as one hears it termed, few MOs, especially classic political MOs, say much about it; that is, develop much cultural symbolism pertaining to it and strive to pattern actual domestic arrangements on that symbolism. The several waves of commune formation in American history have, of course, dwelled on this, and it is becoming increasingly central to the feminist and religious Right movements in America.

The UC, too, has in recent years actively elaborated both ideas about proper domestic life and full-tilt reorganized its members in America from brother-sister communes to husband-wife nuclear families of a special type that are still in the process of emergence. Against the backdrop of several occasions of its spectacular mass marriages, an ethic of the centrality of the nuclear family and of childbearing has been fostered.

The categories of culture I have so far explained and the UC materials I have reported are directed to two generalizations: one, MO cultures differ manifestly in the degree of their elaboration; two, in comparative MO perspective, UC culture is, taken in composite, quite elaborate.

CULTURAL EXPRESSIVENESS

In addition to sheer elaboration or complexity, cultures, including MO cultures, vary in the extent to which their cognitive categories carry what Selznick and Selznick (1964:667) have called "expressive meaning" or "expressive symbolism," and "symbolic value." For them, "the mark of culture . . . is that the ordinary objects and forms of group experience have symbolic value."

To understand the phenomenon of expressive symbolism or symbolic value we need first to step back and reappreciate the existential human situation that gives rise to what Selznick and Selznick (1964:658) call the "primordial culture-creating act." The existential situation of humans is, in their view, one of impersonality, an environment of objects that has no direct and personal relations to humans. However, the special, minded quality of humans renders such an environment objectionable and unacceptable. Humans react against impersonality in the "primordial culture-creating act" which is "the transformation of an impersonal setting into a personal one." Such an act

> is an effort to make the world rich with personal significance, to place the inner self upon the stage, to transform narrow instrumental roles into vehicles of psychic fulfillment. It implicates the self and strives to invest the environment with subjective relevance and meaning. In an older tradition we might have refered to this investment as "the objectification of spirit" [Selznick and Selznick 1964:659]. . . .

> The product of [the culture-creating act] is a world of [expressive] symbols. Culture is created when, in the struggle against alienation, [humans] . . . transform the instrumental and the impersonal, the physical and the organic, into a realm of evocative, expressive, person-centered meanings [Selznick and Selznick 1964:660].

Selznick and Selznick (1964:659) elucidate the nature and importance of the "culture-creating act" by drawing on John Dewey's distinction between "experience-in-general" and "having an experience."

> We all single out events in which we have participated that we remember and speak of as *an* experience. Something aroused and held our interest, touched us deeply, engaged our emotions, focused our attention, stimulated some wholehearted response. *An* experience stands out as a unified segment of experience-in-general, distinguished from a background of the routine, the habitual, the stereotyped, the boring, from all the beginnings that go nowhere, from the aimless, the merely conventional, the indecisive, the unengaging.

In effect, Dewey was distinguishing between existing and living, between "going through the motions" and having a sense of heightened
vitality. The distinction is a normative one, but it is not arbitrary or
culture-bound. Having an experience in Dewey's sense is naturally and
spontaneously valued. It is not the only human value, nor is it always
given highest priority. But it is part of our common humanity that having
an experience, with its qualities of vitality, response, interest, awareness, and meaningfulness, will be prized and sought. And to be denied
the opportunity of experience is to suffer deprivation.

As an inherently valued happening, humans attach symbols to such
experience, the symbols so attached meriting distinction from merely
routine symbol use. It is this special kind of symbol that Selznick and
Selznick (1964:662-63) term "expressive," and speak of as having
"symbolic value." Expressive symbols are themselves in part created

> in order to continue and sustain meaningful experience. The wearing of
> black respects and prolongs the experience of mourning, of confronted
> death. Festivities rich in symbolism can help consummate an experience
> that would otherwise be brief and incomplete. In the presence of the
> symbol, people respond in ways that nurture rather than attenuate the
> experience. Moreover, having had "an experience," [humans] . . . create
> a symbol of it in order that the experience may be re-evoked and relived.
> Durkheim said as much when he suggested that religious symbolism
> arose in part out of the desire to recreate the emotional uplift originally
> stemming from collective excitement.

> [Expressive] symbols help to provide focus, direction, and shape to what
> otherwise might disintegrate into chaotic feeling or the absence of
> feeling. Mass political action gains coherence and discipline from sym-
> bolic leadership, ritual, and exhortation. Without [expressive] symbol-
> ism, it is often difficult to transform an important occasion, such as a
> wedding, into a meaningful experience, as many unconventional and
> secularized couples have found to their dismay. By serving as vehicles of
> response, symbols can help transform a "mere" feeling, a vague somatic
> tension, into genuine emotion. Thus symbols do more than sustain
> emotion. They contribute to the emergence of emotion as a uniquely
> human attribute.

In Selznick and Selznick's (1964:66) view, symbolic expressiveness
is something in terms of which cultures can vary. The possibility of
such variation is the reason they label their theory of culture a
"normative" one, for they do not "shrink from identifying some
cultures as attenuated, some symbols as emptied out, some experiences as truncated or distorted." And in contrast, other cultures may
have "subtle and rich symbolic system[s]." Or as Fine (1979:736)
points out about as seemingly mundane and inconsequential idiocul-

tures as those of little-league baseball teams, some—the more successful ones—"develop . . . a robust culture of baseball-related items."
Such a variable is not to be confused with the moral superiority or
inferiority of the content of a culture. Selznick and Selznick (1964:666-
67) make the difference between and independence of the two quite
plain:

> We take the view that much is to be gained by avoiding the equation of
> the moral and the cultural. Rather, we think the relation between the two
> should be explored. There may well be an empirical tension, though
> probably not a fatal one, between enlightened moral orders and the
> development of culture. To the extent that symbolization of persons and
> groups occurs, there is cultural enrichment. But symbolization can be
> demonic and go hand in hand with cruel and inhuman moral systems.
> Moral enlightenment often depends upon the weakening of symbols,
> upon making profane what was formerly sacred, upon taking people for
> what they are and not for their symbolic status and value. When we look
> at culture with a fascinated eye, it is easy to forget that values realized
> through symbolic systems may inhibit the realization of other values that
> depend upon more instrumental, more rational, more disengaged behav-
> ior.

Bringing all this to bear on MOs and holding aside the question of
sheer cultural elaboration I have just discussed, we may entertain the
possibility that some MOs cultivate and sustain much richer symbolic
lives than others.

It is useful to distinguish two sources of this variation. First, MOs
vary in the degree to which they appropriate existing expressive
symbols into their own schemes and use them internally to enrich the
cultural lives of their members. Many reactive and rejecting political
movements of our times seem to do this very little and appear even
self-conciously to avoid the powerful expressive symbols of the encompassing culture. The UC is decidedly the reverse. Its culture
embraces many of the most evocative and deep of Western cultural
symbols and values: God, faith, the family, spirituality, love, perfection, progress toward an earthly kingdom of God, self-discipline,
anticommunism, among others. Consider the closing words of the UC
promotional videotape "People of the Quest." The Unification Church
(1983) "reaffirms the importance of classic spiritual values: the value of
man as a divine creation; the value of the family as the most important
building block of good society; the value of community service to
establish a healthy nation; the value of a nation's living for the benefit
of the world before its own interests, and above all, the value and law
of love as the altar, purpose, and cornerstone of all relationships." The

very last words of this program are those of the Rev. Moon himself, and spoken by him: "We have one primary goal, the age-old quest for a peaceful world centered on God." After Rev. Moon says this, he and Mrs. Moon are shown singing to one another and kissing.

MOs are differentially creative of their own internal symbolism. Here too the UCers have been busy and are still in the process of generating a rich array of distinctive modes of making experience meaningful and personal. Their world abounds in such cultural concepts as True Parents, True Father, spiritual children, the three blessings, the fourfold foundation, restoration, indemnity, central persons, MFTs (mobile fund-raising teams), heart, and many others.

Associated with but distinguishable from evocativeness is the degree to which a culture embodies conceptions of the ideal that are highly valued and striven for. In positing ideals, the expressive symbols reach beyond the realities of the moment and call people to larger visions and elevating motives to which they are encouraged to subscribe. Some theorists of culture claim that culture is only about valued ideals, all else is merely reactive or instrumental behavior and not culture proper. In fact social organizations differ strikingly in the clarity and force with which they conceive and act to actualize ideals of social and other arrangements and performances.

Almost by definition, one would expect movement organizations to be highly idealistic and optimistic, and expect these to be manifest in a cheerfulness of demeanor. Sadly, this is not my experience of many MOs. Commonly, there is a thorough critique of the present, which implies an ideal, but this critique does not go on to show much optimism about attaining ideals or cheerfulness about living toward them. To the extent one can construe ideals, they are often of a fairly narrow and self- or categorically-interested kind rather than attuned to broad conceptions of common human values. In being so symbolically restricted and dolefully demeaned, however, perhaps most MOs are being but rational; often there is scant objective ground for optimism and cheerfulness.

Numerous observers have noticed the expressive symbolism, idealism, and cheerfulness of UC members. Justified or not, UC cultural values are enormously idealistic and optimistic and members exhibit a distinct kind of positive attitude as a result. As phrased by a long-time and close-up observer of the UC:

> Faith, with its conviction of a transcendent source of renewal and transformation, can work to overcome situations that appear hopeless from the point of view of rational calculations. Such "world-making" faith is convinced that we have access to sources beyond the public

order that sustain the effort to work to transform the world. This, to me, is one of the most impressive things about the Unification movement and is at the heart of the spiritual dynamics that motivate this movement.

In relation to our situation of crisis, the Unification movement believes itself to be inspired by a faith which points the way to a future which will see the Kingdom—or, in their language, "a God-centered world"— realized in the order of space and time. Thus, rather than viewing our cultural situation as a scenario of despair, the Unificationists see a scenario of hope [Bryant 1983:12].

Such optimism and idealism is founded on extremely broad and ultimately justifying conceptions. The UC uses legitimizing symbols much broader than found in many other MOs. The address of Rev. Moon (1983) to the class graduating from the UC seminary in 1983 capsulizes many of these "cosmic-scale" symbols:

People in the world tend to see things primarily from a self-centered perspective. However, members of the Unification Church learn to view everything from a higher and larger dimension. For example: money, power, knowledge—even salvation—are regarded from a worldly view-point as benefiting the individual, or at most the family. How rare it is to find a person who puts even the welfare of the nation above that of the family! But for us the entire cosmos, both spiritual and physical, takes priority over the individual, the family, and even the nation. . . .

Goals such as liberation, freedom, and happiness are generally sought for the sake of a few people rather than the human family as a whole. But unlike the rest of the world, we strive toward liberation, freedom, and happiness not only for all of mankind, but even for God. Anyone who overlooks this difference fails to understand our true nature. . . .

What does history need most? Does it need people with a narrow, worldy perspective, or does it need the Unification Church? If the conscientious people of the world really understood the Unification Church, they would agree that history needs us more than anything else. And if we were to ask God, the answer would be the same.

As sons and daughters of God, we can be proud of our historical mission. When our generation passes away, we must leave behind a worthy history, a secure mankind, and a satisfied God. Such a mission enjoys the protection of history, mankind, and God. For this, we can be grateful in our daily work.

Those of you who are graduating from the seminary today are part of this historical mission. Reverend Moon and the members of the Unification Church have devoted considerable effort to your education, and have high hopes that in your future careers you will become true leaders of tomorrow. We are praying that you establish a royal pattern which will liberate mankind and God, and will defeat Satan and communism. We are also praying that you will establish a new and higher tradition for future history, mankind, and God.

In addition, the expressive symbol of "love," particularly in the sense of giving oneself for the benefit of others, is a key cultural ideal. In comparative movement perspective, this symbol is almost quaint and even embarrassing, most especially among political MOs. It has of course figured to a degree in some Gandhian-inspired movements, such as segments of the American civil rights efforts of the sixties and the peace movement. But, on the whole, most other MOs honor quite different, central symbols, such as justice and freedom.

CULTURAL COMPASSION

Elaboration and expressiveness are formal rather than substantive dimensions of cultural variation. They speak to features of the architecture of culture rather than to the materials of its construction.

I want third and finally to take up the question of content and to focus, I hope not capriciously, on the kind of substance having to do with the degree of civility and humaneness with which MO members treat one another and outsiders. We do not find it difficult to speak of the cultures of some societies as being, for example, more warlike, aggressive, gentle, militaristic, or exploitive than those of other societies. In the same fashion, perhaps it is possible to compare MOs in such terms.

Reversing the Guttman-like logic I used in speaking of cultural elaboration and therefore beginning with the "strongest" state, we may conceive three levels of what I would like to label compassion, or lack of it, in MOs.

In most extreme form, the values of an MO counsel and justify physical violence as an instrument of state and movement policy and as a strategy of member control. Few if any MOs are so indiscriminately belligerent, but some move in that direction. Most seem, empirically, only to encourage and justify "defensive" violence against outsiders and to prohibit all internal violence. In comparative perspective, the UC seems rather similar to most other movements in this respect. In particular, it manufactures parts for weapons of state warfare, elects to support governments that employ violence as an instrument of policy, and supports the rightist administration of the United States of America, a government that is flauntingly proud of its macho lack of compassion.

Second, MOs differ in their promotion and practice of psychic and interactional violence, abusiveness of the human self and social order that does not entail physical violence, but which assaults the integrity of persons and social interaction.

One central form of this is propagation of dehumanizing and demeaning stereotypes of one or more sets of outsiders. Patterns of this include scapegoating, villification, and inferiorization. All movements seek to overcome some sort of evil, but evil can be conceptualized as residing in arrangements and acts rather than in the character of persons. The more compassionate movement culture lodges evil in the former rather than the latter.

Stereotyping and person-based forms of psychic violence can also be practiced against subsets of one's own members in such forms as scapegoating purges and arbitrary categorizations of some members as inferior, using, for example, race, gender, or sexual preference criteria.

Internal authority systems vary in terms of the degree to which the wishes of members are taken meaningfully into account and consent is achieved in the formulation of policy and its execution. At one extreme, self-appointed elites merely propagate and administer policy and rule by intimidation. At the other extreme, there is civil, consented, democratic governance.

Members of all social organizations make mistakes, lie, default, and the like. Deviant behavior among members must therefore be managed and that management can be more or less compassionate.

The physical and mental states of some members invariably go awry. When they do, one easy option is to expel or otherwise "ease out" such problems, forcing other social organizations to pick up the burden. "We are like an army," a leader can declare, and the mentally and physically ill can be left behind.

I am obliged to report that materials available to me regarding these five aspects of interactional and psychic violence in the UC are sketchy and contradictory. Unlike elaboration and expressiveness and some other facets of compassion, these are less "on the surface" of any movement organization, including the UC. They are part of the "internal life" or even the "underlife" of any movement and I must assume that the UC does not differ from other MOs in having an internal life and an underlife that is shielded from observation. And the reliable reports that we have so far on the UC have dealt with the matters just mentioned in highly incomplete ways.

There is also the matter of everyday interactional violence versus compassion in contacts with outsiders. I have already made reference to the quantitative aspect of contact with outsiders—reporting there appears to be a great deal of it, comparatively speaking. Qualitatively, the interactional persona of the modal UC member does seem to lean heavily to the compassionate side. This cultural persona is especially striking as practiced by the students and graduates of the UC seminary, a cadre numbering in the hundreds. Among this elite, leadership is provided by some forty seminary graduates who are (in the early eighties) advanced Ph.D. students in divinity and religious studies programs of leading American universities.

This seminary elite carries the main interactional burden of the many conferences and organizations I mentioned. As one would predict, they are frequently subject to unfriendly inquiry about and commentary on the UC in such face-to-face settings, especially in settings where the object is to present UC ideas per se. In this last, the Ph.D. elite is subjected to severe criticism all day long, day in and day out, for up to 7-day periods several times a year. One can well ask—how many organizations of *any* kind are prepared to place (or do place) any of their members in such a difficult position? But that, too, aside, my interest here is UC member behavior under such stress (as well as in the cultural persona enacted by other members in intercultural contacts).

For whatever reasons, people who attend UC-sponsored conferences, especially those presenting UC doctrines, are prone to publish articles about the experience and these are useful sources in forming judgments about UC interactional style with outsiders. The half a dozen or so of these I have read (along with numerous verbal reports to me from other attendees) always take severe issue with the content of UC ideology but are uniformly impressed with UCers "as people." Praiseworthy qualities often mentioned include member openness to criticism of their doctrines, friendliness, and helpfulness. The Ph.D. student elite is subject to searching criticism of UC theology, but they remain ever "cool," even cordial, and engagingly civil in the face of abrasive and hostile commentary. One writer phrases his more general impressions in this manner, a manner reflective of many other observers: "The people I met were very impressive. They have a commitment to serving God and others, to supporting and loving each other, to chastity, self-discipline, and the sanctity of family . . . that is refreshing in our rather jaded world" (Gaybba 1983:34).

The diversity of personalities one sees acting in this way (and not simply the Ph.D.-earning elite) clues us to the existence of cultural patterning as distinct from converging personality dispositions. The cultural persona displayed by UCers—their distinct order of civility and geniality—are rather like the classic hallmarks of the ideal "cultured person." Selznick and Selznick (1964:657) point out that when we speak common-sensically of some persons being more "cultured" than others we are not only, merely (or even, necessarily) referring to their knowledge of or participation in "high culture," but, instead, of trained differences in capacity for social participation. Some settings more than others produce

> high levels of personal and social competence . . . [and a person who] is marked by sensibility, sophistication, and psychic adequacy. [He/she] . . . understands the nuances of code and custom, the purposes that guide collective action, the spirit as well as the letter of the law [and] . . . is . . . capable of accepting frustration, governing irrational fears, making psychic commitments, sticking to the task at hand, and all the rest. Viewed in this light, the more cultured person is one for whom social participation is meaningful in the sense that he can appreciate, act out, and perhaps teach whatever richness there may be in [an] . . . experience.

Beyond this, observers often mention qualities of warmth and caring, especially in the elite UC members. One observer was so emotionally moved by such impressions that he has described his response in the famous conversion words of John Wesley: "My heart was strangely warmed" (Quebedeaux 1983).

Finally, a cultural scheme may be quite compassionate in the physical, psychological, and interactional senses I have reviewed, but still define the movement's situation in a way that stresses the practical necessity (if not the cultural idealness) of a significant measure of duplicity in its dealings with outsiders. Perhaps the best known instance of this is the so-called entryist strategy sanctified by Lenin for the purpose of infiltrating worker organizations in revolutionary Russia and since employed as a model by numerous Leninist/Trotskyist parties. In entryism, members of a given MO mute or conceal their true political affiliations and beliefs for the purpose of acquiring power and influence in a target association. Phrased more abstractly, some MOs develop exoteric as distinct from esoteric doctrines, tenets, actions, and aims. The former is framed for public consumption and understanding; the latter is directed only to the initiated.

I assess all forms of such double-dealing with the world to be less than compassionate. In several ways over the years it must be said that the UC has practiced duplicity, although it has dropped some forms of it under public pressure. But that historical record of double-dealing is still backdrop to the present and suspicions must linger that there may still be secret and unsavory aims, beliefs, plans, and programs of action. There is a "catch 22" in this. It is difficult for a movement to prove it does not have secret matters. Energetically to deny duplicities and secrets about specific matters and duplicity and secrecy in general are apt to be perceived as "protesting too much" and therefore betraying of guilt. On the other hand, to ignore allegations can also be seen as admission of guilt.

In any event, the historical record poisons the wellsprings of trust among many observers of the UC. I share in this distrust and await further data.

GENERALIZATIONS AND IMPLICATIONS

I have drawn attention to movement organizations as culture-creating and bearing social organizations and suggested that these cultures vary in terms of their quantitative elaboration, qualitative expressiveness, and human compassionateness. Along the way I have made particular reference to the Unification Church in comparative, movement-culture perspective.

The point of all concepts, distinctions, and identified variations is enlightening generalizations, perspectives, and answers to questions. The following are among those I trust we can fruitfully draw from the foregoing.

CULTURAL RICHNESS AND POVERTY

I hope there is now an empirical and not simply normative sense in which we can say that some movements are culturally richer than others. Most are modest affairs in the cultural senses I have elaborated and we can say, therefore, they offer their members relatively little in such ways.

THE RICHNESS OF POLITICAL AND RELIGIOUS MOVEMENT CULTURES

In the spectrum of MOs, religious ones may, on the whole, foster more robust cultures than political MOs. Tentatively assuming this generalization to be true—how might we account for it? Several factors are candidates. First, religious institutions and movements historically antedate political movements. In the struggle to differentiate the two, cultural poverty or starkness was one obvious and easy-to-manipulate differentiator. Politics got "stuck" with the constricted side of the differentiating dialectic. Second, we still live in the shadow of the most culturally robust political movement of modern history, German national socialism, an elaborate and expressive culture that was also so cruel and authoritarian—so lacking in compassion—that it has given political culture a bad name. In the minds of many, robust political culture is still construed as fascist at worse and authoritarian at best, and we cannot lightly dismiss the possibility that robust MO culture in fact always is.

But momentarily assuming that the link between fascism in particular and authoritarianism in general and robust political culture is historically accidental rather than necessary, one implication can be that political movements ought not to be so bashful about constructing richer cultures. In so stating, I do not suggest the willy-nilly appropriation of practices and forms found in other movements. We definitely do not need, for example, social-democratic versions of the Nuremberg rallies, although a fundamental reevaluation of the nature of the "rally" and its features is absolutely in order and a topic of high priority in any effort to enrich political culture.

THE DILEMMA OF CULTURE

There is, nonetheless, a dilemma to be confronted by efforts to enrich movement cultures, perhaps most especially by democratic political movements. To enrich culture is, in one way, to increase demands on members. To increase demands is to restrict the breadth of possible recruitment (Aronowitz 1983a:47). Therefore, the richer the movement culture, the more isolated and enclave-like the movement organization is likely to be or become. And, isolation defeats the outreach and social change aims of the movement. The Democratic Socialists of America (DSA) and the various Leninist/Trotskyist groups illustrate the two contrasting and unsatisfactory solutions to this dilemma.

> The great attraction of the various Leninist organizations is that they insist upon a total commitment from the individual—personal sacrifice of time and money in return for which the organization tries to deliver a coherent ideological and cultural community that meets a wide variety of needs. [The Marxist discourse of such groups as against the popular-democratic discourse of the DSA] constitutes a marker that provides the individual with the security of belonging to a culture. In contrast, the democratic left [as in the DSA] possesses a frail "we," not only because its politics tends, willingly, to leave the hard divisive ideological questions unanswered, but also because it makes membership a matter of paying a minimum annual dues that places little strain on most people [Aronowitz 1983a:47-48].

The perilous path to blaze, therefore, is one that enriches culture in ways that are not also too restrictive of recruitment and therefore productive of movement isolation but which is also not, on the other hand, authoritarian.

RICHNESS AND MOVEMENT LONGEVITY

If cultural richness offers members satisfactions and other adaptive resources, we should expect that movements with richer cultures will be more successful (in several senses of that word) than movements that are culturally poorer.

The most rudimentary meaning of movement "success" is sheer organizational survival for a given period of time, the criteria employed by Rosabeth Kanter (1972) in her comparative study of nineteenth-century utopian colonies. If we scrutinize the specific items Kanter finds associated with such success, we find they consist importantly of the kinds of beliefs and practices I have termed "cultural elaboration and expressiveness."

On the other hand and unhappily, many other of the correlates of longevity-success are negatively correlated with indicators of compassion! As Bruce Hackett has pointed out to me (in conversation), Kanter's findings suggest that in winning the battle of survival, utopian colonies lose the war for the more compassionate world that they were originally waging.

PATTERNS OF CULTURAL ELABORATION, EXPRESSIVENESS, AND COMPASSION

As the form of incongruity we can read from Kanter's findings suggests, elaboration, expressiveness, and compassion do not always vary together. An elaborate culture is not necessarily a compassionate one, for a great many ways in which these three complex components of richness can conjoin. This very lack of conjunction helps to increase the precision with which we can perceive movements in comparative perspective.

With regard to the case I have described—the Unification Church—its cultural pattern as so far developed is relatively elaborate, richly expressive, and only moderately compassionate.

INCONGRUITY AND STRAIN TO CHANGE

Some forms of discrepancy among the three components may be sources of tension and strain to change. Thus in the UC case, the very complexity and emotive power of its culture, combined with the particular symbols that are central to its view, creates, by internal culture logic, pressures toward a greater degree of compassion. Of course, the internal logic of a culture is only one source of pressure for change and there can be countervailing forces that conduce other directions.

Allow me to close with a further observation on the point with which I opened this analysis. I quoted Gary Fine reporting that social scientists have in recent years had difficulty using the concept of culture effectively. That point is especially germane to the subdiscipline devoted to the study of social movements, where the term is virtually never heard. In its place there is much concern with matters such as "ideology" and "commitment," which have a great deal to do with culture, but which are much more restricted and different ideas. I hope most of all that my effort here contributes to reconsidering the range of the basic elements of social movements so as to include more explicit concern with culture and the questions it helps to raise.

NOTE

We are grateful to Lyn H. Lofland, Pam Oliver, and several anonymous reviewers for many helpful suggestions on an earlier formulation of this report. An abbreviated version was presented at the annual meetings of the American Sociological Association, Detroit, Michigan, August 30, 1983.

We want to close by indicating that we do not regard our formulation of modal members as an approach, the six "levels" of MO locals, or the five levels of voluntary association MOs as definitive. They are animated by the matters of purpose and direction just discussed, but there may well be better ways of pursuing these purposes and directions.

10

WHITE-HOT MOBILIZATION: STRATEGIES OF A MILLENARIAN MOVEMENT (1979)

Social movements differ in the level at which they are mobilized at any given moment, at various periods of their careers, and over their life histories taken as a whole. Mobilization thus viewed as a variable rather than a dichotomy encourages us to think in more detail about elements and degrees of mobilization and the factors upon which these in turn depend (cf. McCarthy and Zald 1973).

If we orient ourselves to conceiving the most extreme possibilities of movement mobilization, we may envision a pure, or "white-hot," state of maximum mobilization, which has such features as:

1. The active pursuit of a program of publicity, missionizing, migration, colonization, warfare, or other effort openly, dramatically, and substantially to alter the movement's relation to its host society. In purest form, the effort is to capture the host society.
2. The fielding of a significant full-time corps of totally dedicated members who constitute a major portion of the movement's adherents.
3. The investment of a significant portion of the movement's resources in expanding the number of totally dedicated members.
4. The expenditure of large sums of money ("large" as defined by any given social context) in pursuing and supporting the three lines of activity and arrangements just mentioned and the evolution of devices to generate continual supplies of large-scale funds.

The image, then, is one of well-funded and undivided dedication to altering the movement's position, a dedication that is carried on by an expanding body of true believers. Most movements come nowhere near such a white-hot level of mobilization. Most often, few members are especially dedicated; funding is slim; the program is timid and unacted on; recruitment is haphazard and sparse. But some few movements are, at least for a time, able to achieve white-hot mobilization. By examining such statistically infrequent but contrasting cases we can perhaps learn something about the factors that keep most movements so relatively tame, so lukewarmly mobilized.

I will here examine a single instance of white-hot mobilization, asking: By means of what strategies was it possible to turn a warm into a white-hot mobilized movement? The movement to be analyzed—here called "the DPs"—is the American wing of a Korean-spawned millenarian religion. Followers believe that their leader, Rev. Soon Sun Chang, is the new Christ who will shortly (by 1981, it is hoped) restore the world to an earthly and perfect Garden of Eden. Chang and the believers will preside over an earthly theocracy.

WARM MOBILIZATION

The first DP missionaries arrived in America in 1959 and achieved only a few dozen converts over the first several years. But by continuous, amoebalike division of each budding communal center, by the end of 13 years (in 1971), they had grown to about 500 members spread among about 50 far-flung centers. Headed by Ms. Yoon Sook Lee, the movement existed at a relatively modest level of mobilization. At that time:

1. It lacked a program to alter the movement's position aggressively and dramatically. Mostly, members rather timidly and covertly strove to make converts (Lofland 1966; Bookin 1973). Each center had relatively great autonomy regarding programs of activity and each was directly responsible to the national office.
2. Members lived communally at centers, but most held conventional jobs and practiced their religion during nonworking hours.
3. Recruitment efforts centered on enticing people to attend lectures at the center.
4. Members contributed their incomes to the movement, and these funds supported centers, missionizing activity, and an array of front organizations (Lofland 1977), but no large-scale organizations geared specifically to conversion were mounted.

WHITE-HOT MOBILIZATION

Having grown wealthy on the Korean and Japanese branches of his movement, Chang himself took up residence in the United States in late 1971. He was appalled by the modest mobilization he found and set immediately about whipping more movement out of the American movement by initiating simultaneous changes virtually across the board. The logic of exposition forces a serial accounting of these, but it should be kept in mind that each separate strategy I describe has a mutual dependence on each of the others: they formed a "systemic package" of changes that supported and enhanced one another.

First, he established a set of grandiose and proximate goals the movement had to achieve. He hammered away that there were three 7-year periods on the road to the restored and perfect world to be ruled by DPs: 1960-67, 1968-74, and 1975-81. They were then in the crucial last three years of the second 7-year period. They had to give all to achieve a powerful and famous movement in America. New-member and dollar-raising quotas became omnipresent, and eight elaborate publicity-garnering campaigns and events were staged between 1972 and 1976: an early 1972 7-city speaking tour; a 21-city speaking tour in 1973-74 (starting at Carnegie Hall, with each of the twenty-one stops costing about a third of a million dollars); a 32-city tour in early 1974; a 10-city tour in mid-1974; an 8-city tour in late 1974 (starting at Madison Square Garden, with each stop costing from a third to half a million dollars); a rally for "new hope" in late 1975; a rally at Yankee Stadium in mid-1976; and a rally at the Washington Monument in late 1976.

These and several other events and operations were occasions of maximum movement goal-direction and involvement; each was public, challenging, and exciting. Each provided opportunities for taking initiative in planning, doing huge amounts of publicity, enticing people to attend, staging and managing the events themselves and the expensive dinners that went with each, and so on. The movement was *happening* (greater detail on the astonishing array of what was happening is reported in Lofland [1977] and Bromley and Shupe [1979]).

Each effort was defined as a huge success, of course, and the morale of believers was kept up by those signals of progress and the other devices found commonly in social movements (and all of social life, for that matter, as explained in Blumer [1969b] and Lofland [1966, pt. 3]).

Second, a program of the complexity and expense Chang projected and actually brought off required a reasonably large and well-organized apparatus. He did not have one at the end of 1971, and in order to create it he first purchased an estate at "Tinkertown," near New York City, and set it up as a national training center. Selected members from the dispersed centers were ordered there for training, and they were joined by leaders drawn from foreign wings of the movement, primarily Japan. (They entered the United States on missionary training visas; by 1973 there would be some 600 foreign members in America, many of whom did not speak English.)

In fullest form, this training consisted of several dozen believers undergoing forty days of lectures and lecturing, thirty days of witnessing in New York City, and thirty days of flower and candle selling. They heard lectures on the complex DP doctrines at least three times and were given three chances to pass an apparently difficult written examination.

By such a means, Chang "called out," educated, and increased the commitment of the already most committed DPs. He was creating an elite corps. By mid-1974 perhaps 1000 people had received the Tinkertown training. But more: he did not send them back to their centers. He formed them into bus- and van-going mobile teams. At its height in 1974, there may have been almost 1000 people (about half of whom were foreign members) organized into about three dozen teams evangelizing from state to state, street peddling, and doing advance work and staging chores for Chang's speaking tours and other activities. The centers became "crash pads" of a sort, out of which teams worked in a given area before moving on, although teams often slept in the van, a campground, or a cheap motel. These teams were, in effect, a new organization, a floating and literally deployable corps directly responsible to Chang.

The centers were organized into their own new system. The country was divided into ten regions headed by a regional director, under whom were several state directors, who in turn supervised center directors. Within centers, members were organized into "trinities," groups of eight or so people under a powerful "trinity leader." Paralleling the traditional U.S. army squad, the trinity leader supervised almost all member action. To maximize time for leadership, center directors were ordered not to hold outside employment.

The language of this new organization interlaced military and business terminology. Heads of the mobile teams were "commanders"; there was a "chain of command"; and they had tough "production goals," such as "earn one member per month." In the quest for maximum productivity, the less than properly productive were rotated into different jobs. Their coordinating newsletter reports a vast number of assignments, reassignments, and rotations in this period, suggesting a frantic effort to match job and person to the best effect. (Rotation was also spurred by a desire to put as many people as possible through the Tinkertown training.) Members were organized into various kinds of teams and pitted against one another in productivity contests: Americans against foreigners, centers against mobile teams, new members against old, and so on.

An observer of the early phases of this change in 1972 characterized the shift in this manner: "There was no more activity that was not church-related and organized. The whole operation got much tighter, more goal directed, and local leaders had less freedom. They also seemed to be doing better in terms of getting more recruits to come to lectures and in giving better organized and presented lectures" (Bookin 1973). As Chang summed it up in early 1973: "We must purge your old concepts of the American movement under the Divine Precepts."

Third, all of these and many activities I have not mentioned were very expensive: white-hot mobilization is expensive. By what devices can a movement generate the $15 or so million a year that this one was now spending?

An unknown amount came from the Korean and Japanese branches of the movement. In Korea, a significant portion of believers worked in Chang-owned factories, lived in close-by dormitories, and were paid only token wages. Chang was personally a multimillionaire, and he likely at least primed the pump of the American movement (as he did also in England and elsewhere, it is reported).

It has often been alleged that some money came from the South Korean Central Intelligence Agency and/or the American CIA. Personal interconnections among these three have definitely been established, but the flow of money has not.

These two sources were popular explanations of their wealth at the time the DPs became famous, I believe, because one of their more likely sources of major income was so ingenious, novel, and fantastic: street peddling by a large portion of a rapidly growing number of true believers, previously used with great success in Japan. Items such as flowers, candles, candy, and dried flower arrangements were purchased cheaply in bulk and sold on streets, bars, and in other public places for $1 or a few dollars. Hard workers could gross $80 to $150 a day, clearing at least 60 percent, as all the peddlers had to be self-supporting. On the basis of a very conservative estimate, it can be seen that 500 people netting $100 a day for 300 days a year can produce $15 million a year for a movement. And that is a very conservative calculation. There is no doubt that street peddling produced money of at least this magnitude, and likely more, in every year of this period.

This success on the streets was importantly facilitated by Chang's early edict that all members must wear close-cropped hair and neat and conservative attire. Looking rather like the more familiar Mormon male missionaries of America (with the addition of "blissed out" smiles), and presenting themselves as raising funds for noncontroversial programs, they gained the attention of ordinary citizens, who were quite responsive to their proferred wares. (Innocuous peddling covers included work on a "drug program" or a "youth program.")

Many local groups operated their own economic enterprises: a few hotel-apartment housecleaning and janitorial services, gas stations, and restaurants. All the enterprises were labor-intensive; the labor was essentially free, and the returns were reasonable.

Least significant, converts gave all their possessions. Parents were sometimes milked for more money by such devices as long-distance pleas for funds to pay nonexistent auto repair or medical bills.

The mystery of the movement's wealth is less a mystery when we begin to comprehend the possibilities of selfless and fanatical levels of dedication on the part of even a few hundred educated young people. By giving their all in the public places of a permissive and free society, they could generate astounding resources for the leaders of the movement and for their own local activities. By purchasing slow-moving country estates and other such "prestige" property, on which they made minimum down payments (a 1976 estimate of central movement real estate reported equity of about $10 million in $35 million worth of property), and by mounting flashy publicity campaigns, the DPs could by 1974 appear to be a formidable and large social force. Outsiders beholding this display gauged its substance in the terms with which they were familiar: normal investments, normal returns, paid employees with fringe benefits, and all the rest. People therefore assumed Chang must have vast resources and wealth. Outsiders did not appreciate that fanatical dedication along certain lines could (for a time, at least) leapfrog the ordinary laws of investments, wages, returns, and social display. (Such leapfrogging has, however, its own large price, as we shall see.)

Fourth, recruitment efforts were reorganized in a way that helped to produce a marked increase in membership. The 500 of 1971 jumped to something over two 2,000 in 1974 (augmented by about 600 foreign members).

The new mode of making converts brought prospects along through three stages. Focusing on its operation in and out of "State U City" and "Bay City" on the West Coast—the major producers of new converts—a prospect was, first and commonly, literally picked up hitchhiking or approached on the street and invited to dinner with "the Family" at a commune and/or to hear a lecture on some noncontroversial topic such as "world peace." Once at a DP center, most commonly for a free dinner, he/she was assigned the "buddy" who had been the initial contact and treated with extreme solicitude and "loving" support by the dozens of DPs assembled for the meal. After eating, an entertaining and unoffensive lecture was given on the principles that bound the Family, stressing sharing, loving one another, community activity, and other abstract ideals to which virtually anyone could subscribe. Chang and his movement were never mentioned and even religion per se was deemphasized. Then prospects were invited to a weekend workshop at the Farm, a several-hundred-acre retreat some fifty miles north of Bay and State U cities.

The second phase began with arrival at the Farm. Details of its operation are available elsewhere (Lofland 1977; this vol., chaps. 5 and 6); it will suffice to say here that prospects were effectively encapsulated in a physically exhausting, emotionally arousing, and intellectually reorienting round. A signal feature of DP effort at the weekend workshop is captured in their concept of "love bombing"—intense effort to make prospects feel they were overwhelmingly loved by DPs and to give them a desire to "melt together" (another DP term) with the embracing collective. General DP, unexceptional ideas were stressed in lectures (e.g. the "principle of give and take," in Lofland [1966:14-23]), but many specific, heterodox doctrines, aims, and programs were not.

Prospects who responded favorably (and hundreds apparently did in the early seventies) were invited to stay on at the Farm for various periods. It was in the third phase, if there, that the more specific and "objectionable" doctrines were revealed, in the context of waxing love and commitment. One important step in the process of increasing commitment was going into a nearby city to street-peddle; the fact that one could make $100 a day or so at it was "mind-blowing" and rewarding for many.

It is difficult to separate the power of the conversion organization from the effects of the social trends and changing definitions of discontent that were also occurring between 1972 and 1974. I think we can say, though, that this new conversion organization would not have been as effective had the American mood about public affairs also not changed. It is of fundamental import that all during the turbulent social optimism of the sixties, the DPs did not do well at converting. Politics, disorders, communes, drugs, hippie driftings, and Woodstock celebrations framed the imagination of young people. Despite its dark and violent side, the sixties were an affluent and creative era. Conservatism and sociocultural sterility reasserted themselves, and the sixties literally and socially ended in the Cambodia invasion of 1970. The killings at Kent State and the closing of college campuses closed a period in American life. And as has been documented across numerous societies and historical periods, when avenues of political activity and this-worldly optimism are thwarted, the political impulse is disguised as religion and asserts itself as religious ferment (e.g. Smelser 1963, ch. 10). This is the direction that the eternal discontents of youth began dominantly to take in the early seventies: Jesus freaks and East-West mutant religions abounded. It is in this now-shifted context of fashion in defining discontent that the DPs thrived. Their conservative religious motif fit into the new ideas of plausible public definitions of private stresses.

THE COOLING OF WHITE-HOT MOBILIZATION

White-hot mobilization would appear to be an enormously difficult achievement and an even more precarious state to sustain. Chang stoked up the movement in 1972 and 1973, reaching a peak heat in late 1974 during the 8-city tour starting at Madison Square Garden. He seemed to have extended the movement to about its limits by 1975, for the stresses of its taut stretching began to show.

On the program and goal front, evangelical campaigns were abandoned and resources husbanded for the Yankee Stadium and Washington Monument events that were over a year away. DP strategists openly acknowledged they might not have sufficient resources or membership even to stage the Yankee Stadium rally successfully. Weariness became visible in the ranks, and members began to defect in 1975 and 1976.

The conversion organizations were decreasingly productive. Newer converts were defecting at a higher rate than previously, but new converts tended to balance defectors, keeping the total membership approximately stable, but far below the goal of constant and rapid growth. An emergency missionary program conducted in early 1975 failed to increase converts. Funding apparently continued to be no large problem.

In 1975, a new set of factors began to enter the picture. White-hot mobilization had been achieved in a socially benign context. DPs were unknown; they claimed to be and were publicly thought to be ordinary fundamentalist and evangelical Christians. As time went on, their millenarian, "fanatical," "bizarre," and "cultish" beliefs, aims, and practices became known. Social criticism started and reached a crescendo in mid-1976, embodied in a wide variety of local and federal investigations, convert-parent lawsuits and other actions, and uniformly negative and extensive media coverage (see Lofland 1977; Bromley and Shupe 1979).

In the face of all this, Chang announced an end to the current period of his American ministry and left for Europe, apparently aiming to fan those parts of his movement into white-hot mobilization. The American movement began to cool down to something closer to its previous level of warm mobilization.

GENERALIZATIONS

What might we learn from this case about high levels of movement mobilization? Allow me some unfortunately obvious but still worthwhile tentative generalizations.

1. White-hot mobilization is rare and a function of a rather peculiar conjunction of being able to (a) pose for members a belief in pressing and exciting objectives and achievements that can be attained if they are striven for with all one's effort; (b) deploy members in an elite, indoctrinated, mobile corps; (c) generate large-scale funding; and (d) do the preceding things in an auspicious social context with a conversion organization that can furnish a rapidly expanding membership.
2. White-hot mobilization is self-terminating. Members grow weary. The host society is likely to react negatively and begin to thwart the movement's programs.
3. The recruitment and training of a mobile, elite corps is an important mechanism for redirecting a movement through giving it a "split-level" organization.
4. Irrespective of the effects of the machinations of movement-manipulation factors (funding, conversion organization, split-level organization, etc.), I am impressed with the crucial role of larger social trends and contexts in movement mobilization—and movement fate in general. Chang initiated changes in organization, conversion, and funding at precisely the time (1971-72) when American youth were the most enthusiastic about communal, East-West mutant, fundamentalist Christian, and other such religious views of reality. Significant numbers of youth were still posturing in alienated wanderings about the country. The DP organization was only one of dozens of religious groups that prospered between 1971 and 1974. Good organization, conversion technique, and large funding help, certainly, but only this more fundamental matter of auspicious social context made it possible for these movement-manipulable factors to be effective. We see the importance of context clearly in the fact that, by 1975, fashions in defining discontent had already begun to shift again. The DPs, along with dozens of other religious groups, had to cool down, redirect, and retrench.

NOTE

Background details on the movement here called the "DPs" (but in reality the Unification Church, as explained in the introduction to part 2 above) is available in, among other sources, Bromley and Shupe (1979) and Lofland (1977). The indispensable help of Andrew Ross, Michael Greany, David Taylor, and Hedy Bookin is gratefully acknowledged.

11

MANKIND UNITED (1970)

The socioreligious movement called "Mankind United" was the creation of Arthur L. Bell, an American businessman. Although little is known of his earlier career, Bell claimed to have been born in New Hampshire in 1900, to have grown up in poverty, and to have completed only four years of school. Emigrating to California in his teens, he sold real estate and insurance during the booming 1920s and became a Christian Science practitioner and a devotee of various theological and utopian writings. He was badly hit by the economic crash of 1929, and subsequently divorced his first wife and married, at age thirty-four, a fellow Christian Scientist—a wealthy woman in her early sixties.

Financially supported by his wife, Bell conceived the movement and at his own expense published its text, *Mankind United* (International Registration Bureau 1934). In its 313 repetitious pages, Bell sought to answer the ancient questions of why the world is dominated by war, poverty, greed, and hate, when so many long for it to be otherwise; and how it might be changed so that everyone could live in economic abundance and happiness under the Golden Rule of Christ: "Whatever you wish that men would do to you, do so to them" (Matthew 7:12).

BELIEFS

According to the text, on Christmas Day 1875, a small group of wealthy and humane persons had assembled to ask themselves these same questions. In their opinion, poverty, war, and other evils were totally unnecessary since technology was capable of producing more than enough for all. These evils continued only because "a worldwide organization composed of a small group of families in possession of fabulous wealth" was stifling the economic and moral well-being of humankind in order to bring it to total enslavement. In their mad ambition to control all wealth and power, these "World's Hidden Rulers" or "Money Changers" were the root of all evil.

THE SPONSORS

Wanting to save humandkind, these people pledged their fortunes and lives to overcoming the Money Changers and to instituting a world economy of equality and abundance. They called their organization The International Institute of Universal Research and Administration. Bell referred to them, more simply, as "the Sponsors."

In the following years, the Sponsors gradually expanded their numbers, spied upon the Money Changers, and engaged in the development of fantastically advanced techniques of economic production. Since the World's Hidden Rulers would destroy the Sponsors if they knew of them, the latter had to work in secrecy.

By 1919, the Sponsors' research department had assembled exhaustive proof of the Money Changers' existence and nefarious aims, and had worked out a plan for a worldwide economy in which, working only four hours a day, four days a week, eight months a year, everyone could live in astonishing prosperity. Since then they had been waiting for the most propitious moment to make their discoveries and plans known. To prepare for this "unveiling" the Sponsors had formed a group called "International Legion of Vigilantes." Bell claimed that he was recruited to this organization when it was set up in 1919 and that by 1934 he had been working as a secret agent for fifteen years.

THIRTY DAYS OF PROOF

Recognizing that their claims might seem incredible to the public at large, the Sponsors planned a rapid 30-day program "during which time the Institute's well-guarded sixty years of discoveries and carefully prepared recommendations will be freely offered to the human race." In 2-hour programs repeated day and night, twelve times each twenty-four hours, five days a week, irrefutable and exhaustive proof would be offered as to how the Money Changers worked and how Utopia was possible.

Mankind United was merely a bulletin announcing the imminence of the thirty days of proof. It did not in itself offer proof of anything, but was intended as an "invitation" to those who saw it to take part in the thirty days, and at the end to vote on 100 recommendations. However, the Sponsors had determined that if the enormous power of the Money Changers was to be overcome, it would be necessary to have at least 200 million people listening and voting. Until that number had agreed to participate, the thirty days of proof could not begin. It was in order to register the requisite millions that a part of the Sponsors' secret organization had become public. Once the 200 million had voted for the

Sponsors' program, the Universal Service Corporation would be formed and would thereafter conduct all economic production and distribution. Membership in the corporation would increase rapidly and within a few years, the World's Hidden Rulers would be completely out of business. As H.T. Dohrman (1958) has observed, the new order depicted in detail in *Mankind United* was very similar to the Utopia pictured by Edward Bellamy.

Arthur L. Bell, the argument of the text continued, was selected by the Sponsors to be the first "public" vigilante, and California was to be the first area in which registration was to occur. In his role as a mere functionary of a large and powerful secret organization, Bell disclaimed authorship of *Mankind United,* and the title page proclaimed that the book was "published by the International Registration Bureau (Pacific Coast Division of North America)."

MOVEMENT ORGANIZATION AND CAREER

Equipped with his wife's money, an ideology, and an attractive physical presence Bell set out to build a movement. It was to have an active history of only seventeen years (1934-51), but it provides an intriguing study in the ingenious organizational responses of a leader to changing and adverse circumstances.

POPULARIZING (1934-39)

From the middle to the late 1930s California, deep in the depression, was overrun with salvationist schemes. Into this highly competitive but permissive market, Bell introduced Mankind United. Membership involved merely the purchase of the book, a promise to pass it on to friends, and a willingness to listen and vote during the forthcoming 30-day program. In return for this minimal effort, members were promised a fantastic future gain. At the height of the movement's popularity, in 1938-39, frequent mass meetings were held throughout California and it is estimated that upwards of a quarter of a million West Coast citizens read the book, registered themselves, and attended at least a few meetings. Bell encouraged the formation of local clubs dedicated to promoting the book, and while this was not obligatory such clubs nonetheless flourished. As they grew in numbers, Bell organized them into an elaborate bureaucracy of dedicated workers. As many as 30,000 were actively engaged in the goal of registering 200 million "educated and religious people"—precisely the people, Bell said, whom the Money Changers most urgently wanted to annihilate.

The bulk of membership was drawn from the working and lower-white-collar classes, was primarily between ages forty and sixty, and had completed some secondary education (Dohrman 1958). Females slightly outnumbered males. By and large, members came from those worst hit by the depression—groups who were neither poor in 1929 nor sufficiently wealthy to weather the decade in reasonable comfort. More specifically, Bell sponsored his movement among those portions of such groups that were religiously inclined but disenchanted with established religion. His doctrines were as much economic as religious, but his scheme to make "do as you would be done by" a reality on earth was promoted among persons who were more religious than they were economically or politically sophisticated. For this reason Bell's economic claims encountered minimal resistance (Dohrman 1958).

COMMITTING (1940-43)

When speculation about America's entry into World War II flourished in 1939, and again when war came to the United States in 1941, Bell condemned it as another of the Money Changers' plots to worsen humankind's situation. Communist, fascist, and capitalist leaders alike were merely puppets of the Money Changers, and the latter were pulling the strings to further their plan for world dictatorship. Already by 1939 the federal government had infiltrated the movement and Bell had begun to retrench by discontinuing sale of the book and by calling for the close screening of members of Mankind United.

As support for the policies of the American government increased, membership declined, and in response Bell instituted a series of measures designed to commit the remaining followers. A program to train "instructors" and "election supervisors" to conduct affairs during the imminent 30-day program was instituted. Initially this involved a payment of only $20 per member, but a variety of other monetary requests followed. These culminated in a requirement made in 1943 that members become part of the "50/50 fund" by giving 50 percent of their gross earnings to the movement. The successive demands were made in the context of extreme secrecy and urgency: the 30-day program would begin at any moment, if only the latest monetary goal could be reached. But each time, Bell announced, the members failed and each time he sent them headlong toward a new financial goal which they had to achieve if the war was to be prevented (in 1940-41) or stopped (1942-43), and Utopia begun.

In pursuit of these elusive monetary goals and in scurrying about on a variety of additional and inexplicable "missions" at Bell's bidding, the members lived with an inflated sense of self-importance and with a vivid sense of the urgency of their tasks. The extent of this "urgency" was made clear in December 1942 when Bell and sixteen leaders were arrested on charges of sedition. They were found guilty in May 1943 but, as a result of an appeal, the decision was reversed on procedural grounds four years later. None of them ever served any time in prison.

COLLECTIVIZING (1944-45)

The best defense being offense, in the face of declining membership and government prosecution, Bell adopted a bold but logical organizational strategy to save and consolidate his movement. Late in 1943, he announced to the membership the "literally unheard-of opportunity" to become "student ministers" in "training schools" for those who would form the foundation of the forthcoming Universal Service Corporation. Incorporating a new organization, Christ's Church of the Golden Rule, Bell pressed his followers to give over all their worldly goods to the church and to begin work in one of the large number of businesses he was in the process of acquiring.

Under two years later, by the summer of 1945, he had assembled more than $3.5 million worth of property in California, including a number of office buildings, hotels, ranches, laundries, garages, and the like. Bell's following, however, was now down to about 850 persons, so that only part of these vast new holdings were run by members as utopian Laboratories of Abundant Living.

DECLINE (1946-51)

Conditions at these "model utopias" were apparently more spartan and harsh than many had expected. Late in 1945, the attorney general of California began to receive complaints from members who wanted their worldly possessions returned. The state initiated bankruptcy proceedings, but Bell, in order to retain some control, countered by throwing Christ's Church into voluntary bankruptcy. There followed a protracted process of court-ordered sales of property for the purpose of settling several hundred claims. In late 1951, all claims had been settled, leaving the organization with a few properties and some 300 die-hard loyalists.

In these later years, Bell's followers saw him less and less. Finally, in December 1951, he made an announcement to the faithful remnant. The Sponsors had decided that the majority of mankind was so selfish as to be unworthy of salvation and would, in any case, eventually destroy itself in wars. They had therefore explored possibilities for the colonization of other planets, which they had discovered existing in "another dimension" but "at virtually the same place in the universe." A planet that was physically similar to Earth had already been located and to this new world they were transporting themselves. They had left behind, deep beneath the Earth's surface, automatic machinery which could detect those individuals with a true interest in the Mankind United program. Those who remained faithful would also be transported to the new planet, although the automatic machinery could effect this transition only "during the brief instant immediately preceding one's so-called death." Following the announcement of this final communication, Bell disappeared from the view of members and public alike. Members grew few and old, operating a few remaining businesses, among which was a laundry and a motel. By 1956, less than 100 members remained faithful and the end of Mankind United was reached.

Part Four

MOVEMENT ACTION: DOING PROTEST

INTRODUCTION

MOVEMENT ACTION AND PROTEST

Following on the diverse traditions reviewed in the general introduction and elucidated in this part, "protest action" may be conceived as
one of three basic styles of action, a style flanked on the Right by
"polite," "ordinary," or "diplomatic" action and on the Left by
violent action. It is a style of action that helps define social movement
organizations (although it is not the only kind of action in which such
organizations engage). Citizen organizations other than MOs also at
least occasionally use it, especially its less "serious" forms. This loose
coupling of the several forms of citizen organization and the basic
forms of action is displayed clearly in the practice of "crowd lobbying"
described in chapter 14, where we see mainline interest groups—
including even the top executives of America's most powerful corporations—creeping in cautious and camouflaged ways toward mild forms
of protest action (the rally and march). Or, in a different imagery, many
interest groups carefully incorporate protest forms into their "repertoires of collective action" (Tilly 1981a). Specifically, the creation of
gatherings that have a contentious character communicates *implicit*
protest messages while drawing back from the more explicit threats
inherent in overt protest action (cf. Eisinger 1973; this vol., ch. 14).
Likewise, in chapter 15 on symbolic sit-ins, we discover a number of
staid interest-group organizations mounting at least the shorter-term
and "less flexed" forms of protest occupation of public space for the
purpose of pressing political demands. Conversely, we also see manifestly protest/movement organizations doing a great deal of prosaically
diplomatic and lobbying action along with the centerpiece of protest
action that they are also carrying on.

In broader and comparative perspective, the coupling of organization and action have become ever looser in Western societies since the
sixties, especially at the less serious levels of protest acts, gatherings,
events, and campaigns. In particular, marches, rallies and vigils—the
time-honored staples of MOs—have entered the ordinary repertoires
of the largest and mainline interest groups. Studies of people's atti-

tudes in several nations are finding, too, surprisingly widespread acceptance of (and expressed readiness to participate in) protest acts. Thus, Marsh (1977:51), in his protest "threshold" study, finds among United Kingdom adults:

> Forty-three percent of the population will have nothing more to do with protest than to sign a petition and half of these doubt they would do even that. But 35 percent would go further and engage in lawful demonstrations, and many of them would even operate boycotts against some protest target. The remaining 22 percent would clearly enter the third threshold zone of illegal demonstrations, half of them would stop at unofficial strikes and withholding their dues from the local authority or the inland revenue in protest. But the remainder would go "all the way" and take their politics into the street through the use of blockades and occupations. The conservative manner in which these estimates were constructed encourages the belief that this 22 percent really are committed to the legitimacy of nonlegal protest.

Also indicative, many citizen organizations we would need to characterize as "interest groups" often do not blink at labeling themselves "movements," as among the numerous interest groups in the "freeze movement" of the early eighties. Perhaps in the same way a concept of the symbolic sit-in has been required to distinguish the actions described in chapter 15 from historic sit-ins, we will soon need a concept of the symbolic movement to make the same kind of distinction among organizations (and with a meaning quite different from that provided by Joseph Gusfield [1963] in his treatment of the "symbolic crusade" or movement).

This loosening of the coupling of organization and action makes it especially important for us to have a clear conception of what is involved, by contrast, in the tight coupling of organizational form and action. It is only in terms of contrast that "tightness/looseness" can be gauged with precision and clarity. Several major profiles of coupling are required and an effort to provide at least one of these is offered in chapter 13—on sociologists as an interest group—which can and should be read as an almost ideal-typical outline of the organizational and action features of the classic interest group. Building on Robert Salisbury's (1975) synthesis, I draw out the "diplomatic" action program of one would-be interest group, that of sociologists. Similar tightly coupled profiles are in order for social movement organizations and violent organizations, steps I have not myself taken. (For MOs, this would involve juxtaposition of the kinds of organizational considerations addressed in chapters 7 and 8, with the array of protest actions presented in chapter 12.)

THE PROTEST SPECTRUM

Protest actions vary in two ways that are helpful in locating the chapters of this part in the universe of such action. First, the term *protest action* encompasses six units of social organizational reference: acts, gatherings, events, campaigns, waves, cycles (general introduction). The survey of protest action in chapter 12 is confined largely to the acts, gatherings, events, and campaign levels. The form of camouflaged protest I call "crowd lobbying" (chapter 14) consists of a series of single or a few gatherings that only in a few more complex forms composite into "events." They rarely if ever reach the "campaign" level. Likewise, the symbolic sit-ins described in chapter 15 are (modally) only gatherings and infrequently become events. Only one or two bordered on being campaigns. The empirical studies of this part focus toward the microstructural end of the protest spectrum.

Second, protest actions differ in terms of their "seriousness"—the degree of risk they entail (general introduction). The forms of protest and camouflaged protest that are the objects of my own direct observation here (in chapters 14 and 15) are at the lower end of any seriousness scale. This is hopefully counterbalanced by the picture drawn in chapter 12, which strives to portray a large portion of the gamut of possibilities.

12

SOCIAL STRUGGLE AND THE PROTEST OCCUPATION (1982)

Complex societies are vast and intricate arenas of social struggle—of politics in that term's most fundamental meaning—over the distribution of the scarce resources of class, status, and power. There are three fundamental strategies of struggle in this eternal contest for wealth, prestige, and influence, each with distinctive and implementing forms of social organization.

THE THREE FUNDAMENTAL FORMS OF SOCIAL STRUGGLE

In most societies in what are by definition "ordinary times," the dominant strategy is restrained diplomacy. Its earmarks are staidness, dignity, politeness, and orderliness. Its ideals are codified by Robert's *Rules of Order* and Emily Post's *Etiquette.* Its primary unit of collective action is the *interest group,* by which is meant any formal organization that engages in diplomatic activities designed to protect or enhance the social resources of its members by influencing the policies and practices of other associations (particularly governmental institutions) and by influencing the sentiments and dispositions of the public at large.

Robert Salisbury (1975:209) has provided a useful scheme for ordering the "major categories of strategic activity" we observe among interest groups, categories "defined by the relative specificity of [the] . . . policy objectives." The narrowest, *lobbying,* "involves explicit efforts" to influence specific government decisions. The three major variations on it are professional lobbying, mobilization of constituencies, and informal interaction between interest-group elites and target elites. In *representation,* group spokespeople seek "to be represented explicitly in the institutional mechanisms by which a class of policy decisions is to be determined." *Comprehensive mobilization* is designed to integrate the interest group "with other organizations, such as political parties, in a more or less long-term effort to mobilize broad community support and, in turn, gain control of the full array of governmental policy-making machinery." Phrased in another way, polite or diplomatic struggle involves persuasion and bargaining (Turner 1970). And even though many tactics may be illegal—as in bribery, blackmail, wiretapping, and burglary—these are carried on in a physically peaceful, courteous, and circumspect manner.

For complicated and concatenated reasons, themselves surrounded by centuries of often acrimonious debate, at least some contenders in the arena of society engage on occasion in *protest* or *violent struggle,* the two fundamental alternatives to polite struggle.

Violent struggle refers to the strategy of physically damaging or destroying property or other humans. Its more "primitive" (in the sense of relatively unplanned and short-lived) forms include proletarian and bourbon lynchings, mob attacks, communal and ghetto riots, pogroms, and official riots (as described in chapter 1). More sophisticated (in the sense of planned and long-lived) forms include the bombings and kidnappings of terrorists bands, guerrilla armies, insurrections, dual sovereignty contests, and international war.

Protest struggle stands between polite and violent struggle, a kind of "middle force." As I use the term, protest eschews or at least avoids the extensive physical damage to property and humans found in violent struggle on the one side and the restraint and decorum of staid politics on the other. It is an "out of place" form of struggle in at least the two senses of often being conspicuously out-of-doors or impolitely and ostentatiously intrusive on indoor space. The garden variety form of protest struggle is the *demonstration,* defined by Webster as "the act of making known or evident by visible or tangible means" and a "public display of group feeling." In ordinary usage over recent decades there are connotations of "uninstitutionalized" and "street" actions. Thus, one analyst properly distinguishes demonstrations from "more routine forms of expression, such as regular participation in a town meeting or party convention" (Etzioni 1970:4).

My usage includes but is not coextensive with what is called "nonviolence" or "nonviolent action" as those terms were employed in the American civil rights movement of the 1960s (e.g. Bell 1968) and have been reflected on by philosophers (e.g. Stiehm 1972).

Protest is a broader and more generic phenomenon and antedates nonviolent protest by millennia. A signal feature is an impatience with the encumbrances of institutions and a readiness to act impolitely but not necessarily with violence. Howard Zinn and Kenneth Clark capture this quality when describing the early ethos of the Student

Nonviolent Coordinating Committee (SNCC). As Zinn and Clark are quoted in Piven and Cloward (1977:222), SNCC participants had "an eagerness to move out of the political maze of normal parliamentary procedure and to confront policy-makers directly with a power beyond orthodox politics—the power of people in the streets and on the picket line" (Zinn 1964:13). And Clark (1966:259) said that "SNCC seems restless with long-term negotiation and the methods of persuasion of the Urban League, and it assumes that the legislative and litigation approach of the NAACP" had exhausted its possibilities.

These distinctions among polite, protest, and violent politics or struggle have considerable precedent in the literature, as has been documented in the introduction to this volume. In addition to the materials reviewed there, we may point to the distinctions Arthur I. Waskow (1966:277-78) has drawn among the politics of order, violence, and "creative disorder" in analyzing the American civil rights movement of the early sixties.

> In the politics of order, people divide their attention between the changes to be accomplished and the accepted rules of society about the "legitimate" ways of bringing about change. In the politics of violence, people divide their attention between the changes to be accomplished and those powerful people who get in the way of change—the enemy. In the politics of disorder, people tend to reduce greatly their interest in both the given rules and the enemy; instead they focus very strongly on the changes to be accomplished. To over-simplify a bit, in the politics of order, [people] . . . follow the rules; in the politics of violence, they attack their enemies; in the politics of disorder, they pursue change.

Or, in treating "direct action," (i.e. protest) British political theorist April Carter (1973:24) marks it off "from guerrilla warfare and street fighting . . . [and from], at the other end of the scale . . . political activity relying on speeches, leaflets and general propaganda which are the stock in trade of constitutional pressure groups. . . . [The latter] may well be a prelude to direct action, or an ancillary aspect . . . but they are not in themselves a form of [it], unless undertaken as a challenge to specific laws or the authorities." The important task, of course, is not merely to reiterate these distinctions but to forge on in making analytic use of them.

TYPES OF PROTEST STRUGGLE

If we want to understand *protest* struggle, we need first (or at least early on) to draw a reasonably clear picture not just of it as a global entity but as a complexly constituted creature composed of numerous forms. To what *kinds of actions* (as well as situations and definitions of them) are we referring when we evoke the notion of protest? As obvious as this question may be, relatively little systematic attention has been accorded it. Ralph Turner's (1970) briefly drawn contrasts between persuasion, bargaining, and coercion (and similar contrasts reported in the introduction to this volume), seem to suffice for most analysts. The single most concerted effort has been that of Gene Sharp (1973) in his monumental *The Politics of Nonviolent Action,* a work remarkably disattended by scholars but studied and used quite seriously in some contemporary social movements. Drawing on and modifying Sharp, I propose four major classes of protest politics that can themselves be ranked from lower to higher levels of system challenge and social definition of seriousness.

SYMBOLIC

At the first and lowest level is *symbolic* protest, those orderly and nondisruptive but more or less ostentatious ways in which people collectively draw attention to their grievances. Sharp (1973, ch. 3) treats this class under the label "nonviolent protest and persuasion," calling attention to ways in which such actions also overlap with the devices of polite politics. April Carter (1973:24) also views symbolic protest as "on the borderline of direct action," as is evident in the quote from her, just above. And in the contemporary antinuclear movement one encounters a distinction between "direct and symbolic action," the former often held to be superior to the latter (Chatfield 1980:7).

The three prime forms of symbolic protest are the procession (e.g. marches, parades), the assembly (e.g. the rally), and various kinds of public acts, including picketing. Sharp (1970, ch. 3) lists fifty-four detailed forms of it that he groups, in part, into formal statements, group presentations, symbolic public acts, drama, and honoring the dead.

These modest or even almost polite protest actions are such only in the context of relatively open societies; they are symbolic because authorities and other citizens are prepared to allow people to perform acts that can be symbolic without hindrance. The symbolic nature of the protest resides in the *social response to it* and not only in the act itself. To the degree that audiences define what could be symbolic protest as threatening and as something that must be stopped or interfered with, the protest act escalates to a third class we will discuss, the "intervention." One classic illustration is the response of authorities to civil rights paraders in Birmingham, Alabama in early

1963 and Selma, Alabama in early 1965. Mere symbolic protest (parading) achieved the status of intervention protest by virtue of authorities electing to define parading as intervention (Garrow 1978).

NONCOOPERATION

The second basic form of protest is *noncooperation*, a refusal to provide the actions necessary for a social arrangement to continue. Sharp declares that nonviolent action "overwhelmingly" involves this class and 103 of the 198 methods he describes in his book are so classified. He in turn divides them into their social, economic, or political focus (devoting a chapter to each). The most familiar are in the economic realm, including the strike, slowdown, and boycott, and variations thereof.

ALTERNATIVE INSTITUTIONS

Sharp's third and final class of protest action—the intervention—encompasses two forms I feel ought to be distinguished. I will describe what is for me the fourth, final, and highest form of protest (the alternative institution) prior to the third (the intervention) because I will not be returning to the fourth and it will only clutter discussion to come back to it. Sharp's distinction between negative and positive forms of intervention seems more fundamental than simply a variation on intervention—the way in which he elects to deemphasize the distinction. He defines "positive intervention" as establishing "new behavior patterns, policies, relationships, or institutions which are preferred" (Sharp 1973:357). Following this usage, this class can be labeled *alternative institutions*, subforms of which include alternative communication, transportation, and economic systems and "dual sovereignty and parallel government" (Sharp 1973, ch. 8). To the degree that the protest alternative institution comes to supersede the loyalties of citizens, this is the most serious and consequential type of protest. It can augur quite profound—even revolutionary—change in ways not possible in connection with the other three major classes of protest.

INTERVENTION

The third strongest form, the *intervention,* may "disrupt or even destroy established behavior patterns, policies, relationships, or institutions which are seen as objectionable" (Sharp 1973:357). As Sharp (1973:357) mentions, compared to symbolic protest and noncooperation, "methods of . . . intervention pose a more direct and immediate challenge." They seem more prone to involve violence. Somewhat reordering Sharp's treatment, four patterns of intervention may be distinguished:

1. *Harassment,* in which the objectionable activities of a person are continually called attention to in some extraordinary manner.
2. *System overloading,* in which a too large amount of whatever an arrangement processes is injected.
3. *Blockade,* in which protesters temporarily impede the movement of objectionable people and/or materials (e.g. Taylor 1977).
4. *Occupation,* in which people "enter or refuse to leave some place where they are not wanted or from which they have been prohibited" (Sharp 1973:371).

THE PROTEST OCCUPATION

In twentieth-century America, the protest occupation has constituted the leading edge technique of at least four major social movements and has been an important ancillary device in several others (as well as being an unsung but integral aspect of all American history; see e.g. Cooney and Michalowski [1977]. In sequence, the four major waves of this century have been as follows.

Among industrial workers in the thirties, "sit-down strikes" were the practice of taking over plants or other work places as a tactic in winning union recognition and other advances. Starting sporadically in the early thirties, their number escalated and they became a "fashion" in 1936-37, jumping from 48 affecting 88,000 workers in 1936 to 477 affecting 400,000 workers in 1937. One newspaper remarked on this "strike storm" that "sitting down has replaced baseball as a national pastime, and sitter-downers clutter up the landscape in every direction" (quoted in Fine 1979:331). This technique was augmented by ordinary strikes and pickets, but some analysts have argued that success of the "vast labor upheaval" of the thirties was centrally dependent on the use of the sit-down (Piven and Cloward 1977, ch. 3; Fine 1979:338-41).

Likely most memorable is the use of the sit-in by the civil rights movement in 1960-61, a wave of public accommodation broachings that in a year and a half involved "at least 70,000 sit-inners" in "over a hundred cities and towns in every southern and border state" (Matthews and Prothro 1966:23). Here, also, some observers have claimed that the sit-in as a technique was a critical component of success, although obviously augmented by boycott and parading (Piven and Cloward 1977, ch. 4). The "sit-in" was such an integral part of the civil rights movement that the name of the technique has often been used interchangeably with the substantive name of the movement.

Not quite as sharp in the collective memory is the fact that participants in the student movement of the middle and late sixties often seized buildings as part of their strategy. Beyond the famous episodes at Berkeley in 1964 ("where it all began") (Heirich 1968) and Columbia in 1968, hundreds of campus buildings were occupied over the years of the late sixties. Bayer and Austin (1971:307) report almost 300 were seized/blockaded in *each* of the years 1968-69 and 1970-71.

After several years of relative disuse, the basic technique was taken up by the antinuclear movement in the late seventies, continuing into the early eighties. While no firm figures are yet available (in part because media have elected to downplay or ignore the movement's existence and protest actions [Gitlin 1980:287ff.]), successful and attempted occupations of nuclear-involved places have numbered at least in the hundreds since 1974 and have involved many thousands of protesters (Barkan 1979).

We might think of these as four major waves of protest occupations within and between which smaller eddies and swirls have also occurred. There are, thus, the American Indian occupations at Alcatraz Island in 1969, at Wounded Knee in 1973, and at a variety of other places (Editorial Research Reports 1978:13-14). In 1977, groups of disabled occupied several offices of the federal government, one of them for twenty-six days (Anderson 1977:49). There have been a host of other efforts, many of them localized and brief (see e.g. Cooney and Michalowski 1977).

Thus summed up, let us consider, first, some important ways these waves vary, and second, key features they have in common that set them off from, but informing of, the symbolic sit-ins to which we will come in chapter 15.

It is important to distinguish among protest occupations in terms of the relation between the territory seized and the protest demands being made. In what we might consider the most primordial of relations, the protesters lay an *ownership* claim to the exact territory they have elected to seize. Such has been the case for numerous American Indian protest occupations. Up slightly from that, the occupation lays a claim to the *use* of a place or at least to a place of that *kind* if not that exact place. The Squatters Movement in Britain following World War II, in which the homeless occupied empty houses without legal sanction, illustrates this variation (Carter 1973:16ff.). In both, there is an integral or substantive relation between the act of occupation and the place occupied.

These differ from the pattern in which a place is temporarily occupied to press for expanded public rights of *access*. In the classic sit-ins of the civil rights movement White seats of lunch counters, churches, bus stations, and the like were occupied to gain the concrete right to occupy the specific seat where situated and all seats of "that sort." Here too there was an integral and immediate relation between the protest act and its objective. Wade-ins, ride-ins, and so forth were genotypically identical in this way although phenotypically quite different.

Next, territory can be brought under protester control for the purpose of promoting a demand that lies beyond and is substantively disconnected from the territory occupied. The sit-down capture of factories in the American thirties was not an effort to seize the ownership of factories or gain the right to be in them, but only a device to strengthen one's bargaining position. Student seizure of buildings in the sixties were likewise efforts to gain leverage in struggles with campus officials rather than efforts to live in administration buildings (an *ownership* claim) or gain the right to enter them (a *rights* claim). Both were *tactical* in nature.

Last, in what might be thought a very elaborate variation on the blockade, territory can be occupied for the purpose of preventing an objectionable activity from starting or continuing at that place. As in the initial three patterns above, there is a substantive relation between occupation and territory but it is of a quite different character, at least in the case of antinuclear activists who are its main practitioners. No ownership or rights claim is made on a nuclear site, but the site and the protest act are nonetheless substantively connected because the nuclear activists are directly acting against a place to which they object because of its constitutive activity. As Michael Fink and I spell out in chapter 15, the symbolic sit-ins we observed at the California Capitol were exclusively of the *tactical* type. No claims of ownership, access rights, or constitutive objections were made.

An appreciation of protest occupation history, waves, and variations in the relation of occupation to demand, helps us now to see a number of ways in which these episodes are also similar despite their manifest differences. These need to be elaborated because they provide a set of contrasts with the symbolic sit-ins we will analyze in chapter 15; that is, symbolic sit-ins *do not* have these features and their absence will be central to understanding them.

An initial matter has already been mentioned but its significance has not been drawn out. Protest occupations tend to occur in waves or spurts that last only two to a few years. All parties to them tend to bracket individual episodes together as part of a class of events "of this kind" that "we are experiencing now." In sheer statistical terms, only a few episodes are perceived as isolated or minor.

This wave quality is not a matter of mere, dispassionate cognition. Everyone involved defines the developing wave situation as one of challenge and crisis. Unusual numbers of police or even the military are likely to be mobilized or at least action to do so agonized about by some and demanded by others. On all sides, emotions become highly aroused and the rhetoric inflated.

Standing patterns of setting activity tend to be disrupted: factories stop running; lunch counters stop serving; college administrations stop functioning; construction crews stop building.

The occupations are defined as "third-party relevant" in several senses. "Everyone" in public life, especially people in political offices, feel they can and should pronounce on the occupations, especially on their legality. Segments of *local* populations feel it is appropriate for them to appear at the occupation site and openly to comment on the proceedings, either hostilely or sympathetically. Mobs may harass the occupiers; supporters may develop elaborate support organizations (as in the extraordinary General Motors sit-down strike of 1936-37); crowds may do battle with police or military deployed to eject the occupiers. Irrespective of the content, there is enormous on- and off-the-scene third-party action and attention.

Features such as these make up what sociologists refer to as a "collective behavior situation," a situation in which people collectively move toward:

1. Defining a situation as extraordinary and as reason for suspending the "attitude of everyday life" and the ordinary sense that "nothing unusual is happening" in favor of a definition that "something unusual is happening."
2. Displaying high levels of emotional arousal and, in particular, high levels of fear, hostility, and joy.
3. Acting in ways that are socially defined as unusual, among occupiers, authorities, and others, and aside from and in addition to the unusual acts that constitute the protest occupation per se. (For expanded discussion see ch. 1, this volume.)

The pattern described is the true protest occupation, or more loosely, the classic sit-in or territorial seizure. It has at least two kinds of significance for an understanding of the symbolic protest occupations discussed below in chapter 15. One, for reasons to be elaborated in chapter 15, the symbolic sit-in is a variety of *symbolic protest*—the first or "lowest" class of protest outlined above—and not a type of noncooperation, intervention, or alternative institution—the other three classes. Two, it became possible for the symbolic sit-in to emerge and enter the repertoire of social movement protest actions precisely because of the background of waves of protest occupation just described. Those waves (and eddies) provided the imagery and rhetoric of protest that inspired the crystallization of the symbolic sit-in.

I want to conclude by calling attention to the social importance of what may be thought of as "protest studies." Without arguing the reasons, we may take as a working premise the generalization that polite politics seem unable effectively to respond to the churnings and grindings of modern societies. Violent and protest politics keep appearing, albeit sporadically and in waves. If the world cannot be made safe for and by polite politics and if violent and protest politics seem unavoidable or even inevitable, a key question becomes not *if* but in *what* form and manner. Once beyond polite politics, the initial choice is obviously between protest and violent politics.

For scholarly analysts such as myself, preferring protest to violent politics, a priority concern becomes how to facilitate the former and inhibit the latter. One way to foster the choice of protest politics is to provide increasingly articulate, wide-ranging, and *usable* analyses that are empirical, reflective, and systematic. Despite endless journalistic reports, moral musings, and abstract theorizings, there are few studies displaying these scholarly features of empirical closeness and analytic acuity.

Happily, however, a viable field of something like "protest studies" does seem to be on the horizon and we can envision a day when scholarly treatment of protest achieves the same institutional embodiment and support already enjoyed by the study of polite and violent politics—and which encourages both. (One not-so-whimsical possibility is university departments and institutes of protest studies, paralleling current departments and institutes of political science that ought more accurately be labeled departments and institutes of polite or diplomatic politics.)

I am suggesting, then, that the social arena is made more stable and workable by means of protest, and that one important task of social analysts is to facilitate at least some forms of it by means of activist-usable scholarly analyses.

13

SOCIOLOGISTS AS AN INTEREST GROUP: PROSPECT AND PROPRIETY (1981)

Over the last two decades, American society has changed in ways that significantly alter our relationship, as sociologists, to it. I want in these remarks, first, to depict these changes—the coming of something approaching "the interest-group society"—and second, to point up the new measure of social value that accompanies it. Like it or not, sociologists must develop some sort of posture toward this new interest-group context and its emerging measure of value. As my third task, therefore, I want to outline the three main postural possibilities: continuation of the relatively passive status quo; rejection of politics altogether; and a more assertive interest-group program. In the spirit of exploration rather than advocacy, I shall, fourth, detail some of the things a more assertive posture might mean and require. It is, however, one thing to list aspects of hypothetical programs; it is quite another to mobilize resources for them. Further exploring, I shall, fifth, consider some of the major facilitants and inhibitants of any important upgradings in our collective posture. Finally, I will offer some personal reflections on all this.

THE INTEREST-GROUP SOCIETY

Following more or less established and restricted usage, the term *interest group* refers to any formal organization that engages in activities designed to protect or enhance the social resources of its members by influencing the policies and practices of other associations (particularly governmental institutions) and the sentiments and dispositions of the public at large. Prominent, lay-conceived categories of interest groups are businesses, government agencies, labor unions, and educator, farmer, environmental, senior citizen, "public-interest," civil rights, and women's associations (Ornstein and Elder 1978:35-53).

My use of the term *interest group* and the tradition associated with it is guarded and adapted to the problem at hand. I am aware that the interest-group perspective, so labeled, is currently and decidedly out of fashion among social scientists, especially those who involve themselves in matters of political economy, elite and class-dialectic models of political power (Whitt 1979), and the historical and comparative study of large-scale societies. From those or similar distances, interest groups may indeed be invisible or only insignificant details, and the concept may ring of naive, fifties', pluralism. But when we stand closer and observe people competing for money, power, and prestige, an organizing construct such as interest groups begins strongly to recommend itself as an at least useful if not perfect tool for ordering our observations. (And, despite the label's disfavor, interest-group scholarship is still very much alive and even thriving; it is merely traveling under assumed identities, a major one of which is the so-called resource mobilization approach to social movements [Zald and McCarthy 1979].)

In highlighting interest groups, I am only saying, further, that they are *a* significant feature of modern life, one of special importance to sociologists as such. There are obviously other and perhaps more significant aspects, including my own pet concerns, social and revolutionary movements, classes of associations that operate, by definition, outside the diplomatic and polite realm of the interest-group struggle but which often bear quite momentously on its very constitution.

I must confess my partiality to the root image of society sponsored by the interest-group perspective, an image of scurrying contenders in a vast and intricate arena. That imagery scales down the powerful and scales up the powerless, placing them on the same plane of action despite disparities of resources and organization. This strikes me as a much more potent, fearsome, and optimistic cognitive map—one that heartens the less powerful and frightens the more powerful—than the principal alternative image, that of a hierarchy of strata or classes, the layer-cake view of society.

Be all these matters as they may, in the long sweep of American history, a first and notable feature of interest groups is the "upward secular trend" of their numbers (Salisbury 1975:191). Within this major trend, there are, second, "wave-like spurts" in the rate of their founding (Truman 1971). The most recent wave, occurring in the 1960s and 1970s, has not yet been subjected to precise numerical assessment, but knowledgeable people do not hesitate to characterize it as a "genuine explosion" (Ornstein and Elder 1978:227).

A third salient generalization relates to the sheer range or diversity of interests that have achieved organized expression. Especially in the last two decades, this too has virtually exploded. Nonexistent or extremely obscure only years ago, there are now complex sets of consumer, environmentalist, age-based, educational, "public-interest," civil rights, religious, and many other categories of interest groups. One implication is that an increasing fraction of the total population has likely been drawn into the interest-group struggle for resources. While not yet comprehensively documented, some studies suggest a fourth generalization: the total volume and value of resources (meaning people and money) deployed to activities of an interest-group character has been rising as a portion of total social resources. In vicious circle fashion, as new groups have entered the arena of social struggle, older groups have increased their efforts to compensate for the new competitors. Newer groups react, in turn, and the cycle starts over at a higher level.

A fifth and last generalization of special relevance is that the range of tactics and targets of influence may be expanding. Confining our attention to interaction between interest groups and government (the institution to which all interest groups are said to gravitate), Robert Salisbury's classification of "modes of interaction" summarizes basic target and tactics of influence in a way that helps us to see both expansions and shifts. His "major categories of strategic activity" are "defined by the relative specificity of [the] policy objectives" (Salisbury 1975:209). The narrowest, *lobbying,* "involves explicit efforts" to influence specific government decisions. Three major variations on it are professional lobbying, mobilization of constituencies, and informal interaction between interest-group elites and target elites. In *representation,* group spokespeople seek "to be represented explicitly in the institutional mechanisms by which a class of policy decisions is to be determined." Moreover, *comprehensive mobilization* is designed to integrate the interest group "with other organizations, such as political parties, in a more or less long-term effort to mobilize broad community support and, in turn, gain control of the full array of governmental policy-making machinery" (Salisbury 1975:209).

Each of these three modes of interaction subsumes a panoply of complicated options and processes and the most accurate generalization about trends is, perhaps, movement to deploying a wider array of forms of each in more sophisticated and complex versions. For example, Ornstein and Elder (1978:81) conclude that social changes in the last two decades have "altered the art" of even lobbying "in fundamental ways." The trend is toward efforts to persuade an ever-greater number of skeptical decision makers with ever-better "research" and "reasoned" arguments, with all the organizational and personnel elaborations these require. (Salisbury [1975:209] warns us, however, that lobbying is likely *not* "the most characteristic mode of group-government interaction.")

Shifts of these magnitudes and rapidity move us toward a substantially altered process by which significant social resources are distributed; that is, the process through which social policy is forged. It is a process in which myriad groups contest for protection and advantage at every complicated and tortured step.

THE NEW MEASURE OF SOCIAL VALUE

One critical upshot is a new way in which audiences of interest groups gauge the seriousness with which to take the claims they ubiquitously encounter. As the number, diversity, volume, and range of activity of interest groups expand, the flow of resources is thereby more tenaciously contended. This creates a climate of the *expectation of claims making* on the part of everyone involved in the policy process. Since so many interests are routinely present, it is easy to make the inference that any logically interested interest group that absents itself has consciously elected to do so and has no objective interest in whatever is at issue. That inference is not necessarily true. Any set of interests expressed in a policy process is quite arbitrary, a momentary constellation reflecting only the degree of the advance of "consciousness" and organization at a moment in history. But that is not the operational assumption of competing interest groups and policy framers and implementers. All of them already have enough trouble and interest-group agents at their doors; they are decidedly not inclined to seek additional and theoretically or logically relevant parties to issues.

The demonstration of social value of everything has thus escalated. Under the onslaught of well-articulated, competing claims of value, the very fact of *being a claimant* (or failing to be one) itself becomes an important measure of social value. This shift is easy enough, because there are no clear and agreed-on measures of the value of anything. Instead, there are only competing claims to be adjudicated and placated. Phrased differently, an important social function performed well does not carry its own testimony of merit. Merit, instead, must be accented, highlighted, and broadcast by means of conscious and formal effort directed to strategic audiences. Mere consistent presence is one key aspect of such highlighting. Moreover, because so many groups are now engaged in this new *dramaturgy of value*, interest groups that do not engage in it find themselves greatly disadvantaged. Further, in the escalating climate of the dramaturgy of group protection and promotion, groups that "stand still" in their level of effort are in fact falling behind relative to other groups who are increasing their efforts.

If in the wake of proliferating interest groups there is a new dramaturgy of social value (as well as the need to make more plausible, substantive arguments on any interest group's behalf), there are then questions of if and how sociologists ought to act toward all this in the last decades of the twentieth century.

SELECTED POSTURES

Without overadvocating, we can outline three fundamental possibilities. The first basic direction is to denounce the interest-group society itself and refuse to participate in the social struggle as defined by it. There are, in turn, two versions of this posture. In one, the interest-group struggle is viewed as "sandbox politics." It and the electoral system are bracketed together as two components of an elaborate, ruling-class-sponsored confidence game aimed at diverting attention from the more fundamental problems of the social order, which include the existence of a tight ruling class and control, inequality, and exploitation. Interest-group images and theory are mere species of pluralism, reformism, or economism—all equally bankrupt doctrines relative to a more accurate revolutionist, or at least class-dialectic view.

The other version of "a pox on ordinary politics" fears the fragmentation effects of proliferating interest groups and the presumed paralysis of policy that Balkanization may entail (Ornstein and Elder 1978:228). In the interest of fostering national consensus and policy on a variety of issues, sociologist and other interest groups, it is argued, ought to be prepared to give significant ground or even to stay out of the struggle altogether. Additionally, this posture fits together with stress on sociology as a pure, scholarly pursuit that ought not to be sullied by the assertedly corrupting effects of political action. It might even be argued that the social value of sociology is so great and obvious—unlike other social groups—that no special effort on their part is required. (A subterranean theme crosscutting both these versions of "a pox on politics" is that sociology is not worth defending relative to the merits of the claims of other interest groups.)

A second basic direction would hold that sociologists are already engaged in a great deal of interest-group activity, and it is sufficient to the task. Assessment of the adequacy of the present level of mobilization must be hinged, in part, on evaluation of what *is* the present level *relative to* that of other interest groups, especially those with whom we perforce compete most closely. No one has yet, to my knowledge, come forth with a systematic scale that allows us numerically to calculate levels of mobilization and therefore accurately to compare groups. In the absence of that, I can only offer my own impressions, and those of others who are knowledgeably involved, that on a scale of say 100, sociologists would earn perhaps a 10 relative to the maximum scores of many other groups and relative to scores in the twenties and thirties we would give the other knowledge-producing occupations with which sociologists often compare themselves.

Be this scaling as it may, it can be said without the slightest aspersion on any of our present or past leaders and within the context of the interest-group revolution and the new measure of value I have outlined that maintaining the current level of mobilization among sociologists will mean falling behind. Perhaps sociologists ought to elect to stand still and therefore fall behind in this manner.

We come now to the third possibility: a more self-conscious, multifaceted effort to be collectively and self-interestedly involved in policy processes at all three of the levels mentioned—lobbying, representation in decision making, and comprehensive mobilization.

ASPECTS OF AN INTEREST-GROUP ACTIVISM

Continuing in the spirit of exploration rather than advocacy, let me enumerate some of the obvious things that an activist stance could mean.

First, there is the arena of our relation to the national government. At that level, we might allocate more resources to monitoring legislation, regulation, and relevant programs of funding. Mechanisms for the rapid and nationwide marshaling of sentiment could be devised, a technique called "indirect" or "grass-roots" lobbying and used widely and effectively by interest groups (Congressional Quarterly 1979:20). Two matters recently and continuingly at issue at the national level might have gone more in our favor in the past and might in the future go better if we had "in-place" capacities for such activations. One is the effort of the government to impose onerous regulations on the conduct of social science research, a matter that is by no means settled and likely to be an unending source of difficulty, because, let us be clear, other well-organized and powerful interest groups have a keen interest in hobbling social scientists. The other is the year-in, year-out struggle for funding of basic research in the social sciences, supportive action for which social scientists seem loath to take (Dynes 1979). But, in the words of Russell Dynes (1980a), "it's less a problem that members of Congress are deaf. The major problem is that social scientists are dumb . . . in the sense of being silent and . . . in the sense of not being concerned with their own self-interest."

There are obviously a great many other government actions to which sociologists could reasonably be party—among them, for example, the recent and little-publicized decisions of the Library of Congress to cease cataloging books in the historic fashion.

Further, it is clear that "political action committees" are now a major facet of the interest-group society (Malbin 1980). Sociologists might consider their own, tailored version of this mechanism, one that deals with a carefully chosen set of those officeholders whose behavior impinges most critically on the occupation. The lead effort here is the American Psychological Association's Association for the Advancement of Psychology.

Second, there may be a growing usefulness, in at least some parts of the nation, more carefully to monitor the activities of state government with a keen eye on new laws relating to privacy and freedom of information and the impact, both helpful and harmful, these can have on research activities. For example, some new state laws that protect members of the press from state-coerced revelation of news sources might be expanded to provide protection for the "subjects" of social science inquiries. One important function of the state sociological associations we have seen multiplying in recent years could be that of monitoring state government and mobilizing sentiment when and where needed. Also along such lines, relations among state, regional, and national associations might auspiciously be elaborated, following models of "operational" "second-order," and "peak" associations that have long been used by other interest groups for purposes of forcefully mustering views and other resources (Salisbury 1975:187).

Third, it is often, and I think correctly, said that sociologists are naive in dealing with the media, including the press (Dynes 1980b). Frequently misquoted and misconstrued, many among us try to avoid it. We should be aware, though, that almost all other interest groups have a strikingly opposite policy. In an organized fashion, many seek (and get) reasonably accurate, frequent, and positive coverage of many kinds. For sociologists such a policy might mean, for example, standing committees on relations to the media in all our associations, including the use of those staples of public life, press officers, press releases, and press conferences. (Conventions of the Pacific Sociological Association do not receive media coverage for the simple reason that we do not ask for it. A great many of the matters we discuss at our meetings are newsworthy, nonetheless, and very much to our credit. A host of opportunities to enhance the public appreciation of our work constantly go by the board for such reasons.)

The comments of James Banner (1980:3), spearhead of the newly formed National Association for the Advancement of the Humanities, are instructive in this context. Observing that people in the natural sciences long ago stimulated "science reporting," and that it is now a "recognized and organized field of journalism," he has urged humanists also to launch a "community-wide program to improve press coverage and enhance public understanding of their work, an effort that will require bold departures from customary practices and attitudes."

Fourth, the forging and maintenance of alliances is a prime condition of interest groups' effectiveness, particularly those that are relatively small (Congressional Quarterly 1979:3). Among sociologists, some such exist at the national level, and it is likely that they could be strengthened easily and greatly, and their number expanded. At this time, the coalitional networks in which sociologists as an association participate are mostly those that bring together learned societies, social science associations, and higher-education organizations (Dynes 1978c). Their number could surely be enlarged, as in, for example, seeking charter membership in the newly forming "federation of behavioral and cognitive sciences" that will "represent the interests of those fields in Congress and the federal bureaucracy" (Foltz 1981). Participation in state or regional versions of such coalitions is an obvious extension.

Fifth, the perspectives, theories, skills, instruments, and so forth that sociologists invent and develop have a pronounced tendency to migrate out of the discipline (or should I say to be appropriated?) and to be codified in what become competitor programs and occupations. This happens in part because sociologists are too frequently apathetic about matters of organization, training, and job labeling, both within and without the academy, and too "pure" to so concern themselves (Dynes 1978a). Among the consequences are slow, long-term attrition of our numerical strength and legitimacy. As I have heard it put, "everybody" wants sociology taught as long as it is not taught by sociology departments, and "everybody" wants to hire sociologists as long as they are not called "sociologists." The interest-group implication of this trend is a much more watchful eye on academic planners and nonacademic employers of sociologists. For better or worse, there might need to be issues of certification in some form.

Sixth, many of the things we already do have significance for sociologists as an interest group, even though we do not ordinarily think of them in that fashion. I have in mind the numerous teaching materials and techniques projects of recent years. The classroom is one of the major arenas in which images of our activities are presented and credibility gained or lost. The organized concern we show for teaching is, in such terms, completely justified, even though there are other important reasons to give it much attention. Indeed, a more conscious appreciation of the political character of teaching might stimulate us to take it even more seriously and think about it in new ways.

These points suffice to convey the kinds of things involved in a more active interest-group posture. Measured against the panoply of theoretical possibilities and the "in-place" programs of sophisticated interest groups, however, it is an exceedingly sparse and only suggestive set of items, as even the most cursory reading of the interest-group literature forcefully conveys.

INHIBITANTS AND FACILITANTS OF AN INTEREST-GROUP ACTIVISM

I hope to have treated each of the three basic postures in detail sufficient to convey their nature and implications. I have accorded the third the most attention because it is the hardest to achieve and the most novel; the second is simply what we have, and the first merely dismantles what we have.

In the end, which of these three courses we elect, if any, is a matter of collective moral choice and as such involves preferences themselves not notably subject to processes of reasoning and evidence. But even a question of "ought" or "should" can be informed by a recognition of what "is." It can be folly, or at least a waste of time, to strive for courses of action that are clearly impossible in view of the objective situation at hand. Therefore, before coming to the question of what we *should* do, let us ask what we *could* do; holding aside propriety, let us scrutinize prospect.

Slanting the question in the direction I think we must take most seriously, let me organize discussion in terms of objective features of the situation of sociologists that inhibit or facilitate a greater degree of interest-group activism.

Regarding the former, there is a first and basic fact that significantly increased degree of interest-group activism requires much intensive labor and specialized knowledge. The ordinary interest-group solution to these problems is a complex combination of paid staff and committed volunteers. Regardless of how the two are mixed (and interest groups vary greatly), they are very expensive. An appreciable increase in mobilization would require at least a doubling, and likely a tripling or greater increase, of the rates at which sociologists now "tax" themselves. (Sizable increase may be possible. A late 1980 survey of American Sociological Association members discovered that three-quarters or more of them favored increased political and other such ASA action, and were willing to pay higher dues for it [Brown and Cook 1981].)

Sociologists are small in number and relatively poor in economic resources. In the spectrum of interest groups, these structural facts are great competitive disadvantages that may be insurmountable. Even more ominous, sociology seems likely to decline in both these respects in the years ahead. One recent projection asks not *if* but *when* our junior members "will enter the ranks of the working poor," that is, be working but earn less than the federal poverty threshold (Abbott 1980).

Second, the onset of the interest-group society coincides with one of our weaker periods, one of severe theoretical, methodological, and substantive fragmentation, economic decline, and the broader demoralization and malaise these produce. Collective self-doubt, born of the wider and broader doubts of society as a whole, bodes ill for self-interested collective action. Fragmentation, in particular, is expressed (among other ways) in current contentions among those most active in the American Sociological Association who dispute the very nature of the association's primary mission: "development of the discipline" versus increase of research funding versus "organizational weapons to correct . . . injustices which affect members of the Association and members of the larger human community" (Dynes 1978b), among others.

Third, occupational identities rooted more centrally in formal organizations perhaps supersede and overwhelm identities as sociologists. That is, most sociologists are faculty in higher education, and their most proximate struggles are with their direct employers. Quite reasonably, they look first and perhaps only to that realm of the interest-group struggle.

Fourth, we must be careful not to underestimate the degree to which all of us harbor what Melvin Seeman years ago identified as a "minority-like" adjustment to the situation of being a species of intellectual. The classic minority group themes he documented among professors were "direct acceptance of majority stereotypes," "concern with in-group purification," "approval of conformity," "denial of group membership," and "fear of group solidarity" (Seeman 1958, emphases omitted). The last theme—fear of collective action—is especially striking to me because I encounter it with surprising frequency. Even sociologists who are strong advocates of collective action by *other* social categories become nervous and overreactive when it is proposed for people like sociologists. They tend to think an activist posture must mean things like strikes, boycotts, pickets, or even sit-ins, measures that, they quite correctly point out, seem inappropriate for us. But that collective action for sociologists and other social scientists evokes such images of protest and visions of public hostility directed toward them betrays the same kind of fears and insecurities classically common among a wide variety of ethnic, racial, physical, gender, and sexual minorities. (It is obvious, moreover, the vast bulk of interest-group action has nothing to do with protest; it is dully polite and bureaucratic.)

On the facilitant side and beyond such obvious aspects as having high-level analytic and organizational skills, we can notice, first, the well-developed and "dense" character of our translocal organization. The most evident form of this is the existing scholarly societies, but those are supplemented by rich and strong bonds of personal knowing and trust that lace together every state and the entire nation. Taking a leaf from the resource mobilization notebook on social movements, the "cooptable preexisting networks," as Jo Freeman (1975, ch. 2) labels them, are complex and strong. Both forms could be and are being strengthened in the recent growth of state sociological associations and, within them, as well as in regional associations, the elaboration of several kinds of material, solidarity, and expressive benefits (Salisbury 1975:184) that could serve, in addition, to legitimize the discipline in terms of larger publics.

Second, and drawing further from Freeman, discontents are relatively unactionable in the absence of focusing crises. The trend of national events augurs ironically well in this regard. The general movement to the Right portends the development of crises that could serve to transform the collective fearfulness we see among sociologists to a more assertive anger, mixed with pride, which is then itself organizationed. (Such a transformation from fear and shame to anger and pride has been observed among many stigmatized social categories and accomplished by many methods, "consciousness-raising" groups among them, a measure that is not overly whimsical to counsel for the programs of sociology conventions and other gatherings.)

Third, as sociologists we are rightly trained to construe pleadings of virtue as mere legitimizations of privileges or accommodations to disadvantages. As such, sociologists, more than other professionals, are disposed to regard all moral claims as rhetoric and self-serving mystification that is isomorphic with social location. One consequence is that we tend even to turn that skepticism onto ourselves. Recognizing that we have a social location that "conduces" us to promote the value of sociology, the impulse to plead is blunted or debilitated by our appreciation of our locational corruption. But, as Bennett Berger has had the courage to see and say, the cozy and convenient correspondence between social location and pleading of virtue is not, by the sheer logic of the matter, a dismal and shameful relation. The cynicism with which we regard that relation is merely a disposition we bring to it and not a logically entailed aspect of it. An alternative attitude might be, as Berger (1979:68) puts it,

> *respect* [for] ideas that enable people to get on with their lives more successfully. What, after all (asks the historical relativist), are moral ideas for? To suffer in the name of? Or are they tools, instruments like shovels, rakes, and chain saws, to help people get through their days, and in helping them through to provide some comfort, pride, even ennoblement for having got through safely?

Once freed from an undue skepticism about pleading on their own behalf, sociologists might think more clearly about the kinds of reasonable pleadings they can make. Such pleadings can and do move along a wide variety of dimensions. Let me recall only a few for which I have a special fondness and which might serve to facilitate an interest-group activism.

I begin with the observation that in complexly differentiated societies, ordinary people playing through their ordinary days are enmeshed in devising and enacting ideas and activities that are responsive to immediate exigencies. Immersed in acting, they have little time, training, or disposition carefully to collect information on multiple facets of their situations, to assemble it, to reflect on its meaning, to envision larger contexts in which it might be variously interpreted, and to contemplate feasible and conceivable alternatives to whatever exists. Of central significance, the unavoidable alliances, accommodations, ruses, mutings, euphemizings, and other necessary avoidances of ordinary life prompt people not to "see" many features of their situations and to develop the legitimizing and accommodating meanings to which I have referred. Said differently, the requirements of acting vitiate, nay cripple, the capacity and honesty to reflect.

The sociologist (as well as some other social analysts) is, by definition one would hope, trained to eschew these constrictions of ordinary life when examining it. Instead of quickly assembling practical information clearly directed to a problem at hand, we, at our best, collect data slowly and methodically. Instead of ordering data in a "quick-and-dirty" fashion, we, at our best, agonize over the most informative and meaningful treatment of it and over its accuracy and completeness. Instead of offering fast and firm decisions, we, at our best, insist on reflection, contemplation, or reconsideration. Instead of being practical about what is possible in proximate circumstances, we, at our best, want to be comparative and historical, bringing socially and temporally far-flung but relevant contrast cases to bear, pointing up perhaps currently unfeasible but not totally impossible ways of thinking about and acting toward the matter at hand.

Such contrasts between enmeshed actors and analysts are, of course, not unique to sociologists. The distinctly sociological posture entails, additionally, a focus on social organization, its forms, levels, causes, and so forth. While obvious to us, that focus sets us off from the situationally enmeshed tendency and socially ingrained disposition to use mobile, fleshbound creatures and how they internally vary as the basic unit of perception and explanation. Our special power derives, in particular, from the capacity to move up and down levels of social organization—the familiar interpenetration of biography and history—and to range widely in constructing social-organizational comparisons and contrasts.

Applied full-strength, this mixture of ingredients is a potent concoction. Its effects have sometimes been referred to as the "liberating" vision of sociology (Berger 1963), achieved by establishing a larger and wider understanding of and context for situations than the immediately enmeshed are likely to evolve—wider contexts in which even the basic categories of description and explanation used by the enmeshed are themselves made objects of description and explanation. Further, it is to be hoped that this process is, as Alvin Gouldner has discussed, continuously "reflexive," unremittingly obligated "to transform 'givens' into 'problems,' resources into topics." What Gouldner dubs the "culture of critical discourse" (of which sociology is a major variety) "must put its hands around its own throat and see how long it can squeeze [in] an unending regress" (Gouldner 1979:59-60; see also Hacker 1979; Etzioni 1968, ch. 8; Lippmann 1971).

Allow me to illustrate these contrasts by drawing from my own experience, not because it is any better than a legion of other examples, but because I know it better. The growth of new religions in Western societies has occasioned sharp accusations that their recruiters engaged in "brainwashing," "mind control," "spot hypnosis," or some similar deprivation of free will. People in the new religions have responded with the claim that they are no different than those converted to other religions and, indeed, that they may have been subject to some kind of divine guidance. People on both sides of this conflict are the sorts of "situationally enmeshed" ordinary participants I have described.

Several dozen sociologists in many countries have, over the past several years, scrutinized the changes found when people join a new religion. Working relatively independent of one another, they have constructed pictures of conversion that do not fit the depictions of either side. Careful and prolonged observation and interviewing, methodical treatment of the data, reflection, and a thorough consciousness of past and present contexts of new religions and conversions have produced accounts that are less lurid and dramatic than those sponsored by either side, and more "naturalistic" and even sympathetic than the depictions promoted by either side. I might even venture to say they are truer. (For reviews of the literature, see Robbins et al., 1978; Lofland and Skonovd 1981.)

But of what social value is this kind of distancing operation on social life? Coming full circle, back to the situation of ordinary people in ordinary life, sociological analysis facilitates the breakup of the collective self-deceptions—the ideological logjams—to which all social life is inherently prone. Indeed, as the situations in which people are intimately enmeshed grow ever more specialized and arcane and submerged in increasingly larger scales of social organization (even planetary-scale organization), the intellectual operations of the sociologist that I have sketched grow ever more important because situationally induced irrationality becomes more and more common and its consequences more fateful for all of us (Hacker 1979).

I have carefully inserted the phrase "at our best" in this description of our distinctive task. The degree to which we actually perform each operation at a high level in any given outing, varies. In quest of acceptance by the situationally embroiled, many of us are tempted to take on their perspective—to "lose perspective" as it is appropriately put. To identify that tendency as a temptation and to assert the appropriateness of tension between participants and analysts is, however, to have taken the most critical step in guarding against it.

Our own tendency toward situational enmeshment goes to the root of why our social role is, at its best, exceedingly difficult. As data gatherers and orderers, reflectors, and comparativist-contextualists, the microsituationally ensnarled are not likely to find immediate solace in our productions—as, for example, neither the new religionists nor their antagonists are given much comfort or ammunition by sociological analysis of identity change. Our audiences, therefore, must of necessity be broader than any immediate social organization or topic we analyze.

We need to think through the fact that what we do, in our best moments, sets up a basic, irresolvable tension between us as a social role and everyone else, a tension that marks us off from other interest groups and complicates all our relations. It is not clear to me how we ought to deal with this, aside from being forthright about it and striving to convince people that the larger and longer-term benefits of our enterprise are worth the immediate pain it may cause. Such a proposition is exceedingly difficult to evince persuasively.

These lists of inhibitants and facilitants can obviously be extended indefinitely by artful speculators, and my listing of items in one column or the other can assuredly be debated. Be those niceties as they may, the aspects I have mentioned serve adequately to suggest that an increased degree of interest-group activism is not impossible, but it would require a great deal of travail to achieve and be accompanied by a significant amount of conflict and acrimony in our ranks. If such is a reasonably accurate assessment of the prospect, how then does it and other factors bear on propriety?

PROSPECT AND PROPRIETY

The manner in which I have framed and phrased all this has doubtless already communicated my personal position: reluctantly and ambivalently I fear we must move to a markedly greater degree of interest-group action, if only to hold on to what little we have, which has already begun to slip away. I do not accept either version of the first basic option I mentioned, for, while I do not find the interest-group polity especially attractive, it is preferable to alternative systems so far proposed and to which we could reasonably move from where we are now. Nor, given the rapidity of change, will the second option, the status quo, provide even minimum self-defense.

An important part of my lack of enthusiasm derives from the fact that while I believe the objective need and I know something about what is required and how to go about it, I am not attracted to devoting a great deal of time to advocating, boosting, and performing the necessary work. My disinclination would be of little importance if only a small percentage of us shared it. I suspect, though, that my disposition is the rule rather than the exception. This ought not to surprise us, because we became involved in scholarship and are to one or another degree successful at it because of qualities that lead us away from the glad-handing hustle that is the essence of politics and public relations. I should have listed this alleged feature in the "inhibitants" column above, but I did not in order more forcefully, in closing, to point it up as perhaps *the* central problem of increased mobilization and the key one we would need to remedy.

The concrete work of interest-group activism seems best done by people who are sociable (who "mix well"), who are content to suffer a melange of fools patiently and unendingly, who are happy to attend meetings and conferences into infinity, who can quickly master complex and tedious documents produced by manifold agencies (each with "hidden agendas"), who can handle the stress of frequent, nasty surprises sprung by competitors, enemies, or even friendly interest groups, who do not become too rapidly bleary-eyed under the unbroken onrush of words and paper, who thrive on lunch after lunch and dinner after dinner of rubber chicken meals eaten in hotel banquet rooms under harsh fluorescent lights, who do not mind waiting untold hours in officials' reception rooms and government hearing rooms, who find it exhilarating rather than devastating to be challenged hostilely in public by officials and others who doubt one's pleadings, who can remain optimistic in spite of wavering and uncertain support given by members of one's own interest group, who can remain cool and good-humored in the face of frustrating, drawn-out, and frequently unsuccessful processes of decision making, who are prepared, overall, to give themselves over to the extremely demanding flow of events in the interest-group struggle.

Such are the kinds of situations and demands that the selection, training, and ordinary lives of sociologists do not strongly perpare us for, although everyone is involved in paler versions of such social struggle. Fortunately for our interest-group future, some among us, despite all selection and training, seem to thrive on that struggle, and their increased involvement in it will need to be stimulated. Beyond them, representing interest groups is an emerging occupation, a new kind of profession, one might even say. Contracting with firms offering that service or directly employing one or more of these professionals at appropriate times is a way some other interest groups deal with the reluctance or inability of their members to give time but who are nonetheless willing to provide money.

I want to close by acknowledging that my qualified call for a greater degree of interest-group action is founded on two premises, either or both of which may be untrue and obviate any need for us to act more strongly on our collective behalf. One, I may exaggerate the extent and importance of recent changes in interest groups. Two, all these changes could be true, but they do not have, and will not have, any important effects on us, corporately, as sociologists. Because we are good professional skeptics of all generalizations about social organizations, we want obviously to entertain these two alternatives. I would certainly prefer to be wrong; it would save us a great deal of time and tedious political work or, alternatively, declines in fortune forced from without in the absence of any action by us.

Uncertainty of several kinds may abound in all this, but there is nonetheless at least one nontrivial thing that can be said with certainty: The rapidity and extent of social change is going to force us to devote a great deal more attention to determining the nature of our corporate relation to our society, at many levels, and deciding how we ought collectively to act, including not acting at all.

NOTE

An abbreviated version of this paper was delivered as the presidential address to the Pacific Sociological Association meetings in Portland, Oregon, March 20, 1981. I am grateful to the following people for their cogent suggestions on a draft: Herbert Costner, Russell R. Dynes, Gary Hamilton, Lyn H. Lofland, and John Walton. The approach I employ grows out of several years of direct observation of interest groups as they operate at the Capitol of California and, particularly, from observations made over the calendar year of 1977, during which I did full-time fieldwork on them (Lofland 1982a) and their protest kin (Lofland and Fink 1982). My daily presence was supported by a combination of sabbatical leave, conducive scheduling of my sociology department duties, a faculty associate appointment with the Institute of Governmental Affairs at Davis, and by two small grants from the Davis Division of the University of California Academic Senate. I am very happy to acknowledge these supports.

14

CROWD LOBBYING (1982)

The term *crowd lobbying* refers to the lobbying organization tactic of circumspectly assembling large numbers of its grass-roots constituency at governmental centers for the purpose of promoting policy preferences in direct contact with officials. It is an emerging tactic of interest-group action that ingeniously blends features of two of the three basic genres of struggle explained in chapter 12—diplomatic and protest struggle.

In a narrow technical sense, crowd lobbying is a subform of lobbying, in particular of what Robert Salisbury (1975:209-13) terms "mobilization of constituencies," which involves efforts of lobby leaders to activate their constituency sufficiently to exercise a potential sanction on officeholders, usually an electoral sanction. Such efforts may be indirect and broad, as in mass media appeals, or more narrow, as in "letter or telegram campaigns and the use of 'bus tripping' to bring large numbers of agitated constituents to visit legislators" (Salisbury 1975:212).

Salisbury (1975:212-13) characterizes all mobilizations as "risky," since failure to achieve an electoral sanction "can well discredit the organization"; mobilization is "accordingly . . . approached with caution by most groups." The genius of the pattern of crowd lobbying is that by means of it lobbying organizations are able to have their protest cake and eat their diplomatic cake too.

First, crowd lobbying—the ones that are the subject of this chapter and that I studied for several years at the California capitol, at least— said little or nothing about electoral punishment. Instead they stressed, more positively, their specific policy preferences and their rationales. Electoral consequences that might follow from opposing such preferences were obvious—perhaps so obvious that there was no need to even mention them. Since it makes little or no overt commitment to punishment at the polls, crowd lobbying is not threatened by the possibility of discreditation due to failure to punish.

Second, the *crowd* aspect is the key feature that sets this form of lobbying off from all other forms of the diplomatic interest group struggle. None of the types of diplomatic struggle routinely employ crowds, at least not in the specific sense of assembling them at a governmental center for the purpose of influencing the policy process.

In being so set apart, crowd lobbying adopts a salient feature of protest struggle. Looking back over the subforms of protest outlined in chapter 12, a signal feature of most of them is the *crowd,* a relatively large number of persons gathered face-to-face focused (in the form relevant here) on a common object of attention. In contrast, the central social organizational trend of diplomatic struggle is the 2-person or small-group meeting created by the deployed agents of formal organizations.

The ingenious innovation of crowd lobbying is the adroit and controlled manner in which a social unit associated with protest (the crowd) is, by careful management, shorn of its protest meanings and "smuggled" into the repertoire of diplomatic struggle. In this sense, crowd lobbying is camouflaged protest, a tamed and constrained version of the lowest or symbolic level of protest (described in chapter 12), specifically the *rally* and the *march.* By means of such polite devices as staging indoors, in dignified settings, and constrained crowd expression, a functional equivalent of protest action becomes available to interest-group constituents who feel unrest and discontent but who also find it beneath them and utterly undignified to engage in action suggestive of protest.

A mental experiment will help clarify and sharpen the point. In the monograph *Crowd Lobbying,* from which this discussion is extracted, I describe the 59th "Annual Meeting and Legislative Conference" of the California Manufacturers' Association, a 3-day gathering of some 300 "top corporation executives" (the words of reporter Barbara Bry in *The Sacramento Bee,* March 29, 1977), a gathering of clean-shaven, middle-aged men, almost all of whom dressed in remarkably similar three-piece suits. Mentally picture them marching, with picket signs, and gathering on the lawn outside a capitol building to cheer their leaders' denunciations of pending government regulation and legislation. There were dozens such episodes on the lawns of the California Capitol in the course of a year, but they were not performed by corporation executives or their ilk and the oddity of even the mental image of them doing so tells us why. Respectable and powerful people simply "don't do that sort of thing" because they have the resources of money, time, and hired agents that make it unnecessary for them to do it, that make it possible for them to achieve the same "crowd power" effect in more dignified guise.

The fact that even the wealthy are interested in gathering in crowds (however dignified) for political purposes alerts us to the special meaning of crowds per se. Any reasonably large number of gathered humans sends messages that are not entirely transmittable by any other device of social struggle. The crowd is simultaneously: *personal* in declaring that its members care merely by being there; at least vaguely *threatening* because of the common fear that a crowd might "turn on" people who are not its members; *powerful* in (by its very existence) displaying the capacity to exist, and in so doing auguring the capacity for a wide range of other on- and off-the-scene actions; and the *concrete embodiment* of abstract social categories, an embodiment not achievable in any other manner (there is no other way to make an official perceive, for example, that "the steelworkers are *here*").

This is the sense in which crowd lobbying allows one to have one's cake and eat it too. The manner is polite but the crowd form is protest. By means of the former one smuggles in the latter.

FORMS OF CROWD LOBBYING

Crowd lobbying has the essential features just described, but the activity is not itself homogeneous within the category created by those features. It is mounted in several important subforms that may be arrayed in a hierarchy running from the less to the more complex— from the brief, transient, single, and simple occasion to the long, enduring, complex, and recurrent occasion. These forms are treated in detail in the monograph *Crowd Lobbying* and I will therefore here only provide a schematic overview.

CROWD CRYPTOLOBBYING

Crowd cryptolobbying is the most primitive type of the form. It has political significance and influences the course of events at state capitols and elsewhere but does so in an indirect fashion by only calling public attention to its participants as an entity and affirming certain broad values or voicing a general orientation to public policy and the broad relative roles of political, economic, and other institutions and social groups. Among its own forms are:

1. Annual affirmational assemblies, such as the Host Breakfast of Sacramento and the American Legions' Boys' State, the former of which each year gathers the "decision makers" of the state "to exchange views, establish friendships, and create new areas of good will and understanding" (a statement appearing in a brochure explaining the Host Breakfast).

2. One-time legitimizing crowds that justify the entry of a topic or group into the political arena, such as a week-long "educational program" called "Forgotten Victims Week."
3. Ordinary conventions with political components.

Crowd cryptolobbying provides a cocoon of rhetoric around the more pointedly political process. Such gatherings are rather like the appreciative spectator crowds one encounters at other scenes of struggle. They function as supportive audience to the action, and, while partisan, do not quite enter the fray. Nonetheless, by their very presence, they are an important aspect of the scene.

EMERGENCY MOBILIZATIONS

The simplest form of the overtly political crowd lobbies are isolated mobilizations operating with an "emergency" mentality. Something happening at the Capitol has to be attended to and attended to *now* because of the way in which Capitol officials have scheduled events. Ordinarily, the sense of *now* attaches to a legislative or administrative hearing date, but it might also attach to an assessment of the critical constellation of political forces without a critical date. Forms of these include:

1. The hearing in which distraught crowd members appear at scheduled hearings for the purpose of voicing strong approval or disapproval of speakers and testimony before a hearing board. The formal purpose of such hearings is to collect facts pertinent to an impending decision. Such facts can be presented by anyone who signs up to appear and provide them. The less formal function, however, is to provide a type of orderly and institutionalized display of anger on one or both sides of the matter under deliberation.
2. Defensive celebrations in which a broad range of threats is responded to by preemptively staging one's own positive counterevent in an effort to subdue or thwart the threats.
3. Emergency crowd swarms in which the halls of the Capitol are flooded with emergency-mobilized lobby members making efforts to sway officials' sentiments. One lobby group even refers to such action as "Legislative Swarm Day," a term aptly suggestive of the organized frenzy seen in this pattern.

ANNUAL ASSEMBLIES

The well-organized, recurrent, and political heart of crowd lobbying is the annual assembly. Many of them last but one day, but many others run several days or even an entire week over which a long list of preferred actions is promoted with officials. Differences in the sophistication of these annual assemblies are captured in the titles of its subforms: (1) show-and-tell crowds; (2) slick one-day traditions; (3) two-day elaborations; (4) multiday conferences; and—reaching an almost new order of strategy—(5) the elite crowd lobby.

The fifth and most sophisticated form deserves special mention. Exemplified only by members of the California Manufacturers' Association, it is unique for many reasons, among which is the fact that top state officials visit them in their convention center headquarters rather than they going to the Capitol building or other offices. They come to the Capitol city, 300 strong, from each of America's major corporations, but do not take that last compromising step of setting foot in the petitioned's territory. Instead, the petitioned come, finally, to them!

THE APPARENT INCREASE

Several incomplete types of data suggest that the number of interest groups engaging in crowd lobbying in California (as well as in other states and in Washington, D.C.) has been increasing over the last several decades and accelerating in recent years. One indicator is that the "annual" ones mostly list members below twenty. Only the California Manufacturers' Association seems to be able to boast a number as high as sixty. Another suggestive bit of material is that in the late seventies (the period of my study) several called themselves the "first annual" and other numbers below five.

From a different kind of source, the number of conventions held in Sacramento increased steadily in the seventies. In 1977 and 1978, it was the site of more state and district conventions than any other California city, up from second in 1976. According to the California Association of Convention and Visitors' Bureaus, there were 280 Sacramento conventions in 1977 and 362 in 1978; the latter year was reported to have involved some 400,000 persons (*Sacramento Bee*, March 30, 1978). This association defined a convention as a minimum of 50 people occupying at least 25 hotel or motel rooms, a definition that seriously underestimated activity; several smaller ones and some rather large ones were known to me in 1977 (the calendar year in which I did intensive study) but not to the convention bureau official who compiled statistics. Not all of these were crowd lobbies, but a significant portion were.

Assuming there has been an upward trend, the question then becomes *why?* Several changes concomitant with the spread of crowd lobbying make their apparent proliferation understandable. First, in California, a prohibition on several forms of classic, professional lobbying techniques began in 1975. That prohibition provided impetus to devise alternative methods of contact with officials. The crowd lobby is only one compensatory device. Second, the crowd lobby as an event is facilitated by (if not entirely dependent on) having a lobby organization at the Capitol scene and operating there day in and day out. Such organizations have themselves proliferated over the last several decades and increased steadily through the seventies. The sheer staging personnel has in such a fashion become increasingly available. Third, travel has become easier and less expensive. California, especially, has been blessed until recently with moderately priced intrastate airline travel and a high-speed road system. Moreover, the Mediterranean climate makes the use of such facilities relatively unproblematic. (Correlatively, rapid rises in the cost of transportation ought to inhibit crowd lobbying.) Fourth, there has been a general rise in the level of affluence, an enlargement in the proportion of the population that can afford to be at the State Capitol a day or more at a time.

These factors are mostly on the "opportunity" or "facilitant" side of things. On the more markedly impetus side, there is, fifth, the obdurate fact that the State Capitol is increasingly the locus of decision making that manifestly affects local citizens. Rhetoric about local control to the contrary notwithstanding, the more fundamental fact (of California life, at least) is a broad and deep process of centralizing control over an expanding range of matters. If people are to deal directly with their controllers, they increasingly must go to the Capitol. (Ironically, the "era of Proposition 13" appears to have exacerbated rather than slowed or reversed this centralizing trend by making local government ever more dependent on state funding.)

There are many mediated ways in which to communicate legislative/ administrative preferences to officials: letters, telegrams, telephones, and the like. These have been used in profusion. But in the context of the foregoing factors there is yet another, a sixth and more profound reason for the rise of the crowd lobby: There is no adequate substitute for face-to-face contact. In the end, people prefer to meet their adversaries, their leaders, the people who affect their lives, in the flesh. All else is compromise. Face-to-face contact has an immediacy, a reality, a fullness and richness of input, and a flexibility that none of the mediated modes begins to approximate. It permits a promptness of feedback, assessment, and probing that is discontinuous in character with any mediated device yet developed, a qualitative disjunction long contemplated by social scientists of these matters (e.g. Berger and Luckmann, 1967:28-34).

Seventh, it needs also to be appreciated that we are dealing with face-to-face contact of a special kind: *crowd* contact. Both as cause and as consequence, the crowd is an entity that has a peculiar kind of power and sends a distinctive message to officials who view it. The lobby crowd says that there is indeed "behind" the professional lobbyist a real interest group composed of flesh-and-blood human beings who support the lobbyist's representations. The lobbyist is not merely hired by perhaps dispersed, coerced, or apathetic dues payers or a small number of rich angels: "the people" in assembly back them up. The crowd lobby is thus a psychological presence, a living organism that is there *now* and often promises to be there again next year for an accounting; in some cases it even promises to come on the scene as a crowd at any time an interest group emergency is declared (this seems to be a strong capacity of realtors, in particular).

The crowd also communicates power in a more subtle way: It is a literally and physically large presence in the day of the official. The interest group is not just an idea, a threat, or an abstraction. It concretely "fills up his/her senses" for a time, entering his/her line of vision no matter how the official's body might politely be positioned. It is an expensive but striking mnemonic device (cf. Canetti 1978; Brown 1954).

EFFECTIVENESS OF CROWD LOBBYING

There is, inevitably, the question of the effectiveness of crowd lobbying (and other activities) in achieving goals in the political process. I have devoted relatively little attention to this question because of the impossibility of answering it. The political arena is a vastly complicated field of social forces that are constantly shifting and changing. As such, it is *theoretically* possible to (1) enumerate all the forces, (2) measure their changing strengths over time, and (3) assess their respective effects on decision makers. But it is a *practical* impossibility to do so. The very process of measurement itself would be so obtrusive that it would change the very things it was trying to measure. The answer to the question of effectiveness is that we do not know and we are likely never to know with any important degree of precision.

Yet the prospects are not totally dismal. Miscellaneous observations suggest this imagery: Sometimes a lobbying effort matters and sometimes it does not, and whether an effort has an effect or not is a function of variables that any given actor most often cannot control. The existence of "factors that the political actor cannot control" is critical. Decisions are typically the outcome of a long and tortured course involving many types of input, some occurring quite late and out of the reach of effective action, as described by BeVier (1979) and Bardach (1972), among others. Two of the more colorful, late developing, and arbitrary "out-of-reach" factors in the legislative process, in particular, dramatically illustrate such features. First, some measures get caught up and killed in the personal disputes of legislators; they are weapons of interpersonal retaliation that have nothing to do with the substantive merits or demerits of the measure or the array of proponents and opponents (e.g. the assembly speaker's personal feud with a senator in July 1979, reported in *The Sacramento Union* [July 21, 1979], and the speaker's feud with an assemblyperson over the "Behr Bill" in 1978, reported by Martin Smith in *The Sacramento Bee* [March 7, 1978]). Second, many bills get passed (or passed over) in the last-minute rush of the legislative year; they are virtually unread or unconsidered and are therefore apart from the substantive political process. One such scene was accurately headlined by *The Sacramento Bee* (September 2, 1978): "Near Chaos Rules Last Day of Squabbling Lawmakers." "In the final hours, bills often change shape faster than anyone but a tiny handful could follow" (John Berthelsen, *Sacramento Bee*, September 2, 1978).

At the level of particular measures, then, one practical answer to the question of effectiveness is that it is highly problematic and uncertain. But having said this on the question of *specific* effectiveness, let me "stand back" and consider the possibility that the question as I have posed it is too narrow. More than specific pieces of legislation and administration are at stake in the political process. Rather, crowd and other lobbying establish a *context*—an ambience, a range of plausible alternatives—for considering specific matters. The appropriate frame of reference for asking the question of effectiveness may not be a few decisions won or lost but the *larger and longer campaign for credibility and alternative defining*.

Crowd lobbyings and related activities need perhaps to be set alongside the public relations campaigns of industries in order best to understand them. For example in the late seventies, "Big Oil"—the largest refining companies—began "putting their executives on the speech trail" to promote their legitimacy and point of view (Kelly 1979). They took their cue in part from the statement of John D. Rockefeller, who, in reflecting on his decades-long policy of not responding to press criticism of his empire said: "I shall never cease to regret that we never called in the reporters" (Kelly 1979). In the apt imagery of Roger Cobb and Charles Elder (1972), these are matters of *agenda building*—the structuring of (1) what gets to be an issue in the first place, and (2)the construction of the parameters in terms of which an issue is envisioned.

The question of effectiveness in getting or defeating a limited set of specific measures is therefore minor and narrow *relative to* these larger questions of controlling the content of the agenda and how the items on it are regarded. It is in these more fundamental ways that crowd lobbies are likely of critical importance; that is, highly effective.

Viewing the question of effectiveness in this light and taking note of the rapid spread of crowd lobbying brings us to a generalization about it that we have long accepted about ordinary lobbying: Interest groups that do not adopt some form of it do so at their peril (Milbrath 1968:443). In a political arena where crowd lobbying becomes commonplace, it forms a new standard or criteria of seriousness and credibility. By the same token, at the level of ordinary lobbying, groups *not* practicing it have for decades been disadvantaged in the political struggle specifically and the social struggle more generally.

How serious is a group that does not (read "cannot") assemble its members to communicate its interests? Not unreasonably, officials are reactive rather than proactive, and they react to that which bears visibly (and literally) "down on" them. One primitive but potent medium of visibility is the *crowd*. With the relative decline of the crowd as a common agent of political action in modern life, its relative novelty, when used, might make it all the more potent (cf. Tilly 1978).

The social sources that prompt the growth of crowd lobbying and which in turn increase the requirements for credibility in the political struggle, then, in their own turn present a new set of demands for all lobbying. We have, it would seem, an escalation of requirements for "effectiveness."

CROWD LOBBYING AND DEMOCRACY

The specific and narrow aims of crowd lobbying are obvious. Its larger meaning and importance are perhaps less evident. As public decision making centralizes in ever larger scales and in breadth of political organization, effective channels of communication between officials and citizens unavoidably attenuate. I say "effective channels" to suggest once more that the various mediated means of communication—telephones, letters, newspapers, television—are not fully acceptable substitutes for direct, face-to-face contact. In the end, the important matters of human affairs have to be dealt with "eyeball to eyeball," as one felicitous folk phrase has put it. Crowd lobbying in its several forms can be interpreted as one important form of reaching for such direct contact with people who make decisions that affect one's life in important ways.

In the vastness of the social landscape of complex societies, if officials and citizens are to have such effective contact there are two polar possibilities (with a range of mixing): Officials can go to the citizens or citizens can go to the officials. It is in many ways more efficient for officials to stay put in their place of work (and go on working) and receive citizens intermittently. (The latter hardly excludes the former.)

Moreover, crowd lobbies are in one sense the new form of the *town meeting*, a form appropriate to (1) the highly specialized and differentiated nature of our modern problems combined with (2) the geographically scattered and far-flung locations of those involved in specialized problems. Like the classic town meeting, crowd lobbies are occasions for airing a variety of perceived difficulties, for working toward a stance regarding them, for voicing discontent, and for assessing and perhaps repairing or breaking relations between citizens and officials.

They are social events that *punctuate* the otherwise undifferentiated flow of social life and provide occasions for the assessment of the group's position. Each may be considered a miniature "state of the union" address. Or, in the more pointed language of Karl Rosengren et al. (1975:318-20), each is a *summary event*, a staged occasion in which to give sharpened form to what are otherwise difficult-to-grasp large structures and slow processes that are often imperceptibly impinging on an interest group.

Crowd lobby occasions provide situations in which officials can promote their own "summary event" definitions of issues. Put differently and cynically, crowd lobby appearances by officials are often given heavy coverage by the media, so that addresses to crowd lobbies are attractive to officials for this reason. One need not be merely cynical about this cozy arrangement because it is indispensable to the process of democracy that such publicity occur, that the proposals of officials be known. Without crowd lobbies to provide audiences, officials might well be reduced to the mere issuing of press releases. Better, it would seem, that they stand before citizens when voicing their envisioned solutions and be required as a consequence to "answer up" in relatively immediate ways.

For these and other reasons, crowd lobbying constitutes an ingeniously adaptive and democratic device that springs from the tensions between (1) centralized decision making and (2) a high level of technology that holds together (3) a geographically dispersed and (4) occupationally specialized population.

There are also several negative aspects of crowd lobbying. One is that the capacity for it (or any other collective action) is not equally available to all segments of the population. Relative wealth and freedom to arrange one's own week and "be away" facilitate participation in it, and these, among many other variables, critically shape the capacity, level, and form of collective political action, especially crowd lobbying. Broader, however, are issues of "interest-group politics" per se and questions of the social fragmentation and political Balkanization it raises (Ornstein and Elder 1978:223-30). The rise of interest groups is said to be concomitant with the decline of political parties and therefore the very capacity to forge coalitions of sufficient size, strength, and vision to govern effectively and justly—that is, to achieve widely supported policies that are in the long-term public interest. Too many, too vigorous interest groups fixed on their too-narrow concerns augur the paralysis and/or stunting of policy of the breadth and temporal reach required to deal with the problems of the society (e.g. Lowi 1969).

Finally, although it is not as profound as the two concerns just mentioned, I am intrigued by the question of input overload that might accompany the expansion of interest-group activities. Lobbying activities can expand (crowd lobbying being but one gambit in a rich panoply of strategies and tactics), but the number of most relevant officials does not. "Input" from "the people" might build from a stream, to a deluge, to a flood, but there is a fixed number of hours in the lives of officials. There is, in the logic of the case, an upper limit on the number of crowd lobby and associated events in which officials can participate. It is inherent in the situation that if such events continue to increase, more officials will need to decline "invitations" more frequently. But such refusals go against the rightful democratic demand to "petition the government," especially the *elected* people in it. Discontent will be the upshot, perhaps with the emergence of new policy issues about who gets to see whom, how much, and in what circumstances.

All these crowd lobby and other crowds (and individuals) pressing on officials surely takes its toll. As one member of the assembly declared when explaining why she had decided not to stand for reelection:

> I'm tired of being expected to be up all the time . . . tired of being expected to be enthusiastic and interested in people's problems. . . . I'm tired of placating people so that they will be . . . happy to give me a

contribution. I don't want to stand up at anyone's dinner dance and say that I am happy to be there when I am not. . . . [And] I cannot continue to work seven days a week [*The Sacramento Bee* (June 29, 1980); see also Price and Bell (1980)].

Can public life become *too* democratic in the sense that an impossibly large number of groups can come to feel they have a right to the time and presence of their elected and other officials? Wisely (in the short run) responsive to invitations to appear and to other solicitations—do officials run a high risk of burnout? The rise of interest-group democracy might well be creating an impossibly pressing situation for, especially, elected leaders. Ironically, it is sometimes the organized adoration of constituents that is most oppressive. As the asemblyperson quoted above also exclaimed: "I don't want to be at your dinner—you are honoring me to death!"

NOTE

The larger work from which this chapter is excerpted was supported in part by the organizations listed in the acknowledgment note to chapter 13. Michael Greany superbly assisted me in collecting much of the empirical material referred to in this and the next chapter. The events studied in both chapters took place at diverse and often odd and inconvenient times. I owe a profound debt in Lyn H. Lofland for not only enduring but facilitating and supporting a year of my day-and-night, 7-days-a-week "on call" relationship to the Capitol setting where I observed crowd lobbying and symbolic sit-ins. Edmond Costantini, Joseph R. Gusfield, Fred R. Harris, Lyn H. Lofland, Robert W. Salisbury, and Alvin D. Sokolow read the manuscript in draft and made many very helpful suggestions for revision.

15

SYMBOLIC SIT-INS (1982)

With Michael Fink

In this chapter we depict and dissect a series of sit-ins and associated events centered on the reception room of the governor's office at the Capitol of California over the six years 1975-80. In comparing the pattern of these protests with other forms of social struggle (outlined in chapter 12), we have come to conceive it as the symbolic sit-in, or more technically the symbolic protest occupation (*occupation* meaning "occupancy"). It is a new form of protest that we believe might become increasingly used and significant in the tactical tool kits of future social movements.

As explained in chapter 12, this new form has come into being against the background of the four waves of protest occupation that have occurred in the United States in this century. The exact initiating episodes of symbolic sit-ins are difficult to determine, but those taking place in the reception room of the governor of California in late 1975 must likely be counted as among the pioneers.

FEATURES OF THE SYMBOLIC SIT-IN

In chapter 12, the protest occupation as a general class of activity was delineated and the symbolic sit-in defined only negatively and as a residual phenomenon. Within that context we need now to provide a positive profile of features.

An initial and salient aspect of the Capitol episodes is that they were *called* "sit-ins" or "occupations" by everyone—performers, media, authorities, and others. The imagery and language of "the kind of event this is" was drawn directly from the recent history of protest occupations of the 1960s. All parties used the terms *protest, demands, negotiation, pressure,* and other terms suggestive of protest as distinct from polite politics.

The performers did act in irregular ways—ways that people in polite politics would not deign to act. At the mildest level of irregularity, picket signs were carried inside the Capitol and crowds paraded and stood about singing and chanting in the name of a demand. At its strongest, people slept overnight on the governor's reception room floor, night after night, week after week, and scurried about in raucously vocal crowds somewhat distracting Capitol workers from their ordinary tasks. There are several features these episodes did *not* display that by their absence tell us some aspects that were present.

Drawing from the discussion in chapter 12, unlike classic protest occupations, standing patterns of activity at the Capitol were not disrupted significantly. Attention was accorded protesters, certainly, but nothing approaching the paralysis attendant to the sit-downs of industrial workers, the sit-ins of the civil righters, the sieges of students, or the bivouacs of antinuclearists.

Most took place in or were oriented to the governor's reception room and an understanding of it and its microecological relation to the larger Capitol will help in understanding how these sit-ins were in effect encapsulated while still on display. The governor's complex occupied a large portion of the ground floor of the Capitol annex. Almost the entire south half of the interior space was sealed off in the sense that although there were five access doors, they were locked and unmarked. As such, the governor and his immediate staff could not be approached by simply walking in or even barging in. Three of these five doors opened into a reception and waiting room twenty-four feet square and containing, for most of the 6-year period, two couches, three chairs and tables, and the receptionist's desk and associated equipment. All three doors to the complex, one in each of the three walls adjoining the office complex, were ordinarily locked. Two of them were the routine modes of entrance and they were controlled by an electric lock system operated from behind the receptionist's desk. Thus the reception room was adjacent to the governor and his people but quite carefully sealed off from them.

The wide fourth door of the room opened onto the broad main corridor of the Capitol annex and was across from the bank of elevators that ascended to the five legislative floors, the offices of the senators, assemblypersons, hearing rooms, and so forth. Traffic was heavy in this main corridor—thousands of persons came and went daily—and when the reception room doors were open—as they were during the day—anyone passing by the room could gaze in and see almost all of it at a glance. The room had a "fishbowl" quality: contained but thoroughly viewable. It was a kind of public stage upon which actors might promenade but still not be terribly in anyone's way.

This was a site in which people could protest and be public and quite dramatic about their feelings without at the same time disrupting the ordinary flow of business.

These "microecological" aspects combined with a set of quasi-formal "rules for sitting-in" that the state police had devised after the governor responded to the initial reception room sleep-over declaration of November 20, 1975 by granting permission. The first sleep-inners were members of the United Farm Workers and personally led by the second most prominent person in that organization. The governor was a long-time and active supporter of the UFW; another group might not have been treated so permissively. Once having permitted the UFW, it was inconsistent to deny sit-in privileges to subsequent protesters.

Be that as it may, state police set the parameters and sit-inners largely operated within them. Even though disputed and renegotiated by both sides on occasion, the basic ones were no food in the reception room, no entrance after the building was locked at 10:00 p.m. (although one could leave), and little or no equipment beyond a sleeping bag. Further structuring the situation, a plainclothes policeman was on duty in the room around the clock (rotating in 2-hour shifts) and the bright fluorescent lights were left on all night.

As the existence of rules implies, authorities treated the sit-ins as more or less routine matters rather than as a crisis and challenge. Tempers sometimes flared on several sides, but these were momentary and soon curbed.

Unlike classic protest occupations, almost no "third parties" elected intensively to involve themselves in the episodes. No significant numbers of people either supportive of or hostile to the protestors appeared on the scene. Most often, no one paid much attention to them. Those who did were frequently just curious tourists and groups of schoolchildren who stared at the protesters rather in the way people look at strange animals in zoos. (A small number of seemingly media-stimulated "volunteers" did appear, especially at the longer symbolic sit-in episodes. Their participation was mostly short-lived and they were defined by sit-in leaders and others as "off the wall" and "kooky.")

The willingness of protesters to constrain their protest and "play by the rules" combined with the willingness of authorities to allow mildly irregular, symbolic protest acts in technically trespassed official space provides a new species of protest—the symbolic sit-in. Drawing forward chapter 12's delineation of four levels of protest (symbolic, noncooperation, intervention, and alternative institutions), the symbolic sit-in employs the rhetoric of true intervention but exercises the restraint of symbolic protest. In being restrained and in being permitted by authorities, however, it is fundamentally a form of symbolic rather than intervention protest.

The symbolic sit-in is in one sense an evolved form because it clearly takes its inspiration from, and is part modeled on, intervention occupations of the sixties. But in another sense it is a regressive form because it also in some ways debases or dilutes the earlier meaning of the term *sit-in* and like terms. The truly serious meanings and consequences associated with earlier sit-ins (and antinuclear bivouacs) are removed and that concept and associated terms come to mean only minor embarrassments and inconveniences on hard floors at a state capitol.

Taking all the above considerations into account, we may characterize symbolic sit-ins as protest occupations of places or spaces that draw on the ideology, rhetoric, and posture of historic sit-ins but which lack the classic, additional earmarks of those actions: true disruption of the settings in which they occur, an atmosphere of crisis, the threat of (and actual) violence, and extensive involvement by bystanders and other third parties.

TYPES OF SYMBOLIC SIT-INS AT THE CALIFORNIA CAPITOL

The some two dozen episodes of the symbolic sit-in we selected for description and analysis in the monograph *Symbolic Sit-Ins* varied considerably among themselves. Perception of them as microprotest entities is advanced if they are, in turn, divided in terms of their more conspicuous differences. Grouping them first in terms of what seem to be their global similarities, the episodes so clustered struck us as correlatively varying in terms of (1) duration, (2) size, and (3) level of what we call "flex." The conjoining of the types with their characterizing variations is shown in Figure 15.1.

Total duration refers to the elapsed clock time between the starting and ending of an episode. In terms of statistical frequency, most episodes only lasted a few minutes or hours. In *Symbolic Sit-Ins,* we describe ten "pack-ins" to illustrate subforms of them, but several multiples of that number occurred over the six years under discussion. (Since no one kept records on them, the exact number is not known.) Slightly longer, about a dozen episodes, each, of "lone-ins" and "one-night stands" endured one to a few days. And just a little longer, two episodes of "spirited sieges" went several days. There is then a gap and a jump to staying overnight for weeks, a feat performed by three "long-term vigils."

Sheer size is a significant difference, ranging from the lone protester

FIGURE 15.1

TYPES OF SYMBOLIC SIT-INS

		Variations		
		Total Duration	**Size**	**Flex Level**
Types	**Pack-ins**	hours	crowd	high
	Lone-ins	1 to several days	1 person	low
	One Night Stands	1-2 days	clique, small crowd	medium
	Spirited Sieges	days	crowd	medium to high
	Long Term Vigils	weeks	clique to crowd	low to medium

up to, at some times, several hundred people. Within this, the larger-scale and longer-lasting episodes themselves varied considerably over time in the numbers making up their crowds. The general tendency was for their numbers to fall at night—often down to a token force—and to rise in the daytime, peaking at midday. Within these variations, the tendency was for total numbers displaying these variations to decline over the days and weeks.

There was intraepisode variation in "mobilization" or *flex level*. A low or "unflexed" level of mobilization involved people simply sitting about waiting for authorities to respond to them. In it, people read, chatted, or slept. Most symbolic sit-ins were at this level most of the time—often boring and dull affairs.

Up slightly from this—a middle level—were group discussions and strategy sessions, interviews with media crews who came on the scene, and meetings with authorities. These served to punctuate time but were a relatively small portion of it. The highest level of mobilization seen among the episodes reported here consisted of marching, singing, and chanting crowds and noisy debates with authorities in the presence of the full complement of sit-inners.

MAJOR EPISODES

Although there were many dozens of symbolic sit-ins taken as a general class over the six years 1975-1980, only fifteen can be considered major in the sense that they involved one or more persons sleeping over at least one night. Of those fifteen, eleven ran from one to four nights, involving these groups, issues, and nights:

1975: Sixty members of the United Farm Workers (UFW) demand changes in the Agricultural Labor Relations Board (four nights).

Thirty-five wives of physicians demand reforms in medical malpractice insurance (one night).

Fifteen parents of institutionalized, developmentally disabled children demand better treatment for their children (one night).

1976: One elderly woman protests curtailment of an escort service for senior citizens (one night).

1977: Four farm work families demand access to labor camp housing (two nights).

Some forty deaf or blind people demand continuation of a client assistance program about to terminate (two nights).

Several hundred developmentally handicapped adults led by their caretakers (under the name Title XX Coalition) protest projected cuts in the funding of day care centers (four nights).

Mother with her teenage, developmentally handicapped son protest conditions in the state hospital where he is a patient (one night).

1978: Two dozen members of the Gray Panthers protest closing of a state-funded nursing facility (three nights).

1980: Three antinuclear protesters do a one-night follow-up to a 37-night vigil terminating a month previously.

Six antinuclear protesters sleep over one night commemorating the first anniversary of Three Mile Island.

Four events were much longer, involving these groups, issues, and nights:

1976: A Black physician demands reform in malpractice insurance (fourteen nights):

Five to thirty members of the Network against Psychiatric Assault demand reform of many practices in state mental hospitals (twenty-nine nights).

1977: A few to several hundred members of the United Farmworkers and their supporters demand fair treatment by the Agricultural Labor Relations Board (fifteen nights).

1979: Thirty to more than 200 members and supporters of People United against Ranch Seco (PUARS) demand closing of a near-by nuclear power plant (thirty-seven nights).

In trend terms, we have this sequence for these fifteen major episodes: 1975—three; 1976—three; 1977—five; 1978—one; 1979—one; 1980—two; The numbers are small but they display the classic "collective behavior curve" of a relatively rapid rise to a peak followed by more rapid fall-off and a final "blip," a curve also found in the occurrence of ghetto riots, student protests, and lifestyle fashions and fads (Penrose 1952; Irwin 1977; Spilerman 1976).

The distinctive skewing of the social categories of persons electing to sleep-in also merits notation. Only two approach being mainstream or establishment "social types" of persons—the group of physicians' wives and the lone physician. Even here it is significant that these are the doctors' *wives,* and that the lone doctor was a Black male who practiced in the Watts area of Los Angeles. Three episodes involved farm workers, a troubled and marginal occupation by all accounts and one in turmoil for many years in California. Three additional episodes were mounted by the underemployed "intellectual proletariat" (the antinuclearists) (Widmer et al. 1979). Seven, almost half, were performed by traditionally stigmatized groups that have begun in recent times to develop a political voice: mental patients, the aged, the deaf and blind, and the developmentally handicapped.

SOCIAL REACTION

One important question about sit-ins is what are their effects, or at least, how do people react to them? In order best to answer this question in relation to those observed at the California Capitol, we need to specify elements in terms of which there can be a reaction. A first distinction is in terms of audiences. Sitting-in was an act designed to draw the attention of media and officials. Ideally, one got the attention of both and that attention had a mutually reinforcing effect: The attention of one made the other take the protesters more seriously. Second, the attention drawn can itself be divided into reaction to the cause or *objectives* as distinct from the *tactic* of sitting in itself.

Media reaction to the objectives of the sit-ins may be characterized as positive in the sense that what seemed an ordinary portion of the Capitol press corps would typically appear, collect material, and present it in words and pictures. We say "ordinary portion" to point up that very few stories at the Capitol drew anything near half of the press corps. The run-of-the-mill Capitol news conference staged in the Capitol press conference room (Room 1190), a citadel of polite politics, might draw on the order of a dozen media teams/persons, and sit-ins seem to have about the same attention-gaining potential. That was no mean feat; one was likely to get media attention, billed as a sit-in, complete with an interesting picture.

Distinct from these are questions of reactions to sitting-in per se, irrespective of objectives. Protest occupations started November 20, 1975 and there were three episodes in quick succession. *The Sacramento Bee* responded to them on December 6 of that year with a "let's make light of it" feature headlined, "Check Yer Arms: The Fight to Sleep in [the Governor's] . . . Office." Tongue in cheek, the writer compared the accommodations to a hotel, noting it accepts no reservations, has only one room, and is not listed in Michelin. Calling it the "Governor's Inn," the bathroom facilities were rated as "no more convenient than those at a third-rate rooming house."

Into 1976, *The Los Angeles Times* opened a January 1 story on the phenomenon with the declaration: "It is in the best American tradition to petition your government, but this is getting ridiculous!" Obliquely referring to "pack-ins," the story described demonstrators as "literally shoulder to shoulder" and the reception room as "a madhouse." "A television cameraman climbed on [the receptionist's] . . . desk to get a better shot of the crowd." It was a "giant media event running out of control," because several demonstrating groups were on the scene simultaneously and pressing their case by packing into the reception room.

The mid-1976 long-term vigil of NAPA (Network against Psychiatric Assault) provoked the ire of a state senator who said, for the media, that he was "absolutely outraged by the stench arising from the dirty, disheveled reception room" (*Sacramento Bee,* July 20, 1976). In a letter to the state health director that he made public, the senator requested an investigation into the "health and safety" aspects. Several days later (July 30) a *Sacramento Union* columnist characterized the reception room as a "pig sty," claiming that visitors were "appalled at the degradation" and he called for an end to using the room as a "public camp ground."

Over the Labor Day Weekend of 1976, the carpet of the reception room was replaced with a hardwood floor, an event itself an object of *Sacramento Bee* reporting (September 8) under the headline "Governor's Office Takes a Hard Look." The reporter interpreted the change as an effort to discourage sleep-ins without banishing them and characterized the office as having been the "scene of numerous demonstrations."

There was a lull in episodes in late 1976 and early 1977, but a "spurt" in mid-1977 was accompanied by an upsurge in rallies, pickets, and pack-ins more generally. This moved the editors of *The Sacramento Bee* to editorialize on July 1, 1977. Under the declaration "End the Sit-ins," the unsigned statement claimed "the mass sit-ins and, at times, sleep-ins are no way to air an alleged injustice." Further, the governor had been "overly tolerant" with groups "besieging the reception area of the governor's office," and if he would not speak out against them, "we will: the inside demonstrations are becoming a nuisance and should be curtailed before they develop into a destructive tradition."

As it happened, the incidence of such events declined without official action and there was also little more social reaction until late 1979 when the antinuclear demonstrators occupied the room for thirty-eight days. Early in January 1980, the two upholstered (and decrepit) couches and four cushioned chairs were replaced with wooden benches and matching coffee tables. These were dutifully pictured in the media together with text that drew explicit attention to how this change made life more difficult for prospective sit-inners (*Sacramento Bee,* February 13, 1980; *Sacramento Union,* February 12, 1980). Seeing the new furniture in the reception room for the first time, the governor was quoted as commenting, "this looks bleak."

Over time, the state police "rules" of protest occupations grew more restrictive. Earlier occupiers had eaten in the reception room, used sleeping bags, and the 29-night NAPA protest of 1976 had even had mattresses. In 1977, the state police were attempting to prohibit all such accoutrements, albeit the Title XX coalition of the developmentally handicapped negotiated more supplies on the grounds of having special physical needs.

Taking the themes appearing in the media together with impressions formed from conversations with the variously involved, it can be said that the major reaction to symbolic sit-ins was bemused humor and curiosity. A few people were irked and disapproving, but this was far from the dominant reaction, which was much more benign or even supportive. Several aspects of the sequence of protests (that also serve to elaborate our prior depiction of the symbolic sit-in) make this dominant reaction more understandable. First, there was rarely, if ever, any problem of violence or even threat of violence. Many groups sang and chanted, but such acts were not defined as presaging "stronger" measures. Second, the causes espoused by the various groups were all ones for which there was reasonably widespread public sympathy, support, or indifference. None of the groups promoted "radical" or otherwise unpopular political or religious enterprises. Third, the governor of California seemed to be surprisingly important as a reference point for people in deciding how they ought to feel about the activities in the reception room (*and* a wide range of other matters). During the period in question he obviously "allowed" the protests. In the same period, he was frequently criticized for failing to take positions on a great many matters; people wanted to know how "the Governor felt" and to take that into account in developing their own views. The fact that he even sometimes met with sit-inners (and his staff frequently did) provided them a more than ordinary sort of legitimacy—or at least defined them as benign. (We will take up questions of the policy effects or success of symbolic sit-ins at the end of this chapter.)

DYNAMICS

The longer-running symbolic sit-ins exhibited several kinds of dynamic processes to which we want to draw attention.

THE LAW OF PASSIVE ADVANTAGE

The first of these involves features of the sit-inners' situation as it related to a modification of what Donald Light (1969) has formulated as "the law of passive advantage" in classic protest occupations.

The first relevant aspect of their situation is that they were very much "at the mercy" of officials in several senses. Their enterprise was almost totally geared to achieving meetings with what were defined as relevant officials and achieving satisfactory decisions by, or pledges from, them. While it may not have seemed so in advance and superficially, once embarked, sit-inners saw quite quickly that the advantage lay with the officials in (1) electing to meet with them and (2) deciding whether to concede or simply to stall in the many available ways. In having elected to post themselves on the premises, the advantages of officials set up anxiety and tension: "When is the meeting?"; "With whom?"; "What exactly will be said?"

Second, officials had, for practical purposes, infinite time, but sit-inners did not. This fact was unspoken between officials and sit-inners but clearly known to both. Officials could afford to "normalize" the situation as "just another meeting" in a day full of meetings. Sit-inners were not so comfortably situated and wanted to "get it over with" or at least to "get on with it."

Third, in having been rendered routine or normal in the setting, sit-inners could in theory remain in place the rest of their lives. When officials pleasantly stalled and otherwise sidestepped demands, there came to be problems of deciding between escalating the tactics of demand, redefining the demands, defining the response of officials as satisfactory and leaving, conceding defeat and leaving, or merely leaving. Since none got what they initially demanded while still on the premises, all had to engage in redefinition of their situation and devise ways to leave with dignity. In the longer occupations, a key problem was how to get out without seeming foolish and losing face.

Together, these three situational features provide a variation on Donald Light's (1969:81) "law of passive advantage" in protest occupations. Surveying leading episodes of student seizures of campus buildings in the middle sixties, Light's "law" refers to the superior situation accruing to authorities in being passively open to protesters while allowing them to act (or even encouraging them to act) in highly assertive fashions, thus tending to portray themselves as unsympathetic aggressors. The upshot of such passivity combined with budding aggression is the "stand off" in which the restrained authorities seem increasingly "reasonable" and the occupiers increasingly "unreasonable". In this way, "the longer the stand-off lasts, the more ground the protesters lose." Credibility and the appearance of reasonableness are not as problematic in the symbolic sit-in, but, with modified referents, the law of passive advantage is nonetheless at work. In some ways it operates more poignantly because even though the occupiers were not disruptive or destructive, they were ordinarily quite far from their homes and all the physical and social supports this implies, in contrast to participants in classic protest occupations. Authorities needed only to wait; that is, to act normally.

THE FRAGILITY OF ORGANIZATION

On the surface and at a distance, one might posit that relatively formal, enduring, disciplined, and hierarchical organization is requisite to strategic protest occupations, especially those that involve "sleeping over" for an indefinite series of nights. Organization moving in that direction is evident in the case of the United Farm Workers, which is a large and stable labor union with a relatively elaborate and paid staff structure. That staff core could mobilize members and sympathizers, albeit the mobilizations were for relatively short shifts and only for sporadic and brief periods. (For details see Lofland and Fink 1982, ch. 7, secs. A.2, A.3.) Operating from their nearby lobbying office and performing the core protest occupation acts themselves, staff could (and did) keep the effort going.

Such stability of organization and commitment was the exception. The other major and longer-term occupations were conspicuously more emergent, fragile, and temporary-coalitional constructions. Moreover and also unlike the UFW, it was difficult to identify *the* leader, a feature decisively suggestive of their emergent and temporary nature. Instead, there was a circle of situationally shifting leaders. Among the deaf/blind (who did not even have a name for their coalition), one person emerged as the de facto leader but he was by no means formally *the* leader in press releases and in meetings with officials. Even his de facto leadership seems possibly an artifact of the unique circumstance that the other main leaders in the coalition were deaf and had difficulty speaking effectively in rapid-paced exchanges with officials and among members of the coalition. The Title XX coalition of the developmentally handicapped was markedly stratified, but the organizations and persons that came together in the coalition could not entirely depend on one another to appear each day and the leadership circle itself had no formal head. That circle only labeled itself a "steering committee" and there was no "chair," "facilitator," or other such office. The antinuclear movement is ideologically antihierarchical, (Barkan 1979), and the PUARS episode was conducted along the ordinary lines of that movement. "PUARS" was itself a label for a shifting cast of protesters (with a fairly stable core) who were *not* a preexisting group. Instead, they were drawn from several antinuclear groups in Northern California and formed a new "affinity group" for the occasion, united by their belief in the efficacy of occupying the governor's reception room for the purpose of pressuring him to use his emergency powers to close a nearby nuclear plant. Following antinuclear protocol there was no single or small set of formal leaders (although temporary "spokes" were allowed) and all decisions had to be "put to consensus." Of course, the more assertive, energetic, and articulate did emerge as a de facto leadership, but this was quite different from ordinary formal hierarchy. As critics claim, there was, perhaps, a "democratic fog" (Widmer 1979:14).

One consequence or at least correlate of these trends in social organization was *interactional fragility*. As coalitions of organizations and individuals and therefore very much volunteers for protest, continuing participation was problematic. People were exceptionally free to "pick up their marbles and go home," and components of the protests sometimes did just that. The dubiously legal, clearly déclassé, and physically inconvenient actions in which they were engaging provided significant impetus to drop out. One ironic upshot was that leaders seemed exceptionally polite to one another—almost gingerly polite. None could "order" any of the others to do anything—to continue, to undertake a given action—and "natural" or "personal" leadership (as opposed to formal or bureaucratic) became the basis on which strategy was forged. (We oppose only these types to each other because nothing remotely suggestive of the "magic" of "charismatic" leadership was observed.)

Other terms and phrases useful in capturing the organizational character of the longer-term symbolic sit-ins include: tentative, groping, emergently negotiated, somewhat internally disorganized, and decentralized in terms of the factions composing the protest effort.

It is indicative, finally, that after their respective protest efforts, only the United Farm Workers continued to be locatable as an organizational entity. The deaf/blind and the Title XX coalitions disappeared, as entities, the night its participants left the Capitol. PUARS persisted a few more weeks but then disbanded.

PREPARATION-EVENT PULSES

Some of the symbolic sit-ins exhibited a "pulse" feature in which the protesters launched an action, received the response of officials, paused, launched a new action in response to that response, and so on to one or another type of termination. While displayed perhaps most dramatically by the spirited siege of the Title XX coalition, it is seen less conspicuously in other episodes and in most prolonged fashion in the PUARS vigil. The features of these "pulsations" emerge clearly by asking: Toward what are the occupiers most proximately aiming? In general, the answer is: toward a meeting with officials in which demands are made and negotiated. Such meetings required preparation. Decisions about what to demand, how to demand it, and how to support contentions needed to be planned in advance. Focusing on the PUARS vigil as a prototypical instance, we find it to have been structured around a series of five key and structuring events (i.e. meetings) that initiated a pulse, that is, injected a surge of directed energy into the protest. These are shown in the left-hand column of Figure 15.2 and consist of meetings with and promises by officials. Such meetings and what officials did in them structured the vigil along the particular lines it evolved. It might be said that the PUARS vigil ran thirty-seven rather than some other number of nights because of the particular spacing of and promises made at meetings by officials. In this sequence, there is a certain "stringing along" quality that encouraged the hopes of the vigilers, albeit they were eventually demoralized and redirected their energies.

The pulsing surges of new orientation and energy are shown in the right-hand column of Figure 15.2, where the interplay between structuring events and "pulse period" orientation can be seen. The initial pulse brings the group to the Capitol and the first structuring event, the meeting with the governor's chief of staff on November 29, at which a meeting with the governor is promised for December 4. That promise provides a surge of focus and direction, leading up to December 4, at which time yet a third pause period is initiated, aiming toward December 17. The December 17 meeting precipitated demoralization and the scaling down of demands, building to efforts to extract milder concessions, an effort concluded on December 24, at which time a final, detailed settlement meeting was set for January 2, thus providing an orderly interval for terminating the vigil.

Scrutinized from this distance, slowed down, and viewed in "pulse perspective," the PUARS vigil (as well as many other protest occupations) evinces social motion that seems quite graceful, supple, and interactive. Forging forth, protest occupations encounter resistance, take account of it, reformulate action, and forge forth once more. Successive expansions and contractions are sensitively calibrated to officials' responses and episodes draw to a close in ways and at times that seem reasonable to participants and sympathetic observers alike.

FIGURE 15.2
Structuring Events and Pulse Periods in the PUARS Vigil

Structuring Event	Pulse
	1. Preparing to and occupying the reception room.
1. November 29: Chief promises a meeting with the Governor.	
	2. Preparing to meet with the Governor.
2. December 4: Governor promises another meeting, on December 17.	
	3. Preparing to meet again with the Governor.
3. December 17: Govenor refuses the main demand, gives lesser concessions.	
	4. Demoralization and reformulation of demands.
4. December 24: Meeting with Chief; new, lesser demands granted, final arrangement meeting set for January 2.	
	5. Preparing for final meeting, shift of focus away from the Capitol.
5. January 2: Final meeting; arrangement of details.	
	6. Overnight occupation of reception room ends.

THE CIVILITY MILIEU AS FACILITATOR

At the beginning of this chapter we mentioned several background features that help explain the emergence and restraint of the symbolic sit-in at the California Capitol. These include the facts that (1) sit-inners were promoting causes that themselves had relatively wide social support and (2) they tended to "play by the rules" established by the California State Police, restraining and channeling their protest actions. We want now to introduce another facilitating and dynamic feature, one peculiar to the California Capitol as a social milieu, one we may think of as an unusually strong milieu of civility.

In order best to appreciate this feature let us first highlight how many authorities treated sit-inners in much more than a merely tolerant fashion. It is one thing to permit or allow symbolic sit-ins (and a great deal of the response to them was of that sort), but it is quite another to provide them active and even affectionate support. Major forms of this may be briefly recounted. First, supportive officials often addressed rallies staged by occupiers as prelude to or part of their occupation, most notably in the cases of the United Farm Workers. Second, legislators, in particular, were prone to "stop by" the governor's reception room and give brief "pep talks" to protesters, a phenomenon especially apparent in the blind/deaf effort (see Lofland and Fink 1982, ch. 6, sec. A). Third, in at least one instance, legislators even collected money and handed the cash directly to the occupiers. Fourth, well-situated aides to high officials provided continuing advice and "rumors" of what relevant officials were doing or likely to do. Fifth, and more diffuse and all-pervasive, officials in general were impressively solicitous of protest occupiers in that they took them quite seriously in agreeing to meet with them, listen respectfully, and discuss their demands. The governor's chief of staff and the secretary of health and welfare seemed to do a great deal of this kind of work and be especially adept at it. They were ubiquitous players in several of the episodes. They and other officials were not infrequently subjected to relatively harsh verbal treatment but, overall, they "kept their cool" and "took it."

These and other aspects of officials' behavior make up a reasonably benign and permissive social environment in which to perform protest occupations. Occupiers may not have often got what they wanted, but they were at least treated with a considerable measure of dignity—minor and erratic harassment by the California State Police notwithstanding.

Let us now put this in larger, milieu context. Solicitude and civility in the face of distraught and frustrated citizens was a *broad and pervasive feature of the Capitol milieu.* Stressful contention is endemic to the political process and an ethos of superpolitness and patience had evolved as a means of dealing with, or covering over, the very real, sharp, and consequential matters at issue. People commonly had good reason to be deeply distraught, and the Capitol etiquette of coolness and restraint was geared to control it (cf. Suttles 1970). The civility accorded protest occupiers was not a special treatment of them. It was simply the civility commonly accorded people with whom one disagreed. Ironically and appropriately, the dispute-riddled Capitol environment had given rise to a norm of restraint in the face of abuse that permitted, protected, and perhaps even encouraged a mild degree of incivility on the part of protest occupiers. Accustomed to conflict and disagreement and practiced in handling it calmly, Capitol officials were prepared to deal with occupiers as only somewhat more obstreperous people encountered that day.

REALITY AND DEPICTIONS

Categorizations of social experience unavoidably simplify what is in fact a more ambiguous, elusive, and shifting reality than depicted. Such is the case for what we caption as "symbolic sit-in" as opposed to those that are more substantial. In messy reality, many of the substantial protest occupations in the classic waves (described in chapter 12) do not fall clearly into one or the other of the opposites we have pictured. Instead, they share features of both.

This occurs both in terms of the place in the "wave" that an occupation appears (the later ones being more symbolic) and in terms of the life of a single episode when authorities and protesters negotiate a reconstitution of a substantial into a symbolic sit-in. Although occurring early in its historical wave, such a negotiated reconstitution seems to have happened, for example, in the student occupation of the University of Chicago administration building in May 1966 (Light 1969). Hints of evolving symbolic aspects are seen also in antinuclear actions. Activist-journalist Harvey Wasserman (1979:150) describes an August 22, 1976 Seabrook occupation in these terms:

> We told the police everything we planned to do and gave them no reason to mistrust our word. . . . Everyone had a reasonably good idea of what was about to happen. There was an air of good feeling and self-assurance among both the police and occupiers that made the event seem more like a ballet than a traditional political confrontation.

Likewise, some of the episodes we have described here on occasion moved toward the more substantial or classic form of the protest occupation. It is only for the purpose of clarifying major patterns and dominant tendencies that simplifications of the kind we have practiced in this report are justified. One important implication of this ever-problematic relation between reality and depiction is that we must be continually alert for evolving new patterns whose recognition is inhibited by the forcefulness of existing typifications.

EFFECTIVENESS AND EFFECTS

The single most important question to practical, political actors about protest occupations is likely: Is it effective? Or: How effective is it in its several forms relative to other types of political action, especially relative to "polite politics"? Such specific questions of effectiveness raise the general question of how to assess the effects of action. Scientific assessment of the effects of action in ongoing, natural settings is no mean task. Causal assessment requires, at the most rudimentary, that a situation be "played through" identically in at least two forms, once with and once without the action in question. The requirement of identicality in all but the questioned regard is virtually impossible to meet in any but the most controlled and artificial of circumstances that can and are created for a myriad of laboratory purposes but which are virtually never achieved in social life (Campbell and Stanley 1966).

In life, situations are never the same, or at least we dare not assume they are the same, because *some other variables* might account for the correlation we observe between a social action and an effect.

Despite the unassailable truth of the proposition we can never have confidence in statements about causal links between social actions and effects in natural settings, it is also clearly unacceptable. People almost *demand* assessment of the effectiveness and effects of tactical actions in the social struggle, for it is of enormous practical import. Sensitive to that demand, we elect mildly to pander and do so with a clear vision that what we say has no solid basis and can never have any. Let us, then, speculate.

We begin by distinguishing "effectiveness" and "effects." By "effectiveness" we refer to assessment of the relation between the declared goals of symbolic sit-ins and their achievements over the reasonably short run—a space of weeks. By "effects" we refer to all other consequences of symbolic sit-ins.

At the level of effectiveness so defined, symbolic sit-ins were extremely ineffective. No one, in the space of weeks, got what they started out to get. But perhaps this is too strict a measure of effectiveness. For in processes of negotiation, some efforts got "lesser settle-ments" in the short run, settlements that the protesters, at least, attributed to their efforts. For example, the deaf/blind coalition got access to high-level decision makers, influence in the operation of an advisory council, and so forth. PUARS got a number of conciliatory concessions even if their main objective, the closing of a nuclear plant, was not achieved.

This may also be too strict a measure of effectiveness. Many episodes appeared not even to achieve a lesser settlement in the short run, but need not be counted as total failures. Social life is more complicated than that. Even if a short-run failure, the fact of having made an appearance, of having *mounted a presence* contributes to framing, in authorities' minds, *a context for policymaking.* For exam-ple, some angry gasoline dealers who packed the governor's reception room failed to achieve any immediate policy changes (or even to see the governor), but they did provide one more, however small (but dramatic), piece making up the interest-group struggle picture that authorities (and others) would likely take into account when making subsequent decisions. At this broader level, effectiveness consists of being perceived as present, as a player in the arena, as one of the forces that *builds the agenda of social concerns* (Cobb and Elder 1972). Achieving such a presence probably requires much more than an occasional symbolic sit-in, but even such a sit-in can dramatize an otherwise inconspicuous, sporadic, and unnoticed Capitol residence.

As we expand the meaning of *effectiveness,* we begin to overlap with the encompassing question of *effects.* The first question about effects is: Effects on what? Without pretense to comprehensiveness, several salient classes can be mentioned. One of these has already been discussed under the rubric "social reaction." Effects on the media and citizenry seemed to run largely to bemused interest. We can now go a bit further and suggest that one function of symbolic sit-ins was to provide some expressive and humorous release in the midst of other-wise grim Capitol doings. Symbolic sit-ins might have served tension-release functions not dissimilar to those served by the surprising amount of "horseplay" and zaniness that took place among legislators, especially among members of the assembly. In a situation of intense but rigidly controlled conflict, comic and other expressive activity becomes a strong need and many outlets arise, symbolic sit-ins perhaps among them.

The social-psychological and associated effects on the protesters themselves are difficult to gauge. Degrees of embarrassment, fear, anxiety, and boredom were easy to observe but it seems doubtful that these were lasting emotional states for many, if any, protesters. No one was physically injured (or even underwent threat of it), so permanent traumas of that sort are unlikely.

A goodly proportion of (especially) leaders of the episodes are known to have been involved in political matters months or even years after the symbolic sit-ins. None has appeared conspicuously in more extreme protests, and several of those known to us have been involved in "polite politics" in subsequent periods. That is, there is no evidence that symbolic sit-ins made leading participants either more radical or inordinately prompted them to drop out of the social struggle altogether.

As reported with regard to social reaction (above, this chapter), the editors of *The Sacramento Bee* editorialized their concern that symbolic sit-ins would somehow degrade the political process by "developing into a destructive tradition." This does not appear to have happened.

We might conclude, then, that symbolic sit-ins were mildly effective in policy terms and had relatively modest effects more generally. In so assessing, we imply a comparison: mild and modest relative to what? There are several, and the judgment is the same for each: (1) doing nothing; (2) doing ordinary interest group lobbying and associated action; (3) doing violent struggle. For each, achieving mild or modest effects is not insignificant.

FUTURE OF THE FORM

In view of the fact that protests in the United States are only canvassed and compiled for relatively special purposes and for rather short periods (Etzioni 1970; Bayer and Austin 1971), trends in total volume are difficult or impossible to assess, much less trends in various of the *forms* of protest. Recognizing this, we can only offer the impression or conjecture that the symbolic sit-in is increasing in frequency, despite the fact that they seem to have decreased or even ceased in the setting where we observed them. Some reports suggestive of increase include the apparent widespread but symbolic occupation of post offices attendant to the draft registration days of 1980 (Beck 1980) and the willingness of some nuclear energy agencies to permit long-term and nondisruptive occupations of nuclear-relevant sites, including one in Vernon, Vermont, and San Francisco, California (Perlman 1980).

To suspect the possible increase of symbolic sit-ins is not to imply the decrease of ones that are more substantial. Indications are quite to the contrary. While not defined, attended to, and *reported* in the dominant media of mass communication, protest occupations of the more classic sort continue to take place with some regularity as Americans and other nations move into the eighties. (This, at least, is the picture one forms from following the Left-oriented press in America [e.g. *In These Times; The Guardian; People's World;* see also Gitlin 1980, ch. 11; Terkel 1980].)

The legal aspects are critical to the frequency and even survival of the symbolic sit-in. The restraint of authorities in protest occupation situations that is reciprocated by the restraint of protesters, thereby creating the symbolic sit-in, also creates *precedents of practice* that might well be used in court cases to claim some type of legal status or right. Legal briefs in support of the more substantial forms of protest occupation have existed for many years, notably the sit-down strikes of the industrial workers (Fine 1969, ch. 11) and the sit-ins of the civil righters (Waskow 1966, ch. 16). No special imagination or talent is required to rework and adapt these legal theories for the symbolic sit-in (and at least one law firm is known to us to have experimented along these lines). The artfulness of the arguments devised and the receptiveness of courts are integral to future possibilities for, and the attractiveness of, symbolically sitting-in. It might conceivably achieve the status of leafleting, picketing, and striking, practices all reported to have been illegal at some time in Anglo-American history.

NOTE

The larger work from which this chapter is excerpted was supported in part by the organizations listed in the acknowledgments note to chapter 13. Collection of the empirical materials referred to required more than ordinary indulgence by the people being observed and we are exceedingly grateful for the patience and forbearance extended us by almost all protesters and by members of the California State Police.

Bibliography

Abbott, F.
    1980   "Commentary: When Will Academicians Enter the Ranks of the Working Poor?" *Academe* 66:349-53 (October).

Adler, Peter
    1981   *Momentum: A Theory of Social Action.* Beverly Hills: Sage.

Aguirre, Benigno, and E.L. Quarantelli
    1980   "A Critical Evaluation of Two Major Critiques of Collective Behavior as a Field of Inquiry." Unpublished paper.

Aldrich, Howard E.
    1979   *Organization and Environments.* Englewood Cliffs, N.J.: Prentice-Hall.

Alinsky, Saul D.
    1969   *Reveille for Radicals.* New York: Vintage (originally published 1946).
    1972   *Rules for Radicals.* New York: Vintage.

Almond, Gabriel
    1954   *The Appeals of Communism.* Princeton: Princeton University Press.

Altheide, David, and John Johnson
    1977   "Counting Souls." *Pacific Sociological Review* 20:323-48.

American Sociological Association
    1982   "Revised Code of Ethics." Footnotes, vol. 10 (no. 9, March): 9-10.

Anderson, Maurice
    1977   "Power to the Crips!" *Human Behavior* (July):48-49.

Anthony, Dick
    1978   "Meher Baba and the Baba Lovers." *New Religious Movements Newsletter* 1 (October):4-5.

Anthony, Dick, and Thomas Robbins
    1982   "Spiritual Innovation and the Crisis of American Civil Religion." *Daedalus* 111:215-34.

Armstrong, Edward A.
    1965   *The Ethology of Bird Display and Behavior.* New York: Dover.

Aronowitz, Stanley
    1983a   "Remaking the American Left, Part One: Currents in American Radicalism." *Socialist Review* (no. 67, January-February):9-51.
    1983b   "Remaking the American Left, Part Two: Socialism and Beyond." *Socialist Review* (no. 69, May-June):7-42.

Associated Press
    1975   "Image Resembling Jesus Reported Seen on School Wall" (June 18).
    1977   "10 Million Bathe in Sacred Ganges" (January 20).

Back, Kurt W.
    1978   *In Search for Community: Encounter Groups and Social Change.*
            Boulder, Colo.: Westview.
Backman, E.L.
    1952   *Religious Dances in the Christian Church and in Popular Medi-*
            cine. London: Allen & Unwin.
Bailey, Robert
    1974   *Radicals in Urban Politics: The Alinsky Approach.* Chicago:
            University of Chicago Press.
Bainbridge, William, and Rodney Stark
    1979   "Cult Formation: Three Compatible Models." *Sociological Anal-*
            ysis 40 (Winter):283-95.
    1980   "Client and Audience Cults in America." *Sociological Analysis* 41
            (Fall):199-214.
Balch, Robert
    1979   "Two Models of Conversion and Commitment in a UFO Cult."
            Paper presented at the Annual Meeting of the Pacific Sociological
            Association.
    1980   "Looking Behind the Scenes in a Religious Cult: Implications for
            the Study of Conversion." *Sociological Analysis* 41 (Sum-
            mer):137-43.
Balch, Robert W., and David Taylor
    1977   "On Getting in Tune: The Process of Making Supernatural Con-
            tact." University of Montana, unpublished paper.
Banner, James M.
    1980   "Press Coverage Needed to Improve Public Understanding of the
            Humanities." *Humanities Report* 2 (no. 10):2-3.
Bardach, Eugene
    1972   *The Skill Factor in Politics: Repealing the Mental Commitment*
            Laws in California. Berkeley: University of California Press.
Barkan, Steven E.
    1979   "Strategic, Tactical, and Organizational Dilemmas of the Protest
            Movement against Nuclear Power." *Social Problems* 27:19-37.
Barton, Allen
    1969   *Communities in Disaster.* New York: Doubleday.
Bayer, Alan, and Alexander Austin
    1971   "Campus Unrest, 1970-71: Was It Really All That Quiet?" *Educa-*
            tional Record 52: (Fall):301-13.
Beck, Melinda
    1980   "Signing Up—and Sitting In." *Newsweek* (August 4).
Becker, Howard S.
    1953   "Becoming a Marihuana User." *American Journal of Sociology*
            59 (November):235-42.
    1964   "Personal Change in Adult Life." *Sociometry* 27:40-53.
Beckford, James A.
    1975a   *The Trumpet of Prophecy: A Sociological Study of Jehovah's*
            Witnesses. Oxford: Blackwell.
    1975b   "Two Contrasting Types of Sectarian Organization." In Roy
            Wallis (ed.), *Sectarianism.* London: Owen.
    1978   "Accounting for Conversion." *British Journal of Sociology*
            29:249-62.

Bell, Daniel
    1952   "Marxian Socialism in the United States." In E. Egbert and S.
            Persons (eds.), *Socialism in American Life,* vol. 1. Princeton:
            Princeton University Press.
    1961   *The End of Ideology.* New York: Collier.
Bell, Inge Powell
    1968   *Core and Strategy of Non-violence.* New York: Random House.
Berger, Bennett M.
    1979   "American Pastoralism, Suburbia, and the Commune Move-
            ment." *Society* (July-August):64-69.
Berger, Bennett, B. Hackett, and M. Miller
    1973   "Supporting the Communal Family." In R. Kanter (ed.), *Com-
            munes.* New York: Harper.
Berger, Peter L.
    1963   *Invitation to Sociology: A Humanistic Perspective.* Garden City,
            N.Y.: Anchor.
Berger, Peter, and Thomas Luckmann
    1967   *The Social Construction of Reality.* New York: Doubleday.
Bergesen, Albert J.
    1976   "White or Black Riots." Paper presented at the Annual Meeting
            of the American Sociological Association.
    1980   "Police Violence during the Watts, Newark, and Detroit Race
            Riots of the 1960s." In P. Lauderdale (ed.), *Political Deviance.*
            Minneapolis: University of Minnesota Press.
Bergesen, Albert, and Mark Warr
    1979   "A Crisis in the Moral Order: The Effects of Watergate upon
            Confidence in Social Institutions." In R. Withrow (ed.), *The
            Religious Dimension.* New York: Academic.
Berk, Richard A.
    1974   *Collective Behavior.* Dubuque, Iowa: Brown.
BeVier, Michael J.
    1979   *Politics Backstage: Inside the California Legislature.* Philadel-
            phia: Temple University Press.
Bird, Fredrick
    1979   "The Pursuit of Innocence: New Religious Movements and Moral
            Accountability." *Sociological Analysis* 40 (Winter):335-46.
Bird, Fredrick, and B. Reimer
    1982   "Participation Rates in New Religious and Para-Religious Move-
            ments." *Journal for the Scientific Study of Religion* 21 (March):1-
            14.
Bleackley, Horace, and John Lofland
    1977   *State Executions Viewed Historically and Sociologically.* Mont-
            clair, N.J.: Patterson Smith.
Blumer, Herbert
    1957   "Collective Behavior." In Joseph B. Gittler (ed.), *Review of
            Sociology.* New York: Wiley.
    1969a   *Symbolic Interactionism.* Englewood Cliffs, N.J.: Prentice-Hall.
    1969b   "Collective Behavior." In A.M. Lee (ed.), *Principles of Sociol-
            ogy,* 3rd ed. New York: Barnes & Noble (originally pub. 1939).
    1969c   "Fashion." *Sociological Quarterly* 10:275-91.
Bookin, Hedy
    1973   Private notes and personal communications.

Boulding, Kenneth E.
    1969   "Preface: Towards a Theory of Protest." In Walt Anderson (ed.),
            The Age of Protest. Pacific Palisades, Calif.: Goodyear.
Bowden, Tom
    1977   *The Breakdown of Public Security: The Case of Ireland, 1916-
            1921, and Palestine, 1936-1939*. Beverly Hills: Sage.
Brill, Harry
    1971   *Why Organizers Fail: The Story of a Rent Strike*. Berkeley:
            University of California Press.
Brinton, Crane
    1957   *The Anatomy of Revolution*. New York: Vintage.
Bromley, David G., and Anson D. Shupe, Jr.
    1979   *Moonies in America: Cult, Church, and Crusade*. Beverly Hills:
            Sage.
Brown, H.G.
    1943   "The Appeal of Communist Ideology." *American Journal of
            Economics and Sociology* 2:161-74.
Brown, Roger
    1954   "Mass Phenomena." In G. Lindzey (ed.), *Handbook of Social
            Psychology*, vol. 2. Cambridge: Addison-Wesley.
Brown, W.R., and I.J. Cook
    1981   "The ASA at 75: Results of the 1980 Member Survey." *American
            Sociologist* 16 (May):81-86.
Bryant, M. Darrol
    1983   "Towards Understanding the Unification Movement." Paper pre-
            sented at a Unification Church-sponsored conference on Explor-
            ing Unification Theology, Funchal (Portugal), August 2.
Burke, Kenneth
    1936   *Permanence and Change*. New York: New Republic.
Butler, Edgar, and Robert McGinley (eds.)
    1977   *The Other Americans: Living in Emerging Alternative Lifestyles*.
            Buena Park, Calif.: Lifestyles.
Campbell, Bruce
    1978   "A Typology of Cults." *Sociological Analysis* 39 (Fall):228-40.
Campbell, Colin
    1972   "The Cult, the Cultic Milieu, and Secularization." In M. Hill
            (ed.), *A Sociological Yearbook of Religion in Britain*. London:
            SCM.
Campbell, Donald T., and Julius Stanley
    1966   *Experimental and Quasi-Experimental Designs for Research*. Chi-
            cago: Rand McNally.
Canetti, Elias
    1978   *Crowds and Power*. New York: Seasbury.
Cantril, Hadley
    1940   *The Invasion from Mars*. Princeton: Princeton University Press.
    1941   *The Psychology of Social Movements*. New York: Wiley.
Carney, Tom
    1975   "Is This Woman Really the Voice of the Virgin?" *In-the-Know
            Magazine* (September).
Carr, L.J.
    1932   "Disaster and the Sequence-pattern Concept of Social Change."
            American Journal of Sociology 38:207-18.

Carter, April
  1973   *Direct Action and Liberal Democracy.* New York: Harper & Row.
Case, John, and Rosemary C.R. Taylor (eds.)
  1979   *Co-Ops, Communes, and Collectives: Experiments in Social Change in the 1960s and 1970s.* New York: Pantheon.
Chaplin, J.P.
  1959   *Rumor, Fear, and the Madness of Crowds.* New York: Ballantine.
Chatfield, David
  1980   "Direct Action in the UK." *It's About Time* (August):7.
Christensen, Carl W.
  1963   "Religious Conversion." *Archives of General Psychiatry 9:207-16.*
Clark, Elmer
  1929   *The Psychology of Religious Awakening.* New York: Macmillan.
Clark, Kenneth B.
  1966   "The Civil Rights Movement." *Daedalus 95 (Winter): 250-60.*
Cobb, Roger W. and Charles Elder
  1972   *Participation in American Politics: The Dynamics of Agenda-building.* Boston: Allyn & Bacon.
Coe, G. A.
  1916   *The Psychology of Religion.* Chicago: University of Chicago Press.
Cohen, Albert K.
  1955   *Delinquent Boys.* New York: Free Press.
Cohen, Barbara, M. Colligan, W. Wester, and M. Smith
  1978   "An Investigation of Job Satisfaction Factors in an Incident of Mass Psychogenic Illness in the Workplace." *Occupational Health Nursing* 26:10-16.
Coleman, James S.
  1961   *The Adolescent Society.* New York: Free Press.
Colligan, M., and W. Stockton
  1978   "Assembly-line Hysteria." *Psychology Today* (June): 93ff.
Congressional Quarterly
  1979   *The Washington Lobby.* Washington: Congressional Quarterly.
Cooney, Robert, and Helen Michalowski (eds.)
  1977   *The Power of the People: Active Nonviolence in the United States.* Culver City, Calif.: Peace.
Couch, Carl
  1968   "Collective Behavior: An Examination of Some Stereotypes." *Social Problems* 15:310-22.
  1970   "Dimensions of Association in Collective Behavior Episodes." *Sociometry* 33:457-71.
Crawley, A.E.
  1918   "Processions and Dances." *Encylopedia of Religion and Ethics* 10:356-62.
Cressey, Donald
  1972   *Other People's Money.* Belmont, Calif.: Wadsworth (originally pub. 1953).
Critchfield, Richard
  1978   "Wild at the Carnival." *Human Behavior* (February).

Curtis, Russell, and Louis Zurcher
    1974   "Social Movements: An Analytical Exploration of Organizational
            Forms." *Social Problems 21 (Fall): 356-70.*
Damrell, Joseph
    1977   *Seeking Spiritual Meaning: The World of Vedanta.* Beverly Hills:
            Sage.
Davenport, F.M.
    1905   *Primitive Traits in Religious Revivals.* New York: Negro Universi-
            ties Press.
Davis, Fred
    1979   *Yearning for Yesterday: A Sociology of Nostalgia.* New York:
            Free Press.
Davis, Rex, and J. T. Richardson
    1976   "The Organization and Functioning of the Children of God."
            Sociological Analysis 37 (December): 321-39.
Deal, Terrace, and Allan Kennedy
    1982   *Corporate Cultures.* London: Addison-Wesley.
Delgado, Richard
    1977   "Religious Totalism: Gentle and Ungentle Persuasion Under the
            First Amendment." *Southern California Law Review* 51:1-110.
Denzin, Norman
    1968   "Collective Behavior in Total Institutions." *Social Problems*
            15:353-65.
De Santis, Sanctus
    1927   *Religious Conversion.* London: Routledge & Kegan Paul.
Dohrman, H.T.
    1958   *California Cult: The Story of Mankind United.* Boston: Beacon.
Downes, Anthony
    1972   "Up and Down with Ecology: The 'Issue-Attention Cycle.' "
            Public Interest (Summer): 38-50.
Durkheim, Emile
    1915   *Elementary Forms of the Religious Life.* London: Allen & Unwin.
Dynes, Russell
    1970   *Organized Behavior in Disaster.* Lexington, Mass.: Heath.
    1978a   "Inter Nos." *American Sociological Association Footnotes*
            6(no.1):5.
    1978b   "Inter Nos." *American Sociological Association Footnotes* 6(no.
            3):5.
    1978c   "Report of Executive Officer." *American Sociological Associa-
            tion Footnotes 6(no. 6):9.*
    1979   "Inter Nos." *American Sociological Association Footnotes* 7(no.
            5):5.
    1980a   "Inter Nos." *American Sociological Association Footnotes* 8(no.
            4):12.
    1980b   "Inter Nos." *American Sociological Association Footnotes* 8(no.
            8):3.
Editorial Research Reports
    1978   *The Rights Revolution.* Washington: Congressional Quarterly.
Eisinger, Peter
    1973   "The Conditions of Protest Behavior in American Cities." *Ameri-
            can Political Science Review* 67 (March): 11-28.

Emerson, Joan P.
  1970 " 'Nothing Unusual Is Happening.' " In T. Shibutani (ed.), *Human Nature and Collective Behavior*. Englewood Cliffs, N.J.: Prentice-Hall.
Erickson, William
  1973 "The Social Organization of an Urban Commune." *Urban Life* 2 (July): 231-56.
Etzioni, Amitai
  1961 *A Comparative Analysis of Complex Organizations*. New York: Free Press of Glencoe.
  1968 *The Active Society*. New York: Free Press.
  1970 *Demonstration Democracy*. New York: Gordon & Beach.
Festinger, Leon, Henry Riecken, and Stanley Schacter
  1956 *When Prophecy Fails*. Minneapolis: University of Minnesota Press.
Fichter, Joseph H.
  1954 *Social Relations in the Urban Parish*. Chicago: University of Chicago Press.
Fine, Gary
  1979 "Small Groups and Culture Creation: The Idioculture of Little League Baseball Teams." *American Sociological Review* 44 (October): 733-45.
Fine, Sidney
  1969 *Sit-down: The General Motors Strike of 1936-37*. Ann Arbor: University of Michigan Press.
Firestone, Joseph
  1972 "Theory of the Riot Process." *American Behavioral Scientist* 15:859-82.
Fishman, Mark
  1978 "Crime Waves as Ideology." *Social Problems* 25:531-43.
Fogarty, Robert S.
  1980 *Dictionary of American Communal and Utopian History*. Westport, Conn.: Greenwood.
Fogelson, Robert
  1971 *Violence as Protest: A Study of Riots and Ghettos*. New York: Doubleday.
Foltz, D.
  1981 "Move Afoot for a New Research Presence in Washington." *APA Monitor* (January): 1.
Fox, Jack V.
  1967 *Youth Quake*. New York: Cowles Educational.
Freeman, Jo
  1975 *The Politics of Women's Liberation*. New York: McKay.
Freeman, Jo (ed.)
  1983 *Social Movements of the Sixties and Seventies*. New York: Longman.
Freud, Sigmund
  1922 *Group Psychology and the Analysis of the Ego*. London: Hogarth.
Friedenberg, Edgar
  1965 *Coming of Age in America*. New York: Random House.

Gallup, George
    1977   "Exercising Doubles in Two Decades." *Sacramento Union* (October 6).
Gambrell, Richard
    1979   "Displays of Arousal in Audience Settings." Paper presented at the Annual Meeting of the American Sociological Association.
    1980   "Issue Dynamics in the Student Movement." *Sociological Focus* 13 (August): 187-202.
Gamson, William
    1975   *The Strategy of Social Protest*. Homewood, Ill.: Dorsey.
Gamson, William, Bruce Fireman, and Steven Rytina
    1982   *Encounters with Unjust Authority*. Homewood, Ill.: Dorsey.
Garrow, David J.
    1978   *Protest at Selma: Martin Luther King, Jr., and the Voting Rights Act of 1965*. New Haven: Yale University Press.
Gaybba, Brian
    1983   "A Week Spent with the Moonies." *Theologia Evangelica* 14:29-36.
Gehlen, Frieda, and Stephen Doeren
    1976   "Karate Instruction as a Type of Craze." Paper presented at the Annual Meeting of the American Sociological Association.
Genevie, Louis (ed.)
    1978   *Collective Behavior and Social Movements*. Itasca, Ill.: Peacock.
Gerlach, Luther, and Virginia Hine
    1970   *People, Power, Change: Movements of Social Transformation*. Indianapolis: Bobbs-Merrill.
Gitlin, Todd
    1980   *The Whole World Is Watching: Mass Media in the Making and Unmaking of the New Left*. Berkeley: University of California Press.
Gitlow, Benjamin
    1965   *The Whole of Their Lives*. Belmont, Wash.: Western Island (originally pub. 1948).
Glock, Charles
    1964   "The Role of Deprivation in the Origin and Evolution of Religious Groups." In R. Lee and M. Marty (eds.), *Religion and Social Conflict*. New York: Oxford University Press.
Goffman, Erving
    1953   "Communication Conduct in an Island Community." Doctoral diss., University of Chicago.
    1961a   *Asylums*. New York: Doubleday.
    1961b   *Encounters*. Indianapolis: Bobbs-Merrill.
    1983   "The Interaction Order." *American Sociological Review* 48 (February): 1-17.
Golding, William
    1959   *Lord of the Flies*. New York: Putnam.
Goodman, Felicitas
    1974   "Disturbances in the Apostolic Church." In F. D. Goodman, J. Henry, and E. Pressel (eds.), *Trance, Healing, and Hallucination*. New York: Wiley.

Goodman, Paul
    1956   *Growing Up Absurd*. New York: Vintage.
Gouldner, Alvin W.
    1979   *The Future of Intellectuals and the Rise of the New Class*. New York: Seabury.
Grant, H. Roger
    1981   "Utopia without Colony: The Labor Exchange Movement." *Communal Societies* 1 (Autumn): 44-54.
Greeley, Andrew
    1974   *Ecstasy*. Englewood Cliffs, N.J.: Prentice-Hall.
Gregg, Richard B.
    1959   *The Power of Nonviolence*, rev. ed. New York: Schocken.
Griffin, John
    1961   *Black Like Me*. Boston: Houghton Mifflin.
Grimshaw, A.
    1960   "Urban Racial Violence in the United States." *American Journal of Sociology* 66:109-19.
Gross, Feliks
    1974   *The Revolutionary Party*. Westport, Conn.: Greenwood.
Gurr, Ted, and Charles Ruttenberg
    1969   *Cross-national Studies of Civil Violence*. Kensington, Md.: Institute for Research.
Gusfield, Joseph R.
    1963   *Symbolic Crusade: Status Politics and the American Temperance Movement*. Urbana: University of Illinois Press.
Gusfield, Joseph R. (ed.)
    1970   *Protest, Reform, and Revolt: A Reader in Social Movements*. New York: Wiley.
    1979   "Two 'New Classes' or None?" In B. Bruce-Briggs (ed.), *The New Class?* New Brunswick, N.J.: Transaction.
Hall, Richard H.
    1972   *Organizations: Structure and Process*. Englewood Cliffs, N.J.: Prentice-Hall.
Hamilton, Gary
    1978   "The Structural Sources of Adventurism." *American Journal of Sociology* 83:1466-90.
Harmond, Richard
    1972   "Progress and Flight: An Interpretation of the American Cycle Craze of the 1890s." *Journal of Social History* 5:235-57.
Harris, Sara
    1953   *Father Divine, Holy Husband*. Garden City, New York: Doubleday.
Harrison, Michael
    1974   "Preparation for Life in the Spirit." *Urban Life* 2: 390-401.
Hedeman, Ed (ed.)
    1981   *War Resisters League Organizers' Manual*. New York: War Resisters League.
Heirich, Max
    1968   *The Spiral of Conflict: Berkeley, 1964*. New York: Columbia University Press.

1977   "Change of Heart: A Test of Some Widely Held Theories about Religious Conversion." *American Sociological Review* 83: 653-80.

Herbele, Rudolf
1968   "Types and Functions of Social Movements." In David Sills (ed.), *International Encyclopedia of the Social Sciences* 14:439-44. New York: Macmillan.

Hoffer, Eric
1951   *The True Believer: Thoughts on the Nature of Mass Movements.* New York: New American Library.

Horn, Marilyn
1968   *The Second Skin.* Boston: Houghton Mifflin.

Hughes, Everett
1958   *Men and Their Work.* New York: Free Press.

Infield, Henrik
1973   "Biomandau: A French Community at Work." In R. Kanter, (ed.), *Communes.* New York: Harper & Row.

International Registration Bureau
1934   *Mankind United: A Challenge to "Mad Ambition" and "The Money Changers."* No place given: International Registration Bureau (Pacific Coast Division of North America).

Inverarity, James M.
1976   "Populism and Lynching in Louisiana, 1889-1896: A Test of Erickson's Theory of the Relationship between Boundary Crises and Repressive Justice." *American Sociological Review* 41:262-80.

Irwin, John
1970   *The Felon.* Englewood Cliffs, N.J.: Prentice-Hall.
1977   *Scenes.* Beverly Hills: Sage.
1980   *Prisons in Turmoil.* Boston: Little, Brown.

Izard, Carroll
1977   *Human Emotions.* New York: Plenum.

Jacobs, Norman
1965   "The Phantom Slasher of Taipei." *Social Problems* 12:318-28.

James, E.O.
1961   *Feasts and Festivals.* New York: Barnes & Noble.

James, William
1902   *The Varieties of Religious Experience.* Garden City, N.Y.: Doubleday, Dolphin.

Janowitz, Morris
1968   *Social Control of Escalated Riots.* Chicago: University of Chicago Press.

Jenkins, J. Craig
1983   "Resource Mobilization Theory and the Study of Social Movements." *Annual Review of Sociology* 9:527-53.

Jenkins, J. Craig, and Charles Perrow
1977   "Insurgency of the Powerless: Farm Worker Movements (1946-1972)." *American Sociological Review* 42 (April): 249-68.

Johnson, Donald
1945   "The 'Phantom Anesthetist' of Mattoon." *Journal of Abnormal and Social Psychology* 40:175-86.

Johnston, Hank
   1980   "The Marketed Social Movement: A Case Study of the Rapid
             Growth of TM." *Sociological Perspectives* 23 (July): 333-54.
Jorgensen, Danny L.
   1982   "The Esoteric Community: An Ethnographic Investigation of the
             Cultic Milieu." *Urban Life* 10 (January): 383-407.
Jules-Rosette, Bennetta
   1975   *African Apostles: Ritual and Conversion in the Church of John
             Maranke.* Ithaca, N.Y.: Cornell University Press.
Kanter, Rosabeth Moss
   1972   *Commitment and Community: Communes and Utopias in Socio-
             logical Perspective.* Cambridge, Mass.: Harvard University
             Press.
   1973   *Communes: Creating and Managing the Collective Life* (ed.).
             New York: Harper & Row.
   1979   "Communes in Cities." In J. Case and R. Taylor (eds.), *Co-Ops,
             Communes and Collectives.* New York: Pantheon.
Kelly, Brian
   1979   "Nobody Cared When Energy Was Cheap." Reprint of article in a
             Chicago Sun-Times series. Sacramento Union (August 7).
Kephart, William M.
   1974   "Why They Fail: A Socio-Historical Analysis of Religious and
             Secular Communes." *Journal of Comparative Family Studies* 5
             (Autumn): 130-40.
   1982   *Extraordinary Groups,* 2d ed. New York: St. Martin's.
Kerckhoff, Alan, and Kurt Back
   1968   *The June Bug.* New York: Appleton.
Kerckhoff, Alan, Kurt Back, and Norman Miller
   1965   "Sociometric Patterns in Hysterial Contagion." *Sociometry* 28:2-
             15.
Klapp, Orrin
   1964   *Symbolic Leaders.* Chicago: Aldine.
   1971   *Social Types: Process, Structure, and Ethos.* San Diego, Calif.:
             Aegis.
Kluckhohn, Clyde
   1962   "Values and Value-Orientations in the Theory of Action." In T.
             Parsons and E. Shills (eds.), *Toward a General Theory of Action.*
             New York: Harper & Row.
Knight, James, T. Friedman, and J. Sulianti
   1965   "Epidemic Hysteria: A Field Study." *American Journal of Public
             Health* 55:858-65.
Knoke, David, and David Prensky
   1982   "What Relevance Do Organization Theories Have for Voluntary
             Association?" Paper presented at the Annual Meetings of the
             American Sociological Association, San Francisco.
LaBarre, Weston
   1962   *They Shall Take Up Serpents.* Minneapolis: University of Minne-
             sota press.
Lakey, George
   1973   *Strategy for a Living Revolution.* San Francisco: Freeman.

Lang, Gladys Engel, and Kurt Lang
    1981   "Mass Communication and Public Opinion: Strategies for Re-
            search." In M. Rosenberg and Ralph H. Turner (eds.), *Social
            Psychology.* New York: Basic Books.
Lang, Kurt, and Gladys Lang
    1960   "Decisions for Christ." In M. R. Stein, A. Vidich, and D. White
            (eds.), *Identity and Anxiety.* Glencoe, Ill.: Free Press.
    1961   *Collective Dynamics.* New York: Crowell.
LaPiere, Richard
    1938   *Collective Behavior.* New York: McGraw-Hill.
Lawson, Ronald
    1980   "A Decentralized But Moving Pyramid: The Evolution and Con-
            sequences of the Structure of the Tenant Movement." Paper
            presented at the Annual Meetings of the American Sociological
            Association, New York City.
Le Bon, Gustave
    1960   *The Crowd: A Study of the Popular Mind.* New York: Viking
            (originally pub. 1895).
Lenin, Vladimir I.
    1970   "The Urgent Tasks of Our Movement." In idem, *Selected Works,*
            vol. 1. Moscow: Progress.
Lifton, Robert Jay
    1961   *Thought Reform and Psychology of Totalism.* New York: Norton.
Light, Donald W.
    1969   "Strategies of Protest: Developments in Conflict Theory." In
            James McEvoy and Abraham Miller (eds.), *Black Power and
            Student Rebellion.* Belmont, Calif.: Wadsworth.
Lindesmith, A.R.
    1968   *Addiction and Opiates.* Chicago: Aldine.
Lippmann, Walter
    1971   "The University." In C. Anderson and J. Murray (eds.), *The
            Professors: Work and Life Styles among Academicians.* Cam-
            bridge, Mass.: Schenkman.
Lipsky, Michael
    1968   "Protest as a Political Resource." *American Political Science
            Review* 62 (December):1144-58.
Lofland, John
    1966   *Doomsday Cult.* Englewood Cliffs, N.J.: Prentice-Hall.
    1968   "The Youth Ghetto." *Journal of Higher Education* 39 (March):
            121-43.
    1970   "Mankind United." *Man, Myth, and Magic,* vol. 13. London:
            BPC.
    1976   *Doing Social Life: The Qualitative Study of Human Interaction in
            Natural Settings.* New York: Wiley.
    1977a   *Doomsday Cult,* enlarged ed. New York: Irvington.
    1977b   "Becoming a World-Saver Revisited." *American Behavioral Sci-
            entist* 20 (July-August): 805-18.
    1979   "White-Hot Mobilization: Strategies of a Millenarian Move-
            ment." In Mayer N. Zald and John D. McCarthy (eds.), *The
            Dynamics of Social Movements.* Cambridge, Mass.: Winthrop.

1981a   "Sociologists as an Interest Group: Prospect and Propriety."
         Sociological Perspectives 24 (July):275-97.
1981b   "Collective Behavior: The Elementary Forms." In Morris Rosen-
         berg and Ralph Turner (eds.), *Social Psychology*. New York:
         Basic Books.
1982a   *Crowd Lobbying: An Emerging Tactic of Interest Group Influ-
         ences in California*. Davis: University of California at Davis,
         Institute of Governmental Affairs.
1982b   "Crowd Joys." *Urban Life* 10 (January): 355-81.

Lofland, John, and Michael Fink
1982   *Symbolic Sit-Ins: Protest Occupations at the California Capitol*.
         Washington: University Press of America.

Lofland, John, and Michael Jamison
1984   "Social Movement Locals: Modal Member Structures." *Socio-
         logical Analysis* 45 (Summer): 115-29.

Lofland, John, and Lyn H. Lofland
1984   *Analyzing Social Settings*, 2d ed. Belmont, Calif.: Wadsworth.

Lofland, John, with Lyn H. Lofland
1969   *Deviance and Identity*. Englewood Cliffs, N.J.: Prentice-Hall.

Lofland, John, and James T. Richardson
1984   "Religious Movement Organizations: Elemental Forms and Dy-
         namics." In Louis Kriesberg (ed.), *Research in Social Move-
         ments, Conflicts, and Change*. Greenwich, Conn.: JAI.

Lofland, John, and Norman Skonovd
1981   "Conversion Motifs." *Journal for the Scientific Study of Religion*
         20 (December):373-85.

Lofland, John, and Rodney Stark
1965   "Becoming a World-Saver: A Theory of Conversion to a Deviant
         Perspective." *American Sociological Review* 30 (December):862-
         74.

Lofland, Lyn H.
1973   *A World of Strangers: Order and Action in Urban Public Space*.
         New York: Basic Books.

Lopreato, Joseph, and Letitia Alston
1970   "Ideal Types and the Idealization Strategy." *American Sociologi-
         cal Review* 35:88-96.

Los Angeles Times
1977   "A Festive Strike in France" (May 25).

Lowi, Theodore J.
1969   *The End of Liberalism*. New York: Norton.

Lucas, Rex
1969   *Men in Crisis*. New York: Basic Books.

Luckmann, Thomas
1967   *The Invisible Religion: The Problem of Religion in Modern Soci-
         ety*. New York: Macmillan.

Lynch, Frederick
1977   "Field Research and Future History: Problems Posed for Ethno-
         graphic Sociologists by the 'Doomsday Cult' Making Good."
         American Sociologist 12 (April):80-88.
1979   "Occult Establishment or Deviant Perspective? A Sociological
         Analysis of a Modern Church of Magic." Manuscript.

McCall, Michel
    1970   "Some Ecological Aspects of Negro Slum Riots." In J. Gusfield
            (ed.), *Protest, Reform, and Revolt*. New York: Wiley.
McCarthy, John D.
    1982   "Social Infrastructure Deficits and New Technologies: Mobilizing
            Unstructured Sentiment Pools." Paper presented at the Annual
            Meetings of the American Sociological Association, San Fran-
            cisco.
McCarthy, John, and Mayer Zald
    1973   *The Trend of Social Movements in America: Professionalization
            and Resource Mobilization*. Morristown, N.J.: General Learning.
McFadden, Cyra
    1977   *The Serial*. New York: Knopf.
McLeod, W.R.
    1975   "Merphos Poisoning or Mass Panic?" *Australian and New
            Zealand Journal of Psychiatry* 9:225-29.
McLoughlin, William G.
    1959   *Modern Revivalism*. New York: Ronald.
    1978   *Revivals, Awakenings, and Reform*. Chicago: University of Chi-
            cago Press.
McPhail, Clark, and David L. Miller
    1973   "The Assembling Process." *American Sociological Review* 38
            (June):721-35.
McPhail, Clark, and Ronald T. Wohlstein
    1983   "Individual and Collective Behaviors within Gatherings, Demon-
            strations, and Riots." *Annual Review of Sociology* 9:579-600.
Malbin, M.
    1980   *Parties, Interest Groups, and Campaign Finance Laws*. Washing-
            ton: American Enterprise Institute for Public Policy Research.
Marsh, Alan
    1977   *Protest and Political Consciousness:* Beverly Hills: Sage.
Marsh, Peter, E. Rosser, and Rom Harre
    1978   *The Rules of Disorder*. London: Routledge and Kegan Paul.
Martin, Thomas, and K. Berry
    1974   "Competitive Sport in Post-Industrial Society." *Journal of Popu-
            lar Culture* 8:107-20.
Marx, Gary
    1979   "Conceptual Problems in the Field of Collective Behavior." Paper
            presented at the Annual Meeting of the American Sociological
            Association.
Marx, Gary T., and James Wood
    1975   "Strands of Theory and Research in Collective Behavior." In A.
            Inkeles (ed.), *Annual Review of Sociology*. Palo Alto, Calif.:
            Annual Reviews.
Marx, John, and D. Ellison
    1975   "Sensitivity Training and Communes." *Pacific Sociological Re-
            view* 18:442-62.
Matthews, Donald R., and James Prothro
    1966   *Negroes and the New Southern Politics*. New York: Harcourt,
            Brace, & World.

Matza, David
    1964   "Position and Behavior Patterns of Youth." In Robert E.L. Faris
            (ed.), *Handbook of Modern Sociology*. Chicago: Rand McNally.
Mauss, Armand L.
    1975   *Social Problems as Social Movements*. Philadelphia: Lippincott.
Meyers, Robert C.
    1948   "Anti-Communist Mob Action: A Case Study." *Public Opinion
            Quarterly* 12:57-67.
Milbrath, Lester W.
    1968   "Lobbying." In David Sills (ed.), *International Encyclopedia of
            the Social Sciences*, vol. 9. New York: Macmillan.
Miller, Jerry, and Robert Evans
    1975   "The Peaking of Streaking." In R. Evans (ed.), *Readings in
            Collective Behavior*. Chicago: Rand McNally.
Miller, Mike, et al.
    1979   *The People Fight Back: Building a Tenant Union*. San Francisco:
            Organized Training Center.
Moon, Sun M.
    1983   "Founder's Address." *Unification News* 2 (no. 7, July):13.
Morán, Rolando
    1982   "EGP Leader Interviewed." *Guardian* (October 6).
Morris, Aldon
    1981   "The Black Southern Student Sit-In Movement." *American Soci-
            ological Review* 46 (October):744-67.
Mosse, George L.
    1975   *The Nationalization of the Masses*. New York: New American
            Library.
Murray, Robert K.
    1955   *Red Scare*. New York: McGraw-Hill.
Nelson, G.K.
    1969   *Spiritualism and Society*. New York: Schocken.
Obershall, Anthony
    1973   *Social Conflict and Social Movements*. Englewood Cliffs, N.J.:
            Prentice-Hall.
Ornstein, N.J., and S. Elder
    1978   *Interest Groups, Lobbying, and Policymaking*. Washington: Con-
            gressional Quarterly.
O'Toole, Roger
    1977   *The Precipitous Path: Studies in Political Sects*. Toronto: Martin.
Park, Robert E., and Ernest W. Burgess
    1924   *Introduction to the Science of Sociology*. Chicago: University of
            Chicago Press.
Penrose, L.S.
    1952   *On the Objective Study of Crowd Behavior*. London: Lewis.
Perlman, David
    1980   "Diablo Canyon Plant Raring to Go." *San Francisco Chronicle*
            (July 28).
Perry, Joseph, and M.D. Pugh
    1978   *Collective Behavior: Response to Social Stress*. St. Paul: West.
Peterson, Severin
    1971   *A Catalog of the Ways People Grow*. New York: Ballantine.

Peven, Dorothy
    1968   "The Use of Religious Revival Techniques to Indoctrinate Person-
            nel." *Sociological Quarterly* 9:97-106.
Pfeiffer, Paul
    1964   "Mass Hysteria Masquerading as Food Poisoning." *Maine Medi-
            cal Association Journal* 55:27.
Piven, Francis Fox, and Richard A. Cloward
    1977   *Poor People's Movements: Why They Succeed, How They Fail.*
            New York: Random House.
Plutchik, Robert
    1962   *The Emotions.* New York: Random House.
Pratt, J.B.
    1920   *The Religious Consciousness.* New York: Macmillan.
Price, Charles M., and Charles G. Bell
    1980   "Why the Voluntary Exodus of So Many Assembly Members?"
            California Journal (September):27-29.
Pruden, Durward
    1936   "A Sociological Study of a Texas Lynching." *Studies in Sociology*
            1:3-9.
Quarantelli, E.L., and J. Hundley
    1975   "A Test of Some Propositions about Crowd Formation and Be-
            havior." In R. Evans (ed.), *Readings in Collective Behavior,* 2d
            ed. Chicago: Rand McNally.
Quebedeaux, Richard
    1983   "Are You a Moonie?" Paper presented at a Unification Church-
            sponsored conference on Exploring Unification Theology, Fun-
            chal, Portugal, August 5.
Quinn, Sally
    1975   "They Simply Adore Lana." *San Francisco Chronicle* (April 16).
Rambo, Lewis R.
    1982   "Current Research on Religious Conversion." *Religious Studies
            Review* 8 (April):146-59.
Rankin, A.M., and P. Philip
    1963   "An Epidemic of Laughing in the Bukoba District of Tanga-
            nyika." *Central African Journal of Medicine* 9:167-70.
Raper, Arthur
    1933   *The Tragedy of Lynching.* Chapel Hill: University of North Caro-
            lina Press.
Richardson, James T.
    1979a   "A New Paradigm for Conversion Research." Paper presented at
            the Annual Meeting of the International Society for Political
            Psychology.
    1979b   "Cult to Sect." *Pacific Sociological Review* 22 (March):139-66.
    1983   "Financing the New Religions." *Journal for the Scientific Study
            of Religion* 21 (September):255-68.
Richardson, James T. (ed.)
    1978   *Conversion Careers.* Beverly Hills: Sage.
Richardson, James T., R. Simmonds, and M. Stewart
    1978   "The Evolution of a Jesus Movement Organization." *Journal of
            Voluntary Action Research* 7:93-111.
Richardson, J.T., M. Stewart, and R. Simmonds
    1979   *Organized Miracles.* New Brunswick, N.J.: Transaction.

Robbins, Thomas, Dick Anthony, and James Richardson
    1978   "Theory and Research on Today's New Religions." *Sociological Analysis* 39:39-122.
Roberts, Ron E., and Robert Kloss
    1979   *Social Movements.* St. Louis: Mosby.
Rochford, Edmund B.
    1982   "Recruitment and Transformation Processes in the Hare Krishna Movement." Doctoral diss., University of California at Los Angeles.
Rose, Jerry D.
    1982   *Outbreaks: The Sociology of Collective Behavior.* New York: Free Press.
Rosengren, Karl, P. Arvidson, and D. Sturesson
    1975   "The Barseback 'Panic.' " *Acta Sociologica* 18:303-21.
Ross, Andrew
    1975   Private notes and personal communications.
Ross, E.A.
    1908   *Social Psychology.* New York: Macmillan.
Rothschild-Whitt, Joyce
    1979   "The Collectivist Organization: An Alternative to Rational-Bureaucratic Models." *American Sociological Review* 44 (August):509-27.
Rudé, George
    1964   *The Crowd in History.* New York: Wiley.
Salisbury, Robert
    1975   "Interest Groups." In F. Greenstein and N. Polsby (eds.), *Non-Governmental Politics.* Reading, Mass.: Addison-Wesley.
Schein, Edgar
    1961   *Coercive Persuasion.* New York: Norton.
Schuler, Edgar, and V. Parenton
    1943   "A Recent Epidemic of Hysteria in a Louisiana High School." *Journal of Social Psychology* 17:221-35.
Schwartz, Michael
    1976   *Radical Protest and Social Structure: The Southern Farmers' Alliance and Cotton Tenancy, 1880-1890.* New York: Academic.
Seeman, M.
    1958   "Intellectuals and the Language of Minorities." *American Journal of Sociology* 64 (January):25-35.
Selznick, Gertrude, and Philip Selznick
    1964   "A Normative Theory of Culture." *American Sociological Review* 29 (October):653-69.
Selznick, Philip
    1960   *The Organizational Weapon.* New York: Free Press (originally pub. 1952).
Sharp, Gene
    1973   *The Politics of Nonviolent Action.* Boston: Sargent.
Sheatsely, Paul, and Jacob Feldman
    1964   "The Assassination of President Kennedy." *Public Opinion Quarterly* 28:189-215.
Shibutani, Tamotsu
    1961   *Society and Personality.* Englewood Cliffs, N.J.: Prentice-Hall.

Sinclair, Thorton
1938   "The Nazi Party Rally at Nuremberg." *Public Opinion Quarterly* 2:570-83.
Skolnick, Peter L.
1978   *Fads: America's Crazes, Fevers, and Fanciers from the 1890's to the 1970's.* New York: Crowell.
Skonovd, L. Norman
1981   "Apostasy: The Process of Defection from Religious Totalism." Doctoral diss., University of California at Davis.
Smelser, Neil J.
1963   *Theory of Collective Behavior.* New York: Free Press.
Smith, Michael D.
1975   "Sports and Collective Violence." In D. Ball and J. Loy (eds.), *Sport and Social Order.* Reading, Mass.: Addison-Wesley.
Smith, Thomas S.
1968   "Conventionalization and Control: An Examination of Adolescent Crowds." *American Journal of Sociology* 74 (January):172-83.
1974   "Aestheticism and Social Structure." *American Sociological Review* 39 (May):725-43.
Snow, David A., and Richard Machalek
1984   "The Sociology of Conversion." *Annual Review of Sociology* 10:167-90.
Snow, David, and Cynthia Phillips
1980   "The Lofland-Stark Conversion Model: A Critical Reassessment." *Social Problems* 27 (Fall):430-47.
Snow, David A., L. Zurcher, and S. Eckland-Olson
1980   "Social Networks and Social Movements: A Microstructural Approach to Differential Recruitment." *American Sociological Review* 45 (May):787-801.
Snow, David, Louis A. Zurcher, and Robert Peters
1981   "Victory Celebrations as Theater: A Dramaturgic Approach to Crowd Behavior." *Symbolic Interaction* 4 (Spring):21-42.
Somit, Albert
1968   "Brainwashing." In David Sills (ed.), *International Encyclopedia of the Social Sciences,* vol. 2. New York: Macmillan.
Spilerman, Seymour
1976   "Structural Characteristics of Cities and the Severity of Racial Disorders." *American Sociological Review* 41 (June):771-93.
Stahl, Sidney, and M. Lededun
1974   "Mystery Gas: An Analysis of Mass Hysteria." *Journal of Health and Social Behavior* 15:44-50.
Starbuck, Edwin
1911   *The Psychology of Religion.* New York: Scribners.
Stark, Rodney, and William Sims Bainbridge
1979   "Of Churches, Sects, and Cults: Preliminary Concepts for a Theory of Religious Movements." *Journal for the Scientific Study of Religion* 18 (June):117-31.
1980a   "Toward a Theory of Religion: Religious Commitment." *Journal for the Scientific Study of Religion* 19 (March):114-28.

1980b   "Networks of Faith: Interpersonal Bonds and Recruitment to Cults and Sects." *American Journal of Sociology* 85:1376-95.

1981   "Secularization and Cult Formation in the Jazz Age." *Journal for the Scientific Study of Religion* 20 (December):360-73.

Starr, Paul

1979   "The Phantom Community." In John Case and Rosemary Taylor (eds.), *Co-Ops, Communes, and Collectives: Experiments in Social Change in the 1960s and 1970s.* New York, Pantheon.

Staudinger, Nick

1982   "New Terrorist Threat in West Germany." *Sacramento Bee* (December 16), Associated Press.

Stiehm, Judith

1972   *Nonviolent Power.* Lexington, Mass.: Heath.

Straus, Roger

1976   "Changing Oneself: Seekers and the Creative Transformation of Experience." In John Lofland (ed.), *Doing Social Life.* New York: Wiley.

1979a   "Inside Scientology." Paper presented at the Annual Meeting of the Pacific Sociological Association.

1979b   "Religious Conversion as a Personal and Collective Accomplishment." *Sociological Analysis* 40:158-65.

Strauss, Anselm

1958   "Transformation of Identity." In A. Rose (ed.), *Human Behavior and Social Processes.* New York: Houghton Mifflin.

Suczek, Barbara

1973   "The Curious Case of the 'Death' of Paul McCartney." *Urban Life* 1:61-76.

Sutherland, Edwin, and Donald Cressey

1966   *Principles of Criminology,* 7th ed. Philadelphia: Lippincott.

Suttles, Gerald.

1968   *The Social Order of the Slum.* Chicago: University of Chicago Press.

1970   "Friendship as a Social Institution." In George McCall et al., *Social Relationships.* Chicago: Aldine.

1977   "Foreword." In John Irwin, *Scenes.* Beverly Hills: Sage.

Tan, E. S.

1963   "Epidemic Hysteria." *Medical Journal of Malaya* 18:72-6.

Tarrow, Sidney

1983a   "Struggling to Reform: Social Movements and Policy Change during Cycles of Protest." Ithaca, N.Y.: Cornell University Center for International Studies Occasional Paper No. 15.

1983b   "Resource Mobilization and Cycles of Protest." Paper presented at the Annual Meetings of the American Sociological Association, Detroit, Michigan.

Taylor, C. L., and M. C. Hudson (eds.)

1972   *World Handbook of Political and Social Indicators,* 2d ed. New Haven: Yale University Press.

Taylor, David

1975   Private notes and personal communications.

1978   "The Social Organization of Recruitment in the Unification Church." Master of Arts thesis, University of Montana.

Taylor, Richard K.
    1977   *Blockade: A Guide to Nonviolent Intervention.* Maryknoll, N.Y.:
            Orbis.
Terkel, Studs
    1980   "Across America There's a Flowing of Life Juices . . . A Long-
            Buried American Tradition May Be Springing Back to Life."
            Parade (October 12).
Tierney, Kathleen
    1980   "Emergent Norm Theory as 'Theory': An Analysis and Critique
            of Turner's Formulation." In M.D. Pugh (ed.), *Collective Behav-
            ior: A Source Book.* New York: West.
Tilly, Charles
    1978   *"From Mobilization to Revolution.* Reading, Mass.: Addison-
            Wesley.
    1979   "Repertoires of Contention in America and Britain, 1750-1830."
            In M. Zald and J. McCarthy (eds.), *The Dynamics of Social
            Movements.* Cambridge, Mass.: Winthrop.
    1981a   "Introduction." In L.A. Tilly and C. Tilly (eds.), *Class Conflict
            and Collective Action.* Beverly Hills: Sage.
    1981b   "The Web of Contention in Eighteenth-Century Cities." In L.A.
            Tilly and C. Tilly (eds.), *Class Conflict and Collective Action.*
            Beverly Hills: Sage.
Tilly, Louise A., and Charles Tilly (eds.)
    1981   *Class Conflict and Collection Action.* Beverly Hills: Sage.
Toch, Hans
    1965   *The Social Psychology of Social Movements.* Indianapolis:
            Bobbs-Merrill.
Tonabene, Lyn
    1967   "I Passed as a Teenager." *Ladies Home Journal* 64 (June):113-18.
Travisano, Richard
    1970   "Alternation and Conversion as Qualitatively Different Transfor-
            mations." IN G.P. Stone and H. Farberman (eds.), *Social Psy-
            chology through Symbolic Interaction.* Waltham, Mass.: Ginn-
            Blaisdell.
Troeltsch, Ernst
    1931   *The Social Teachings of the Christian Churches.* New York:
            Macmillan.
Truman, D.B.
    1971   *The Governmental Process: Political Interests and Public Opin-
            ion.* New York: Knopf.
Truzzi, Marcello
    1972   "Occult Revival as Popular Culture." *Sociological Quarterly*
            13:16-31.
Tumin, Melvin, and A. Feldman
    1955   "The Miracle at Sabana Grande." *Public Opinion Quarterly*
            19:124-39.
Turner, Ralph
    1953   "The Quest for Universals in Sociological Research." *American
            Sociological Review* 18 (June):604-11.
    1964   "Collective Behavior." In R. E. Faris (ed.), *Handbook of Modern
            Sociology.* Chicago: Rand McNally.

1969   "The Public Perception of Protest." *American Sociological Review* 34 (December):815-31.
1970   "Determinants of Social Movement Strategies." In Tamotsu Shibutani (ed.), *Human Nature and Collective Behavior*. Englewood Cliffs, N.J.: Prentice-Hall.
1981   "Collective Behavior and Resource Mobilization as Approaches to Social Movements: Issues and Continuities." In Louis Kreisberg (ed.), *Research on Social Movements, Conflict, and Change*, vol. 4. Greenwich, Conn.: JAI.

Turner, Ralph, and Lewis Killian
1957   *Collective Behavior*. Englewood Cliffs, N.J.: Prentice-Hall.
1972   *Collective Behavior*, 2d ed. Englewood Cliffs, N.J.: Prentice-Hall.

Unification Church
1983   "People of the Quest." New York: Holy Spirit Association for the Unification of World Christianity. Videotape.

United Press International
1978   "Girl Attempts Demon Exorcism" (February 14).

Useem, Bert
1983   "Additions to the Repertoire." *Critical Mass Bulletin* 8 (Fall-Winter):27.

Useem, Michael
1973   *Conscription, Protest, and Social Conflict: The Life and Death of a Draft Resistance Movement*. New York: Wiley.

Wallis, Roy
1974   "Ideology, Authority, and the Development of Cultic Movements." *Social Research* 41:299-327.
1977   *The Road to Total Freedom: A Sociological Analysis of Scientology*. New York: Columbia University Press.

Waskow, Arthur I.
1966   *From Race Riot to Sit-In, 1919 and the 1960s: A Study of the Connections between Conflict and Violence*. Garden City, N.Y.: Anchor.

Wasserman, Harvey
1979   "The Nonviolent Movement versus Nuclear Power." In Severyn T. Bruyn and Paula M. Rayman (eds.), *Nonviolent Action and Social Change*. New York: Irvington.

Westley, Francis
1978   "The Cult of Man." *Sociological Analysis* 39 (no. 2):135-45.

Whitt, J.A.
1979   "Toward a Class-dialectic Model of Power: An Empirical Assessment of Three Competing Models of Political Power." *American Sociological Review* 44:81-99.

Widmer, George, et al.
1979   *Strange Victories: The Anti-nuclear Movement in the U.S. and Europe*. New York: Midnight Notes Collective.

Williams, F.E.
1923   *The Vailala Madness and the Destruction of Native Ceremonies in the Gulf Division*. Port Moresby: Baker.

Wilson, Bryan R.
1959   "An Analysis of Sect Development." *American Sociological Review* 24 (February):3-15.

1961   *Sects and Society*. Berkeley: University of California Press.
Wilson, James Q.
1961   "The Strategy of Protest: Problems of Negro Civic Action."
        Journal of Conflict Resolution 3 (September):291-303.
1973   *Political Organizations*. New York: Basic Books.
Wood, James L., and Maurice Jackson
1982   *Social Movements*. Belmont, Calif.: Wadsworth.
Wolfe, Tom
1971   *Radical Chic and Mau-Mauing the Flak Catchers*. New York:
        Farrar, Straus, & Giroux.
1976   *Mauve Gloves and Madmen, Clutter, and Vine*. New York: Far-
        rar, Straus, & Giroux.
Worsely, Peter M.
1957   *The Trumpet Shall Sound: A Study of Cargo Cults in Melanesia*.
        London: Gibbon & Kee.
Wuthnow, Robert
1978   *Experimentation in American Religion*. Berkeley: University of
        California Press.
Zablocki, Benjamin
1971   *The Joyful Community*. Baltimore: Penguin.
1980   *Alienation and Charisma: A Study of Contemporary American
        Communes*. New York: Free Press.
Zald, Mayer, and Roberta Ash
1966   "Social Movement Organizations: Growth, Decay, and Change."
        Social Forces 44:327-40.
Zald, Mayer N., and John D. McCarthy (eds.)
1979   *The Dynamics of Social Movements: Resource Mobilization,
        Social Control, and Tactics*. Cambridge, Mass.: Winthrop.
Zinn, Howard
1964   *SNCC: The New Abolitionists*. Boston: Beacon.
Zurcher, Louis A., & David A. Snow
1981   "Collective Behavior: Social Movements." In M. Rosenberg and
        R. Turner (eds.), *Social Psychology: Sociological Perspectives*.
        New York: Basic Books.

Index